W9-DFW-665

F.V.

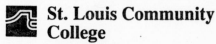
St. Louis Community College

Forest Park
Florissant Valley
Meramec

Instructional Resources
St. Louis, Missouri

THE NAKED
AND
THE UNDEAD

Thinking Through Cinema

Thomas E. Wartenberg, Series Editor

THE NAKED
AND
THE UNDEAD

Evil and
the Appeal of
Horror

Cynthia A. Freeland

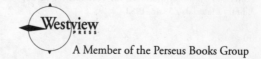

A Member of the Perseus Books Group

Thinking Through Cinema

Copyright © 2000 by Westview Press, A Member of the Perseus Books Group

Published in 2000 in the United States of America by Westview Press, 5500 Central Avenue, Boulder, Colorado 80301–2877, and in the United Kingdom by Westview Press, 12 Hid's Copse Road, Cumnor Hill, Oxford OX2 9JJ

Find us on the World Wide Web at www.westviewpress.com

Library of Congress Cataloging-in-Publication Data
Freeland, Cynthia A.
   The naked and the undead : evil and the appeal of horror / Cynthia A. Freeland.
      p.   cm.— (Thinking through cinema)
   Filmography: p.
   Includes bibliographical references and index.
   ISBN 0-8133-6702-6
   1. Horror films—History and criticism.   2. Evil in motion pictures.
I. Title.   II. Series.
PN1995.9.H6F755 1999
791.43'6164—dc21   99-35593
                                                                        CIP

10   9   8   7   6   5   4   3   2   1

To Krist

CONTENTS

pαrt thrεε
Sublime Spectacles
of Disaster

pbotos

PREFACE AND ACKNOWLEDGMENTS

Prefaces to professors' books on horror have two common refrains, so I'll get straight to those. Yes, I've been an almost lifelong fan of horror—ever since my parents refused to let me see *Psycho* (wisely, I now think—I was nine at the time). My love of horror was heightened by living in Pittsburgh while George Romero was filming *Dawn of the Dead* at the Monroeville Mall, where I sometimes shopped. I got to see early revivals of *Night of the Living Dead* at the Pittsburgh Playhouse, where I hooted along with other fans at the in-joke when horror TV show host "Chilly Billy" made a guest appearance as a newsman. And yes, my spouse, Krist Bender, has had to put up with some very graphic and unpleasant dinner-table conversations. His support (technical, intellectual, and emotional) is much appreciated, especially given his dislike of horror films.

To make my horror sensibility clear at the start, I will say that my favorite horror director is David Cronenberg, and my favorite film of his is *Scanners* (I make a case for it in Chapter 3). But I decided to write in this book only about movies I love, and this means that I have genuine affection and respect for *all* the films I discuss here (even *The Texas Chainsaw Massacre, Part 2* and the *Hellraiser* films). Because I have little patience for Jason, Freddy, or Michael Myers and happen to dislike Brian De Palma's movies, you will not find them here. I regret that I have not had the space to discuss some other horror movies and directors I like very much; this includes Sam Raimi's *Evil Dead* and most of the films of Dario Argento.

Since in my view, crucial pleasures of horror involve audience participation and critical response, it has been especially important that I've shared the horror experience over the years now with many close friends. My memory of certain movies is tied up with the concrete circumstances of watching and discussing them. I will quickly thank here John Clobridge, Jo Tyler, Lynn Randolph and Bill Simon, Doug Ischar, Angela Curran, Erwin Ferguson, Jon Jarrett, Jack McNees,

James Gustin, Steve Koch, Lynne Brown, Nancy Tynan, and Krist Bender. I owe a special debt to Mark Seidman, who first took me to *Eraserhead* and made me sit through *The Texas Chainsaw Massacre* at the drive-in.

Marian Luntz prompted me to start writing about feminism and horror when she invited me to curate a film series for the Museum of Fine Arts, Houston, in 1991. Through her invitation, I had the pleasure of organizing "Fatal Subtraction: Three Decades of Women in Horror, 1960–1990." There, along with an appreciative audience, I first got to see movies like *Peeping Tom* and *Repulsion* on the big screen. My debt to other feminists writing about horror will be obvious in the text below; my criticisms represent serious engagement with their views.

Although I had a glimmering of how my interest in horror connected up with my more typical philosophical interests in Aristotle's *Poetics* and classical tragedy, I was thrilled to see Noël Carroll work out these links in his 1990 book, *The Philosophy of Horror*. I learned much from him about how a philosopher could write about this questionable genre. My style and approach are not the same as Noël's, but I am indebted to him, and to Bob Solomon, for telling me I was—I must be—writing a book on horror. I also had the chance to learn more about how a philosopher writes about film, both directly in seminars and indirectly in books, from Stanley Cavell (who might be appalled at my choice of movies). Tom Wartenberg gave the final push by soliciting the book for his Westview series, "Thinking Through Cinema," and I am very grateful to both him and to Westview's Laura Parsons and Sarah Warner for their enthusiasm and assistance.

Most recently, my thoughts on evil have been stretched and refined through my Houston Teachers Institute seminar, "Addressing Evil." I am grateful to all the teachers in my seminar and to Paul Cooke and Bill Monroe for inviting me to participate in it.

My colleague Anne Jacobson has constantly pushed me into learning more about the new sciences of the mind; she has had a major impact not just on several of my chapters here but on the book's entire outlook. Her friendship and support have been invaluable. Elizabeth Miller answered questions about *Dracula*, and Matthew Rexer shared his peerless knowledge of the *Hellraiser* movies. Aaron Smuts and Steven Schneider offered useful comments on several chapters. Although my parents, Alan and Betty Freeland, are wary about my interest in monstrous mothers and fathers, they tried to see what I'm up to here, even to the point of helping proofread and edit several chapters. Mary McDonough was a steadfast on-line friend as the writing struggled on, chapter by chapter. I offer a sincere thank you to all these people.

Drafts of chapters were read on many occasions where discussion prompted new angles or revisions. I thank audiences at the College of Charleston, Davidson

College, the University of Kansas, the University of Texas, the Houston Public Library, the College of the Mainland, the Society for Women in Philosophy, the Society for the Study of Contemporary Visual Arts, the American Society for Aesthetics, and Mt. Holyoke College.

Finally, I gratefully acknowledge support from a University of Houston book subvention, which made it possible for me to hire Laurel Lacroix. Laurel assisted more than ably—enthusiastically—with the editing, filmography, video and DVD research, and image production. Her knowledge of *Frankenstein* saved me from some major errors.

A Note on Images

Most images reproduced here are screen captures using a computer-video connection. Where available, DVD formats were used to obtain the highest-quality image. I thank Sarah Gonzales of Rounder Graphics for technical advice and Krist Bender and Laurel Lacroix for patient assistance. Screen captures enabled me to be more precise in my selections than would otherwise have been possible. There are obvious limitations and distortions, but any film image reproduced in a book is but a sketch alluding to the real thing, the movie. If one of my discussions or an image here inspires a reader to watch the movie and ponder it further, I will have succeeded.

Cynthia A. Freeland

INTRODUCTION
Evil in Horror Films—
A Feminist Framework

Most people have a certain understanding of what a horror film is, namely, that it is emotionally juvenile, ignorant, supremely non-intellectual and dumb. Basically stupid. But I think of horror films as art, as films of confrontation . . . . Just because you're making a horror film doesn't mean you can't make an artful film. Tell me the difference between someone's favourite horror film and someone else's favourite art film. There really isn't any. Emotions, imagery, intellect, your own sense of self.

—**David Cronenberg**[1]

This is a book about how horror films prompt our reflections on evil and its allure. I want to focus on broad themes raised by some significant and—to use director David Cronenberg's term—"artful" horror films. I will look at films made by great directors like Alfred Hitchcock *(Frenzy)*, the late Stanley Kubrick *(The Shining)*, and Roman Polanski *(Repulsion)*. I will discuss popular films *(The Silence of the Lambs)* and lesser-known films *(Peeping Tom)*, vampires and slashers, gory horror *(Hellraiser)* and subtle horror *(Dead Ringers)*. I will move from the gothic European crypts of *Frankenstein* and *Dracula* to the contemporary American world of *Henry: Portrait of a Serial Killer* and on into the future of humans in outer space in *Alien*.

This introduction describes my methods and the general grounds for considering horror films in a philosophical way. The topic of evil is a huge one that has been addressed over centuries by philosophers, theologians, psychologists, political scientists, and, of course, artists in many media. Horror films continue the traditions of Sophocles, Dante, Milton, Shakespeare, Bosch, Goya, Mozart, Verdi, Kafka, Dostoyevsky, and many others by offering fictive or symbolic representations of evil. Monsters are at the heart of horror, and monsters are usually—though not always—evil.

One recent book on the topic of evil, C. Fred Alford's *What Evil Means to Us*, suggests, however, that the meditations of horror movies are vapid ("stupid" or "juvenile," to use Cronenberg's terms).[2] Alford argues that contemporary culture offers few and only shallow resources for symbolizing evil. He sees this as harmful and dangerous, because symbols of evil are essential to enable all of us to grapple with very basic human limitations and fears, especially the fear of death. Religious frameworks for addressing evil are not as dominant, nor as satisfying to many people, as they once were; but rich and persuasive new frameworks have not sprung up to replace them. If reflections on evil must be fundamentally *moral* in nature, then scientific accounts of evil—even social scientific ones from fields like psychology or criminal justice—will also not suffice.

Horror films provide one very large, popular, ongoing, and accessible body of material for symbolizing evil. The question is, do they do so interestingly? Can they offer rich, varied, subtle, and complex views on the nature of evil? Do they afford us ways of meditating on death, the limitations of the flesh, and our tiny place in the cosmos or on ways to create values once religion has lost its grip? I think so, and I plan to argue for this claim here. Alford thinks not. He considers vampires, for example, vapid figures of evil compared with the richly complex Satan of a great work like Milton's *Paradise Lost;* vampires are mere consumers of the flesh, not tempters of the soul. I disagree: Vampires and other monsters, in excellent films, can promote quite subtle reflections on evil. In horror films, evil may be very diverse and shifting: It can be localized in a monster like a six-foot cockroach, or it may dwell inside us humans—within a mad scientist like Dr. Frankenstein or a psychopathic killer like Hannibal Lecter. It may be the project of evil corporations, as it often is in Cronenberg's films, or evil may be a more floating, generalized cosmic condition, as in *Eraserhead*.

Another criticism of horror films inverts Alford's claim that the symbols of evil in horror movies are too shallow. Perhaps instead horror films are too *interesting* in their depictions of evil. Monsters are often creative, fascinating, sympathetic, complex, and deeply insidious in their vile programs and agendas. A monster like Lestat (Tom Cruise) in *Interview with the Vampire* is very seductive and entertaining. But, as Hannah Arendt famously argued in her book *Eichmann in Jerusalem: A Report on the Banality of Evil*,[3] an overemphasis on monsters falsifies the nature of modern evil, which is often bureaucratic and almost faceless. Arendt argued that evil in the Nazi period was "banal"—Eichmann was a middle manager "just doing his job" and seeking promotion, not a foaming-at-the-mouth horror-movie monster. Modern evil is often characterized as indifference to suffering rather than as the active pursuit of it by an extraordinary monster like Pinhead in the *Hellraiser* series—an update of Lucifer with his nail-studded head, maniacal laugh, and S&M paraphernalia. Pinhead is recognizably monstrous, whereas Eichmann could pass as the man next door. Perhaps, then, horror-movie evil is *too* imaginative, creative, and intriguing. There may be something to this criticism, but it, too, like Alford's, misrepresents and oversimplifies the horror film. I will argue here that some films (like *Henry: Portrait of a Serial Killer*) do suggest we consider the banality of evil. And other movies also offer hints of real-life, and not wildly fictive, kinds of evil: problems like child sexual abuse, scientific hubris, racism, or corporate greed.

In reviewing the many ways horror films present evil, I will regard these films as artifacts structured so as to stimulate both our emotional and our intellectual responses. I draw on recent cognitivist film theory and maintain that horror films are designed to prompt *emotions* of fear, sympathy, revulsion, dread, anxiety, or disgust. And in doing so, they also stimulate *thoughts* about evil in its many varieties and degrees: internal or external, limited or profound, physical or mental, natural or supernatural, conquerable or triumphant. Horror films are stimuli that tend to work effectively in certain ways or that reliably elicit certain kinds of emotions and thoughts; but they do not function on merely passive audiences. Rather, these films (like others in different genres) require those of us in the audience to be active as we exercise our various mental abilities.[4] We are *thinking* as we follow features of the film that guide our emotional response: We make judgments and evaluations as we watch, react, and listen. We may experience standard or predictable emotions (fear, revulsion, dread, relief), but then we also reflect on why and whether it is right to do so. Is it right, for example, to sympathize with the serial killer Mark Lewis in *Peeping Tom*, or to approve of Susan Tyler's genetically engineered cockroaches in *Mimic*? Among other things, we think about what the film is saying about the nature of evil, and about how well it functions as a movie: Is it subtle, interesting, innovative within its genre? Just how complex our thinking about horror can be is best shown by illustrations—a task that the rest of this book aims to complete.

Feminism and Horror

My readings throughout this book will be feminist. Some people assume that the horror genre is antiwoman—and, to be sure, women have always been targets of monsters, from vampires to slasher killers. I will argue, however, that in their reflections on evil, horror films often question the traditional values and gender roles associated with patriarchal institutions such as religion, science, the law, and the nuclear family. This kind of challenge to dominant values was evident in the first modern horror masterpiece, Mary Shelley's *Frankenstein*, and it remains a factor in recent horror movies like the *Alien* series or *The Silence of the Lambs*. As a feminist, I face certain obvious challenges, though, in making my case. Since *Psycho*'s infamous shower scene, the big screen has treated us to Freddy Krueger's long razor nails emerging between Nancy's legs in the bathtub *(A Nightmare on Elm Street)*, Brian De Palma's exhibitionist heroine being power-drilled into the floor *(Body Double)*, and Leatherface hanging a woman from a meat hook *(The Texas Chainsaw Massacre.)* Even in films with a strong heroine like *Alien* and *Aliens*, the feminist message seems qualified by the monstrousness of the alien mother, the objectification of Sigourney Weaver in her underwear, and her character Ripley's forced assumption of a maternal role. Despite all this, there has been some feminist work on horror, and I believe there is room for more.

I do not presume any one account of feminism (radical, liberal, Marxist, postmodernist) or any one theory of sexual or gender difference. I seek to avoid universalizing assumptions about gender as I ask how a given film depicts gender in relation to its larger themes about good and evil. *Repulsion* and *The Silence of the Lambs*, for example, both offer kinds of feminist visions in horror, but in quite different ways. I consider psychoanalytic feminisms to be theoretically ill-grounded and too reductive; their prominence in film theory is disproportionate to their general importance in feminist theorizing. Cognitivists like me who seek to diagnose the gender ideology of a film may adopt the viewpoint of a Marxist or liberal feminist; in either case, one could be critical, though of different aspects of the film and to different ends. Much current film theory is interested in the psychology of viewer interest and response. I am more interested in what the movies *say*, in how they are structured to present certain contents. Some of the questions I ask will take the place of others posed on the more problematic basis of depth psychology or psychoanalysis. Questions common in feminist film theory (about "the gaze," the sadistic male viewer, the masculine narrative order, and so on) will be replaced here by questions about whether a film presents women as primarily suffering and tortured physical beings or whether they are also shown to be alert, curious, intelligent, capable of independent investigation, and so forth. I also ask about whether the women characters help move the narrative along or are simply targets of the horrific spectacle. The most serious questions I want to consider are about where the film narrative locates the sources of evil and how evil is analyzed or described in relation to gender.

More About the Cognitivist Framework

Like ancient Greek tragedies, horror films are works that involve disturbing an audience. They are "difficult" works with a kind of negative aesthetic aim. Tragedy, according to the classical account of Aristotle, aims at evoking pity and fear, whereas horror aims to evoke fear, terror, disgust, and other associated emotions. Both genres pose a problem about why we would enjoy them, since they are painful to watch. Plato thought that tragedy ran the risk of desensitizing audiences to proper value commitments by fostering too much emotion; and many modern critics similarly argue that horror movies can be corrupting and degrading influences on audiences. Aristotle famously defended tragedy in his *Poetics* as having redeeming moral and social value because it provides an intellectual engagement with the artistic features of a play, such as its plot and thought. He argued in effect that tragedy depicts ways in which good people cope or are damaged by the limitations life can pose for them.[5] Faced with death, disaster, or unintended evil effects, a good person's character should persist and not be ruined.

The cognitivist approach in film studies is continuous with previous discussions of other kinds of artworks in the Western aesthetic tradition. These range from Aristotle's account of tragedy in the *Poetics* and Kant's treatment of beauty and the sublime in his *Critique of Judgement* to more recent works like Kendall Walton's *Mimesis as Make-Believe: On the Foundations of the Representational Arts*, which analyzes our responses to fictions of many sorts.[6] Philosophers have typically supposed that it is appropriate for aesthetic theory to discuss aspects of the psychology of our response to artworks and have done so within various evolving theories of the psyche. Aristotle and Kant, for example, both had faculty theories of the mind that separated imagination from conceptual or scientific thought. Their theories of the mind had an impact on the other branches of their philosophies, including their ethics and aesthetics. Over the centuries, philosophers have treated emotions and imagination in very different ways. Some have held that there is a sharp separation between affect and intellect; Aristotle and Kant differed on this point. But in most cases, philosophers have emphasized that our aesthetic responses somehow draw upon both aspects of our psyche. In other words, paintings, tragedies, sculptures, or even landscape gardens have been seen as particular kinds of phenomena intentionally created and well structured to produce certain kinds of effects on *both* our emotions *and* our judgments—effects variously labeled *katharsis*, aesthetic distance, the free play of the imagination, and so on.[7]

Current cognitivism continues this tradition of philosophical aesthetics by drawing upon recent scientific accounts of human psychology and the human mind to describe our responses to artworks. Obviously, we humans are capable of being frightened, excited, horrified, and the like by artistic representations, including horror films; cognitivists try to analyze how this occurs. Cognitivism is not a single method dominated by any one figure or school. Thus, David Bordwell and Noël Carroll write, "We think that cognitivism is best characterized as a stance. A cognitivist analysis or explanation seeks to understand human thought, emotion, and action by appeal to processes of mental representation, naturalistic processes, and (some sense of) rational agency."[8] Cognitivists acknowledge and draw upon recent scientific theories of the mind. The science of the mind is as old as Aristotle; it took important steps in the late nineteenth century with Freud, the Gestalt psychologists, William James, and others, but it has been under constant development and has taken even more enormous strides in the late twentieth century. Different fields such as neuroscience, cognitive linguistics, primate biology, artificial intelligence, psychiatry, and robotics are all making distinct and remarkable contributions to our understanding of the mind, its evolution and development, its physiological base in the brain and body, its manifestations in language, and its breakdowns in diseases like schizophrenia, autism, or various aphasias. Experts in psychology, mass communication, and vision now study our human perception and response to films in empirical ways—even measuring, for example, how our bodies might respond to an on-screen stimulus like the appearance of a gigantic monstrous dinosaur or, to change genres, a pair of naked bodies encoiled in sexual intimacies.

Some initial efforts along these very empirical lines, such as psychologist Ed S. Tan's treatment of film as an "emotion machine" in his book *Emotion and the Structure of Narrative Film: Film as an Emotion Machine,* are very interesting and suggestive.[9] Despite the fact that his book title smacks of reductivism, Tan actually urges the need for refinement and subtlety and for more specific studies of particular genres in relation to their unique audiences. Tan makes the point by noting that people vary along a dimension he calls "cinephilia": There are some people who are especially knowledgeable about film and likely to spend time attending movies. They particularly appreciate films as aesthetic objects, and Tan comments that "[a]ppreciation of the film as artifact can be measured."[10] Although this seems an initially odd claim, we probably all recognize that people who go to more movies do know more and react differently to them than people who go to few. Similarly, Tan points out that different kinds of people are likely to prefer and attend films of different genres and that emotional and cognitive response may vary according to both the genre and the specific audience in attendance. Horror, as I know from my own experience from years of being a fan, definitely does attract a distinctive kind of audience.[11] Some people tell me that they never go to horror films and simply cannot stand them; others of us are more dedicated to the genre and enjoy or even love it. We are obviously more knowledgeable about it. Horror audiences are participatory. We may clap, laugh uproariously, or otherwise respond in surprising ways to things that we recognize as allusions, in-jokes, or sight gags, while our more weak-stomached friends (or spouses we have dragged along) find the movie frightening or simply disgusting.

Since I am a philosopher and not an empirical psychologist or social scientist, I do not propose to wire people up to measure their heart and breathing rates or to assay their responses scene by scene by means of detailed questionnaires. My own reliance on cognitivism is like that of other philosophers who have entered the field of film studies in recent years (such as Richard Allen, Gregory Currie, Noël Carroll, Murray Smith, and Carl Plantinga). We share with a psychologist like Tan something other than a particular method of empirical research. We emphasize a view that cognitive science supports: the intricate intertwining of our human intellect and emotions. An emotion like disgust—say, when we suddenly witness on-screen the human bodies being "cocooned" by the alien monster's larvae in *Alien Resurrection*—may seem quite physical, uncontrolled, and not very "intellectual" at all. Yet even this sort of reaction does involve thoughts ("How frightening for those poor people who are victims and are actually awake at the time!"), classifications ("The Alien is like a wasp."), recommendations ("The crew had better get out of this ship, and fast!"), questions ("How can humans cope now that Ripley is dead?"), and judgments ("Those Aliens are nasty killers who ought to be exterminated."). Horror films may evoke quite complex and subtle combinations of feelings and emotions; I think that such responses can be of philosophical interest. Perhaps ironically, recent cognitive science dovetails with a view of thought, emotion, and human response to art that recalls Aristotle's back in the ancient world—since he, too, thought that an emotion included elements of physiology, judgment, and tendencies toward action and that artworks like tragedies might prompt such complex responses from audiences.

There have been several recent noteworthy cognitivist forays into the horror genre, and it will be helpful to distinguish my aims and framework from theirs. I will mention two examples. First, in his important book *The Philosophy of Horror, or Paradoxes of the Heart*, Noël Carroll argues that the genre of horror can be defined in terms of the characteristic emotions it is designed to elicit from audiences.[12] The most obvious list of such emotions includes fear, repulsion, dread, and disgust. A key question to answer about horror films involves the "paradox of the heart" referred to in Carroll's subtitle: Why do we enjoy being scared, repulsed, or disgusted by scary books or films? Carroll's answer is plausible and well developed. He describes a notion of "art-horror," a special aesthetic response to a representation or a fiction in an artwork. "Art-horror" involves real emotions like fear or sympathy: We may really be frightened or disgusted by a film; we may have a rapid heartbeat and hold our breath when the heroine goes into that dark basement or attic. But this experience or emotion is unlike the horror we would ourselves feel in response to a real-life threat, because we are reacting of course to a story. The film, along with its slasher, dinosaur, mad scientist, or evil "blob," is a *representation*. It is just simply true of humans that we may enjoy or feel other responses to such representations. As Aristotle said in the *Poetics*, the enjoyment of imitations seems to be natural from childhood.

Art-horror, in Carroll's view, accompanies the cognitive challenges of a plot; we enjoy following a narrative as it shows how characters learn about and confront a monster—perhaps overcoming it, perhaps not. Carroll argues that the emotions of horror are prompted mainly by monsters, so that these creatures are essential to horror. He defines monsters as entities that are supernatural or not believed to exist by scientists, and he explains that they are threatening primarily because they are "impure" or, in his words, "categorically interstitial." Another feature of our intellectual engagement with horror, then, is the cognitive challenge of trying to understand and conceptualize such interstitial beings. Here we are guided by the film narrative as the plot unfolds and characters suffer, whether justly or not; fight, whether valiantly or foolishly; uncover or collude with the threat, and so on.

Carroll's account is a cognitivist one, and so is mine, but we differ on many details. For one thing, I aim, as he does not, at producing more extended readings of individual horror films, and feminist readings at that. I also want to suggest that the more intellectual aspect of our engagement with horror films is focused on issues about evil and that it involves more than plot. In Carroll's account, horror focuses primarily on the nature of monsters, disturbing and interstitial beings. I assume a different perspective, considering monsters as beings that raise the specter of *evil* by overturning the natural order, whether it be an order concerning death, the body, God's laws, natural laws, or ordinary human values. The spectacles of horror—the gruesome wounds, slimy beasts, undead vampires, or exploding heads—may be more central even than plot to forcing our confrontation with evil.

In another recent book, *Moving Pictures: A New Theory of Film Genres, Feelings, and Cognition*, Torben Grodal offers a different account of the cognitive appeal of horror.[13] Like Carroll, Grodal thinks that horror narratives elicit judgments, along with feelings and emotions. But his focus is not so much on monsters and the challenges of conceptualizing them; rather, in Grodal's view, horror thematizes certain universal human concerns about autonomy in the face of threats from within or without. He writes that "the explicit motivation for horror fiction . . . is a desire for cognitive and physical control."[14] So, for example, a horror film might be about our loss of cognitive control in a "paranoid narrative" where rational explanations make no sense of the cosmos in light of the existence of ghosts, zombies, and the like. This is the case in the film *Them!*, where giant ants attack humans. Grodal explains that "the extreme effect of alien, nature-based subjectivity on the humans is 'paralysis,' lack of flexible human subjectivity."[15] Or alternatively, a horror film might thematize our loss of individual bodily control, as Grodal illustrates with the example of *Coma*. Here, evil doctors are harvesting human body parts from healthy people to sell on the black market. They drug the heroine, a woman doctor, once she uncovers their dastardly plot, and she is unable to speak or act so as to convey her knowledge as they proceed to make plans to operate on her.

Grodal only discusses horror as part of a short (sixteen-page) chapter that also considers crime and thriller movies, so it is not surprising that his analysis of the appeal of horror is cruder than Carroll's. It is less clear in Grodal's treatment that horror movies are aesthetically constructed artifacts and also not clear why we would enjoy many of them. He suggests that we enjoy films like *Coma* because they frighten us, only in the end to reinforce our "desire for control." In *Coma*, the doctor is rescued in the nick of time before the tainted anesthetic is administered. Thus, Grodal writes that "from the point of view of emotion-engineering in visual fiction, fear and terror caused by cognitive dissociation and/or violence have the morally dubious advantage of creating high levels of arousal and strengthening the viewers' wish for emotional autonomy and control by aversion."[16] Grodal's analysis implies that horror movies provide a sort of tonic for the ego: We go to them and get frightened about losing control, so we gird our loins, so to speak, emerging from the theater all prepared to do battle against threats! This might seem counter to the more natural construal, that a film like *Coma* would make us even more paranoid than we might already be about the manipulations of the medical establishment in an era where it has turned into big business. Since I do think that horror can offer social critique (David Cronenberg's horror movies, for example, often focus on the medical-business alliances of our modern era), I do not make this suggestion merely facetiously. (Think of all the women who claimed to be unable to take a shower after seeing *Psycho*.) Grodal's account just seems too skimpy to tell us much that is interesting, and it also forces a single overly restrictive goal onto a particular genre—horror—that offers a lot of variety and complexity.

I have mentioned these two previous approaches to horror, Carroll's and Grodal's, so as to illustrate key features of a cognitivist account. As I noted earlier, cognitivism in general treats emotions as part of our cognitive outlook on the world; emotional arousal accompanies audience members' active interpretation and thinking about a film. Too many accounts of emotions or of responses to films fail to bring out these aesthetic and cognitive dimensions. We can *learn* even as we react to the most blatantly scary and manipulative scenes in films that shock us and make us jump or recoil at a physical level. I will proceed along similar lines, but in my view, it is more philosophically interesting to consider horror movies that are about evil rather than to focus on the nature of monsters or on an alleged aim of cognitive control. Also, unlike Carroll and Grodal, I write as a feminist, so my focus and emphasis will be distinctive. One worry about Grodal's analysis is that many horror films (Cronenberg's included) do not offer the kind of resolution or happy ending that *Coma* does. That is, they seem to challenge a viewer's hopes for or beliefs in our own possibilities of control or autonomy, undermining the grounds he offers for their appeal. And in any case, "control" is a rather vague and general notion. The seductive threat to our control from vampires is very different from the physical threats posed by giant spiders, aliens, or demonic forces of possession; mad-scientist films might carry social critiques that are distinct from those suggested by the slasher genre. Both Regan in *The Exorcist* and Rosemary in *Rosemary's Baby* lose control, they are both young and female, and each film presents horror in a quasi-theological context. The two films were made in roughly similar time periods and set in a similar cultural milieu. Yet they differ in important ways. They ask different questions and depict very different kinds of avenues of response to demonic evil. Regan (at least prior to the many *Exorcist* sequels!) seems to be cleansed and rescued, whereas Rosemary is doomed. Horror movies are a good case in which the devil is almost literally in the details.

Carroll's treatment of horror is book-length, wide ranging, subtle, and superior to Grodal's, but even so, I find his attempt to hang his definition of the horror genre on the one central notion of monsters too restrictive. If monsters are really "*super*-natural," as he thinks, then a real-life monster like Bob Rusk in *Frenzy* does not quite fit the paradigm. For similar reasons, Carroll has to stretch things a bit to make a movie like *Jaws*, with a shark monster, or Alfred Hitchcock's *The Birds*, fit his definition. I consider horror narratives to be centrally concerned with evil, but I do not aim here to defend this assumption by developing this as a general definition of horror. Horror has too long and complex a history for me to feel confident about any one definition. The genre is just slippery: It blends at the edges with many other genres such as science fiction and the thriller. It is also important to recognize the dazzling diversity of horror's subgenres: Gothic, mad scientist, alien invader, slasher-psycho, rape revenge, B-movie, cult film, monster, vampire, werewolf, possession film, zombie, comedy, Japanese horror (the original *Godzilla*), and so on—even music video horror (Michael Jackson's *Thriller*)! In light of all this genre diversity, I do not aim at anything like a definition. Rather, I propose an approach that may help in looking for meaning in individual films.

In fact, my view that horror concerns evil could in principle encompass both Carroll's and Grodal's suggestions, that it is about monsters or about issues of autonomy and control. After all, monsters are usually (though not always) evil in horror movies, and the loss of control, too, is often attributed to something evil or adds up to an overall existential condition of evil. But the theme of evil as treated by some horror movies makes them more philosophically interesting than these other accounts suggest. So here is an extra reason for them to have appeal: They challenge, puzzle, and stimulate us as we see or feel horrific things happening to people—often to good people—and we ponder whether we also might be fated to confront or succumb to such evil. There may be key formulas or scenarios (vampires), prominent directors (Hitchcock, Cronenberg), or distinct social contexts (*Them!* versus *Henry: Portrait of a Serial Killer*) that affect meaning and impact in this genre. Similar factors operate in other genres, such as the Western, where themes of good and evil are also paramount.[17]

Films within a single subgenre like the vampire film may present male monsters as distinctive as Klaus Kinski's emaciated Nosferatu, the campy Bela Lugosi, the languid Frank Langella, the sinister Christopher Lee, and the macabre but hilarious ball-goers of Roman Polanski. A quite horrific and gory movie can also be wildly funny (*The Texas Chainsaw Massacre, Part 2; Frenzy; An American Werewolf in London; Blood Simple*). Horror films can be eerie and subtly creepy (*The Dead Zone*), or they can revel in over-the-top hair-raising outrageous effects (*Hellraiser; Cujo; Evil Dead II: Dead by Dawn; The Texas Chainsaw Massacre, Part 2*). They can be depth-psychological "family romances" (*Repulsion, Peeping Tom*) or virtual cartoons (*Predator 2*). They can be historical costume dramas (Werner Herzog's *Nosferatu*, Francis Ford Coppola's *Bram Stoker's Dracula*) or technophilic futuristic visions (*Robocop, Alien*). They can be vividly realistic (*Jurassic Park*) or ridiculously fake (*Godzilla*). They can be incredibly original (*Scanners, Brain Dead*), mindlessly imitative (*Silent Madness, Orca*), or a little of both (*Body Double*).

A comprehensive approach to cinematic horror would have to be historically aware and also broad and open enough to work for all of these varieties of horror. In light of these observations, the task of building a "feminist cognitivist theory of horror" may seem monumental. And in fact, this is not my aim in this book. I do not propose to analyze the nature of horror any more than to suggest that there is an "essence" that defines the genre. Rather, I want to show that at least some horror films, the ones I discuss, are very interesting for philosophers and for feminists in general to consider. I would hope that as film theorists, we can avoid overgeneralization along with reductivism. Because of the horror genre's complexity, history, and variety, I do not aim at a putatively complete "feminist theory of horror."[18] Horror originated from the Gothic novel, a fact important for feminists to note because of the unusual prevalence of women as both writers and readers within this genre.[19]

I will return to this and other aspects of horror's history in later chapters. The astounding variety of styles, nuances, and tones within this genre leads me to be skeptical about any particular feminist theory of horror, just as I am doubtful about aspects of the earlier cognitivist accounts given by Carroll and Grodal. Feminist theories too often become overly general, whether they associate gender with a certain kind of looking, monstrousness, the victimization of women, or some alleged psychological work such as "abjection" (for more details, see the next section).

My strategy will be to select certain films that I consider especially good and worthwhile and to emphasize these films, placing special weight on the interplay between cinematic, emotional, and cognitive dimensions as I focus on their attitudes toward evil. I will also explore their "gender ideologies" or use of "gendered concepts"—terms I will explain more as I proceed. To produce my feminist readings or interpretations of various horror films, I focus on their representational contents and practices, describing how these elicit characteristic affects (terror, dread) as well as how they prompt our thinking about the various evils they represent. I want to examine how horror films answer questions about evil in relation to issues of gender, sexuality, and power relations between the sexes. There does not seem to be any one path or method to do this; rather, I proceed by examples, actually looking at various crucial sorts of film elements, whether of narrative, characterization, spectacle, or more general "cinematic features" (point of view, special effects, lighting, musical score, and so on). Some of a horror film's key elements will concern its representation of women and monsters, but there are many dimensions involved in how a film is structured and how it works. A cognitivist supposes that we can explain the psychodynamics of viewing movies by actually describing the nature of films as artifacts that function for certain purposes to elicit a fused cognitive/emotional response. The effects of such artifacts may be studied by examining the construction of these artifacts as well as their role in culture. To study their construction, I will look at such standard features as plot, characters, and point of view. To study their role in culture—that is, to inquire about this as a feminist—I will examine their gender ideology. This is what I mean to do in producing feminist philosophical readings of the horror films I discuss.

The strategy I favor is one that revises and updates a somewhat old-fashioned feminist approach to film studies, the "images of women" approach.[20] Using this approach, we would analyze a genre of horror like the slasher film, say, by observing the images of women that are presented in these films. Thus, typically, young women are shown either as tomboys or as teenage sex fiends who somehow deserve their dismemberment at the hands of a Jason or a Michael Myers. To explore a film's gender ideology, I ask various questions that would also be asked in the images of women approach: How does the film depict/represent women—as agents, patients, knowers, sufferers? What role do women play vis-à-vis men in the film? However, I will go beyond this rather simple set of questions in two main ways.

First, a cognitivist recognizes that films are complex functioning artifacts composed of a wide variety of elements that affect our thoughts and emotions. These include more than simply the "images of women," understood as the representation of female characters in the movie. Films also include technical and formal features such as editing, visual point of view, lighting, sound, and costuming, as well as features shared with literary works such as plots, dialogue, audience point of view, and narrative structure. Horror films are good or operate effectively by producing thoughts but also by eliciting emotions, sometimes very strong ones like fear, dread, or disgust. These effects can be produced by pacing, visual displays, or music, as much as through the narrative and depiction of characters. I want to consider many such devices. Still, narrative is the most important element, because in most cases, it is what provides the background or structure of a film.[21] This includes what Noël Carroll has called the film's rhetorical strategies, such as the elicitation of audience presumptions in completing gaps in the story.[22] Thus, in my approach we will ask questions like these: How do the film's structures of narrative, point of view, and plot construction operate in effecting a depiction of gender roles and relations? Does the film offer a "heroic modernist" narrative of mastery, centered upon a male character, offering up either a clear resolution or a noble tragedy? Or is there a non-standard, postmodern narrative centered upon female characters, offering a more open-ended and ambiguous conclusion? Does the film reference historical or genre precedents—say, a particular earlier vampire film or the mad scientist genre in general—and if so, how does it comment upon, replicate, parody, or revise the gender thematics of its predecessors? What are the film's implicit rhetorical presuppositions about natural gender roles and relations? Does the film present possibilities of questioning or challenging these presumptions?

Second, unlike the sometimes simplistic feminism we can find in the images of women approach, I seek to use feminist ideological critique of horror to offer a "deep" interpretive reading. By this I mean to refer to a reading that asks hard questions about the gendered concepts of the film. The phrase "gendered concept" is explained by Carolyn Korsmeyer in a fascinating article about the aesthetic theory of taste. She writes, "By this phrase I refer to concepts that, lacking any obvious reference to males or females, or to masculinity or femininity, nevertheless are formulated in such a way that their neutral quality and universal applicability are questionable."[23] To scrutinize a film's use of gendered concepts, I will question its gender ideology. This is a notion I borrow and develop from Marxist theory. An ideology is a distorted representation of existing relations of power and domination. Although such relations empower only certain people and prop up the status quo, they are presented as natural and beneficial to all. In the particular context of feminist analysis, the ideology under examination is one that sustains the power relations of patriarchy and male domination (together with any relevant associated relations of class or race dominance). Often such relations are represented on film as natural or inevitable. Feminist ideology critique is a critical or deep interpretive reading that criticizes or analyzes a film's presentation of these naturalized messages about gender roles and the power relations between the sexes. I want to study the messages that a film may offer about gender—either about what is taken for granted and accepted as true and natural or about what it challenges its audience to question. Films (including horror films) often convey messages that perpetuate the subordination and exploitation of women; they sustain the current understanding of gender hierarchy or genderized roles and relations by portraying these as normal. But I find it more interesting that often in good horror movies like *The Silence of the Lambs*, the film itself raises questions about ideology or about these supposedly "normal" relations of gender dominance.

An interesting and creative feminist reading of a film may look below its surface representations of male or female characters to consider gendered concepts in such notions as reason, science, nature, creativity, intelligence, care, and so on. To explore the ideology, we search for gaps, presumptions, or even what is "repressed" in it. It is important to look at what a film may show as blocked, omitted, or avoided in our standard representations of gender and the relations between the sexes. My strategy accords with advice laid out by the French feminist Luce Irigaray in her critical exploration of central gendered concepts or gender ideology in the discourse of the male Western philosophical tradition.[24] Irigaray highlights these through her disruptive feminist readings of classical texts, and she speaks of "jamming the theoretical machinery itself, of suspending its pretension to the production of a truth and of a meaning that are excessively univocal."[25] In a similar way, I want to do disruptive readings of horror films as texts. Irigaray is a psychoanalyst and philosopher who emerged from within the Lacanian psychoanalytic tradition, but she has produced powerful feminist critiques of the most basic assumptions of Freudian and Lacanian psychoanalytic theory, and I do not believe that her recommended strategies of reading (whether of philosophy, literature, or film) must rely on any specific psychosexual assumptions. As strategies of *reading* they work much like deconstructive textual strategies that are logically separable from particular psychological assumptions. A brief example may help show this.

In her book *Men, Women, and Chain Saws: Gender in the Modern Horror Film*, Carol J. Clover has done something like an Irigarayan deep reading that highlights gender ideology and the use of gendered concepts in recent popular teenage slasher movies.[26] Clover does this by criticizing an existing form of discourse in the depiction of women and girls in slasher films. She points out the obvious: that these films show young women as somehow bad—too sexy and alluring—before they are attacked by a male. (Even such recent movies as *Scream* and *Scream 2* do this). Clover argues, more deeply, that though slashers often feature one central heroine, they nevertheless reinforce cultural messages (ideologies) about the virtues of masculinity by presenting a villain who is defectively masculine—often someone pudgy, awkward, shy, or seemingly impotent—and by making the heroine (the "Final Girl," as she calls her) virginal, "pure," and more masculine than feminine. I call this a deep reading because it shows up a continuing ideology: The apparently male villains are bad because the relevant concepts like "impotent" or "pudgy" are culturally coded as feminine. Similarly, the concepts like "mechanical," "strong," "resourceful," or "active" that name attributes of the "Final Girl" are coded as masculine.[27] In Clover's reading, despite the fact that they present intriguing heroines, slasher films uphold gender ideology by upholding traditional "male" virtues and derogating or punishing "female" traits.

My readings ask questions about films' representations of evil in the world and in relation to gender roles and relations, the horrific monster, and the type of resolutions presented. Cognitivism about horror raises questions about how horror constructs narratives of evil and presents gender ideology. I believe that my cognitivist framework offers a flexible, nonreductive, and potentially illuminating framework for constructing creative feminist readings of horror films.[28] We must recognize that horror movies often have very complex, mixed representations of women as well as of larger issues about the nature and existence of evil. I will construct readings that focus on gender representations within certain horror films. Different feminist readings of the same horror film could probably be constructed. But this is part of my point: Horror films can stimulate thought and reflection. Of course, horror films are not all equal. It would be absurd to claim that every horror film has something particularly exciting or illuminating to say on the subject of gender or on the other topics of my book—evil, power, morality, human limitation, and so on. My readings do not purport to be final or "complete"; it will be enough for me if I can show that it is possible for feminists and philosophers to take horror movies seriously. To echo director David Cronenberg's words, quoted as the book's epigram, I, too, "think of horror films as art, as films of confrontation."

Methods I Do Not Use

Marxist Ideology Critique

My approach differs from traditional forms of Marxist ideology critique. Marxist lines of interpretation emphasize the role of capital so much that they ascribe great power to the productive apparatuses of Hollywood and correspondingly little power to audience members.[29] But I believe that audience members do have the power to create individual, often subversive, readings of films. Viewing this from my cognitivist framework of general psychological processes, it may be that horror directors expect or rely on the power they exert over audiences, but that is neither to say that the filmmaker controls or dictates the audience responses nor that audiences are unintelligent. Horror movie viewers are often highly sophisticated and critical; horror movie screenings tend to be more participatory than those for other genres of film. Cult phenomena like *The Rocky Horror Picture Show* make this clear. Although it is undeniable that some horror films like those in the *Alien* series are popular and big-budget items with major stars and broad releases, horror often has an uneasy relation to the Hollywood mainstream. As recently as 1996, Cronenberg, though a well-established and highly touted film director, had great trouble securing the American release of his controversial semi-horror film *Crash*.

Similarly, in his book *A Philosophy of Mass Art,* Noël Carroll notes that ideology critique as practiced by humanities scholars often implicates "the masses" in a kind of dumb victimization that patronizingly suggests they require professorial liberation and enlightenment. (At the same time, unfortunately, this also suggests that they might just absorb the academic critique in the same dumb, passive way!) Carroll acknowledges that a number of rhetorical functions are played by diverse types of mass art, not all of them very savory, but he holds that audiences are not merely passive victims of such rhetoric. He provides a detailed analysis of the controversial and overused concept of ideology that concludes by emphasizing that the core notion of ideology has two aspects: an epistemological one (an ideology presents false information) and a dominance one (the false information serves the ends of a dominant class or group). To show how a given form of mass art (like horror) is ideological in this sense would require empirical studies and support, and Carroll does not oppose this approach. But like me, he also advocates the option of exploring how the genres function or are intended to function to interact with audience capacities for both feelings and thoughts.

This kind of cognitivist strategy provides a new framework for ideology critique that acknowledges both the structures of texts and the psychological abilities of audiences—including their critical abilities. Like Carroll, other cognitivists I have mentioned before in this book, such as Ed S. Tan and Torben Grodal, would emphasize these dual aspects as a framework for exploring horror films. We must look at both the aesthetic features of representations and the audience's cognitive and emotional responses to them.

In my view, feminist critique aims to uncover ideologies in horror films (and elsewhere) of traditional patriarchal dominance relations. But I believe that individual viewers (perhaps in particular, feminist viewers) may either see through such relations or reread the intended ones in subversive ways. Even when a film presents a problematic image of women, the audience reaction may subvert or undercut it. Douglas Kellner and Michael Ryan, in their book *Camera Politica*, adopt a more standardly Marxist view of film ideology than my own. They discuss sexist ideologies of horror films in the early 1980s, which they interpret as expressing male backlash against feminist advances of the time.[30] Perhaps I would agree with them about some movies such as *Fatal Attraction*, but not about others.[31] Kellner and Ryan are highly critical, for instance, of the bondage scenes in *Cat People;* their discussion seems to assume that the filmmakers had an agenda that would determine audience responses by buying into their assumed agreement or shared resistance to new feminist values. Yet when I saw the film in a crowded theater in New York City at the time of its release, the audience hooted loudly and derisively at just these scenes (the phrase "catcalls" took on new meaning in this context!). That is, they seemed to see through this maneuver of the filmmakers so as to resist the film's surface ideology. As we will see throughout this book, horror films often do solicit just such subversive audience responses.

Psychoanalysis

Similarly, my cognitivist account allows for more individuality of critical reaction from the audience than many current feminist psychoanalytic theories of horror. Feminist studies grounded in psychoanalytic theories of human motivation emphasize viewers' allegedly primal motives and hence assume that there are universal sorts of interests in watching horror films. Typically in these accounts, women are described as castrated or as threats evoking male castration anxiety. In psychoanalytic theories, it is also standard to presume some connection between gazing, violent aggression, and masculinity and to suggest that there are particularly "male" motivations for making, watching, and enjoying horror films. Such approaches seem flawed to me, both because they downplay our intellectual engagement with horror movies and because they tend to be simply too reductive.

Feminist psychoanalytic approaches to film were launched by Laura Mulvey's influential essay "Visual Pleasure and Narrative Cinema" in 1975.[32] Mulvey's model draws upon theoretical work of Jacques Lacan, particularly his construals of castration anxiety and visual fetishism. She associates Lacan's notion of the "Law of the Father" (the symbolic order or patriarchy) with such traditional film features as narrative order and plot resolution, arguing that the narrative forms characteristic of mainstream Hollywood cinema differentially use women and serve men. There is a dual analogy between the woman and the screen (the object of the look) and between the man and the viewer (the possessor of the look). A tension arises in the viewer between libido and ego needs, and this tension is resolved by a process of identification, whereby the [male] viewer identifies with the [male] protagonist in the film. Thus possessing the film character of the woman by proxy, the viewer can proceed to focus energy on achieving a satisfactory narrative resolution.

Mulvey's view is still enormously influential and oft-cited, although it has also come in for a number of persuasive criticisms by other feminist film theorists, and she has even revised it herself.[33] For example, Linda Williams scrutinizes Mulvey's straitjacketed association between males and the pleasures of looking or spectatorship, pointing out that often in horror, contrary to mainstream cinema, women may "look" to find the monster or *do* possess "the gaze."[34] The fates of women and monsters are often linked, since both may somehow stand outside the patriarchal order. I also find Williams's own account too limited. She argues that women who possess the gaze in horror and who become aligned with monsters are typically shown to represent threats to patriarchy and hence to require punishment. Thus, Williams accepts the basic idea that horror films reinforce conceptions of the active (sadistic) male viewer and the passive (suffering) female object. Women are punished for their appropriation of "the gaze," and a sort of masculine narrative order (what Lacan would call the Law of the Father) is restored. I do not think that this sort of explanation will work to capture what is interesting about many of the horror films I will discuss. Clarice Starling is certainly not punished in *The Silence of the Lambs*, for instance, and there are even ways in which the film undermines the message of her affiliation with the patriarchal world of the FBI. Nor does *Repulsion* restore the patriarchal order when Carol Ledoux gets apprehended at its end; to say this is to deny the numerous and disturbing ways this film chooses to occupy her point of view and shows that her responses have legitimacy in a world tainted with profound evil.

More recently, feminist film theorists have turned to the work of one of Lacan's successors, the French feminist psychoanalyst Julia Kristeva, author of *Powers of Horror: An Essay on Abjection*.[35] Kristeva's views have been adapted to film studies by Barbara Creed in her book *The Monstrous-Feminine: Film, Feminism, Psychoanalysis*.[36] Kristeva locates the sources and origins of horror not in castration anxiety but in the pre-Oedipal stage of the infant's ambivalence toward the mother as it struggles to create boundaries and forge its own ego identity. The mother is "horrific" in the sense of being all-engulfing, primitive, and impure or defiled by bodily fluids—particularly breast milk and flowing menstrual blood. Kristeva uses the term "abjection" to designate the psychic condition inspired by this image of the horrific mother. For Kristeva, horror is fundamentally about boundaries—about the threat of transgressing them and about the need to do so. Hence, she emphasizes the duality of our attraction/repulsion to the horrific.

Creed thinks that horror texts all serve to illustrate "the work of abjection"[37] and that they do so in three basic ways. First, horror depicts images of abjection, such as corpses and bodily wastes; second, horror is concerned with borders or with things that threaten the stability of the symbolic order; and third, horror constructs the maternal figure as abject. In applying this theory to a movie like *Alien,* Creed stresses the film's repeated birth scenarios and numerous versions of the engulfing, threatening, voracious, horrific Alien mother. She emphasizes that horror importantly concerns not just women as victims—women who are attacked because they present a horrific vision of a castrated body—but also monstrous women who threaten to castrate men. Thus, like Williams, Creed shows that women can be allied to monsters.

Despite details of their different pictures, each of these psychoanalytically grounded views construes the familiar tensions of horror in terms of an opposition between "female" and "male" aspects, understood or defined within the terms of a certain allegedly true theory of depth psychology. There is a tension between spectacle or the horrific feminine (associated with the castrated woman, pre-Oedipal mother, or castrating woman) and plot or narrative resolution (associated with the patriarchal order that the child achieves after resolving the Oedipus complex). A general or universal psychological theory grounds their analysis. To back up her speculations, Creed, for example, appeals to both universal cultural practices and classical mythology. Psychoanalytic feminist film theorists speculate about why "we" are interested in horror and more basically about why certain things are horrifying. These kinds of questions require an answer in terms of a specific psychoanalytical theory, which remains the basis for explanations offered of our interest in certain films. For instance, here is Creed on *The Exorcist*:

> Regan's carnivalesque display of her body reminds us quite clearly of the immense appeal of the abject. Horror emerges from the fact that woman has broken with her proper feminine role; she has "made a spectacle of herself"—put her unsocialized body on display. And to make matters worse, she has done all of this before the shocked eyes of two male clerics.[38]

Psychoanalytic feminist film interpretations are significantly constrained by the theoretical vocabulary and framework of psychoanalysis. Psychoanalysis is not only very internally divisive but it is far from achieving anything like general acceptance as a psychological theory. It has been subject to forceful critiques from a variety of directions (by Frederick Crews, Adolf Grünbaum, Gilles Deleuze and Felix Guattari, Luce Irigaray, Geoffrey Masson, and others).[39] There are new grounds in recent cognitive science for skepticism about such key psychoanalytic assumptions as the role of repressed memories or the basis for dreaming.[40] But typically in film studies, psychoanalytic interpretations are advanced a priori rather than in an open-minded spirit of testing how well they actually work. At first it may seem that a Kristevan reading is illuminating for *Alien*, with its many birth scenarios and theme of monstrous mothering. But I will argue in detail later on that such a reading fails to attend to numerous *cinematic* aspects of the film and also misses the complexity of its moral messages about corporate science; these make the film an interesting and potentially feminist successor to Mary Shelley's critique of mad science in *Frankenstein*.

The notion of abjection expands in Creed's interpretations to become almost vacuous. It is simplistic and reductive to understand in advance that all the varieties of horrific monstrousness we can think of or witness on film are really just "illustrations" of the "work" of abjection. This includes an astonishing variety ranging from *Alien*'s monstrous mother to the disintegrating cannibalistic zombies in *Night of the Living Dead*, from Seth Brundle's hideously gooey and amoral fly to the *Hellraiser*'s S&M-style Cenobites. In what sense is a psychological theory of abjection "explanatory" when it becomes so broad? Such an account misses out on the specifics of what is evil in these films, and why it is so, and how the accounts differ; it discounts the possibility of their posing distinctive ways of questioning gender ideology. A cognitivist allows that there can be unique, distinctive, sui generis human fears of a variety of things, things that are evil in different ways and for different reasons. Fear of something nasty like bugs or larvae may be rational, or it may indeed be irrational, but for reasons having nothing to do with the archaic mother.[41] To treat evil in every case as a sort of psychological remnant of the failure to separate from the mother is simply too reductive. Why must we accept or assume that all other fears can somehow equal or be reduced to fear of the primal mother? Such an assumption is unilluminating for feminist or any other purposes.

Some of the most basic assumptions of psychoanalytic feminist film theorists—that it is conceptually useful and appropriate to distinguish between male and female viewers or between heterosexual and homosexual men or women— have been placed under attack in recent theoretical work in queer and performance theory by writers like Judith Butler and Eve Sedgwick.[42] A focused awareness of issues in queer theory could lead, for example, to intriguing complexity in discussing movies like *The Hunger*, *Interview with the Vampire*, and *The Silence of the Lambs*. Taking gender transgression as a topic, I could note the obvious problems with the homophobic depiction in *The Silence of the Lambs* of the "Buffalo Bill" character, who is seemingly punished for his desire to "dress as a woman." We could go on to ask whether the vampire films present attractive and subversive visions of a new polymorphously perverse sexuality, thus validating homoeroticism—or perhaps instead subtly condemn such sexuality as perverse by showing it belongs only to undead monsters.

Even if at times there are insights produced by psychoanalytic readings of horror films, they do not require grounding in some particular psychogenetic theory that allegedly explains viewers' interests and responses in general filmic narratives and representations. It is entirely possible to construct a theory of horror that emphasizes these same tensions—between plot and spectacle—without genderizing them. And this is what I propose to do using cognitivist psychology. As far back as the ancient world, Aristotle's account of tragedy in the *Poetics* recognized a tension between the aesthetic effects evoked by spectacle in tragedy and its narrative structures.[43] Carroll's *The Philosophy of Horror* follows Aristotle and similarly pays central attention to the dichotomy horror typically depends upon, a dichotomy between the cognitive pleasures of following out the narrative and the emotional pain of art-horror associated with monsters and spectacles.[44] As feminists thinking about horror, we can attempt to grasp these same tensions and offer reasonable explanations of how a variety of films offer their unique visions of evil in relation to gender.

PART ONE

Mad Scientists and Monstrous Mothers

chapter ONE: Dr. Frankenstein's Progeny

In this chapter, I will consider what is probably the most famous horror story, *Frankenstein*. I will begin with Mary Shelley's 1818 masterpiece, then contrast it with two prominent film versions—the James Whale Universal Studios classic (1931) and the recent major studio effort directed by Kenneth Branagh, *Mary Shelley's Frankenstein* (1994). In the former, Boris Karloff offers his famous portrayal of the monster, and Robert De Niro takes on the role in Branagh's very different version. My focus will be on how these works present complex and differing pictures of good and evil in relation to the monster and his maker. Mary Shelley's book offers an influential depiction of what happens when science oversteps its proper boundaries: Nature can turn fierce to protect her prerogatives, especially when they concern a primitive female capacity for reproduction.

Most film versions of the novel gloss over Mary Shelley's nuanced portrayals of Victor Frankenstein and his creation. Whether either the man or his monster is more good than evil is difficult to decide when reading the book. The most striking differences between the novel and film versions concern the monster. Most *Frankenstein* movies are so clear about the Creature's horrible hideousness, violence, and repulsiveness that he has become one of our defining cultural icons of monstrosity. Stitched together from assorted parts of dead criminals, he is a scarred, shambling, and usually silent mess. In film portrayals like Karloff's, he is "a savage animal" who appears almost simple-minded and can only growl and grunt. Karloff manages, despite all these obstacles, to make the monster sympathetic, but still he goes on murderous rampages and violates the innocent—whether small children or the hero's fiancée. In striking contrast to this typical movie depiction, Mary Shelley presents the Creature sympathetically as having a significant interior life. Most important—and surprising for those who have never read the book—he narrates a good deal of the story.[1] The Creature evolves from goodness into vileness because of his treatment at the hands of humanity. His unnaturalness condemns him to being seen as loathsome, and in the end even he finds himself abhorrent. Branagh's film version comes much closer to allowing the Creature an interior life and moral complexity. Although the movie was badly received by critics and has many flaws, De Niro's performance in this challenging role is remarkable, and the film is well worth discussing.

As I begin with Mary Shelley's novel, I will explore two important contexts for its treatment of nature: the Romantic movement in literature and the Scientific Revolution. I will look at *Frankenstein* with the aid of feminist readings of each of these movements. From both perspectives, we will see that the story's treatment of the feminine in relation to "Nature" is ambiguous. To begin with, *Frankenstein*'s vision of a powerful Nature seems a tribute to feminist goals, since Nature exacts particular respect for the female's unique power of reproduction. Yet there are distinct problems with the novel's views about Nature and gender. A female and sublime Nature is more mystified than respected; and the sublime mysteries of Nature are also linked in troubling ways to the allegedly irrational nature of individual women. Women are valued for an emotional perspective that corrects the excessive rationalism of the male scientist. This is a trope that continues in mad-scientist movies right up to today. Such a picture of women, however, is sentimental and perpetuates gender stereotypes.

Additionally, much depends on how the story treats the "sin" of the male scientist. Monsters are alien and other, not just to the women they threaten but also to the men who create or trap them. In the next two chapters, I will trace other versions of the mad-scientist story, explaining how the *Frankenstein* paradigm is modified in subsequent horror narratives. In Chapter 2, I will consider what happens in horror films when both the monsters and scientists are *female*. Significant changes occur in the depiction of evil and in audience sympathies and emotional responses. Most notably, monstrous female reproduction shifts to the subhuman species, usually "bugs" or sometimes lizards. The female scientist—one combining "femininity" with numerous valued male traits—must correct what has gone wrong with Nature and restore what is properly "female." In Chapter 3, I will look at four of David Cronenberg's films featuring "monstrous flesh." His movies offer updates on the basic pattern of male mad scientists experimenting with female reproductive power. Such overstepping is, even more than in *Frankenstein*, graphically punished. But again we will see that it is hard to pin down the point these films are making. Is Nature feminine and somehow innately good, or is there a sort of monstrousness or evil that goes with each gender?

Mary Shelley's *Frankenstein*

Nature and Romanticism

Monsters in horror are linked to conceptions of nature in general and, in particular, *female* nature. Often, as in *Frankenstein*, monsters are produced by failed male attempts to regulate that nature by controlling or imitating reproduction.[2] Eighteenth-century concepts of the natural and the unnatural, as of art and science, evolved within new paradigms of humans' roles in the cosmos. Artists were held to be individual geniuses who drew upon a special inspirational relation to Nature in order to express their deep and private feelings in beautiful forms. The complement of this overvaluation of sublime Nature as an artistic resource was that scientific rationality required a masculine disciplining of wild rebellious Nature—often through the exploitation of new technologies. I want to explore the role of gendered concepts in *Frankenstein* as they are related to contemporaneous notions of art, science, nature, the unnatural, and the monstrous. This will pave the way for my consideration of where evil really resides in the novel.

Frankenstein is associated with Romanticism and the pursuit of the sublime in art. Both genres, Gothic and Romantic, offer intriguing pictures of male evil in relation to female victims, on the one hand, and to an alternative powerful female presence in sublime Nature, on the other.[3] Anne K. Mellor explains:

> Masculine English Romanticism has long been associated with a love of nature, or more precisely, with the epistemological relationship of the perceiving mind to the object of perception. When the fully conscious poetic mind grasps a nature that is entirely unmediated by language—or wholly constructed by its own linguistic tropes—it experiences what the Romantic writers called "the sublime."[4]

The sublime has its threatening aspects, but it ultimately empowers the (male) poet. Mellor comments that "for Wordsworth, the experience of the sublime entails isolation, a struggle for domination, exaltation, and the absorption of the other into the transcendent self."[5] The male Romantic may be a hero, but in Mary Shelley's version of Gothic literature (as in work by some of her predecessors like Ann Radcliffe), he is presented as having dual aspects. He is both passionate and threatening—much like the Romantic artist and much like both Victor and his Creature. Mary Shelley shows him—at least in the guise of her passionate creator Victor Frankenstein—to be a tragic figure destroyed by the powers of a sublime Nature that becomes not empowering but terrifying, overwhelming, and destructive.[6]

Romantic poets and authors often revisited stories from the Western tradition, as if to reconceive classical notions of heroism. The old tragic hero was endowed with a new Romantic passion through an emphasis on his individual tragic consciousness: Prometheus being punished for his heroic gifts to mankind, Satan's rebellion in *Paradise Lost,* or Adam and Eve's expulsion from the Garden of Eden. These epic figures are obviously referred to in *Frankenstein*—its subtitle after all, is *The Modern Prometheus.* The monster listens and is moved as Milton's poem is read aloud by the De Lacey family, and he later speaks of himself as a creature who has been spurned by his creator and expelled from human society. The Creature's jealousy outside the cottage is compared to Satan's envy of Adam and Eve in Paradise. But the scientist, too, is a heroic sinner, like Milton's Satan: Victor's "pregnancy" and creation are said to be like Satan conceiving sin. Some critics point out that in Mary Shelley's day, there were well-known paintings of Milton dictating to his daughters, and this presented a quite popular view in the late eighteenth and nineteenth centuries of his daughters as repentant and obedient—like Eve making amends to Adam for her sins.[7] By comparison, and perhaps as protest, Mary Shelley reworks male tragic heroes like Satan, Adam, and Prometheus to clarify their meaning in terms that speak to women. She depicts family devotion and domesticity as antidotes to isolated male hubris, and she also addresses the female author's special concerns about reproduction and sexuality.[8]

We can see parallels between Mary Shelley's vision of Nature in this novel—it is often associated with a fruitful land and domestic harmony—and Wordsworth's picture of Nature as a living organism or sacred all-creating mother. But Nature for Mary Shelley is most beneficent when it is tied to pictures of domestic, peaceful family life. Solitary encounters with Nature are not always so tranquil, nor is Nature so amenable to exploitation as a resource for poetic contemplation by the exalted masculine self. In *Frankenstein,* she implies that Nature is a sort of sacred mother who will exact revenge if her proper role is usurped by a mere mortal man. He is in danger if he pursues solitary creativity so far that it becomes an end in itself—an unnatural form of reproduction. A poet like Wordsworth sees the male artist as having the emotional depth and expressive power to depict and sustain a passionate relation to Nature. By contrast, feminists now see *Frankenstein* and Mary Shelley's later works as female reworkings of the standard male paradigms of Romanticism.[9] I will next consider more details about the depiction of Nature in this work and how it provides a response to the Romantic writers.[10]

Nature in the Novel: The New Science

Muriel Spark has claimed that *Frankenstein* delivered the death stroke to Gothic romance because of its *realism*.[11] The novel, despite its more purple passages, attempts an atmosphere of journalistic reporting, especially as it emphasizes contemporary scientific developments, most notably the freakish experiments by associates of Luigi Galvani on corpses of prisoners executed by the state.[12] Although I do not fully accept Spark's claim, since the novel still contains many Gothic elements, there are important ways in which *Frankenstein* does revise paradigmatic Gothic scenarios: First, in the gender ambiguities located in and around its conception and representation of monstrousness, then in its visions of both the monster and the scientist—stand-ins for female and male, respectively—as inquirers. These are part and parcel of Mary Shelley's rethinking of the male myths of Romantic artistic passion and creation.

In Shelley's novel, various concerns or reservations about the new science are represented in fictional form. *Frankenstein* reflects a number of developments of, and reactions to, the Scientific Revolution. Shelley shows an awareness of the major new scientific research of the time period: of new work in chemistry (by Humphry Davy), physiology, electricity (Luigi Galvani had published his *Commentary on the Effects of Electricity on Muscular Motion* in Bologna in 1791, giving rise to the term "galvanism"), the evolution of plant species (Erasmus Darwin), mechanistic theories of the human body (Julien Offray de La Mettrie), and the weaponry of war.[13] Mary Shelley was not alone in voicing concerns about whether the rising new sciences of the day offered unqualified benefits. Ludmilla Jordanova in her book *Sexual Visions: Images of Gender in Science and Medicine Between the Eighteenth and Twentieth Centuries* describes similar concerns that were raised in other early works of horror by American writers like Poe and Hawthorne.[14] For example, Jordanova traces discussion of man-as-machine back to sources in the early periods of modernism from Enlightenment writers such as Descartes and La Mettrie, whose *The Man Machine* (1747) "created a veritable sensation."[15] She also compares some themes in *Frankenstein* to Hawthorne's story *The Birth-Mark*:

> It has been suggested that the "mad scientist" is a literary type in Gothic and Utopian novels, and there do indeed appear to be a number of recurrent themes that bear . . . on the relationships between science, medicine, and gender. Five issues in relation to the "mad scientist" are of especial importance here: masculinity; power, control, and over-reaching; secrecy; experimentalism; and science and magic.[16]

Exploring issues like the five that Jordanova enumerates, feminist philosophers and historians have argued that in Western thought, and more explicitly during the early period of modern science, rationality and science were represented or gendered as *male*, and nature as *female*.[17] Often this involves not just value differentials but power differentials as well. Irrational and wild nature requires training, domination, or ordering by the male scientific mind. The term "penetration" is often used with an almost deliberate sexual innuendo. Evelyn Fox Keller in *Reflections on Gender and Science* notes that there are familiar accounts of ways in which "the institutionalization of science in seventeenth-century England" involved social and political contexts. She argues that this science also "evolved in conjunction with, and helped to shape, a particular ideology of gender. . . . We cannot properly understand the development of modern science without attending to the role played by metaphors of gender in the formation of the particular set of values, aims, and goals embodied in the scientific enterprise."[18]

The transition from alchemy to the new science brought with it new conceptions of the scientist's relation to nature: from a sort of eroticized respect to a controlling goal. This shift is reflected in numerous of Bacon's phrases that Keller quotes: Science will involve a "Masculine birth in Time" that will issue in a "blessed race of Heroes and Supermen." This will provide a force that can "hound," "conquer and subdue Nature," "shake her to her foundations," "storm and occupy her castles and strongholds."[19] Such vigorous, aggressive language can also be seen in Victor Frankenstein's pledges to root out the secrets of perpetual life by pursuing "nature to her hiding places."[20]

Enough has been said so far for me to argue that the concerns of Mary Shelley in *Frankenstein* are more general than just to narrate an entertaining or scary tale and that they have a legitimate basis in some of the assumptions about science and nature in her time. But what exactly is she saying about these topics? Are her points ones that feminists will wish to endorse? These issues are harder to resolve, and I turn next to assess them as they arise in *Frankenstein*.

Good and Evil in *Frankenstein*

To begin to address themes of good and evil in the novel, let us consider how *Frankenstein* treats the dualities commonly associated with science and nature. I have described the early modern period's views about the "maleness" of science and "femaleness" of nature. These and other dualities are discussed by Val Plumwood in her recent book *Feminism and the Mastery of Nature*.[21] Plumwood argues that certain forms of dualistic thinking are "key ones for western thought, and reflect the major forms of oppression in western culture."[22] A partial version of Plumwood's list will be an aid to begin thinking about how these gender associations are present (or not) in *Frankenstein*'s account of good and evil. Her list includes the following:

culture/nature
reason/nature
male/female
mind/body (nature)
master/slave
reason/matter (physicality)
rationality/animality (nature)
human/nature (non-human)
civilised/primitive (nature)
production/reproduction (nature)
self/other[23]

At first glance, this list seems to capture the basic groupings and gender associations that are at work in Mary Shelley's novel. The Creature exemplifies animality, primitiveness, and physicality, whereas Victor represents the forces of civilization, rational production, and culture. Victor is part of a happy family and has prospects of marriage, as opposed to the wild and isolated monster. The Creature is "other," since he is forced outside the human community and is depicted in association with rugged and uncultured nature. But second consideration should make us pause. I have been contrasting Victor with the monster rather than with a woman like his fiancée, Elizabeth. This sets up a dualism in which the monster is the *feminine* member of the pair. Where does this leave Nature—or, for that matter, the women in the book?[24]

Plumwood did not include "good" and "evil" as dualities on her list, but this is another pair that we may want to ponder. In *Frankenstein*, the treatment of evil is fascinatingly complex. And this complexity infects the monstrous Creature and our responses to him. *We cannot presume that the Creature brought to life by Dr. Frankenstein is evil.* Mary Shelley's novel is unusually sympathetic to this monster. The location or "gendering" of monstrousness and evil is much more slippery in the novel than most stereotyped movie versions suggest. Mary Shelley offers at least two other candidates for monstrous evil as she juxtaposes the repulsiveness and violence of the Creature against the unnatural experiments of the mad scientist and also against the elemental, fierce powers of a sublime female Nature.

The first and most obvious monster in the book is of course the Creature. Although he eventually becomes frightening and murderous, the monster begins with a good and innocent nature; he is sensitive to emotions of love and beauty.

Even Victor realizes that the "fiend" is "a creature of fine sensations."[25] But the Creature is hideous and loathsome. He has been manufactured from beautiful parts, but the sum is far, far less than these parts. Victor describes him as a huge being with watery eyes, a shriveled complexion, and straight black lips. He is so ugly that people run away at the first sight of him, and he cries out in horror after glimpsing himself in a reflecting pool. Because he is so foul and disgusting in external appearance, the Creature is rejected and scorned; because he is so pathetically isolated and lonely, he becomes murderous. Even so, he still has hopes of society, looking first to an unspoiled child like William and then to his creator to construct a female companion. All these hopes are brutally dashed.

But is this monster truly male? Of course, the Creature is referred to as "he" and is described as male especially as "he" seeks a female companion or wife to comfort him in his isolation. But the gender associations from Plumwood's list should make us pause before making this link. As an outsider to culture, the Creature is also "other" to most of the "normal" men in the book. He is identified with the feminine in his desire for family and social bonds. This identification is reinforced as the monster is associated with images of a powerfully sublime and female Nature, as he ranges about on snow-capped jagged Alps or on Arctic ice. He may even be a personification of Nature's female power when he acts as the agent providing punishment for the hubris of the male scientist.

Yet another strong reason for construing the Creature as "feminine" comes from extratextual evidence about the author and her own attitudes toward both pregnancy and artistic creation. Anne Mellor comments, "From a feminist viewpoint, *Frankenstein* is about what happens when a man tries to have a baby without a woman."[26] The focus on pregnancy, birth, mothering, and reproduction in *Frankenstein* is hard to ignore. One surface explanation is that it reflects deep concerns the author had herself, not only in general, due to the death of her own mother after childbirth, but more particularly at the time of writing the book. Perhaps Mary Shelley's own voice can be heard here as she deals with the difficulties of becoming both a mother and an author. Mellor interprets Shelley's general anxiety about creative production as linked to concerns over biological reproduction. Shelley spoke later about the difficulty it caused her to "dilate upon" her "hideous progeny."[27] The dates of composition of the book almost correspond to the dates of an actual pregnancy of Mary's, and it is also relevant that she had experienced a constant stream of difficult and tragic pregnancies.[28] More particularly, the monster in the novel can be seen as representing aspects of Mary Shelley's own character, since she was also in a significant sense born motherless, nameless, and illegitimate. Further, at the time of writing the novel, she was unusually conscious of the physical deformities of her frequent pregnancies.[29]

There is much to be said against the Creature. He commits numerous murders, beginning with Victor's beautiful and bright young brother William; the Creature explains that he did not mean to kill him but only had sought a companion. Still, when the child recoiled, the Creature grabbed and choked him, then felt glad after he realized what he had done! The Creature proceeds to kill Clerval, Victor's best friend, and fulfills his promise to Victor ("I will be with you on your wedding night!") by killing Elizabeth, apparently before the marriage has been consummated. All this accumulated grief kills Victor's father. Victor realizes that the monster is watching as he mourns by his family's graves and "gives a loud and fiendish laugh."[30] Despite all this, there is room for considerable sympathy for the Creature. This is especially so in his dialogues with his maker, whom he repeatedly chides for abandoning him at birth, condemning him to a life outside of human society, with no companion to share his lonely state.

We could even propose that the Creature's very monstrousness is a result of his gender and moral indeterminacy. He exhibits a combination of the goods and evils affiliated with each gender in the novel: a desire for domesticity coupled with an extreme thirst for knowledge, the raw power of female Nature as against the uncaring violence of men. The slipperiness of the monster's status regarding good and evil and the uneasy gender affiliations in the novel reflect his monstrously undecidable, unnatural status between life and death. Few film versions I have seen convey this indeterminacy of evil in the novel. This may be understandable, because subtle moral positions are harder to construct and maintain narratively within the time limits of feature film. A complex narrative must evoke shifting sympathies and must require that audiences have varied cognitive and emotional responses to the subtly changing and even elusive nature of evil. Although far from perfect, Branagh's film manifests this complexity better than others, and this is why I plan to discuss it below.

Gender and moral ambiguities in *Frankenstein* carry over to infect Victor Frankenstein, the second plausible candidate in the novel for monstrousness. He is excessively *male;* he is depicted as insane in that he has a demonic, unnatural desire to penetrate Nature's secrets so as to circumvent death and procreate without a female. His quest for knowledge drives him further and further away from family, love, and marriage. He is immoral; he acts upon his desires without considering the consequences. In mad-scientist stories, the scientist is typically a male figure who begins with plausible and commendable goals. Greatness on the part of men, mere mortal humans, might seem to lie in ambitious, enlightened aims and scientific rationality; but such rationality is shown to lead the man (and it is usually a man) into crossing the borders that separate man from nature. Depending on how this scientist is treated by the narrative, the story or film presents a picture of men as evil pre-

cisely because of their excessive rationality—such rationality becomes effectively irrational. Victor Frankenstein becomes excessive in his aim of recreating life and defeating death forever. In the context of the story this hubris is a "sin." The
Prometheus myth and the rebellion of Satan in *Paradise Lost* are obvious forerunners of Mary Shelley's novel. Victor unleashes a monster upon humanity, and this
monster ultimately wreaks violence against the very people Victor most loves.
Victor constantly blames himself for creating a monster, but he somehow evades responsibility through his numerous bouts with "brain fever." The narrative arc of the
story is one of recognition, repentance, and punishment.

The novel casts serious doubt on the claim that Victor is truly rational, powerful, and civilized. Similarly, it casts doubt on who has more power, Victor or the
monster. Is Victor the master of his Creature—is he really the "male" in this pair?
Although the Creature has begun by promising fealty like Adam's to God, he becomes more and more a rebellious Satan, the powerful one in their relationship.
And in the end, Victor hunts the monster rather than the reverse. After the loss of
his family and bride, Victor's solitary object of desire is the monster. He takes on
the quest to destroy what he has created after it has killed everyone dear to him
and has left him with nothing. As Victor lies dying, telling his tale to Captain
Walton, whom he has encountered on a ship frozen in ice during an Arctic expedition, he says, "I feel myself justified in desiring the death of my adversary."
According to Victor (in Walton's narration), the Creature "showed unparalleled
malignity and selfishness in evil," so now, Victor feels that he himself was innocent and can die in "reason and virtue." Walton seems to concur. But when the
Creature is discovered at Victor's side, he is uttering such "expressions of grief and
horror" that Walton feels compassion. The Creature repents and asks the dead
Victor to pardon him. And significantly, the Creature has the last word as he explains to Walton that he pitied Victor and abhorred himself. The Creature asks
despite all this, "Am I to be thought the only criminal, when all humankind
sinned against me?"[31]

By the end of her novel, Mary Shelley has created sympathy for her mad Victor
Frankenstein. He is a tragic figure who, only too late, comes to see and regret his
error. Along with this shift, there may be a shift during the story from an initially
sympathetic to a more horrific portrayal of the monster. Recent studies of the
original manuscripts of *Frankenstein* have revealed ways in which Mary Shelley's
sympathy with the monster was edited out by her husband, Percy Bysshe Shelley,
as he imposed his reading of the story onto Mary Shelley's original text.[32] Percy
apparently empathized with Victor Frankenstein, whom he saw as an innocent
victim, so he subtly altered various scenes to make the monster more monstrous,
his motives less intelligible. This helps explain some tensions in the novel, for of

course the male scientist is also monstrous and the monster is victim of his own creator. The author clearly implies that Frankenstein has overstepped the bounds of Nature, has peered too closely into Her secrets; in this and similar cases, Nature strikes back, and She is sublime and forceful. The monster's crimes accumulate, and he is finally shown as the Gothic male who threatens the heroine. This threat takes on a specifically erotic form; he will rape or steal the hero's human partner, Elizabeth, on their wedding night. The Creature thus functions as a sort of evil twin of the male scientist, an externalization of this figure's evil agency—suggesting that this human man, too, might pose a threat to his fiancée.

The central theme in any mad-scientist story like *Frankenstein* concerns the proper boundaries of science and human rationality, or the scientist's relation to nature. This brings me to the third possible candidate for monstrousness in the book, a sublimely powerful and dangerous Nature.[33] Victor describes his own illicit inquiries as attempts to know the secrets of a feminized Nature whom he has pursued "to her hiding places."[34] The death that particularly motivates his researches is that of his own mother; after that trauma, he pursues and eventually discovers the "cause of generation and life."[35] At rare times, Victor glimpses Nature as soft, sweet, and reassuring, a place of bounty for humans. But more often, Nature is hostile, as is his monster. Mellor comments: "Nature pursues Victor Frankenstein with the very electricity he has stolen: lightning, thunder, and rain rage around him. The November night on which he steals the 'spark of being' from Nature is dreary, dismal, and wet: 'the rain . . . poured from a black and comfortless sky.'"[36]

Nature in her fiercest retributive mode is closely tied to the monster; Her monstrous powers are linked to those of the Creature, who ranges in the remotest areas of the Alps, the Russian steppes, and the Arctic. In his first long and accusatory dialogue with his maker, the Creature proclaims that "the desert mountains and dreary glaciers are my refuge" and "caves of ice are a dwelling to me."[37] He is envious of the De Lacey family, as they all seem able to live in harmony with nature. Nature's benevolent side seems reserved for already domesticated or civilized humans. Victor is forced by his violations of Nature and civil society to move to more and more isolated, remote, and inhospitable environs. When the Creature demands a mate, Victor travels to do this dirty job to a remote and desolate island off the coast of Scotland, where people are almost reduced to inhumanity by the harshness of the terrain and conditions. And at the end, Victor follows the Creature, who "seeks everlasting ices of the north."[38]

The *Frankenstein* story is unlike its forerunners in mythology or religion. Instead of being punished by a divine agency, Victor Frankenstein is punished by Nature herself as his own illegitimate creation comes back to destroy everything he loves. The powers of Nature are construed as female: Nature preserves Her own proper domain of reproduction with the ultimate punishment of death. Nature in the novel has dual aspects. Although She may be benign, a backdrop for idylls and bountiful harvests, when She exacts revenge or retribution, Nature is monstrously fierce or even evil. The shifting symbol of the moon is very specifically associated with the monster in the novel. The "moon's bright disk" might on its own seem calmly beautiful and benevolent, but no sooner does it appear than Victor usually sees "the fiend" silhouetted against it and it has become dim. Such shifts depicting Nature as ominous or monstrous may accompany the narrative switches in point of view that I have just been describing. As Nature grows more threatening, the novel provides a more sympathetic picture of Dr. Frankenstein as someone who suffers at Her hands. He stands in for the Romantic hero as he gradually acquires consciousness of his overreaching and begins to repent.

I have now described a trio of candidates for monstrousness in *Frankenstein*. First, there is the monster, who is indeterminate in numerous ways. He is in part gendered female by his outsider position and by his association with nature rather than culture. Second, there is the male scientist, with his hubris and excessive, antisocial masculine rationality. Third, there is Nature, waiting with Her wrathful punishments for the human who has crossed Her limits and has threatened to limn her secrets. (Mellor comments, "Appropriately, Nature prevents Frankenstein from constructing a normal human being: an unnatural method of reproduction produces an unnatural being.")[39] There is a doubling between Victor Frankenstein and his Creature, as well as between their paired and doomed inquiries: The scientist attempts to probe nature's innermost secrets, and the monster attempts to understand human culture.[40] Both fail; there is no happy ending in the novel—neither of the story itself nor of the searches for knowledge depicted within it. With its complex narrative structure, *Frankenstein* opens outward onto a blanket condemnation of any human search for knowledge passing beyond certain boundaries, and it withholds any ultimate moral resolution with its final vision of the monster, who does not die but rather vanishes from view across the ice.[41]

Film Versions of *Frankenstein*

There are nearly countless celluloid renditions of Mary Shelley's story. It was one of the earliest movies ever to be filmed, in 1910, by none other than Thomas Edison.[42] Later versions range from lurid Hammer films to the semipornographic *Frankenhooker* to a wide range of comedies like *Abbott and Costello Meet Frankenstein* or Mel Brooks's hilarious *Young Frankenstein*. Any selection is arbitrary, but I have chosen two films that I consider particularly excellent for their portrayals of the monster: the 1931 classic with Boris Karloff and Kenneth Branagh's 1994 version. These are also intriguing to compare because they are so very different in era and style. My question is whether even a very good film version of *Frankenstein* can convey the slippery, indeterminate nature of evil as Mary Shelley's novel does. I will consider how the film medium works to portray not only the monster but also his master and Nature herself. We have seen how feminist treatments illuminate Mary Shelley's novel: It is plausible to see that she wrote as a woman about issues that concerned her, both about artistic creation and natural reproduction. Feminist literary critics scarcely ever mention film versions; perhaps this reflects skepticism about whether any film directed and produced by men can capture the feminism of the book. If part of the book's feminism lies in its sympathy for the monster and if this is absent from the film versions, we will have one simple answer to my question.

Mary Shelley's novel has too complex a narrative and is too long to be translated wholesale to the screen. The film medium must make selective cuts, but it still offers many advantages over the novel in its power of vivid characterization and in depicting action, movement, and scenes with strong visual impact. I will consider two primary aspects of the films I have selected. First, how do they depict the story's key characters? Crucial here is how sympathetically the scientist is portrayed and how the monster looks and acts. And second, how do the film narratives present several key moments to stimulate the audience's thoughts and strong emotional reactions? I will zero in on two primary plot scenarios: the scene of creation in the laboratory, and the films' conclusions and what they suggest about Victor himself. My questions will help us reach a final assessment of the films' treatments of good and evil in *Frankenstein*.

Frankenstein 1931 and 1994

In both the 1931 movie and Branagh's 1994 remake, the scientist Frankenstein is young and handsome: Colin Clive in the earlier version and Branagh himself (aged thirty-four) in the later one. Yet right from the start in the James Whale movie, there are indications something is very wrong with him.[43] (Confusingly, he is named "Henry" not "Victor" in the 1931 version, whereas "Henry Clerval" becomes "Victor Moritz.") Whale's film invokes devices of theater and is often interestingly metarepresentational. This aims less, I think, to depict characters than to toy with the audience—as if to play along with their fears by sometimes distancing them or winking at their expectations of being shocked and scared. The movie begins, for example, with a curious introduction in which a man parts a theater curtain and warns the audience that it is about to be shocked and horrified.[44] After this metatheatrical introduction, the story itself starts with a funeral. Stark black-and-white photography reveals a grim scene in a mountain setting as a bell tolls. The style is German expressionist or early film noir: In the dim setting, we witness an almost mad juxtaposition of crosses, priests chanting, women sobbing, and words muttered about grave robbers and corpse stealing. (Incidentally, the opening of *The Texas Chainsaw Massacre* is so similar that it is hard not to see connections; I will discuss that film later in Chapter 8.)

Within this framing, which virtually screams "Gothic" at the viewer, we first see Henry Frankenstein—and he can hardly be a normal sympathetic human being. Henry and his mad assistant Fritz watch the funeral from a short distance, then approach to do some nefarious digging. As Fritz does the dirty work and uproots the corpse, Henry Frankenstein looks straight into the camera and intones, "He's just resting—waiting for new life to come!" Again, this address to the audience invites immediate involvement and a feeling of direct participation. There are several more metafilmic moments in the movie, such as the scenes in an anatomy lecture where a skeleton bounces as brains are displayed. This bobbing animated skeleton, which frightens Fritz, seems a reference to the flickering medium of film we are watching.

Doubts about Henry Frankenstein's sanity pile up very quickly in this movie, reinforced by conventions of lighting. The grave scene shifts to a domestic, well-lit interior, contrasting normalcy with deviance, domestic life with death, healthy daytime with deathly night. We observe a conversation between Henry's fiancée Elizabeth and their friend Victor Moritz. Henry has written that he is on the verge of a major discovery, so major that he has even "doubted his own sanity." He warns her that his work comes before even her and speaks oddly in his letter about how "winds howl in the mountains." Elizabeth and Victor visit Dr. Waldman, Henry's professor at the university, who reports that Henry had an "insane ambition to create life." He was "brilliant yet so erratic," with "a mad dream." By this time, there can be little doubt that Henry Frankenstein is a menace! The film provides no normalizing discourse about him, no earlier introduction to his past, no hints about his motivation to create life. Also, we do not see Henry going to the university and learning things gradually. We are plunged *in medias res* to find Henry on the brink of his monstrous creation.

By contrast, in the novel and in Branagh's film, Frankenstein's motivation is strongly set up as a reaction to his mother's death. (Branagh's film even shows that scene in gory detail.) Branagh's film begins with the framing device of the novel, an introduction to the very act of storytelling, with the saga of Captain Walton's frustrated Arctic expedition. Walton (Aidan Quinn) faces mutiny as his ship is trapped in the ice, yet he insists on pursuing his expedition to be first to reach the North Pole. We see his men suddenly notice a strange apparition materializing across the ice, a feverish and nearly frozen Victor Frankenstein. Parallels between Walton and Frankenstein are driven home in the movie, as Victor talks to the captain and says, "You are just like me!" The monster's existence is previewed, and his violence is hinted at when the sled dogs who go chasing after him are violently tossed back like rag dolls. But the appearance of the monster is forestalled; we only get sounds of harsh breathing and point-of-view shots of him running across the ice. Branagh here invokes more modern horror movie conventions used to depict villains since *Halloween*. Such delays make the monster a curious object of the audience's ambivalent desire.

Next, Branagh's film, much like Shelley's novel, flashes back into an extended narrative of Victor's life, clarifying how his ambition leads to destruction and death. This film is far less Gothic than its predecessor and makes Frankenstein a more well-rounded and sympathetic character. We see Victor's warm relationship with his mother, his developing love for his "more-than-sister," the adopted girl Elizabeth (Helena Bonham Carter), and his earnest scientific researches. Victor is not mad or unbalanced, just a bit of a drudge because he prefers to stay indoors with his dusty books and experimental puppets rather than run outside in the gorgeous Alpine scenery. On the one day when he is persuaded to "go out to play," he brings a kite and performs a scary experiment with an odd passing electrical cloud(!).

Branagh's film sets up the key motivation for Victor's mad project with a depiction of his mother's agonized death in bloody childbirth. We see lots of red blood in full living color as it flows over her as well as her doctor husband (Victor's father). The cause of her death has been shifted from the novel, perhaps to allude to the duality of birth, perhaps to allude to Mary Shelley's own mother's early death after bearing her. There follow extended scenes of Henry's departure for Ingolstadt and his early debates with his anatomy professor about the proper role in science of imagination, alchemy, the spiritual, and so on. Victor begins to collaborate in secret with the sinister-looking Dr. Waldman (John Cleese), who reveals the secrets of reanimation through electricity. But even Waldman refuses to divulge his final secret because it "produces abominations." Remarkably, Victor remains somewhat sympathetic. He is still not mad or excessive as Colin Clive seems to be, but he is rather bold, original, and ambitious. (Victor may just be a legitimate scientist seeking to make an impact on his field, as Branagh seeks to pump life into the classics by bringing them to stage and screen.) This impression is reinforced by the film's allusions to our own modern science—as when Victor pledges that a day will come when a heart can be transplanted and still live. Such references, in addition to the truly hideous death of his mother, make Victor's overall ambition to avert death seem much less outrageous.

The Laboratory and "Birth" Scene

I shift now to look at the mise-en-scène and narrative in what we could justly call the central moment in each film: the creation or birth of the monster. In Whale's fast-paced film, we are positioned along with the innocent Elizabeth and Victor Moritz when they first see Henry's laboratory looming rather like an ominous Dracula's castle. Whale continues the expressionist blackness of his earlier grave-yard scene. Perched in a very Gothic setting atop a cliff, Henry's laboratory tower is revealed to us in flashes of lightning during a pounding thunderstorm. Inside, the lab looks much like Dracula's castle (in the film from the same studio and year): It has steep winding stairs and enormous high ceilings. A delirious Henry exclaims: "This storm will be magnificent. All the electrical secrets of heaven!" Many scenes have striking vertical compositions that emphasize the tall lines of the tower wall and underline the demonic, overreaching ambition of the scientist who works here. (This is a visual trope that Branagh updates in his movie.) Lit with small pools of lantern light, the lab is rife with ominous shadows; the black-and-white photography is stunning. Henry says to Fritz: "Just think of it. The brain of a dead man waiting to live again in a body I made with my own hands. . . . *with my own hands.*" When Victor and Elizabeth arrive with Professor Waldman, Henry admits them so that they may watch his triumph: "You said I was crazy—we'll see about that!" There is another brilliant metafilmic moment as Henry says to his visitors (and presumably to the audience as well): "Quite a good scene, isn't it? One man *crazy*—three very sane spectators!"

After this buildup, the creation scene itself is surprisingly brief. The body Henry has assembled is lifted on a gurney amid a bizarre set of pulleys and flashing tubes reminiscent of *Metropolis* (a movie Whale admired). Raised to the opening in the roof, this body is struck by a huge bolt of lightning, then lowered. There is a moment of high anticipation while we wait, again echoing the scene's internal spectators, until the Creature's finger finally moves (Photo 1.1).

When his creature finally is thus "born," Victor shouts with gleeful and crazed passion, "He's alive, he's alive!" He is so overwrought that he collapses. The movie suddenly cuts to a setting that again dichotomizes good/bad through the light/dark contrast. We recognize how unnatural and "dark" the birth scene was as we are suddenly shown a bright, domestic morning scene at the baronial Frankenstein home. This is like the first cut I mentioned earlier that shifts from the darkness of the grave to the bright light of domesticity. Now Elizabeth and Victor reassure Baron von Frankenstein that his son will soon be well. The baron worries about when the wedding will take place and insists that the delay must be because "there's another woman—and I'm going to find her!" In the logic of this

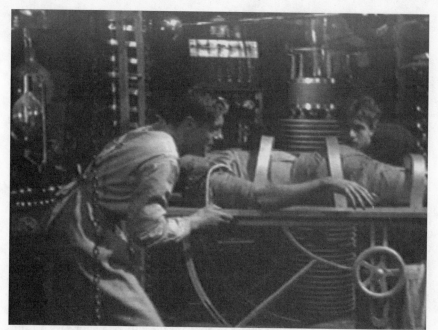

PHOTO 1.1   *Henry Frankenstein (Colin Clive) is overwhelmed by the birth of his Creature in* Frankenstein *(1931).*

film, then, the Creature functions as the "other woman" who keeps Henry from his proper role in producing a legitimate heir.[45] We see no more of the monster at the creation scene beyond his somewhat delicate though huge hand and fingers. This is worth commenting upon: Like Branagh's film, with its initial hints of a brutal unnatural force running amok on the ice floes, the Whale film also arouses audience curiosity about this "other woman," along with trepidation about how the monster will really look. The monster becomes an object of strong desire.

The laboratory creation scene in Branagh's film is brilliant. To build up to its frenetic pace, we have seen a Victor who becomes increasingly mad in his desire to subvert death. He watches his adored Dr. Waldman being killed while trying to inject a peasant with a smallpox vaccination. Victor will not abandon his efforts to revive Waldman, despite Clerval's cries to stop. The bloody scene of Waldman's death is shown in a sort of surgery theater; we see it from above as the camera quickly recedes upward, giving a God's-eye vantage point of Victor that will become a repeated trope in the film. Victor raises his fists to the sky and screams angrily, "Heaven!" Frankenstein, as in Whale's film, is dwarfed by larger forces, whether of God or Nature, and though he cannot conquer them, he will not accept being cut down to size. He rebels. He reads Waldman's journals, discovers the final dark secret of reanimation, and begins his own ghoulish process of recovering bodies. He persists in the face of Clerval's protests and explains that the "chance to defeat death and disease, to allow people who love each other to be together forever" is a chance worth taking, despite Clerval's warning that "there [will] be a terrible price to pay." By now we can see the mad gleam in Victor's eye and realize that the more ordinary Clerval is the good, sane one. This is reinforced by a quick succession of scenes: Victor cutting open Waldman's skull ("the very finest brain"), finding body parts in morgues ("raw materials," he reminds himself), buying amniotic fluid at scenes of birth, and testing his electric eel shock technique by throwing gross, meaty limbs into baths that sizzle.

As in the Whale movie, Clerval and Elizabeth visit the lab and try to dissuade Victor. Here, too, Elizabeth represents the norms of decency and domestic affection. She is shocked to find him feverishly filthy and recoils in horror. "What's happened to you? How can you live here like this!" The female seeks to provide the emotional balance to civilize and domesticate the overreaching male scientist. Victor tells her to go away and behaves violently, another sign of his male aggression run amok, his separation from the usual social norms that would drive him toward a more normal partner than the body on the gurney. Victor says it is impossible to be with her because his work (his other lover?) must come first. The scene is very melodramatic, with Wagnerian musical accompaniment, and leads directly to the laboratory creation scene.

Even more frenzied and overwrought than Whale's, Branagh's creation scene is filmed with dozens of quick cuts, each shot full of movement across the frame. Victor races along his attic hall, cape flying before he discards it to appear barechested and vigorous. While pulleys move, bottles clank, and blue volts of electricity rise in glass tesla tubes, the naked body on the gurney is raised into a copper vat. Electric eels dispense their powerful shocks, a brown saclike bellows "breathes" air or heat, and finally Victor stares close-up at the Creature's eyes. The eyes are seen through a porthole in the vat: This, our first glimpse of the monster, occurs nearly an hour into the film. "Live, live, live, live," Victor chants, then "*Yes!*" (much in the old Colin Clive mode) as it opens its eyes briefly. Nothing more occurs, though, and Victor walks away in despair; but, like us, he is brought suddenly to attention by a sharp and surprising snap of the monster's fingers, which we also see close-up through a porthole (in a clear allusion to the Karloff monster's birth scene). The next sequence drives home the fact that this is a real birth scene, as the vat is smashed open (the "water breaks") and Victor lifts out his huge new "baby," smacking its chest to clear its lungs. We watch an extended scene of birth struggle while Victor works to "deliver" his huge, naked, and hairless "baby"

PHOTO 1.2   Victor Frankenstein (Kenneth Branagh) and his newborn Creature (Robert De Niro) in Frankenstein *(1994).*

by lifting it out of the slime (Photo 1.2). Giving birth is not only very hard labor here; it's messy, too.

These initial scenes do not reveal much of the monster except his huge and powerful body. After an accident with the pulleys lifts this massive body high up into the attic, we again zoom down on Victor from a God's eye point of view as, stricken, he stares and asks: "What have I done? What have I done?" He abandons his new baby and writes in despair in his journal that the reanimant had massive birth defects and was "malfunctional, pitiful, and dead." Now the audience's sympathies are redirected back to Victor. He realizes his atrocity and begins to have a nightmare about the monster opening his bed curtains and confronting him. This sequence is shot so that the viewer cannot tell whether it is a nightmare or real, and it reveals our first vision of De Niro as the monster. Shown (as he typically will be in this movie) in a sudden flash of lightning, he is hideous, with great red scars across his face and body. He is also scary due to his sheer size and power. He vanishes, and Victor next seems to dream of the good professor Dr. Kremp remonstrating with him: "Do you really think this thing will thank you for its monstrous birth? Made from bits of thieves, bits of murderers, evil stitched to evil stitched to evil stitched to evil. Evil will have its revenge. You fool! How could you know what you'd unleashed? God help your loved ones!"

Shifting Sympathies for Frankenstein

From the moment of creation of his monster in Mary Shelley's novel, Victor Frankenstein becomes so seized with guilt that he is incapacitated. He both abandons his newborn offspring and seeks to return to the human society he has spurned—but too late. Right from the start, Whale's movie makes clear the madness of its scientist "hero." And yet, after the creation and the escape of the monster, the movie's point of view and its expectations of audience sympathy begin to shift. Henry Frankenstein appears less mad and more dispassionate, a scientist objectively studying the character of his experimental product, recognizing his limits after it kills Fritz, and becoming deathly afraid of what he has done. He seeks normal society again and admits to Elizabeth, "It's all my fault," as the monster becomes murderous. But once more (as in the book) he collapses in regret, leaving it to Professor Waldman to destroy the Creature "painlessly." After this second collapse, Henry is whisked back to the family estate, and we next see him for the first time domesticated in a lovely sun-drenched pastoral setting, on a picnic with Elizabeth. Henry has thus become "normal" in the film's visual idiom, where dark equals bad and light equals good. He says it is "like heaven to be with you again." In a speech we might almost read as his confession of infidelity and request for forgiveness, he says: "My work, those horrible days and nights, I couldn't think of anything else. When will our wedding be? Let's make it soon." This leads to more images of beatific nature, from the orange blossoms that Elizabeth will wear in her hair to bucolic country scenes of peasants dancing. We will see how these sympathies play out after the monster's rage is unleashed and how the film's plot is resolved.

Branagh's film similarly begins to shift in its depiction of the scientist from the creation scene on. This gradual return of sympathies toward Victor begins in the film, as in the novel, when Victor becomes perilously ill and must be nursed back to health by Clerval. He makes up with Elizabeth and returns home to Geneva, seeking domesticity and normalcy, only to find that the monster has begun to wreak its revenge by killing innocent victims, including his darling little brother William. Victor now is shown as the suffering victim of his own scientific hubris. He meets with the monster to find out what will appease it and plans the filthy work of making a companion for it. Once again his scientific obsession alienates the good, domestic, emotional Elizabeth, until he ultimately recoils in horror from his task and returns to find balance with her. He begs her forgiveness in a stagy scene, which Branagh frames so as to make Victor's confessional mode transparently clear. The lovers are shown in an exchange of one-shots, her beautiful head framed against a sunlit doorway with ominous bars at one side, his tearful face and abject shoulders posed in center right against a crucifix in the upper

PHOTO 1.3 Victor (Kenneth Branagh) confesses his sins to Elizabeth in Frankenstein (1994).

left (Photo 1.3) as he confesses (literally!): "I have done something so terrible, so evil, and I am frightened. . . . I don't know what to do." The scene is accompanied by maudlin violin music. Elizabeth, now a comforting Holy Mother, embraces him and forgives him in front of an altar with candlesticks beside the crucifix: In this movie, Elizabeth exemplifies a redemptive, Mary-like female compassion. She says, "Whatever you've done, whatever has happened, I love you."

The Monster

I will now look more closely at how the movies treat the monster himself. Film versions dwell in loving detail on the mad scientist's lab, with its bottles, tubes, and electrical devices, the gradual assembly of the Creature after scenes of grave robbing and corpse dismemberment, the great shock of lightning, and the gradual or sudden awakening of the monster. Little of this is in Mary Shelley's novel. Victor is deliberately reticent about his dangerous secret, and the details of his construction process are vague, involving only sinister allusions to "vaults and charnel houses."[46] In fact, there is scarcely one short paragraph describing Victor's experiment and its successful culmination. Certain sequences in most film versions, including the nightmare confrontation that Branagh shows, probably come not from the novel but from Shelley's preface to a later edition of the book, where she looks back on the creation scene and imagines it more vividly.[47]

I have described the way these two films treat the actual process of creation as a cinematic playground; in most *Frankenstein* movies, the creation scene is central. In these two movie versions, we can also see changing views about the embodiment of a human being and about allegedly "natural" sources of good and evil. There is at least one thing in most film versions that we do not find in the original novel: a physical or material explanation for the Creature's malign nature. In Whale's 1931 version, Dr. Frankenstein's nefarious assistant Fritz is sent to steal a brain for the Creature but returns with the wrong brain. Instead of stealing the brain from a paragon of virtue, he has nabbed one from a horrific diseased criminal. (We have earlier seen it in its vat, clearly labeled "abnormal brain.") Thus, in the 1931 movie, the Creature is doomed from the start. Branagh's film takes a different but related tack. His Creature is given the lofty and noble brain taken from Victor's teacher Dr. Waldman. But the Creature's body is from the very criminal hanged for murdering Dr. Waldman, a criminal who cursed all doctors and scientists as evil! Hence, this Creature is also condemned by his material nature to have a deep dualism and to be destructively self-conflicted. The film emphasizes this physicalist explanation when the monster asks about his material origins during his dialogue with his creator. The two film versions suggest that good and evil have a physical basis in the body, whereas Mary Shelley's book adopts an altogether social view of the Creature's evil. She assumes a more Rousseauian view of people's innate goodness and of the Creature as a natural innocent. Only his mistreatment turns the monster to crime.

The early 1931 *Frankenstein* features the best-known and now iconic monster as played by Boris Karloff. Karloff's makeup was designed by Jack Pierce, who explained why he made the choices he did: "I made him the way the textbooks said he should look. I didn't depend on imagination. In 1931, before I did a bit of designing, I spent three months of research on anatomy, surgery, medicine, criminal history, criminology, ancient and modern burial customs, and electrodynamics."[48] Pierce designed the flat-topped skull based on the most direct way a surgeon would cut it to take out a brain and put bolts in the monster's neck to allow for the electrical connections that animated him. He also arranged for the monster's arms and legs to look unusually long. Karloff added the wax on the eyelids that gave the Creature both an ominous and yet sad look. Gregory Mank comments: "From the beginning, Karloff's approach to his 'dear old Monster' was one of love and compassion. To discover and convey such sympathy was an outstanding insight—considering that rarely has an actor suffered so hideously by bringing to life a character."[49] The part was turned down by other actors (notably Bela Lugosi and John Carradine) because it was not a speaking role, but Karloff is universally respected for having made it into an amazingly expressive part nonethe-

PHOTO 1.4 *The Creature (Boris Karloff) with little Maria (Marilyn Harris) in* Frankenstein *(1931).*

less, one that justly earned him instant and lasting fame. This "other woman" does have a strangely perverse beauty, with his delicate eyes and graceful hands. There are few more wonderful moments in cinema than Karloff's tentative and contorted smile as he meets the little girl playing with flowers by the lakeside (Photo 1.4). In the original film, he did not utter a word and was reduced to "barking," as one reviewer put it. The monster's levels of conscious awareness are hard to discern; he clearly kills the girl by accident rather than through evil intention, and it is hard to know what his purpose is in stalking Elizabeth at the end. In the final scenes, the villagers searching him out are portrayed as a vicious unruly mob; sympathy is still being created for him, even as he manhandles the puny Henry. And when he bellows like a caged beast, the monster's final moments in the fire are painful for the audience to endure. Still, despite this sympathy, the movie's finale suggests that all is well with him dead and gone and Henry happily married, on the way toward creating a real heir through natural reproduction.

De Niro is fascinating to see as he takes on a role with so much prior history. His appearance, makeup, and clothing are very distinct from Karloff's. De Niro's

Creature, too, is huge and shambling (due, as we know, to his mismatched legs). His face and head are covered with huge and ugly welts of blister-red scars and stitches. Although these eventually fade and his hair grows in, he is still undeniably hideous, and his scarred mouth in particular causes him to speak distortedly. His hands are not delicate but rather are massive and dirty. Most striking of all are his mismatched eyes, one dark and one pale icy blue, with flaws or specks in it. They give his face a particularly sinister look. Having borrowed Victor's greatcoat, he sometimes resembles a flying bat as it flaps about him. He nonetheless does evoke sympathy. After the scene of Victor's nightmare, our first view of him is as a newborn waking on the street, cold and hungry, rooting through garbage for food. Mistaken for a cholera carrier, he is chased and viciously beaten by villagers. Alone and abandoned, brutally attacked, he is touchingly happy to find shelter amid the pigs at the De Lacey family's little hut. Like Karloff, he is the beast quieted by Orpheus as he comes alive to the sound of the old blind man's flute.

> Branagh says that he was particularly interested in the horror genre, and in going back to the source material. He claims that his Creature is much nearer to the novel, and that "he had to be hideous, but also tremendously sympathetic because of his terrible plight. I wanted a wise, articulate and multifaceted Creature who could be angry yet have a sense of humor, however darkly ironic."[50]

Most important, De Niro's Creature *speaks*. He has a strange and stilted eloquence reminiscent of the old-fashioned language used by Mary Shelley's monster. De Niro's monster uses his lips and voice slowly and awkwardly, as if still learning how to make the muscles move. His short phrases have an archaic and almost elegant simplicity and dignity. But the film, like the novel, presents the monster's narrative through Victor's version and experiences. This should alert us that sympathies for the monster may get manipulated in relation to those for or against the scientist. For example, when the Creature confronts Victor after the critical moment of the death of little William, we see the monster—as we do in at least half a dozen other moments in the film—suddenly illuminated in a sharp flash of lightning. He looks huge, pale, and ominous, his scars ghastly against his white flesh. He points to the mountains and orders Victor to meet him "on the sea of ice." It is only then, as they eventually meet and talk in the ice cave (as befits the Creature of the novel), that we hear much of the Creature's point of view; but by this point he has been taken over by his murderous rage, and we see him through Victor's horrified eyes. To Victor, who is astounded to find his "baby" has grown able to talk, the monster says: "Yes, I speak. And read. And think. And know the ways of man." He explains how he came to murder little William, and referring to

Justine, the woman mistakenly hanged for William's murder, the monster asks Victor: "Now two people are dead because of us. Why?" He questions his creator relentlessly. "What of my soul? Do I have one? Or was that a part you left out? Who are these people of whom I am comprised?" He asks where his head, heart, and hands have come from. Victor, appalled, says he doesn't know. The monster continues. "Did you ever consider the consequences of your actions? You gave me life, but then you left me to die. Who am I?" Victor answers, "You. . . . I don't know." "*And you think I am evil,*" responds the monster, slowly and starkly accusing. It is at this point that he demands a companion. Although he has much justice in his complaints, his expectations appear unreasonable and also monstrous.

The moral status of the Creature in this key scene where we hear him speak is still unstable, perhaps as in the novel. He has seemed good in that while he hid in their pig shed, he helped the De Lacey family by chopping wood and digging potatoes. He is also shown sympathetically as he suffers expulsion from this half-family existence through a misunderstanding. Even more alone now after his loss, the monster sobs heartbrokenly, isolated out in nature in a snowy field at the foot of a great tree. The monster reads Victor's journals and understands who he is and how he was made. Backing away from the journal's drawings and sketches, he tears open his cloak to look at his sewn-together chest, and roars with agony and horror at himself. At this point, he is a pitiful center of abject awareness, but he is suddenly transformed into the raging monster-movie beast. He attacks and burns the De Laceys' cottage, and, silhouetted against the blaze, he bellows in rage, "*Frankenstein!*" This also sets up the audience for the scene when the Creature finally meets his maker, where he will make his dual nature very explicit. Not only is Victor responsible for his "bad genes," so to speak, but also for poor fathering. "I have love in me the likes of which you cannot imagine. And rage the likes of which you would not believe. If I cannot satisfy one. . . . I will indulge the other." De Niro's lines are always slow, careful, and deliberate. It is as if the monster thinks through each thing he says and speaks in a heartfelt manner. His threat makes Victor's blood run cold, even though Victor (like us) sympathizes with his plight. At this point, Victor agrees to make the monster a mate.

The Narrative Resolution

I now consider the way each film resolves its narrative. This involves two primary scenes: the monster's threat to the scientist's bride and the ultimate conclusion with the monster's death. The novel and Branagh's film version suggest that the Frankensteins' marriage is never consummated. In Whale's film, Elizabeth ultimately escapes the Creature alive, but only after a close call. On her wedding day, she feels the threat of the monster and senses impending doom. She stands amid her bridesmaids and says, reverting to the "other woman" theme: "Something is going to happen. I feel it. Something is coming between us." She begs Henry, "Henry, don't leave me!" In this movie, the Creature finds his way into her bedroom and chases her with incoherent growls. They struggle and she faints, but she is only dazed, not dead. Henry and the townspeople chase the monster out into the mountains with bloodhounds. Again the movie sets up our feeling of compassion for Frankenstein, as he and the monster fight one-on-one. This must be an individual confrontation because Henry has said: "There can be no wedding while this Creature of mine is still alive. I made it with these hands and with these hands I must destroy it." The struggle continues melodramatically as the Creature drags Henry across cliffs to a gigantic windmill at the top of a rocky pass. Eventually, Henry is tossed onto the windmill's blades and falls to the ground below. But he does not appear to be dead because the peasants plan to take him home. The movie strongly suggests the Creature's demise, as he becomes trapped by a beam in the windmill during a blazing fire. But this is not *the* ending of the film. Presumably Henry has suffered enough and learned his lesson, because the wedding is going to take place. Giggling maids bring wine for Henry, who is still in bed, and his father drinks a toast: "Here's to a son of the house of Frankenstein" (presumably a legitimate and human baby, not a monster).[51]

In Branagh's film, the Creature has become genuinely monstrous when he murders Elizabeth. The erotic and romantic interlude in the wedding chamber is interrupted at a crucial moment as Victor rushes outside to seek the monster. Next comes a sequence that is very powerfully crafted. From the end of the bed, we see Elizabeth, alone, abandoned, desolate. She falls back, and we look down on her from above for a moment. Lightning flashes, and her expression becomes one of horror. Instantly, the point of view shifts so that we see what she sees: the monster glaring in at her from a skylight above, backlit against a flash of lightning. In another instantaneous cut, we look down upon her and see his powerful filthy hand cover her mouth, her eyes wide in terror. He caresses her face tenderly, transfixed by her beauty—perhaps still sympathetic and redeemable. He says, "You are lovelier than I ever could have imagined." But Victor bursts in with pistols brandished; the monster is startled, then enraged, and he crushes her chest and tears out her heart. In a shockingly bloody scene, shifting us from the Romantic period to post-1990s horror-film visual vocabulary, he extends it to Victor across the room and screeches, "*I keep my promises!*"

This scene in Branagh's film clearly asks the audience to take the side of Victor against the fiend. It is impossible not to be horrified when the monster kills poor Elizabeth. Now Branagh's movie degenerates into a bizarre, Hammer Studios style revision of Mary Shelley's plot. Victor decides to reanimate his bride, even though Clerval warns him that he will "lose his soul" and begs him to let Elizabeth rest in peace. But Victor proceeds, and we see another frenetic laboratory scene where he is utterly mad—he even chops Elizabeth's head off with a giant cleaver and sews it onto the one he had started preparing for the monster. Bonham Carter reappears as a ghastly and stitched-together yellow version of herself, sans hair. Victor pleads with her to say his name and dances with her in a macabre waltz; her body is that of a limp puppet. The monster approaches to claim her, and she dimly recognizes who he is and what has happened to her. Caught between these two madmen, looking in pathetic horror to accuse Victor for what he has done, Elizabeth fittingly chooses to douse herself in flames and runs through the house, burning it down as her twice-earned funeral pyre.

This over-the-top scene sets up the final sequence where Victor, who has perhaps become a somewhat sympathetic figure, but only because he has finally absorbed the lessons of his sin, confides everything to Captain Walton in the ice-bound ship and dies. Branagh's film differs from the novel, in that the scientist closes his external narrative with dire warnings to chasten the next male overreacher. Captain Walton listens to Victor's story as he slowly fades into death, saying, "I am so very tired." Victor has become grayed and covered with hoarfrost. Walton goes outside as his men nervously seek the monster out on the ice, but they, as do we, suddenly hear him roaring from within. Rushing back, Walton finds the Creature sobbing beside Victor's corpse. Now both Victor and the monster are shown sympathetically. This is the monster's finest moment in this movie. "Who are you?" Walton asks, and the Creature sadly replies, "He never gave me a name" (Photo 1.5). His plight is dramatized as we recognize that he is alone, with no hope of acquiring clues about his identity or any nurture from the "father" for whom he weeps. De Niro's face is shown in close-ups, with its mutilated and sadly eerie eyes. While the men build a bier for Victor on the ice and Walton reads from a biblical text about wisdom and evil, the Creature is again shown alone, silhouetted in his greatcoat, sobbing in an uncontrollable animal-like paroxysm of grief, like a great dog howling beside his dead master. The ice breaks up suddenly, and although Walton begs the Creature to "come with us," he refuses. "*I have done with man,*" the Creature replies, and then in another close-up, we see his agonized face as he lights both himself and Victor's body with a torch. The Prometheus reference cannot be far from the literary Branagh's mind, even though it is not mentioned in the film (even as a subtitle). The ending of the film is positive in the sense that Walton has decided to turn back toward home; unlike the novel, Walton has learned his lesson and calls off the ill-fated voyage to the North Pole. Yet the ending is also bleak and sad. As the film concludes, we see the dim flames in a shadowy mist across the vast dark northern ice.

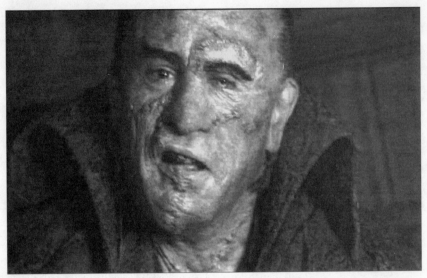

PHOTO 1.5   *The Creature (Robert De Niro) mourns his "father" in* Frankenstein *(1994).*

Conclusion

I chose here to discuss these two film versions of *Frankenstein* expressly for their prominent treatment of the Creature as a not altogether monstrous being. Yet both fail to present him as a being like Mary Shelley's Creature, full of pathos and possibility, a forlorn creature lost to the world of human society through no fault of his own, only of his birth. Whale's movie is far from the novel, yet even here, the mute monster has moments that elicit compassion. Branagh's film is flawed by its frenetic pace, vacillating depiction of the hero, and overwrought sound and cinematography, but it is redeemed by De Niro as the monster who finally speaks and questions his maker on film. It is of course always a risky, and often a fruitless exercise, to compare books with movie versions, and "classic" books pose an even greater threat for this project. Yet this topic interests me for several reasons. The movies in this case are far better known than the book, and some, at least the 1931 version, have achieved a "classic" status of their own. The movies miss out, however, not just on the book's subtleties but also on the major facts that concern its *feminism*. As I showed in the first part of this chapter, the book is a major feminist contribution to horror in several senses: dealing with female concerns, presenting complex gender dynamics, and critiquing masculine paradigms of the Romantic artist and masculinist views of science.

Frankenstein the novel certainly addresses problems of female artistic creation in terms that pose hard questions about male creation in art and science, about the natural versus the artificial, and about how to care for one's offspring. The two films I have discussed here can also be seen as reflections concerning the act of creation itself. This is evident in the way each movie is metafilmic. Whale's version is so partly because of the allusions to other classics like *Metropolis* and partly because of its frequent use of devices that call attention to the film medium and to the specific aims of horror. Branagh's film seems consciously self-referential in other ways, heavily conscious of its obligation to "make the classics live." Branagh as director is ironically like the character he plays in this film, approaching his task as if he must force a dead and inert thing to live, wake up, move, and talk! Why else would there be so much racing, swirling, dancing, rising, leaping, flying, shouting, swooping, crying—even so much romancing and sex and, ultimately, gore? The other challenge Branagh has to deal with is a lengthy history of horror films, something Whale was just starting to invent. Whale was alluding to German expressionism and the familiar tropes of the Gothic novel; his artistic struggles involved getting Universal Studios to agree to his vision. Branagh alludes not just to a whole history of prior *Frankensteins* but also to the British Hammer Studios tradition and to recent horror films like *Nightmare on Elm Street* and *Halloween*.

The last and central problem we face in thinking about this story concerns, of course, the monster. Karloff defined the monster so that even the best subsequent movie versions have not made much of a dent in the popular visualization of Frankenstein's monster. De Niro will not be likely to affect this stereotyping, either, because his Creature defies expectations we have come to have of the Frankenstein monster as he talks, thinks, learns, cries, smiles, hopes, and suffers. That he holds audience attention on the screen in opposition to Branagh's frenetic and self-absorbed acting job as Victor is due not only to his marvelously scripted lines but also to the delivery, acting, makeup, and filming, especially close-ups of his damaged lips and mismatched eyes. De Niro mesmerizes us in this role. It is a ridiculous and best-forgotten mistake, however, to turn him into a Freddy or Jason figure by making him rip out Elizabeth's heart; fortunately, he is redeemed by the tragic heights he reaches at the very end of the film.

Branagh's film also comes closer to the novel's association of the monster with the sometimes equally monstrous powers of nature. It is easy to ridicule this film's *Sound of Music* panoramic camera approach to sublime Alpine scenery, but some moments in the film are visually spectacular: Victor's vertiginous classroom in Ingolstadt, the laboratory creation scene, the cholera panic in the city, the meeting in the ice cave, and the concluding mists that envelop polar ice. Even the more prosaic scenes with the De Laceys are effective, as the family toils in a Millet-like wintry field at dusk or the monster weeps against a snow-laced tree, its gnarled roots framing his distorted body. The polar scenes of mist and crashing ice floes are true to the book; the ending scenes that set an excruciatingly sad monster adrift on the ice are among the best in the film. Whale's 1931 movie is composed of contrasts of black and white as evil and good, dark illicit penetration versus light at the dawn of an "appropriate" marital sexuality. Branagh's film, obviously, is in color and cannot use these same visual tropes. He employs color well: Brilliant reds stain both Victor's mother and the torn body of Elizabeth. Nature here is also full of contrasts, sometimes beautiful but also icy and blindingly bright. Like the monster himself, whose ultimate status is hard to fix, Nature here is in the end cruel and cold. Yet she offers possibilities of escape toward a better home for Walton if he will admit his limits. These are not possibilities open to the monster, so he aptly vanishes, his flame disappearing in Nature's mists. The visualization of this ambiguous ending in Mary Shelley's novel is one last virtue worth mentioning about Branagh's film. Whale's film shows the monster doomed to die—we are not supposed to know yet what we learn later in *Bride of Frankenstein* about his escape hatch through the floorboards. Branagh's film, like the novel, shows a monster who recedes into the distance, lost, unknown, unfixable, a flame of light that will slowly be extinguished.

chapter TWO: Women and Bugs

Monstrous Mothers:
Female Agency in Recent Horror

There's something going on in horror that I call the "women-and-bugs" phenomenon. "Bugs" play a part in some of the most frightening and disturbing images in recent horror movies: Geena Davis's nightmare of giving birth to a slimy maggot in *The Fly*; the six-foot flying cockroaches of *Mimic*; the gruesome metamorphoses of the gorgeous half-alien female in *Species*; the bald green beautiful Borg Queen in *Star Trek: First Contact*; the big fat Brain Bug (Photo 2.1) in *Starship Troopers*. And we must not forget all the horrific scenes in the *Alien* series: the cocooned humans, the slithering brown egg masses, the fierce and fearsome mother Alien.

In the films I will discuss in this chapter, female monsters or "queen bugs," offer new but nasty examples of female agency in horror. Furthermore, the bugs are pitched against female protagonists who lead the human defense against them. I want to consider whether these examples represent a *feminist* development in horror. Can there be feminist horror—and if so, what sorts of monsters and heroines will it offer? To answer these questions, I will focus on two primary examples, the *Alien* series and *Mimic*. I will explore how these films revisit *Frankenstein* to offer new treatments of its themes of good and evil, monsters and mad science, and the relation of women to nature. I will also contextualize this subgenre by tracing some of its roots in 1950s horror classics like *Them!*, with its giant ants. Along the way, I will have more to say about method in film studies. A cognitivist

PHOTO 2.1   *The nasty Brain Bug in* Starship Troopers *(1997): A feminized vision of alien evil?*

approach helps make clear that even bug films can offer thought-provoking moral messages, about women, evil, and social and political issues.

Background: Male Monsters, Female Victims

In horror classics of the 1930s and 1940s, there are few female agents and many female victims. The paradigm scenario has a male monster attacking a screaming (and preferably nubile) young woman. Dracula, Frankenstein's monster, the Wolfman, King Kong, the Mummy, and the Creature from the Black Lagoon are all typical horror movie villains. Clearly male, their attacks on women have an erotic element. The trend continued into the 1960s, although the supernatural monsters changed to slashers in films like *Peeping Tom* and *Psycho*. In the 1980s and 1990s, the psychopaths shifted into surreal monstrous men like Pinhead and Freddy, lascivious sadists with a crude sense of humor. Other villains like Jason, Leatherface, and Michael Myers may not relish women victims more than men, but they are still male themselves and pretty messed up about sex. I will examine representatives of these sorts of male monsters later on in this book.

There are exceptions, though, to the general rule. Women have sometimes also been monsters and agents of horror.[1] As early as Sheridan le Fanu's *Carmilla*, written in 1872, there was a threatening female vampire. Hammer Studios brought us lots of buxom and blond fanged females, in movies like *The Vampire Lovers* and *Kiss of the Vampire*. There is a later variant in *The Hunger*, and there are strong female vampires like Claudia in Anne Rice's *Interview with the Vampire*. Witches are another female horror paradigm, with variations like Carrie in the famous Brian De Palma film that bears her name. And we shouldn't forget the miscellaneous female monstrosities in classics like *Attack of the 50-Foot Woman*. (We also should not forget that the gender of the slasher in horror often turns out to be a surprise: "Jason" was really not the boy but his mother in the first *Friday the 13th*, reversing the way Norman Bates turned out to be his own "mother" in *Psycho*. The female slasher of *Dressed to Kill* is really the male psychiatrist played by Michael Caine, and so forth.)

There is something new, though, about the victims in horror since the 1970s. Often a girl or young woman fights back and triumphs over the monster in the end. This is the phenomenon that Carol J. Clover has dubbed the "Final Girl" and has studied in her book, *Men, Women, and Chain Saws: Gender in the Modern Horror Film*.[2] Such "fighting back" was heralded by *Carrie*, where the victim was a sort of witch, whom we paradoxically cheered on in her horrific final rampage. Jamie Lee Curtis in *Halloween* has a different fate from that suffered by her mother, Janet Leigh, in *Psycho*. In *Nightmare on Elm Street* Nancy is smart and gutsy, as is Kirsty in *Hellraiser*. When Kirsty's boyfriend tries to use the magic box to send the hideous Cenobites back to Hell, Kirsty grabs it back and does the job herself. The character Stretch in *The Texas Chainsaw Massacre, Part 2* not only survives the horror of the cannibal family but ends the film atop a small mountain wielding her own chain saw in victory.[3] But in Clover's analysis, the "Final Girl" type of female agency in recent horror is misleading and not particularly feminist. Women and girls are still punished for their sexuality, since the Final Girl survives "because" she stays "pure" and virginal. And further, the "girl" only succeeds by manifesting male, or "boy," types of virtues, like rigging bombs or jump-starting cars.

I want to look in a different direction in recent horror from Clover's "Final Girl" movies. My interest is in films that feature both a female monster and a strong female protagonist. Here femininity or "femaleness" remains an issue right through to the end—for both the monster and the victim/heroine. The women in these movies do not fit Clover's description of the "Final Girl." I admit that my "women-and-bugs" label is loose and not biologically accurate. I use "bugs" in a nontechnical sense that I hope will not cause entomological offense, including in the category

lizardlike beings, arachnids, and extraterrestrial crawly things like the Alien. (I re-
mind you that in *Aliens* the Marine Corps grunts ask the lieutenant at their briefing
if this is going to be "another bug hunt." He replies, "Yes, a xenomorph is involved,"
and snickering, they say, "Another bug hunt."[4]) There are plenty of other "critters" in
horror: rabbits, cats, dogs, birds, pumas, bats, wolves, alligators, sharks, killer
whales, rats, you name it (even tomatoes). So why bugs? They do not invoke the old
Adam and Eve story of the snake, nor do they play upon noir-ish tropes of lithe female predatoriness like *Cat People* did. We need to consider why female bugs are so
horrible, and why it takes a female hero to defeat them.[5]

Method: Some Options

As I explained in the Introduction, my own approach to film studies is cognitivist.
That means that I regard films as complex artifacts that present ideas and prompt
various judgments and emotional responses from their audiences. Of course, like
other horror films, women-and-bugs films aim especially at evoking fear or
dread. But they may inspire other feelings such as elation, sympathy, moral outrage, anger, and even humor. They may also encourage a range of thoughts on
various issues, as I shall try to describe further below. Our responses to a scene in
a women-and-bugs film may be simple and relatively predictable, like reflex
jumping at sudden movement. Probably everyone in the audience recoils during
Mimic when the baby roach that Dr. Susan Tyler is slowly unwrapping in her dark
lab at night suddenly "stings" her or when one of the Alien babies drops on top of
the bed Ripley and Newt are sleeping under in *Aliens*. But on the whole, these
movies call for more complex responses. Good horror films produce their effects
through their narrative structures as well as through other artistic choices. And
these films have complex concerns that go beyond the issues often focused on by
psychoanalytic theorists, beyond any form of personal psychodynamics. As we
watch them, we engage in various acts of interpretation and hypothesizing that
lead to understanding, prediction, and moral assessment.

For example, we can judge of *Aliens* that the situation of the people in the alien
cocoons is dreadful and that the crew should kill them out of pity. They are human, to be sure, but a merciful death is the best one can do for them. Or we can
agree that Ripley has been right to warn the corporate military bosses who think
they can capture *this* alien to use it as a weapon; only a very evil and nefarious
military-technical complex would believe this is a good goal. Again, it is wrong for
Bob (the FBI agent) to try to keep Dr. Pat Medford (the ant specialist) from going
down into the ants' nests in *Them!*; or we may feel that Dr. Susan Tyler is justified
in genetically engineering cockroaches in *Mimic*, despite the risks, because she

must stop the horrible plague that is killing children. Finally, the new genetically engineered Ripley in *Alien Resurrection* has a frightening bond to the Alien mother that may make her dangerous and unpredictable to her human friends. And so on. Emotional responses to horror scenes like these, even if they involve an element of almost physical or reflex reaction, can play a part in reaching a rational assessment of a film's narrative components and its overall message. Such responses in fact resemble our reactions to challenging situations or "paradigm scenarios" in real life.[6] Emotions in situations of real danger or fear can cue our actions, reactions, and our moral judgments.

In the Introduction, I explained my disagreement with psychoanalytic feminist approaches to horror. One particular complaint I have is that they tend to ignore or downplay the complexity of the moral messages in horror; they may altogether neglect horror films' political or social dimensions. An account confined to personal psychodynamics, particularly one phrased in terms of neurotic personality processes (such as suture, regression, transference, castration anxiety, fetishism, and the like), is inadequate to plumb the complexity of a movie and discounts the role of the audience's intelligence. To interpret our responses to a film in terms of psychopathology raises doubts about whether any meaningful moral assessment can occur as we view a film. From a psychoanalytic perspective, the audience's interest in a horror movie like *Alien* (whether in the spectacle of the monster or in the vision of the heroine) is always somehow neurotic and dysfunctional. This blocks the possibility of learning a meaningful lesson, evaluating a possible female heroine, or having reasons to be satisfied at the end, say, when Ripley blasts the monster into space and contentedly goes to sleep with her cat. Too often, psychoanalytic feminist accounts of horror films are reductive because they just do not consider that horror films like *Alien* can have interesting visual and technical, let alone social or political, dimensions. Since at least one prominent recent feminist psychoanalytic book on horror addresses *Alien* in detail, I shall take that account up next in order to explain my disagreement with this general approach in more detail.

Feminist Psychoanalysis: Barbara Creed on *Alien*

I want to consider here the construal of *Alien* offered by Barbara Creed in her recent book *The Monstrous-Feminine: Film, Feminism, Psychoanalysis*.[7] According to Creed, "*Alien* presents various representations of the primal scene."[8] This refers to the Freudian claim that all children have memories or fantasies of witnessing a "primal scene" of sex between their parents. Let us assume for the moment that this is so. A further Freudian assumption is that this scene presents an "archaic mother." The child's first view of the mother is shocking because of her absence of a phallus, so the child posits a powerful archaic mother who *does* possess the missing phallus. Here, Creed departs from Freud in a presumably feminist revision involving a third assumption. She argues that the monstrous phallus of the archaic mother does not cover up the mother's missing phallus but rather her *vagina dentata* (toothed vagina). A creature like the Alien monster is horrifying because it confronts us with images of this aggressive, destructive archaic mother, through either the Alien baby's nasty way of insinuating itself down people's throats into their stomachs ("raping" the victim) or the big monster Alien's toothily phallic head.

Creed now has enough laid out to claim that the archaic mother is the "backdrop for the enactment of all the events" in the movie *Alien*.[9] In supporting this statement, however, she switches suddenly away from her *vagina dentata* assumption to introduce yet another claim: "The central characteristic of the archaic mother is her total dedication to the generative, procreative principle."[10] We have now accumulated a significant diversity of hypotheses about the nature of an alleged archaic mother. It (a) possesses the missing phallus, so is castrated; (b) possesses the *vagina dentata*, so is castrating; and (c) is driven by the generative procreative principle.

Creed also spends much of her book describing how horror films illustrate Julia Kristeva's concept of "abjection." This concept is quite complex (and vague), but it basically involves a deep revulsion and aversion toward a mother (or anything else) seen as disgustingly dirty, slimy, putrid, and so on. Abjection concerns our feelings about an earlier primal state of union with the mother before bodily fluids became separate and disgusting or forbidden. So we must add "abjection" as hypothesis (d) to our list, as yet another claim or characteristic about the alleged archaic mother. The Alien as archaic mother is also horrible in the sense of being *abject* because it is slimy, nasty, and creepy-crawly. Its jaws leak fluid, its indeterminate genital parts lay large slimy eggs, and its very form is shifting. When it cocoons a human, the human is trapped in a sticky white substance so as to lack physical independence and to be "bound" back to the mother.

Adding to Freud and Kristeva, Creed also uses Lacanian psychoanalytic theory. She invokes Lacan's account of the mirror stage, or of the way images of the self are constitutive of personal identity. This leads to hypothesis (e), which concerns not simply the archaic mother herself but how a viewer *looks* at her in watching a film. Creed reaches this claim after summarizing five "looks" that a Lacanian theorist maintains are possible in relation to films or the screen.[11] The last of these looks is one Creed adds herself: "The horror film puts the viewing subject's sense of a unified self into crisis, specifically in those moments when the image on the screen becomes too threatening or too horrific to watch." Looking away from the screen in horror is necessary, in other words, to allow for a process of reconstitution of the self, which "is also reaffirmed by the conventional ending of some horror narratives in which the monster is 'named' and destroyed."[12]

Even if we were willing to accept these fundamental and quite disputable psychoanalytic assumptions about the nature of the archaic mother, the role of the mirror stage, or the determinative psychic role of the primal scene, Creed's use of the archaic mother concept is just too vague, general, and reductive: It is so open-ended that it can explain almost anything in a trivial sense. Indeed, Creed seems pleased about this as she writes about the numerous aspects of the archaic mother. This concept conveniently fuses all the distinct theories she employs, even though she admits, "It is difficult to separate out completely the figure of the archaic mother, as defined above, from other aspects of the maternal figure: the maternal authority of Kristeva's semiotic, the mother of Lacan's imaginary, the phallic woman, the castrated and castrating woman."[13]

This convenient assemblage allows Creed to make vast generalizations such as this: "The archaic mother is present in all horror films as the blackness of extinction—death."[14] This claim seems odd, too, given that in her book, the archaic mother is meant to be just one among seven possible types of female monstrousness. It would lead one to doubt, with reason, the claim that the seven are truly distinct. Why else could she generalize like this? The archaic mother hypothesis is especially handy since, as Creed notes, its many aspects can be either positive *or* negative. As a negative force, the archaic mother encompasses horrors such as a bird's mouth, a pulsating womb, the shark's maw in *Jaws*, or the spider in *The Incredible Shrinking Man*. As a positive force, the womb is not empty but full, and it evokes a terrifying female who does not depend for definition on the male.[15]

Notice the extraordinary reduction and leveling of films in Creed's proposed analysis.[16] All horror films are about the same thing, and they all work in the same way. Creed is talking about depth psychology, not about psychology on a more presumably superficial level. Hence, there is no reference to differences among viewers, the effects of marketing and advertising, or the social aspects of film-going. Fears in horror films are always fears not of *things*—however evil and frightening they might be—but fears of what things *represent*. And it turns out that they all represent one thing, the archaic mother. Yet some things are just frightening, and with good reason: Giant ants or spiders or sharks or blobs, and the representation of these things on film, are also frightening as we imagine the characters dealing with them. We do not need to invoke the further, and reductive, hypothesis that they are frightening for some one alleged thing that they *represent*.

Alien: Another Look

Creed's study of *Alien* ignores many significant aspects of its plot and themes. Despite its gut-wrenching power, this is also an intellectual movie of sorts. What does Creed think about the film's revisionist approach to the *Frankenstein* theme of male violation of nature or of its political hints about how an evil corporation in the background is at fault, driving this space expedition for purposes of exploitation, war, and greed? What is the impact of setting the story in outer space on a ship named the *Nostromo* (named after the title of the Joseph Conrad novel), rather than having the aliens invade earth, as they do in so many horror movies, from *Day of the Triffids* to *Independence Day*? Have humans asked for trouble by raiding space for their own greedy ends, like old colonialists in the era of Joseph Conrad?

Also disturbing about Creed's archaic mother hypothesis is the simplistic attitude it manifests toward the art of cinema. Apart from discussing the alleged voyeurism of viewing, Creed's book makes little reference to film technique, style, or cinematography. Any aspects she does notice, for instance, the special effects used to depict the Alien Mother or the stage sets for the ship where the eggs are first encountered, are just grist for her mill, grinding out the same end result repeatedly like a mechanical refrain: archaic mother, archaic mother, archaic mother. But *Alien* is a tremendously exciting and visually spectacular film right from the start—as we meander through space and see the eerie white struts of a spaceship that gradually materialize into angular sans serif letters that spell out the film's title. The opening sequence almost instantly sets the mood for a chilling and adventurous story. As it develops, the movie's timing and pacing are superb. Slow scenes of awakening and of the crew's casual friendly interactions lead on into suspenseful moments of exploration and then into horrific sudden jolting visions of the Alien monster and of deathly fights. There is a marvelous ensemble of actors. Add to all this the magnificent stage sets, stunning special effects, and well-chosen music. All the cinematic components work together with the narrative, plot, and laconic script to give this movie its distinctive impact and meaning. They *all* contribute to our understanding of the role and meaning of the heroine Ripley. I will zero in on just one example to explain more of what I mean. In the sequences near the end of *Alien*, the editing of sights and sounds interacts with acting and plot to create an unforgettable heroine.

Near the end of the film is a notorious scene where Ripley (Sigourney Weaver) undresses after she seems to have defeated the Alien. According to Creed, our views of Ripley's body as she undresses at the end of *Alien* (and her adoption of the little orange cat) can be explained

by a phallocentric account of female fetishism . . . . The visually horrifying aspects of
the Mother are offset through the display of woman as reassuring and pleasurable
sign . . . . Compared to the horrific sight of the alien as fetish object of the monstrous
archaic mother, Ripley's body is pleasurable and reassuring to look at. She signifies
the "'acceptable' form and shape of woman."[17]

According to Creed, Ripley has been too masculine in combating the beast and
we need to see her nearly naked female body for two reasons: to be reminded that
she is female and to make up for our horrific visions of the Alien (a.k.a. archaic
mother). Both filmic images speak to an apparently universal audience neurosis
and fetishism. There is no reason to deny that these shots of Ripley's body are very
voyeuristic. Ripley strips off not one but several layers of clothes. She ends up so
skimpily clad that we can see her breasts jiggle and virtually peek into the crack at
the top of her buttocks as we eye her from behind and her bikini underpants slip
down. But Creed ignores where this scene is placed in the *narrative* of the film,
and in so doing, she misses many of its most significant aspects, including its
emotional tone and resonance. These make a difference in what the audience can
infer and judge, so I shall say more about what has preceded the scene, and then
return to it with my own account.

In the scene before this striptease, Ripley has rigged the ship to explode so as to
kill off the Alien. She aims to escape in the small shuttlecraft along with the only
other remaining members of the ship's seven-person crew. Just as she is throwing
all the switches to launch the ten-minute countdown, she hears their screams over
the ship's telecom system. She rushes to their aid, to find only their ravaged bleeding bodies. Ripley is now alone with the Alien monster, the only human within
millions of miles of empty dark space on a ship about to explode. As she runs toward the shuttle to escape, she encounters the beast—at least, she sees its shadow
and glimpses its savage head lurking around one corner. During this entire cat-
and-mouse sequence, the film's sounds and sights are enormously effective at
building tension. The ship's lights strobe, steam hisses out of ventilators as cooling
systems shut down, and alarms screech. A mechanical female voice announces the
countdown to Armageddon. The pacing is frenetic and so are the visuals; this part
of the film is almost literally a light show. Moments of blurry screen movement as
we hear Ripley's panting or screaming are juxtaposed against still moments when
her face is caught like a rabbit in headlights by the flashing strobes. We see her at
times spotlit in blue and sweating, then we cross-cut to scary glimpses of the
Alien's big brutal head. It goes without question that we empathize with her in
these scenes. They continue earlier scenes that build a picture of Ripley's distinctive traits. Like Captain Dallas (Tom Skerritt), she is brave; but unlike him, she is

cautious. Like the science officer, Ash, she is smart; but unlike him, she is human and has a conscience. Like the only other woman, Lambert (Veronica Cartwright), Ripley is frightened and can cry, but she does not dissolve into tears when there is grave and imminent danger. Like the enraged Parker (Yaphet Kotto), she is determined to get even with the Alien; but unlike him, she keeps her head when facing the monster. All told, Ripley is an admirable human being and not, like Clover's "Final Girl," merely an amalgam of stereotyped masculine traits in female disguise.

This breathless escape sequence leads into two more scenes that, amazingly enough, raise the levels of tension even higher. Ripley has reached seeming safety on the shuttle, and the film's music signals a momentary respite. But as there is just one minute left for her to move away from the ship before it explodes, a new panic arises about whether she can escape the blast. Now Ripley displays other virtues and skills by working dexterously under extreme pressure. Again she is smart and quick but not stereotypically male: She hits buttons and turns switches with her long graceful fingers. She does manage to get the shuttle free. Then she (and we) watch as the ship detonates. At this point, the film as light show climaxes; it is at its most purely visual and cinematically spectacular (especially when seen in a theater on the large screen and with Dolby sound). There are long yellow-blue lines of light across the full screen followed by wondrous and loud billowy nuclear explosions of reds and yellows. The explosions are punctuated by blinding flashes of white light. The dramas of exterior space are intercut with tight close-ups of Ripley's face as she sits at the shuttle controls. These shots are extraordinary because she looks consumed in ecstasy as she is bathed in white light. Her head is slanted back at a forty-five-degree angle with eyes closed, lips slack. She moans slightly; in short, she looks orgasmic. I propose that the sexuality in these scenes is visual testimony to the prowess of the filmmaker at his movie's climax—he has his most satisfying creative bursts in this sequence! Creed, by isolating and discussing only the very final scenes when Ripley strips off her overalls after this grueling sequence, ignores this entire cinematic tour de force. It may indeed be that the film is sexist, but if so, it is in ways that are more complex and also more intrinsically linked to its artfulness than the Freudian formulaic analysis of voyeurism can capture.

And now I also want to suggest a different reading of Ripley's striptease before the final combat sequence. These scenes set up another bizarre sexual interaction of sorts in her ultimate confrontation with the Alien. We should keep in mind the beast here is clearly *male* in *Alien* (Ripley says on the shuttle, "I got you, you son of a bitch"—it will be a female and a "bitch" in the later films).[18] This scene is thus a variation on the typical horror movie cliché of male monster as erotic threat. But the sexuality in the scene is rather bizarre. In her final fight with the Alien, after she has donned a huge insulating space suit and helmet, Ripley utters small moans and mumbles over a space of several minutes. This part of the script is quite unusual. On the one hand, Ripley does seem "masculine" in that she is brave, heroic, mechanically adept, and a rational, careful planner. But on the other hand, she is also very "female" in her manner. As she plans some sort of action to take against the Alien, it is hard to make out her words. She keeps up a continuous mutter to herself and says things like "lucky lucky" and "oh oh" and even "I want to fuck you"(!) as she plans how to open the airlock and blast the Alien out into space. Thus, her final dance with the beast is a heavily sexualized battle. But I am not sure that femininity is especially marked here. If it is, it is a femininity with deep-reaching historical roots—like that of the martyr in the Roman Circus who becomes almost male as she fights the wild beasts and emerges victorious. The acts and bravery of female martyrs are like the male warrior's vision of the ecstasies of mortal combat.[19] After all, both sex and this kind of fighting are intensely intimate and private physical encounters.

Unlike Creed, then, I would argue that in the context of *the scene I have just described*, the sight of Ripley's body is not reassuring. Quite the contrary, it induces empathic fear on her behalf. Just as she finally feels herself safe and free of the exploded mother ship, the Alien's arm drops down into her face, and we realize that it, too, is on the shuttle. (It has apparently gone to sleep in the wall spaces of the shuttle. We see its jaws snap in a seeming dream.) Now she is the typical female victim of a (probably male) monster—a monster that has already reached out a seductive tentacle to wrap around the legs of the only other female victim, Lambert. But is the scene really only about sex and erotic threats? Beyond the stereotype, we should note that Ripley's flesh is indisputably *human*: pink, soft, natural, jiggling. Such flesh contrasts sharply with the adult Alien's flesh: blue-black, steely, hard, unnatural, almost mechanically designed. This scene thus echoes the film's opening scenes where the vast dark and empty body of the mechanical ship is contrasted with the small, pale, and nearly naked humans. It is relevant to note that Kane (John Hurt), with his pale and somewhat delicately pink body, is also treated in a similar way as Ripley. He is also shown almost naked, clad in a "diaper," tremendously vulnerable and exposed as he is invaded by the Alien baby parasite. Here, too, this human's pinkness is juxtaposed against the monster's unnatural color, at this stage a nasty yellow-green, and his smoothness to its rough scaliness.

Just as this scene brings out Ripley's human vulnerabilities, so in other scenes does she exemplify a human being's best traits, in contrast to those of the Alien, and also in contrast to the "inhuman" people (whether the android science officer

Ash or the corrupt corporation representative Burke in *Aliens*). *Alien* is about individuality, survival, and being human. The distinctness of fine actors helps show their separateness. Many of the people who die are too individual: They insist on going alone to do things. It could be described as a Hobbesian movie with a Marxian twist, in that the most sinister threats are posed by the greedy higher-ups within the Company (a military-industrial bureaucracy). Ripley as security officer tries to prevent the alien "infection" by maintaining quarantine, but she is overruled by science officer Ash, who follows his private "eyes-only" Directive #937 from the Company to get aliens back for scientific study at all costs: "All other priorities are rescinded. Crew expendable." Similarly, in *Aliens*, Ripley and her surrogate daughter, Newt, are nearly made victims of the alien parasites because the Company's representative, Burke, wants to profit by smuggling the aliens out through quarantine in their host bodies. Ripley comments to him: "You know, Burke, I don't know which species is worse. You don't see them fucking each other over for a goddamn percentage." As I read at least these first two movies in the *Alien* series, then, they are about what it means to be *human*. Ripley's femininity is relevant to this to be sure, but perhaps even more relevant is her *humanity*.

Ripley is horrified to discover that Ash, the science officer, actually admires the Alien: "I admire its purity . . . no conscience, remorse, or delusions of morality." This is an important line because it allows the audience to take a different perspective for a moment about this monster: It is indeed terrifying, but it also intelligent and has its own elegance, awesome power, and force. The visual realizations of H. R. Giger's artistic design are splendid and spectacular.[20] We both want and yet fear to look at this creature more. Its lines are long and elegant, its skin is smooth with the gemlike quality of beautifully tooled metal. But any human sympathy should make plain how immoral such respect is, given the Alien's malignant nature: It destroys all other life forms it encounters. This is confirmed by the film when we realize that the radio signal was a warning note left by the previous Alien victim and when we see Ash revealed to be an android—not a real but a mechanical man. He bleeds white, colorlessly, not the red blood of humans. As the other six members of the *Nostromo* crew are picked off one or two at a time, Ripley by contrast is a superior representative of humanity. She shows both fear and courage (a realistic combination Plato and Aristotle would approve of as true courage). When the only remaining crew members are Ripley, Ash, Lambert, and Parker, she is the most heroic: Ash seems to have given up figuring out a scientific way to kill the Alien (we later learn why); Parker is consumed by rage; Lambert cries and shakes in fear; only Ripley can think things through and plan to carry them out. As senior officer, she can give the orders. To complain that this exemplary human cannot be truly female is to give up the claims of feminism in advance! (I do think that such criticisms are better justified about the latest film in the series, however; see below.)

In the *Alien* series, the heroine herself is not the overreacher, but there are still echoes of *Frankenstein*. Evil science is used in the service of a vast capitalist military-technical machine, and its misguided attempts to control or use a monstrous nature put humans at dire risk. The heroine is the one who must correct the problems that corporate science causes. She is the one who clearly sees the danger of such over-reaching and meddling with nature. By choosing to make the agent of justice a woman, the series offers an interesting continuation (with revisions) of Mary Shelley's thematic opposition between "good" femininity and "evil" masculinity. That is, masculine overreaching must be countered by feminine features aligned with domesticity and sociality. Such a view has its dangers and limitations, as I argued in Chapter 1. And there are the other problems I have remarked upon concerning visual voyeurism and the filmmaker's use of Ripley as an orgasmic respondent to his own art. But we are unfair to Ripley if we view her as either just a reassuring fetish object or a "final girl" who only survives by becoming virtually masculine.

Later films in the series continue the Frankenstein theme as they represent the evil "Company" looking for the latest and best weapon of destruction. As in *Frankenstein* (and in other films like *Species* and *Species II*), the (male) scientists in the military-industrial complex become too enamored of their unnatural monster. In *Aliens*, Burke wants to bring samples of the Alien babies back to earth to study and market them; he is the only evil human in the film, and he betrays all the others. In *Alien Resurrection*, the corporation scientists have not simply encountered the Alien monster out there but have deliberately re-created it from Ripley's DNA (which became blended with it through her impregnation in *Alien³* with the larva of a queen Alien). Once again, the scientists are the sleazeballs of the film; one of them remarks: "The animals themselves are wondrous. They'll be invaluable once we've harnessed them." This series "punishes" the male scientists by the most direct means of death at the "hands" of the very monsters they have created or sought to appropriate. Such moments are obviously just retribution (and prove audibly satisfying to audience members).

Why does only Ripley, the strong, smart woman, survive? Why does the Ripley character change as the series evolves? First she adopts a cat and then a small child; next acquires a lover; then progresses to self-immolation and rebirth as a genetically altered half-breed clone of herself. Depth psychology leaves us little room for interesting analysis of how the *Alien* series has developed in the nearly twenty years since it began. In Creed's view, this is all a matter of competing views of maternity and the maternal body. Here is what she says about *Aliens*:

Throughout, *Aliens* opposes two forms of mothering: Ripley's surrogate mothering
in which there is no conception or birth and where the female body is unmarked; and
Mother Alien's biological, animalistic, instinctual mothering where the maternal
body is open and gaping. . . . Mother Alien represents Ripley's other self, that is,
woman's, alien, inner, mysterious powers of reproduction. It is the latter, the female
reproductive/mothering capacity *per se,* which is deemed monstrous, horrifying, abject. Like Mother Alien, Ripley also transforms into an indestructible killing machine
when her child—even though a surrogate offspring—is threatened.[21]

Further, Creed writes that the heroic, self-sacrificing Ripley at the end of *Alien*[3] "is
betrayed by her body, unable finally to preserve her own flesh from contamination by the abject, alien other—the monstrous fecund mother."[22]

Notice how these comments equate all the movies. Yet many viewers feel
strongly that these films are very different. Some prefer the first movie as a strikingly original departure in sci-fi horror. Some think James Cameron's direction in
Aliens made that movie more thrilling; I have heard it called one of the best movie
sequels ever made. Most fans of the series will agree that the last two films went
downhill. Why are the films different as films, if their horror is the same? Isn't it
an insult to the heroism of Ripley to keep saying that she is just an alternative or a
parallel to the Alien archaic mother?[23] My questions are ones Creed does not raise
and would presumably not find interesting, because they turn away from focusing
on the deep psychological truth of the structures that impel us to react as we do to
the primal scene of the Alien Mother herself.

What can an audience get out of assessing a strong heroine in a bug movie? As
an action hero, Ripley offers interesting possibilities for complex audience identification and empathy. She is simply more human than Arnold Schwarzenegger,
Bruce Willis, Steven Segal, or most other male heroes in action films. Sure, Ripley
can kick butt, drive a tank, lob grenades, punch computer code, face off with the
Alien, or dive suicidally into the flames. Yet she also cries, quakes, has nightmares,
trembles, and is sometimes weak and deeply afraid. This emotional vulnerability
makes her a more interesting and believable character in many ways than her
male action counterparts (some of whom, like Robocop and the Terminator, are
ironically enough in search of human emotions!). Moreover, she is a strong advo-
cate of basic human values like companionship, camaraderie, and caring for others. Indeed, her ability to show some sympathy and caring may make her a better
combatant and leader than most of the men she outlives. She cares about people
enough to think their options through and to never give up on rescuing someone.
She berates the inhuman corporation man for aiming only at his own greedy
goals—in her book, he is no better than the Alien. She earns the trust of fright-

PHOTO 2.2   *The new cloned Ripley (Sigourney Weaver) lolls with her own Alien kind in* Alien Resurrection *(1997).*

ened little Newt so she can find out what the girl may know about the space colony and the Aliens.

In my view, then, Ripley's genetic merger with the Alien Queen in the most recent entry in the series was a mistaken step backward, pushing her into the inhuman mold of the android Schwarzenegger plays in *Terminator*. She has an excuse for her inhumanity now as she simply becomes a big bug herself, a strong tough fighter with inhuman abilities of sense and smell. (This is foreshadowed perhaps by the final scenes of *Aliens*, where she dons a giant mechanical body to use in her last fight against the "bitch.") These "male" aspects do not fit with her sudden and literal descent into the maternal realm of the Alien nest, where she wallows voluptuously among the creepy tentacles and eggs (Photo 2.2). *Alien Resurrection* is an unimaginative parody of its predecessors, an emptied-out formulaic genre exercise. This seems to be admitted when the two inhuman female heroes comment knowingly at the end of the film: "So you did it. You saved the Earth." Ripley speaks with such deadpan irony to Call (Winona Ryder) at the end of the movie that is hard to avoid taking the whole thing as a put-on. *Alien Resurrection* offers no truly interesting female characters on the side of either good or evil.

A Different Take on Bugs

I don't think we need or benefit from the archaic mother hypothesis. Bugs in movies, like bugs in the world, can sometimes be very nasty vermin.[24] They can undermine the foundations of our homes, eat our clothes, ruin our food, eviscerate books in our libraries, defoliate our trees, despoil our gardens, spread human diseases, and deliver painful bites or stings. Bugs live in filthy sewers, dark scary tunnels, or wet storm drains. They are unpredictable and nonhuman in their appearance and movements. They are neither soft and cuddly like kittens nor beautifully effective killers like falcons or cheetahs. They fly at you or squiggle past you, they eat putrid things in foul ways, their eggs and cocoons are slimy, brown, and pulsating. Eventually, they will consume our corpses.[25]

But why then *women* and bugs? I will grant this much to the archaic mother hypothesis: A main reason bugs are horrible in the movies is that they are "queens" who are frightening because of their reproductive powers. They combine a primitive instinctual drive to reproduce with a tendency to dominate the male of the species. Like the praying mantis, they destroy or else simply abandon their mate after he has done his duty. Males are only minimally necessary to them. In *Species,* the lizard lady, clothed in the external garb of a blond bombshell, literally rapes and then murders her male lovers if she scents out their genetic inadequacy. In *Mimic,* the cockroach attackers are all females who keep just one fertile male ready to service them in their nest. In *Them!,* the queen ants are twice as large as the males and can live on for years to lay many eggs and prosper long after their mates have fallen from the sky. The Borg Queen is the only interesting member of a species that is nothing more than high-tech futuristic ants. She combines the efficiency of their mass personality with a unique desire for seduction and novelty.

Here is what psychoanalysis misses out on. The bug movies are interesting not because they conjure up bug queens as images of the archaic mother driven by reproduction but because they creatively explore the *consequences* of bugs' revised sexual arrangements. Sexuality is always linked to larger issues about social frameworks. The bug movies are hence also about science and nature, politics, war and weaponry, good and evil.[26] Large-scale bugs are truly frightening monsters because of their alternative social structures, communicative ability, swarm behavior, and amazing physical powers. The old scientist in *Them!* explains to a blue-ribbon panel of military experts at the White House that ants are formidable foes, "ruthless, savage, and courageous fighters . . . the only other creatures on earth, other than man, who make war." They can lift twenty times their own weight, and they turn captives they do not kill into slave laborers. Chemical weapons and biological warfare are in the bug arsenal, too, as they use stingers to dispense ruinous acids or spit out poisonous sprays. The arachnids in *Starship Troopers* shoot "bug plasma" out across interstellar space like nuclear warheads. Unlike our troops in Operation Desert Storm, the giant ants of *Them!* do very well in harsh desert conditions. The bugs' intelligence operations are phenomenal. They perceive through clever radarlike antennae or bulging composite eyes. They communicate through whistles and clicks. Big bugs can emit bad odors, and the roaches of *Mimic* deposit huge mounds of sticky excrement. Bugs come equipped with hard armor on the outside. Their weaponry is vast and varied: fierce slashing mandibles, quick thrusting tongues, lacerating arms, or strong crushing jaws. Their motives are brutal. In *Mimic,* the wise old scientist quotes Hobbes's remark that human life is nasty, brutish, and short. "Ants would put it more succinctly," he says. "Can I eat it, or will it eat me?"

Not all "bugs" or bug films are the same. We can better understand what is unique about films like the *Alien* series by contextualizing these films in the horror tradition, especially in relation to a film like *Them!,* made in 1954. I next go back in time to explore some background of modern women-and-bugs movies by looking at two interesting examples from the 1950s.

Bug Films of the 1950s

The ants of *Them!* are very similar to the Alien in size, shape, and threateningness. They, too, are female, crawl out of dark holes, lay eggs in vast numbers, protect their babies fiercely, crush and kill innocent people (including the entire crew of a naval destroyer), and menace us with their poisonous body acids. But *Them!* is a movie with themes that are characteristic of the 1950s.[27] It is about the indiscriminate victims of war in a thermonuclear age and the threat of communism. Not only are the ants products of nuclear tests, signifying an early awakening of environmentalist consciousness, but they also symbolize the cold and faceless efficiency of the Soviet army and intelligence machine. *Them!* asks if the ants will beat the individualistic Americans, making us extinct within a year, because *they* have a form of perfect communication and cooperation—unlike *us.*

Them! is also striking (and surprising, given our stereotypes about the 1950s) because it presents a female scientist in a prominent role. Spunky women start to appear on the horror scene in these 1950s films. To match the "formicologist" in *Them!* there is an "ichthyologist" in *Revenge of the Creature* (1955). In each film, the female scientist is a smart and sensible character. However, she must be made unusually attractive in order to counteract her anomalous status qua scientist. I want to consider these women to think more about female heroic agency in bug movies.

In the scene of the scientists' arrival in *Them!*, the male heroes, a policeman and an FBI agent, wait to meet a plane and wonder why two Department of Agriculture scientists, "the Doctors Medford," are being flown in to deal with the mysterious tracks they have found after some thefts and murders in New Mexico. First, we see a somewhat paunchy older male scientist descend the plane's ladder. He absently greets the locals and then shouts for "Pat." Expecting another man, the police agents turn and are delighted to see a woman's beautiful legs, her feet clad in high heels, on the ladder. The voyeuristic scene is extended for the audience as well, as she pauses mid-descent and exclaims, "I'm stuck!" with only her elegant legs on view. The men's response is very 1950s: "If she were the kind of doctor that takes care of sick people, I could get a fever real quick."

In *Revenge of the Creature,* the female scientist is introduced as we hear a radio interviewer tell his audience that he is talking about the Gill Man with an expert who is, amazingly enough, "one of the prettiest young women I've ever had the pleasure to meet." We see "Miss Hobson" with her pert blond curls and little hat, smiling as she stands beside the aquarium tank. She patiently explains what ichthyology is and why they are trying to revive the Gill Man by moving his body through the water in the tank. There was also a beautiful heroine in the first *Creature* movie, but she was the usual damsel in distress destined to be a victim. She went along on the Amazon trip with her boyfriend largely as his assistant and was never presented as having scientific credentials. Julie Adams in this role existed largely, we suspect, to tempt the Creature by swimming languidly in her stunning white suit straight into his watery domain. Like any green-blooded male, he immediately lusted after this lovely human female, and most of the threat and suspense in this film ensues from his pursuit and abduction of her.[28] Similarly in the sequel, the now tank-bound creature spends most of his time mooning with his fishy goggle eyes toward the heroine through the portholes of his tank. Once he escapes, he also ogles her in a shower scene that anticipates the more famous one to come five years later in *Psycho.*

Significantly in both *Creature* movies, the woman is a voice of balance poised between two competing male heroes. She is aligned with the "good" hero who is a scientist out for knowledge, rather than with the "bad" hero who is a mere adventurer out for fame and money.[29] The movies do not seem to acknowledge the fact that both men are exploiting the Creature in similar ways. In the second film, as in the King Kong movies, the heroine does show moments of sympathy for this poor Creature, who has been ripped from his natural habitat, moved thousands of miles, and made into a high-priced zoo spectacle for entertainment in a Florida aquarium. Even beyond this, he has been treated cruelly by the scientist's bizarre educational techniques. We really cannot be sure about his levels of consciousness, but he *looks* intelligent and perceptive. As he reaches for the food the woman offers him, the male scientist tries out operant learning techniques by shocking him painfully with a giant bull prod. Simultaneously, the woman says "no," reinforcing the 1950s message that it is the female role to train male creatures to limit their desires. These painful (and scientifically ill-judged) scenes now seem disturbing, and they make it almost impossible not to cheer later when the Creature escapes. In this movie as well, Helen, like Kay in the first film, is shown as expressing pity for the creature, particularly for his isolation and loneliness.

In *Revenge of the Creature,* the woman's goal of being a scientist will and obviously "should" be subordinated to finding love and marriage. To get married and bear children will require her to give up her scientific ambitions. She lies on the beach mulling over her options with her boyfriend as he explains all this to her. He says: "It's tough on you girls. I'm not saying it should be. Just that it is." Although in this scene she seems undecided and in other scenes she is a strong figure, not just smart but quick on her feet in verbal duels, we later learn that they are engaged. She has obviously made up her mind in a direction the filmmakers expect the audience to consider appropriate.

Them! is a far better movie in almost every respect: plot, pacing, dialogue, cinematography, acting. Its view of the woman scientist will strike us in the 1990s as more contemporary. Joan Weldon, as Dr. Pat Medford in *Them!,* is quite different from the female ichthyologist. Although she is often coded as "feminine" by her attire and attractiveness as she accompanies either her famous father or the male FBI agent (James Arness) like a sidekick, she nevertheless is also a strong, smart, and brave character who is a dedicated scientist. Her knowledge is essential to defeating the giant ants. Even after a romance is hinted at between her and Bob, the FBI agent (she tells him to "call me 'Pat' if the 'Doctor' bothers you"), she is never compelled to sacrifice her science—and indeed that would appear unlikely, given her clear dedication.

This is all the more surprising, given that the movie includes a conventional scene showing Pat as female victim. She ventures out into the New Mexico sands wearing her inappropriate high-heeled shoes and suit, only to become the typical screaming damsel who spots a giant ant, is attacked by it, and then is rescued by the male hero. However, later she dons fatigues and intrepidly enters the ants' nests alongside the men. Bob tries to prevent her, insisting, "This is no place for you or any other woman!" but she simply silences him with her forceful logic in a brisk no-nonsense voice (Photo 2.3). "Listen, Bob; someone with scientific knowledge has to go down there, and my father is physically unable to.... There's no time to give you a fast course in insect pathology." This Dr. Medford even assumes command in the expedition, since she is the only one who can recognize

PHOTO 2.3   *Dr. Pat Medford (Joan Weldon) directs Bob (James Arness) in the battle against the giant ants in* Them! *(1954).*

the queens.[30] Upon finding them in their egg chamber, she gives the orders in no uncertain terms: "Destroy everything in here. Burn it. I said burn it!"

I see this increasing respect for the female role as correlated to another important feature of the villains in women-and-bugs movies. *Them!* opens with the specific threat that bugs pose to human children. Its initial and still strikingly suspenseful sequence shows a small girl wandering in a stark desert setting. In his book *Terror and Everyday Life: Singular Moments in the History of the Horror Film,* Jonathan Lake Crane comments that the plane and the flying ants emphasize the indiscriminate threat of nuclear bombs, where no one is spared, however innocent.[31] Children are also central in the climax when troops battle the colony of giant ants in the storm drains under Los Angeles. Two small boys have been cornered there, so the army cannot use gas in their attack. There are frequent cross-cuts from the action and suspense of the search in the tunnels to the mother waiting outside, sobbing and frightened. Much of the fearfulness of the film's final scenes depends on the threat to the boys, and one hero is killed by the ants while saving them.[32]

Them! seems to end, though, with everything put right. The two children who were the focus of the rescue efforts have been restored to their mother, and there is a strong hint that the woman scientist has been provided with a suitable mate of her own. (Mysteriously, though, we never do see the little girl from the beginning again.) By making children seem so central to both women and men, this film seems to assure its audience that "normal" female reproduction and "normal" parenting will replace the abnormal methods of the queen ants.[33] The challenge posed by the group-think ants has been met, as all the relevant American bureaucracies learn to get along, communicate, trust each other, and share control against a common enemy. The fledgling queen ants are all destroyed before any can develop their wings enough to fly away. True, old Dr. Medford concludes the movie with a dire message about the unknown evils that science may have wrought. Even though his words of warning are enforced by "dramatic" music in the score at the end, the film's optimism overall works to undermine this warning and suggests it is merely a formula.

One reason for the strong presence of female figures as heroes in the bug films becomes clear in *Them!:* A specific threat in these movies is directed at *children. Them!* sets up a dialectic that reappears thirty-two years later in *Aliens* and forty-three years later in *Mimic.* Women are allowed by the logic of these films to don military garb and behave aggressively for a primal reason: protecting babies. It is no accident that the main threat to children comes from giant queen ants who are mothers; they fly through the air breeding new queens to cover all areas of the country. Similarly, in *Aliens* after Ripley adopts the little girl Newt, she is far more aggressive than in *Alien* (Photo 2.4). She wears heavy weaponry, acts physically tougher and angrier, and fights the "bitch" Alien mother as she and the Alien mother each protect their offspring. This difference is signaled best perhaps by the fact that she wears only a white space suit at the end of *Alien* but dons an entire giant metal robotic body at the conclusion of *Aliens.* And most recently in *Mimic,* Dr. Susan Tyler genetically engineers cockroaches for much the same sort of goal—in order to save human children from a plague spread by normal roaches.

To speak about reproduction as the central issue of women-and-bugs films is, however, to risk another kind of reductiveness. We should not overlook further aspects of femininity that are very significant in these films, aspects that stem from the *Frankenstein* tradition. Like the women in Mary Shelley's novel, women in 1950s horror films often bring humanity to situations that have gotten out of hand due to the impersonal aims of a (male) scientific-military technocracy. The rationality of science in films like *Revenge of the Creature* or *The Day the Earth Stood Still* is excessive, cruel and pitiless—so much so that it is actually bad as science. Mark Jancovich points out that in these movies, "feminine" qualities such as

PHOTO 2.4   *Ripley (Sigourney Weaver) protects Newt (Carrie Henn) from the Alien Mother in* Aliens *(1986).*

feeling, intuition, interaction, and imagination are often valued. Further, he notes that "women's involvement is often central to defeat of the menace."[34] This is true as early as *Them!* when Pat Medford must identify the queens. Also noteworthy is that the men, too, at the start of *Them!* show great concern for the little girl in shock and that some of the men near the film's conclusion argue against a utilitarian military leader who wants to gas the tunnels, despite the risk posed to two boys. The heroes point to the children's mother; individual human emotions outweigh the policy of "greatest good for the greatest number."

Despite these hints of a feminist revision of stereotypical male values, we can still criticize the presentation of femaleness in these 1950s films, just as I did for *Frankenstein*. It seems good that women are valued for certain alleged features, yet their treatment in these older horror films is essentializing. That is, though women may not have a biological destiny, certain emotional stereotypes are attributed to the feminine, and women must again serve men by "humanizing" them.[35] Let us move now to my final and very recent example of a women-and-bugs film to see whether this trend continues.

The New *Frankensteins*

I have just described some 1950s antecedents of the modern women-and-bugs films and a rationale for their visible female heroes. I pointed out that these movies begin to depict strong women in the context of fights with female monsters over which species' offspring will survive. Their concern for monstrous reproduction and the female socializing of men into true humanity makes these films heirs of an even older horror tradition, the mad-scientist story stemming from *Frankenstein*. In these movies, we also often find the message that a scientist overreacher can violate natural processes only with dire results. But the monsters created here are female, and the particular form that human destruction will take is their monstrous repro-duction—leading to an infestation of all-powerful and mostly female bugs. The women-and-bugs movies offer a kind of inverse of *Frankenstein,* since they are about ways of bypassing the masculine role in reproduction.

An interesting recent entry in the women-and-bugs genre is *Mimic,* because here the heroine who fights the bugs is also the scientist overreacher who has cre-ated them. She violates nature by genetically manipulating cockroach DNA, com-bining it with that of the termite and the mantis—surely a recipe for verminous disaster! It does indeed lead to bad effects: unanticipated six-foot monster roaches who can masquerade as people and who see humans as tasty meat. The female scientist who created the bugs must then figure out how to destroy her own mon-strous progeny. In *Mimic,* there is even an explicit allusion to the *Frankenstein* theme. A point I want to emphasize in discussing this film is that once again, there are social aspects of the depiction of the monstrous bugs that go beyond the im-mediate personal or psychodynamic threat they pose as monstrous mothers. We shall also see how the heroine's "femininity," as with Ripley or Dr. Pat Medford, plays a key part in the narrative of combat and victory against the bugs.

Mimic

Mimic (Guillermo del Toro, 1997) starts, like *Them!,* with a threat to human chil-dren. This is not shown through graphic attacks but is sketched in the film's bril-liant and chilling credit sequence. As the credits roll, we see static, almost Victorian, images of impaled bugs. These are juxtaposed against huge news head-lines that scream disaster and death. Next we see a pretty woman (Mira Sorvino) visiting a bizarre hospital ward. Rows of children lie in a chamber that once again, like the credit sequence, has archaic and Victorian overtones. In this vaulted and beehive-like hall, there are rows of beds with floating oxygen tents. Topped by tall white shrouds, they look eerily like insect cocoons. Seen closer up, each cocoon contains a small child who gasps for breath. Some children turn away to die as their relatives plead tearfully with the woman visitor for help. Thus, from the start of the film with this almost wordless mini-narrative, we can infer two things. First, the situation is dire; and second, this woman is someone of importance and power who can act to change things. Further, because of her tears, she is obviously compassionate. Warm and human, she hardly fits our stereotype of the hubristic Victor Frankenstein. Instead, the suffering shown here prompts us to endorse the judgment that this woman must help if she can.

In flashbacks and voice-over narration, we watch as Dr. Tyler releases her genetically engineered "Judas" species of cockroaches into the sewers of New York City. Clearly she does so with the lofty and seemingly supportable moral aim of killing the normal roaches that have been spreading the hideous plague that is killing all the children of the city. The story of this new Frankenstein breeding program is told from the perspective of a seemingly successful outcome, as Dr. Tyler stands and speaks beside her husband, Dr. Peter Mann (Jeremy Northam), a Centers for Disease Control doctor. They are appearing at a news conference to announce their victory over the plague. But the camera zooms in to show the face of a wise-looking older man in the audience who ominously shakes his head, a dire forecasting that all is not well with this solution. This note of warning is cross-cut with scenes depicting the couple's exhilaration as they celebrate together at home. They embrace in the bathtub and imagine having children of their own in the near future. *Mimic* is typified by such swings of mood and also by shifts from light to dark and from public to private settings.

This initial ominous hint is fulfilled when Dr. Tyler's "Judas" insects, which were meant to destroy their fellows and then die off, mutate and reappear as fearsome six-foot variants who "mimic" or disguise themselves as men in overcoats. Now Susan's mentor, the wise older scientist (F. Murray Abraham), says, "So, you think your little Frankensteins have gotten the better of you." She protests, "But they all died in the lab!"—to which he replies, "Yes, Susan, but you let them out in the world. The world's a much bigger lab."

The *Frankenstein* allusion is visually reinforced in various ways, too. Not only do the credits and the bizarre hospital chamber offer filmic references to a scientific past, but Susan's laboratory is anachronistic for a researcher allegedly at the forefront of work on genetic engineering. Like Dr. Frankenstein, Dr. Tyler works alone on a stormy night in a lab that looks like one minimally updated from a Dr. Jekyll and Mr. Hyde movie: It is shadowy, containing wooden furniture and old specimen cases, not the sleek modern white and steel outfittings we might expect. She does not have a cadre of postdocs running experiments under her supervision. The scenes of her working alone late at night, of course, also emphasize her vulnerability as a woman. Susan, like Pat Medford of *Them!* and Ripley in *Alien*, becomes a potential victim of the bugs. The brilliant Mexican horror director Guillermo del Toro choreographs these lab scenes with clever sadism and suspense, as a shadowy and unidentifiable bug figure flits in and around, even across the ceiling, undetected by Susan. There are many more Hitchcockian moments of ghastly humor throughout the movie.

Just as *Them!* began and ended by highlighting threats to children, so do Dr. Tyler's concerns about and relations with children drive much of her action in *Mimic*. Besides aiming to save the lives of all the children of New York City, Susan has an affinity with small children, particularly boys. Her encounters with children emphasize her feminine and maternal side, which she has not lost despite being a top scientist. Two young helpers comb the subways for unusual bug specimens for her. She says to a friend that it is better for them to be occupied in this way than to be in a gang. It is a mark of the change of times that here, unlike in *Them!*, the movie kills off these two children in an unexpectedly horrifying scene when they first encounter the Judas roaches. We cannot see who their attackers are or exactly what happens; but we do see a frighteningly sudden and vicious attack with rapid cuts between their twisted, screaming faces, their spurting blood, and their mangled corpses. Despite this violence, *Mimic*, like both *Them!* and *Aliens*, foregrounds a threatened symbolic child who is ultimately saved. This is Chuy, the apparently autistic grandson of a Latino shoeshine man (Giancarlo Giannini). Chuy rarely speaks except to identify people's shoes, but he is not frightened when Susan questions him. He is the first person to observe the giant mutant roaches, but he can only call them by his own label, "Mr. Funny Shoes." He even seems to communicate with them by clicking spoons.

As I have said, *Them!* dealt with the indiscriminate destruction of atomic weaponry, concerns about nuclear environmental impact, and the need for bureaucratic cooperation to ward off the clonelike Communists in the Cold War. *Alien* and *Aliens* offered cynical analysis of the small person's victimization by the larger forces of amoral corporate greed. *Mimic*, made in 1997 after the fall of communism and the end of the Cold War, focuses on a new set of social issues and a new war, in which the enemies are epidemic disease and social ills brought to the United States by immigration. Set in the urban blight of New York City, *Mimic* takes for granted its many scenes of grim poverty and urban filth. Chuy and his grandfather, Manny, live in a bombed-out area across from a mission for the homeless run by an aged Asian priest. These scenes emphasize that social problems and poverty affect immigrants, the elderly, the lower classes, and nonwhites most severely—that is, those who stereotypically live in closer contact with roaches (and who, by implication, are also carriers of disease). The mutant

roaches begin their inroads on humans and establish colonies by killing off un-
named and unnoticed homeless people: the mentally ill, alcoholic bums, kids
from poor neighborhoods, and bag ladies.

It is surely significant to note, then, that from the threatened heroic small group
highlighted in this movie, the heterosexual white couple survives, whereas the savvy
black male subway cop (Charles S. Dutton) and the gentle Mexican shoeshine man
are hideously massacred and devoured by the Judas roaches. After he realizes Susan
is the person who created the mutant bugs, Manny excoriates her as the typical scientist who did not think about the consequences of her acts, and Leonard, the black
subway cop, agrees that she did not care about their children. Also significant is that
these two men each die sacrificing themselves, Manny for his grandson Chuy,
Leonard to save the others. He even goes down singing.[36]

Despite *Mimic*'s dire prognosis about the measures needed to cleanse the world
of urban blight, the film does conclude with an optimistic note on the racial-ten-
sion front. Several scenes in the movie highlight the white couple's desire to reproduce. As already noted, in the introductory film sequence after their press conference, they are shown embracing in a bathtub and imagining their future
children. Later, we see Susan one morning waiting for the results of her home
pregnancy test. She happily scans her abdomen's reflection in the mirror while
bouncy music plays on the soundtrack. A phone call interrupts with dire news of
a sewer bug discovery, and at the same time, Susan learns that the test is negative.
She is despondent enough that the film seems to hint she may have fertility problems, though Peter promises her that "we'll keep trying." This suggests that the
white race cannot quite live up to its evolutionary imperative—or perhaps that
the couple are being punished for Susan's transgressions. Her only "babies" are
the monster bugs out in the sewers. The point is highlighted by the visual juxtaposition of her home pregnancy test kit with the two test strips in her lab in the
scene that confirms her worst suspicions about the genetic identity of the new giant "baby" bug (Photo 2.5). She remarks when first opening up the box holding
the monstrous bug, "You're just a baby!"—right before it viciously stings her.

Concern for children is again brought out in the rather sappy final moments of
the film. Trapped alone with Chuy and an immediately threatening roach, Susan
cuts her own hand so that the roach will scent her and spare the boy. Like Ripley
in *Aliens,* she has become fiercely protective of this one symbolic child, and like
Ripley at the end of *Alien³*, she offers to sacrifice herself instead. But this does not
prove necessary; and in the end, a miraculously saved and reunited Peter and
Susan embrace. Their horrendous battle with the bugs has ended with a huge explosion, roasting all the subways (and, we presume, all the roaches in them) in
one massive fireball. The camera pans down to highlight little Chuy nestled be-

PHOTO 2.5   Dr. Susan Tyler (Mira Sorvino) studies a baby mutant roach in Mimic (1997).

tween them. Clearly implied here is that they are the adoptive parents of this now fatherless and homeless Mexican boy. (No doubt they will also find a special school for autistic children in order to help him realize his full potential.)

I emphasized that in *Them!* the FBI agent must accede to the woman scientist's demand to go down into the ants' nest to destroy the queens. In *Mimic* when the victims are trapped in the subway car and one of them must leave to try to rewire it, Susan volunteers, saying she knows more about what's out there than the others. But her husband goes instead, after pointing out that she is the key person who absolutely must get out of the trap, because she is the one who must put a stop to what's happening. Like Victor Frankenstein, Dr. Tyler bears responsibility for her interventions in nature. Unlike him, she is never shown as mad, excessive, or hubristic—unless we are to take the small hints of disapproval she gets from her mentor figure seriously. But even he confesses that since his own grandchildren are probably alive today because of her, it would be hypocritical of him to chastise her. Rather than trying to create a new human baby in an illicit way like Victor Frankenstein, Susan has worked to save human babies, but in doing so, she has "mothered" a vile species that she cannot control and that must be aborted. Dr. Tyler is just another woman driven by the one primary goal of rescuing children. If she cannot have children of her own, she will take care of the children of others—the sick children she sees at the film's start, the little boys on her bug exploration team, or the small and frightened "special" boy Chuy.

Conclusion

Is female agency in recent horror films, whether of female scientists or of evil female queen bugs, a significant feminist development? My basic hypothesis has been that it is easier for filmmakers to depict females as heroes combating horror if the monsters are also female, especially if they set up a primitive female contest in the reproductive and mothering arena. After all, when is it ever deemed appropriate in our culture for women to exhibit aggression and even ruthless destruction, if not to protect their babies and children? Such movies may reinforce unsavory conservative notions of women's roles and downplay male interests in reproduction and caring for offspring. Through their depiction of the more disgusting biological aspects of creatures that reproduce on a massive scale, these films may reinforce negative images of women's biological nature as primitive and driven by this one chief end. Certainly a film like *Species* would fit into this latter category, with its seductive blond villainess who uses men and then destroys them in her quest for a perfect mate who will help her fulfill her inner, ugly, and nasty drive to reproduce. It is interesting in this regard, though, that back in the 1950s, things were apparently different, in that the men in *Them!* are equally concerned with protecting and salvaging both the girl at the start of the film and then the two children in the tunnel later on.

The depiction of females as agents in these movies could thus be criticized as underscoring a biological and essentialist account of women. The recurring emphasis on childbearing and nurturing reinforces not only a strict biological conception of female nature but also a vision of women's narrow domestic social roles. It is hard to avoid the same kind of ambivalent evaluation of women-and-bugs films that I reached concerning *Frankenstein*. Women and female traits are valued here as the corrective that will balance or make up for male scientific and technological excesses and violations of nature. This suggests that women still play a supportive role as understudies of men.

However, our assessment need not be so completely negative. As a continuation of the *Frankenstein* theme, these movies do highlight significant moral contributions that women can make toward resolving some of the problems of hubristic science. Science in these films is confronted with questions that are legitimate and important ones, and often *women* raise them. In *Revenge of the Creature*, Miss Hobson is doubtful about the value of the scientist's cruel tests of the lonely creature. *Them!* raised warnings about the environmental impact of nuclear testing. The *Alien* series links science (as it has become linked in fact) to broader forces of military technology and capitalism. *Mimic* links science (as it has become linked in fact) to social programs of disease control, economics, demographic study, and population analysis. In each of these films, the women who are the heroes are morally defensible in their behavior. Their femaleness is linked to admirable traits that are, to be sure, worrisome if they are essentialized or seen as women's sole prerogative, but that are nevertheless bona fide human virtues: compassion, caring, planning for a better future, and, even under some conditions (as in *Alien³*), self-sacrifice. (Remember that Ripley turns down the promise that she can be operated on so as to be "normal" and even have children because she knows she cannot trust the sickly sweet human version of Bishop.) I have tried to suggest in particular that in the first three *Alien* movies, Ripley is a viable and attractive female agent in a horror film. This does not mean that her treatment in these films is fine or that the development of the Ripley character in the series is without flaws.[37] A major issue to be pondered is whether the films' treatment of social themes and issues is intriguing or rather just simplistic. Perhaps *Aliens* delivers a reductive anti-technology, anti-corporation message that is purely ironic given its big-budget status; and the do-gooder white, individualistic liberalism of *Mimic* speaks for itself. What we are getting here is, at any rate, not the dark vision of uncanny horror that we will see developed in other films that I examine later in this book.

One remaining topic for assessment in my women-and-bugs movies concerns the nature of their female villains. A big problem with bugs in horror movies is that it is very hard to make insects interesting as villains. Think how dull the bugs are, for example, by comparison with the eloquent Pinhead or the metaphysical vampires Lestat and Louis in Anne Rice's novels. It is hard to do much with a monster who doesn't talk and has an altogether alien psychology. *Starship Troopers,* with its inordinate parodies of the war-film tradition, plays upon this very fact: Bugs are perhaps the one enemy we can teach our children to hate without worries about dehumanization, since the inhumanity of bugs is a simple matter of biological fact.

In assessing villains or monsters for feminist purposes, we can pause for a moment to contrast these films with ones with more traditional male monsters and think about how the monsters function in them. Male personalities simply seem to have been more deeply explored in horror, which is probably no accident, given that most of the writers, directors, special effects creators, and producers are men. This may not change until the economic conditions of female participation in the horror-film industry also change. Male monsters have been developed so as to allow them on the whole more internal complexity. They may be inadvertently evil and disgusting, hence a locus of sympathy, like the Wolfman or the Frankenstein monster. Or they may, like Dracula, Hannibal Lecter, Pinhead, or Lestat, be seductive Nietzschean types who violate the usual social norms and offer women victims escape from their humdrum mortal existence. I shall be moving on to discuss such seductive and heroic male monsters in Part 2 of this book.

Horror audiences are usually interested in villains or monsters. Noël Carroll argues in *The Philosophy of Horror* that monsters are central in horror because people want to learn more about them.[38] Monsters are the focus of the cognitive pleasures of horror. In films this is also true, but we must add in the relevant visual pleasures as well. Even if bugs cannot be psychologically interesting, they can be very visually interesting. In these films, we learn about bug behavior and psychology by seeing the bugs, just as we learn more about what they want and how they might be defeated. The Alien monsters have always been fascinating to look at.[39] The fact of their metamorphoses makes them unpredictable, and there is much to get to know about them. *Mimic* is an interesting and different sort of bug movie rooted in the *Frankenstein* tradition. Director del Toro may not provide the bad bugs with a very clear psychology or complex motivations, but it is worth saying that the giant Judas roaches of *Mimic* have an astonishing visual realization, combining eerie beauty with hideous horror. It is hard to believe that a truly revolting cockroach could have a beautiful visage enabling it to conceal itself and mimic its own predator, man. The film's extraordinary verve, pacing, and visual style make it more interesting to consider than the somewhat simplistic social messages in it would suggest. Also, since fire is the common denominator used to destroy the bugs in all the films I have discussed here, the filmmakers have the opportunity to engage in visual pyrotechnics; flames even look impressive in the black and white of *Them!*

Of course it is unclear whether as feminists we should ask for more female villains in movies. There *have* been genres with female villains, notably film noir, with its femmes fatales. Films like *Species*, *Angels and Insects*, or *Star Trek: First Contact* owe much to this tradition, with their very fatal yet seductive insect femmes. I would count the Borg Queen as the most intriguing villain on my list; she seeks novelty and has a complex strategy of seduction that differs according to her intended victim, whether it be Data or Captain Picard. But the Aliens, giant ants, or giant cockroaches are not at all cast in a seductive mold. Their agency is limited to the drive to reproduce and to destroy other species that might get in their way.

Species and *Species II* are perhaps the oddest and most genre-bending entries into the recent women-and-bugs subgenre. Played by supermodel blond beauty Natasha Henstridge, the lizard lady who is a human-alien blend is a bombshell and femme fatale in the most literal sense. The two films do interestingly different things with this basic premise. In the first film, the scientist who has created Sil by combining human and alien DNA (Ben Kingsley) loves her as his daughter and creation; but, like Victor Frankenstein or the scientists of *Alien Resurrection*, he will be destroyed by his offspring when she metamorphoses into her lizard manifestation at the end of the movie. The men who lust after her are also destroyed in gruesome and graphic ways during the sex act. The lizard or alien version of Eve/Sil is another H. R. Giger design, much like the Alien only with a more humanoid shape, including large and pulsating breasts (from which tentacles occasionally emerge). She is simultaneously hideous, seductive, and elegant with her flowing green tentacle locks of hair. Notably, this alien body is prone to developing wavy appendages, phalluses gone wild that can pierce human bodies in any of a variety of alarming ways. On the one hand, *Species* suggests that a woman this beautiful is bound to be dangerous and that in fact such a woman is really bent on just one thing—using men for reproductive ends. But on the other hand, she is also a victim and seems to be in pain when her lizard side emerges foremost.

This victim side is especially brought out in *Species II* when Eve is shown much more like the Creature in *Revenge of the Creature*. This time, she is both pitied and befriended by a female scientist, Dr. Laura Baker (Marge Helgenberger), a woman who is almost a mother or sister figure and who has always cared for her. Eve escapes and finally mates with one of her own kind, but in this film *his* sexual attentions kill *her* off. Indeed, she is just the latest in a vast line of big-breasted female victims who suffer hideous fates after he rapes and instantly impregnates them. Eve helps to save her caretaker doctor/"mother" from him just before she dies. She is thus morally exonerated in the end. *Species II*, I might add, is an unbelievably bad movie with a terrible script, characters who seem to be important but who go nowhere, illogical actions and plot motivations, gratuitously excessive scenes of violation of women's bodies, and an only thinly veiled pornographic aim. But its scenes of lizard sex are so visually extraordinary that they might just (barely) make the movie worth watching.

One thing I have shown here is that a cognitivist approach to women-and-bugs films provides insight by looking beyond the psychological dimensions of horror to consider the themes, messages, and moral dimensions of these movies. Because most of the films I have discussed here present an interesting social issue in the context of effective suspense and have intelligent dialogue, good acting, and beautiful cinematography, they are well worth our attention. They challenge the audience to respond on many levels—emotionally, visually, intellectually—as we form judgments about their messages. *Them!* is about the horror of giant ants but is also about bureaucracy, Cold War efficiency, and caring for our children in an individualistic society. The *Alien* series is about the threat to human values in an era of corporate and individual greed, when science is serving the ends of a vast faceless military bureaucracy. Within this context, once again, individualism is a value, but it must be coordinated with human compassion, caring, and camaraderie. And *Mimic* is about new urban social problems, including poverty and immigration. It unfortunately provides, yet again, a purely pat and individual resolution to a large and complex set of social problems. In sum, not all bug movies are alike, and their themes do range beyond the issues of reproductive success or the threats posed by an alleged archaic mother.

chapter
thRee; Monstrous Flesh

Monstrous Flesh in David Cronenberg's Films

In this chapter I will examine four films directed by David Cronenberg: *The Brood* (1979), *Scanners* (1980), *The Fly* (1986), and *Dead Ringers* (1988). I will discuss these films in pairs, considering first the mental horrors of *Scanners* and *The Brood* and then the broader horrors about personhood that are central to *The Fly* and *Dead Ringers*. Cronenberg's films are variations on the continuing and central themes of mad science in relation to monstrous flesh. He reflects on the risks and dangers of human embodiment. As he does so, he introduces a "cool" horror, stemming from his films' distinctive cinematography, settings, art design, music, dialogue, actors, and characters. This Canadian director is self-conscious about the horrific: His movies give us a theatricalized version or performance of horror. They force us as audiences into reflexive awareness of our interest in the spectacles of horror and in the actual "mechanics" or mode of delivery of these spectacles.

Cronenberg's movies are heirs or updates of *Frankenstein*.[1] They link mad science to capitalism, corporate technology, and control, hence his horror takes on a significant dimension of social critique. Mad scientists no longer work alone in Gothic laboratories during thunderstorms at night. Instead, they meet in boardrooms of anonymous-looking corporations or run tastefully decorated clinics in the woods.[2] The messages of these films are complex, so they cannot be subjected to simplistic ideology critique as misogynistic thrillers or nihilistic ventures into explosive violence.[3] Nor should they be read in reductive psychoanalytic frameworks. They present crucial ambiguities in their subtle treatment of gender issues against a larger background of themes concerning the body, life and death, science and nature, and good and evil.

All four films I am examining here are variations of the "mad-scientist" genre and as such are successors to *Frankenstein*. In each film, a male researcher crosses certain natural limits, provoking the eruption of monstrous variations of the body and the flesh.[4] The horror here is often associated with the female body and its ability to reproduce. Each film offers a strong and intelligent female protagonist "contaminated" by and expressive of the film's source of horror. In three of the films, as in *Frankenstein,* horror develops from male attempts to harness, reconstruct, or emulate female powers of procreation. Reproduction goes amok—disastrously so and as a kind of punishment for the men who meddle with life's natural processes. Most of these films' male protagonists also experience disorienting descents into horror as they lose control over their own psychic or bodily identity. As in *Frankenstein*, moral complexity and ambiguity abound in these films' assessments of their central male researchers. The general tone of the movies is one of pity and sympathy rather than (or in addition to) revulsion and moral outrage. Horror in Cronenberg's films, as in Mary Shelley's novel, takes on tragic dimensions.

Like *Frankenstein*, Cronenberg's films do not present simple dichotomies of good and evil. For example, the concluding epic battle between the good and evil telepathic brothers in *Scanners* has a disturbingly ambiguous outcome; and even the mad scientist who is responsible for the scanner psychopathology becomes pitiful at the end. In *Dead Ringers,* the Mantle brothers' descent into drug addiction, madness, and murder-suicide is disturbing and grotesque, yet as Cronenberg has insisted, *Dead Ringers* as a whole is and aims to be a very *sad* film.[5] If horror is treated like a disease or a deformation of bodily norms, then we may be repulsed by and yet pity its victims. There is no more monstrous male villain than the horrific man-fly Jeff Goldblum becomes in *The Fly*, and yet even in his final and most inhuman incarnation, he elicits sympathy (tribute in part to the marvelous special effects work in this film by Chris Walas, Inc.). The women in Cronenberg's films also vary tremendously and take on a variety of moral shadings. They may be innocent victims *(Scanners)*, but they also collude in their oppression *(The Brood)*, are forced into lethal choices *(The Fly),* or become objects of deadly male envy *(Dead Ringers)*.

Cronenberg's movies are fascinating meditations on the nature of our human identity as *embodied*. He comments: "[M]y films are very body-conscious. They're very conscious of physical existence as a living organism."[6] That they are *horror* movies reflects the fact that our human embodiment is fraught with danger, limitation, and risk. Often the horror of Cronenberg's films ensues from people's attempts to exceed the boundaries of "normal" embodiment. He might even be described as the filmmaker of the mind-body problem par excellence; his filmic topics constitute a sort of library of classical issues in the philosophy of mind.[7] Most of his movies have plots revolving around what Cronenberg has termed "the new flesh."[8] This notion was explicitly introduced in *Videodrome*, where the lead character, Max Renn (James Woods), imagines reconfigured bodies with new gender identities and combinations, new sexual capacities, and, naturally, new psychological experiences and desires. Cronenberg explains:

> The most accessible version of the "New Flesh" in *Videodrome* would be that you can actually change what it means to be a human being in a physical way . . . . Human beings could swap sexual organs, or do without sexual organs as sexual organs per se, for procreation. We're free to develop different kinds of organs that would give pleasure, and that have nothing to do with sex. The distinction between male and female would diminish, and perhaps we would become less polarized and more integrated creatures.[9]

The new flesh takes human evolution to further stages and presents novel possibilities for pleasure, perception, and interpersonal relations. Yet such altered embodiment is never the source of simple and unattenuated joy; it always presents risks. The director says: "I don't think that the flesh is necessarily treacherous, evil, bad. It is cantankerous, and it is independent."[10] As the body and human flesh shift, they acquire wonderful new possibilities with exhilarating but also horrific aspects.

Because Cronenberg is a writer-director who often works with the same production team, including designer, composer, and cinematographer, his films have strong continuities of style and tone as well as thematic unities or patterns.[11] In calling Cronenberg's movies very "cool" I mean several things. First, literally, they often have wintry settings; there is snow, ice, and a sort of brittleness in their bleak Canadian landscapes.[12] This is reflected by the coolness shown by many of his actors and actresses (perhaps most extraordinarily by Deborah Kara Unger playing the wife in *Crash*). The interior settings are also very cool, from the open natural wintry spaces of *The Brood* to the watery aquarium colors of the Mantle twins' apartment in *Dead Ringers*.[13] (We could think as well of the ultramodern sleek leather and metal furnishings in black and gray in the Ballards' apartment in *Crash*.) The characters in these movies may experience strong emotions or sensations, but they are somehow dampened and known only at a distance. The movies are cerebral, with much discussion among educated and articulate people. The films' plots are intricate, and many crucial elements are presented in subtle ways, leaving the audience to draw its own inferences. Finally, in these films the camera is often very distant. It stays far from a scene and is set at odd angles, watching scenes from below, above, or on the side.

Another part of Cronenberg's cool style involves the realism or naturalism of the horrors manifested in his movies. This realism distinguishes Cronenberg's horror films from others that also depict internal transformations, like those in the more expressionist Gothic and Europeanized werewolf and vampire traditions.[14] Cronenberg's films differ significantly from other movies where monsters come from an outside force like a giant ant or cockroach or are created from dead flesh in the lab like Frankenstein's monster. The horrific transformations of Cronenberg's films may have a supernatural element that requires representation through means that seem excessive or extreme (psychic abilities in *Scanners* and *The Brood*, for example, or the drugged visions of *Naked Lunch*); yet these horrors are still treated very naturalistically. Cronenberg comments:

> The very purpose was to show the unshowable, to speak the unspeakable. I was creating certain things that there was no way of suggesting because it was not common currency of the imagination. It had to be shown or else not done. I like to say, during the course of the film, "I'm going to show you something that you're not able to believe, because it'll be so outrageous or ridiculous or bizarre. But I'm going to make it real for you. I'm going to show you this is for real!"[15]

The settings of Cronenberg's films are almost as distinctive as the forms of horror that evolve within them. His characters are usually middle-class professionals (architects, teachers, surgeons, scientific researchers, journalists, and the like). All of his horrific characters, men and women alike, work at jobs in realistic urban settings that often require the performance of identity in ritualized situations that do, after all, compose our normal everyday working life. These locations include warehouses, construction sites, corporate meeting rooms, high-rise apartment buildings, medical-board hearing rooms, lawyers' offices, subway stations, or the fast-food courts in shopping malls. We see children at school and on playgrounds, people driving cars that slide on icy roads, small-town doctors' offices, even (in *Videodrome*) an optometrists' convention. This public dimension sets horror in a normal world that has become strange, and it adds another layer of interest to these movies in their attention to issues of artistic construction, theatricality, and performance.

Not surprisingly, themes about embodiment and the new flesh offer the director endless possibilities for virtuoso display on the screen.[16] The contrast between the often extreme bodily transformations in Cronenberg's film plots and the cool realism of his style is what I call his theatricalization of horror—his treatment of horror as a form of shocking and yet pleasurable cinematic spectacle. The performance of horror and monstrous flesh come together in the sequences of Cronenberg's films that *display* horror and treat our own interest in it as an issue by highlighting internal audiences for this horror. These horrific scenes are especially jarring because they contrast so sharply with his cool style. Within all this coolness, eruptions of truly gross and extreme forms of horror, like the scene of the exploding head in *Scanners,* seem all the more shocking. The flesh-burning last battle of *Scanners* takes place in a posh corporate office suite. Horror in these movies occurs within and disrupts the everyday. These are neither the Gothic settings of *Frankenstein* nor the sewers, spaceships, and subway tunnels of the women-and-bugs movies. The violent flowering explosions of red within sterile or neutral settings seem all the more outrageous and jarring. It is almost as if the horrific scenes in Cronenberg's movies are a violation of the taste of the filmmaker. Such scenes play with the expectations and mores of the audience.[17] It is horrific when the characters killed in *The Brood* get their heads violently bashed in within the ultranormal settings of an upper-class home or a tidy schoolroom. It is horrific when Nola shows Frank her monstrous external "baby" and licks its bloody sac while wearing a beautifully draped white natural linen dress that is almost fit for a nun.

Cronenberg has a taste for gory and excessive scenes; it would be hard for anything to top his early film *Shivers,* with its nasty, slimy, creeping, fecal yet aphrodisiacal parasites! He can show bizarre and often hideous changes that affect the body in graphic detail, but he can also attempt to convey more intangible features of the new flesh, such as its altered powers of perception or emotional expression. Changes may be depicted from the point of view of those who experience them, or they may be observed by witnesses. A common thread is that scenes of very graphic horror are highlighted reflexively as images through the inclusion of devices that call attention to the film process itself. We repeatedly see scenes in his movies of cameras, films, photographs, monitors and screens, enactments on stage, artists and galleries, scientific presentations, lectures, or devices like eyeglasses and peepholes. Internal or on-screen audiences are included in almost all his films, duplicating us as we become witnesses to the transformations or horrors that imagination can give rise to and make real through this magical medium of film. Although in these movies the catalyst for transformations may come from without—from an evil scientist, for example—the horror that arrives actually erupts from *within* the person. Given the generally realistic style of Cronenberg's films along with the fact that we share their characters' experiences of transformation, our acquaintance with even quite extreme forms of horror becomes more intimate, believable, and unsettling. Through empathic understanding of the horror in Cronenberg's movies, we can sometimes feel or imagine what is at stake an assault on the very nature of a person and on our human emotional and psychological integrity.

Scanners and The Brood

In the first two Cronenberg films I will examine, *Scanners* and *The Brood*, the director reflects on what it is to have a *mind*. In these films, as in *The Dead Zone*, a film Cronenberg directed based on the Stephen King novel, human minds become abnormal. This happens through a terrible car accident in *The Dead Zone*: After waking from a ten-year coma, Johnny Smith (Christopher Walken) finds he has become a psychic who can predict the future—especially future deaths and disasters. But in the other two films, whose scripts Cronenberg wrote himself, alterations in fundamental mental powers occur through the intervention of "mad science." The psychically deformed individuals of *Scanners* have unusual telepathic powers resulting from their mothers' use during pregnancy of an experimental tranquilizer, Ephemerol. Here, the mad scientist is Dr. Paul Ruth, who developed that drug and remains fascinated by its abnormal effects. In *Scanners, individuation* and *insanity* are the key issues. By contrast, *The Brood* focuses on the relation between the body and *emotions*, particularly anger and rage. Dr. Hal Raglan, the mad scientist in this film, is a psychiatrist running the Somafree Clinic of Psychoplasmics, where he trains patients to develop an unusual ability to express anger through physical growths extruding from their bodies. Most spectacular among his patients is Nola Carveth, who gives birth to monstrous and murderous children. Significantly, in both films the scientists are destroyed, like Victor Frankenstein, by their own unnatural offspring.

Mental derangement has of course been dealt with by other film directors, but the derangement in Cronenberg's films is distinctive because of physical manifestations in bodily symptoms. For example, the scanners' telepathic powers put them into contact with the entire bodies and nervous systems of other people. They are victimized by their telepathic powers and suffer hideous, cringing awareness of the sounds of other people's voices. Nola in *The Brood* can externalize her anger by giving birth to literal creatures of her rage, but once started, the physical processes cannot be stopped. Her "Brood" enacts their nasty physical revenge on anyone who crosses her.

Scanners: Psychic Derangement and Exploding Heads

Scanners, made in 1980, is one of Cronenberg's earlier films and among the first he was able to shoot using a well-known cast and a reasonable budget. It was mar-

PHOTO 3.1   *One of the more notorious gory scenes in* Scanners *(1980).*

keted as a sensational horror film with shocking scenes of gore (Photo 3.1). That this brilliant film has not been much discussed is perhaps a function of the fact that its gore is very extreme and distinctive. It is among the most notorious of all horror films for its classic scene of an exploding head. Although the effects used for the film (and for this scene in particular) may now seem technically limited, it seemed shocking and quite realistic at the time of the film's release. The exploding head scene, which occurs early in the movie, introduces the power of the evil scanner Darryl Revok (Michael Ironside) in the most graphic way possible.[18] Subsequent gory scenes also highlight the scanners' powers to destroy other people's bodies through telepathic links that are more than a matter of mind reading: They can establish direct contact with another nervous system, take control of it, and manipulate it. This ability is showcased by the film's inclusion of several bloody explosions, scenes of people set suddenly aflame, and an extended final scanner duel that is literally skin-peeling, vein-bursting, and eye-popping. Perhaps critics feel that a movie with such extreme visions of bodily horror cannot be taken seriously.[19] How, after all, can a philosopher write thoughtfully about a movie with an exploding head?

Scanners is especially interesting for its treatment of mad science in relation to questions of good and evil. It considers both the possible benefits and the costs of interfering with natural female reproduction. Here, as in Cronenberg's other films, horror occurs in a public, not a private, setting. The mad scientists are not solitary schemers but rather representatives of larger forces that go beyond their control. In *Scanners,* there are two evil corporations, each represented on screen in realistic detail. We see establishing shots of the exteriors of their corporate headquarters and a proliferation of equipment (uniforms, trucks, helicopters, offices, boardrooms, and so on) bearing distinctive corporate logos. First, there is ConSec, an international security firm "specializing in weaponry and private armies," which has hired Dr. Paul Ruth (Patrick McGoohan) to do research on the "telepathic curiosities known as scanners." Second, there is Biocarbon Amalgamate, the firm run by the evil scanner Darryl Revok. He wishes to use his telepathic powers to control the world by manufacturing the drug Ephemerol and sending it out to doctors who will create "an army of soldier scanners" by prescribing it to their pregnant women patients.

Scanners is set within a city, contrasting urban detritus and commercialism with mysterious industrial parks where the business of its nefarious corporations is carried out in peaceful-looking rural locations. The film's opening sequence is especially brilliant. It uses the food court, escalators, and artificial lighting of a shopping mall to create horror out of the most mundane setting. This movie was released shortly after the megamall was used to very different eerie effect in George Romero's *Dawn of the Dead* (1979). In Romero's film, the mall was played for comic effect, as zombies wandered aimlessly through well-stocked stores or attacked equally expressionless mannequins. In *Scanners,* the mall is more ordinary and populated with normal shoppers; this works to make it all the more ominous.

In the film's taut four-minute opening sequence, we watch a young derelict (Stephen Lack) stumble into a mall's fast-food restaurant. The soundtrack plays eerie music with echoing chords. The man is filmed from below against repeated rows of hanging lights that glow eerily white against the red reflective surfaces of the restaurant. He is filthy and disheveled, perhaps psychotic, perhaps alcoholic. He filches a cigarette and eats leftover hamburgers while two matronly women eye him in alarm and disgust. As he stares back, we hear their voices discussing him. The sound track plays repetitive chords, and we begin to hear a sort of low growl or bubbling noise, a bit like sonar on a submarine. One of the women becomes ill and collapses into convulsions on the floor. The sound levels increase while the young derelict seems disturbed and in pain; sounds appear to come from inside his head as he attempts to block them out. Then two men who may be security police but who wear no uniforms chase the derelict in a sequence that leads up an escalator into the mall. They shoot the man with a dart, and he becomes unbalanced; again, the scene is shot from below, and we see floating eerie neon lights overhead against numerous red or steel surfaces. Finally, the man collapses into a bundle of dirty clothes that is caught and pounded against the end of the escalator. By this point, the music is loud, throbbing, and repetitive.

This four-minute opening sequence is full of mystery, ambiguity, and suspense. Who is this man, and what is wrong with him? How did he hurt the woman, and why is he being chased? Who is good here, who evil? Who merits our sympathy? Horror is previewed in this scene as some sort of new and potentially dangerous psychic ability; the odd sounds and eerie music signal that something is very strange. The horror is not presented discursively or through dialogue but rather immediately through its effects on the sick woman and through the emotional tonalities of the film, particularly its unnerving sounds and eerie lighting. Only after the psychic derangement has been *shown* to us does the ability in question get a name—"scanning"—as it is further explained in the next sequence. A doctor (McGoohan) diagnoses the disorder of Cameron Vale, the man we saw in the opening scene, who is now cleaned up but straitjacketed like a mental patient in a hospital bed. The doctor, Paul Ruth, introduces himself as a "psychopharmacist specializing in the phenomenon of scanners." Dr. Ruth is working with ConSec in order to release the power of scanners (though we soon learn that the corporation wants to use these telepaths for weapons with enormous power to do harm). Dr. Ruth tells Vale that he is a "scanner" and that this is the source of all his agony but that it also "can be a source of great power." He has in particular the power for intense union with others. But this power can be terribly frightening and disturbing. Vale suffers like a schizophrenic person from his inability to shut out people's voices.

The two sequences that open *Scanners* have first shown the horror of scanners and then given the phenomenon a name and brief characterization. The next two sequences provide *displays* of the horrific side of scanner power through Cronenberg's theatricalization of horror. Horror is showcased in scenes that take the form of demonstrations or performances. On-screen audiences and situations of recording make the witnessing of horror a reflexive event for the film's audience. In the first of these scenes, Dr. Ruth calls in a group of people to demonstrate the nature of scanner power and to begin showing Vale how to control and focus it. The usual strictures of theatrical performance are violated here. The audience files in but sits in its seats with nothing to watch. The performer is silent and only they seem to speak. As they occupy rows of chairs opposite the bed, we hear many voices, but they are not actually speaking. Vale, still straitjacketed on the bed, writhes in agony until the doctor administers a hypodermic that silences the voices. He is on display, but only we know why. Indeed, we become the true audience, since this performance is really given for us. Watching the film, we are echoed by the video camera that is aimed at Vale like a gun, recording the demonstration for ConSec. The setting as a whole and the experiment are ominous, making us pity the scanner. Yet even as we watch him, we also share some of his experiences. We, too, wait for Dr. Ruth's explanations and, like Vale, we are assaulted by the cacophonous voices he cannot escape. The entire situation seems dark and strange: We see outside shots of a dim old warehouse building at night; the people in the audience wear official-looking identification badges but shift restlessly in their seats; and the camera overhead records every move that Vale makes. Dr. Ruth is simultaneously kind, cool, and detached.

With no transition, the scene shifts to an altogether new setting as people once more file in, this time into a theater of some sort to watch a different demonstration of the phenomenon called "scanning." Here, too, we in the movie audience are doubled by an audience in a theater as it gathers to watch the phenomenon that we also seek to understand. Again our situation is ambiguous. We watch the demonstration unfold from a position well back in the theater. A man explains that he will demonstrate the phenomenon by scanning each audience member individually. He warns them that this may cause discomfort, such as headaches or nosebleeds. The room seems tense and filled with anxiety—like the situation of audience members at a horror movie waiting for unexpected effects to burst out at them from the screen. (Viewing the sequence multiple times does not really remove this tension; anticipation of the exploding head on-screen heightens it.) We learn that the setting is the high-tech security corporation, ConSec, and that the audience has been carefully screened and briefed. This sequence shows the power of scanning at its most disturbing, because something goes badly awry in the demonstration. Focusing his mental powers on what seems to be a random volunteer from the audience, the ConSec scanner encounters resistance; we again hear the characteristic sonar sound of the scanner at work as the two men visibly struggle for power, their faces grimacing. The ConSec scanner finally begins to convulse and lose control, until he is suddenly killed when his head explodes. The people in the audience shriek and leap up from their seats, and surely any horror film audience will also at least squirm at this moment. Security men rush to capture the "ordinary" man and attempt to shoot him with a hypodermic. Although he seems innocent at first, in the ensuing sequences we see more of this man's evil power as he psychically deflects the needle, then compels all his guards to kill either themselves or one another. All this occurs with virtually no dialogue, just the growl-like sounds that emanate from him along with his dark, evil gaze.

The plot of the film concerns the efforts of Cameron Vale, the "good" scanner, to understand who he is and to confront the "evil" scanner Darryl Revok. Revok's demonic nature has been directly presented in the murder scenes I have just described. But next it is explained or demonstrated to Vale by Dr. Ruth in another sequence that highlights issues of recording and presentation. Vale switches from being a filmed object to a film watcher as Dr. Ruth screens an old black-and-white psychiatric film that shows a younger, more maniacal Revok being interviewed in an asylum. Dr. Ruth intones, "[A]t age twenty-two he was extremely self-destructive, now at age thirty-five he is simply destructive." Vale learns that the powerful Revok is leading an evil scanning conspiracy and that he has sought out and murdered other scanners who will not join in his efforts to "bring the world of normals to their knees."

Guided by Dr. Ruth, Vale seeks the help of a small circle of other "good" scanners, led by the beautiful Kim Obrist (Jennifer O'Neill). He learns more about Revok's evil plans, but Revok in turn tracks and captures both Cameron and Kim. In its climactic scenes, the film turns out, in true epic fashion, to be a story about a family. Revok explains to the incredulous Vale in the final scene that Dr. Ruth was the man responsible for scanners. He developed the drug Ephemerol as a tranquilizer and tested it on his own wife during her pregnancies. But it unexpectedly turned his two sons—and then a generation of other children from the first test market—into scanners. One of the two original scanners turns out to be Cameron; the other is Revok. That is, the two men are brothers, and Dr. Ruth is their father.

Because Cameron will not accept this newfound filial relation and join in Revok's plans to conquer the world, Darryl fights it out with him, good against evil, "doing it the scanner way" and threatening to "suck your brain dry." In this concluding battle, the special effects go wild as veins bulge and burst, facial skin boils off, palms and indeed whole bodies flame up, and eyes pop from their sockets. The film's conclusion, however, is ambiguous. Kim awakens from a drugged sleep and warily enters the room to find one scanner body dead and burned like a Pompeii victim on the floor. The other man is huddled in a corner in his coat. When this man turns and speaks to her, he has Revok's body but Vale's voice and innocent blue eyes. The man says "It's me, Cameron. We've won." The abrupt conclusion of the film and Kim's questioning gaze leave room for doubt about who exactly the "we" is.

Despite its gory scenes, Scanners also has sequences of enormous power and beauty, even of subtle mystery. These include striking shots of a modernist subway station where sleek steel cars speed by amid sparks and the exteriors of ConSec, with white birches etched against a wintry pale-blue sky. There are four wonderful actors in terrific roles: Patrick McGoohan as the conflicted mad scientist Dr. Paul Ruth; Jennifer O'Neill as the elegant Kim Obrist, paranoid, but with reason; Lawrence Dane as the traitorous corporate representative Braedon Keller; and especially Michael Ironside as the devilishly brilliant scanner Darryl Revok.

The action is swift and taut, the dialogue is crisp, and the smaller parts are also wonderfully played (Robert Silverman as the scanner sculptor Benjamin Pierce and Mavor Moore as Trevellyan, the corporate chief of ConSec). Stephen Lack as the hero and central figure, Cameron Vale, is often criticized for wooden acting and bizarre line readings in the film. Although there is some merit to this criticism, I am not disturbed by his demeanor, because Lack plays a scanner who has lived a destitute life in the streets, unable to hear his own voice. Everything is new to him, and it would not be surprising that he finds talking difficult and speaks with unusual and flat cadences.

Scanners is filled with strong and gory horrific images: The exploding head is the most famous, and I have already commented on how the horror in certain scenes is extreme and theatricalized. But other scenes of horror in the film are much more subtle. These include moments of revelation, as when we realize that the ConSec security chief Keller is working with Revok, or that Revok is really Cameron's brother. One of the most horrific scenes occurs in a doctor's waiting room where Kim and Cameron have gone to find out why Ephemerol is being delivered from Revok's corporation. They learn that the doctor is turning more babies into scanners by treating his pregnant women patients with Ephemerol. Cameron learns this during an off-screen encounter; Kim (and we) make the discovery more directly when she is scanned by an *unborn fetus*. The scene is one of quiet horror; Kim gets the discomfort and characteristic nosebleed of the scanner victim and looks around in the room to see only a pregnant woman, oblivious. Then both she and the camera focus in on the woman's round belly as we infer the ominous truth about the real identity of the scanner.

These recurring tropes of watching, performing, recording, and audience encounters with horror are very significant in *Scanners*. I have already mentioned the camera that records Dr. Ruth's earliest efforts to "indoctrinate" Cameron (camera-on) Vale, the audience in the ConSec theater, and Dr. Ruth's use of the film that reveals Revok. There are many more scenes of recording, watching, and monitoring. Keller spies on Ruth and Vale by watching the films through closed-circuit camera as they are being made in the warehouse. Dr. Ruth stages another demonstration of Cameron's powers when Vale is instructed to alter the heartbeat of a man. The other man is wired so that we can watch the scanners' powers in action by observing movement on the medical monitoring screens.

Similarly, the ConSec computer personnel watch monitors along with the security chief Keller when (like us) they all realize that Cameron is accessing their mainframe by telephone dial-up from outside. His mental states are shown to us directly in the form of changing information on the screen. We then shift to witness Cameron's perceptual experiences of accessing the computer from within by traveling its circuits. When the ConSec men attempt to shut him down by pushing the destruct switch on their computer, we again watch this sequence from two vantage points, their "external" one within the computer control room and Cameron's "internal" one, which is actually outside at a phone booth. Cameron sees circuits being closed as he is rushing to escape and has to burn his way out of the system. Sparks follow his escape route along the telephone wires and finally fall near him as he hangs up the smoking phone in a booth outside a gas station. This scene recreates the explosion sequence of Hitchcock's *The Birds*. A man pumping gas runs off just as the station goes up in flames, and Kim and Cameron must race away from their phone booth before it explodes.

This should be more than enough to defend the serious interest of a movie with an exploding head. This scene in *Scanners*, which Cronenberg originally intended to open the film, is very typical of his style of horror. His movies highlight the very nature of witnessing horror as a spectacular theatrical event, and often, as in *Scanners*, they include scenes of audiences watching a demonstration or film that somehow goes wrong or is disturbing. *The Brood* opens with a very intense and strange psychiatric demonstration, which I will discuss further below. *Crash*, too, has a dramatic performance before an audience when Vaughan enacts one of his obsessed recreations by staging the fatal crash of James Dean. *Dead Ringers* has six striking sequences of Elliot Mantle giving speeches before large audiences and also includes scenes of its actress heroine being made up and of highly staged operations in a surgical "theater." Seth Brundle's journalist girlfriend Veronica in *The Fly* videotapes his experiments in order to report on them for her magazine. In these scenes of *The Fly*, as in Cronenberg's other films with astounding special effects transformations, horror is not simply shown, but it is shown *as watched*—by the characters, but also by us.

Mad Science and Monstrous Anger in *The Brood*

The Brood, like *Scanners*, presents horrors of the mind. Once again, the central figure, Nola Carveth, is someone who has uncanny powers to project her mental states outward to achieve horrific physical effects destructive to others. Whereas *Scanners* focuses on the possibility of sharing or capturing other people's thoughts, *The Brood* is about the externalization of feelings, especially anger. Nola's anger stems from the abuse she suffered as a child from her mother. When released during her treatment at Dr. Hal Raglan's Psychoplasmics Clinic, this anger takes the form of monstrous external births of dwarfish children who enact her rage by killing those she hates—her mother, her father, and then her daughter's teacher, whom she suspects of involvement with her husband. Much of the

PHOTO 3.2   Dr. Hal Raglan (Oliver Reed) treats a patient before an audience at the Somafree Clinic in The Brood *(1979).*

film is told from the point of view of Nola's husband, Frank. His primary concern is caring for and protecting their little daughter, Candice.

The Brood opens with an encounter on a stage between two men (Photo 3.2); we cannot tell for some time whether this is a play or some other form of bizarre demonstration. The older man (Oliver Reed) speaks with assurance and has a powerful build. He sadistically taunts a younger man, who is thin and soft-spoken, about his lack of virility. The younger man's skin gradually erupts in ugly sores and boils as he tries to protest and express his anger. Only when the lights go up in the theater do we learn that we have been witnessing a doctor's radical psychotherapy techniques in action (in a scene reminiscent of the medical school demonstrations of Jean-Martin Charcot or Sigmund Freud). What we have seen is a demonstration of Dr. Hal Raglan's "psychoplasmics" techniques at a theater in his Somafree Clinic. One audience member proclaims in reverential tones, "The man is a genius"—and he could be speaking of Dr. Raglan's theatrical art as much as of his therapeutic strategies.

Eventually the film's hero, Frank Carveth, learns more about Dr. Raglan's controversial techniques as he tries to protect his daughter from the abuse she experiences from Nola during visits to the clinic. At the same time, there are several bizarre murders with suspects who seem to be small children. When one of the children is found dead at the scene of the crime, a postmortem reveals many abnormalities, including lack of a navel. Frank visits his lawyer to seek advice in a custody battle but is told that Dr. Raglan is legitimate, a "bona fide M.D. and all." Nevertheless, things do not seem right at the Somafree Clinic. An ex-patient of Dr. Raglan's shows Frank the lymphomas that have grown as the result of his treatment there, and finally Frank learns that Dr. Raglan is dismissing all his patients but Nola, whom he now regards as his "queen bee." Something about Nola's treatment has made her very special to Dr. Raglan.

In the film's ultimate confrontation, Frank visits Nola, in violation of her isolation regime in therapy. Their daughter has disappeared and Frank thinks Nola may know where she is. Nola does, but because she is suspicious about his relationship with Candy's teacher, she begins to get angry. Dr. Raglan warns Frank to keep her calm because if "the Brood" acts now to express Nola's anger, they will kill Candy, who is trapped in their special cabin. Frank realizes that these dwarfish, monstrous children are the offspring of Nola's anger. This is confirmed when she becomes enraged and gives birth to another one before his (and our) eyes (Photo 3.3). Frank recoils in disgust—quite reasonably!—and Nola's rage activates all the children of the Brood, who attack and kill Dr. Raglan just as he is about to get Candy away from them. Frank strangles Nola in order to rescue Candy. Father and daughter drive away together, but in the film's last scene, the camera zooms in to show small boil-like patches erupting on Candy's skin: The mother's heritage is there waiting to erupt in some future disaster awaiting this little girl.

Since the central scene and site of horror in The Brood are located in Nola's monstrous process of birth, it is not surprising that a psychoanalytic account has been offered focusing on how the film presents women and birth as messy, bloody, disgusting, or "abject." Nola externalizes her anger by giving birth to "the Brood" of the title, monstrous and murderous children. Feminists have used psychoanalytic concepts like abjection to describe the film as evincing disgust over the natural processes of reproduction.[20] Thus, Creed treats the film as a case of a more general pattern in horror films depicting monstrous females. This is understandable, given the film's notorious climactic scene of disgusting birth. Psychoanalytic feminist approaches have been applied to Dead Ringers as well, with its also notorious "gynecological instruments for operating on mutant women" and to Videodrome, with its shocking scenes of a vaginal opening in Max's (James Woods's) chest.[21] But in general, I believe that the psychoanalytic accounts miss much that is significant in these movies. Despite some imagery of

PHOTO 3.3   *Nola Carveth (Samantha Eggar) gives birth to a monstrous baby in*
The Brood (1979).

monstrous femininity, the larger issue in all these movies is the body—what we
could call the metaphysics of the body.[22]

For example, there is a specificity to the uses and depictions of the body in *The
Brood*: The movie has a lot more to it than the one scene of monstrous birth. It is
about the emotional expression of *anger* and its ramifying consequences in fami-
lies. It is about anger's destructive path to child abuse, the derangement of love in
a marriage, and the bitter enmities of divorce (Cronenberg has called it his
Kramer v. Kramer)[23]—as much as about some primitive condition of identity versus separation from the mother. Creed's view is that Cronenberg uses the birth
scene to show that reproduction is itself monstrous; since women are shown here
as wild animals so at home in nature that they are thereby repulsive to men. Creed
goes so far as to suggest that Nola's rage originates in "her husband's disgust at her
maternal, mothering functions."[24] To believe this claim requires us to ignore the
entire plot and narrative of the film. Nola is monstrous in quite specific ways, because her "children" are unnatural, ugly, and bent on destruction. She has used
them to kill three people and now they threaten even her own daughter. Her

monstrousness is a specific kind of evil within her rather than something innate to female nature or to birth and motherhood. Cronenberg has commented on this as follows: "My general feeling was that the kind of rage Nola had was an all-purpose one—genderless. Her rage goes beyond certain moral categories, so the resulting creatures were primal, nearly foetal, nearly formless. Just pure anger."[25] Nola's rage in the film is shown to be due to her experiences of child abuse, not "because of" her husband's disgust. If he is at all disgusted with her initially, it is the more ordinary, non-"deep" disgust of a divorced man who fears his child's welfare is not being served by the woman he used to love. His visceral disgust only arises in the culminating scene, where her rage, again, has a very specific target as it begins to build. Medea-like, she seeks to kill her own child in revenge against her ex-husband for his imagined betrayal with the schoolteacher. Creed also comments that the men in the movie are weak, but this again completely ignores Dr. Raglan's role in the film. He is shown as monstrous in relation to other patients as well as Nola and is viewed as responsible for Candy's great danger. As the doctor/guru figure here, he is both physically and psychologically compelling, in a sense the "father" of the Brood.

Thus, though a Kristevan interpretation may seem initially illuminating as a comment on horrific aspects of the climactic birth scene,[26] to focus on this is to miss many other aspects of the movie. In particular, since the film offers a critique of the mad psychotherapist, Creed's interpretation ignores the role of the villain Dr. Raglan in the movie, a feature linking it to the mad-science tradition. An intelligent man working in the horror genre, Cronenberg is aware of continuities of his movies with the *Frankenstein* tradition. All his films are about the dire (or mixed) consequences of scientific research programs gone awry.[27] Nola may be monstrous in *The Brood*, but so is Dr. Raglan, who elicits her monstrous births. Indeed, because she is a victim, he may be the more evil of the two. Dr. Raglan is, like Dr. Paul Ruth in *Scanners*, a sort of mad genius. Aiming to help people, he has taken his quest too far and has ended up creating monsters—Nola is just one of several. Indeed, often it is the men in Cronenberg's movies who are monstrous, like Cameron in *Scanners*, Bev and Elliot Mantle in *Dead Ringers,* or Seth Brundle in *The Fly*. These men with decaying bodies are shown as far more monstrous than the women in these stories. In the end, the mad scientists are punished for their hubris. But as with *Frankenstein*, the moral assessment of the films is not one-dimensional. Dr. Ruth became pathetic in his final moments, and Dr. Raglan seems sympathetic in the end, too, as he realizes he has gone too far with his experiments and tries to save little Candice from the Brood. His death at the tiny hands of a horde of monstrous screaming children—the death of a huge muscular man with a beefy head, carrying a gun and wearing a massive coat of animal skins—has a kind of fittingness, but it is also quite grotesque. Monstrousness is not the whole of the story for Cronenberg. Both his male and female monsters alike remain sympathetic, and the point of view is often theirs. Thus, their downfall is one we can sympathize with and not simply celebrate as just.

Dead Ringers and The Fly

The *Frankenstein* theme is also present in both *Dead Ringers* and *The Fly*. These films foreground the loss or tragic impossibility of a love that cannot be sustained, as the men in the movies deteriorate, losing their identities. Each film features male scientists whose innovative research takes them into fatal excesses: Seth Brundle in *The Fly* is a physicist, and the Mantle twins of *Dead Ringers* are doctors who are also medical researchers. Whereas in *The Brood* and *Scanners* the scientists were destroyed by their own progeny, in these films each man is ultimately the agent of his own death. Seth Brundle (Jeff Goldblum) in *The Fly* cannot wait to test his new teleporting equipment, so his DNA is accidentally fused with that of a fly. As a result, he experiences tremendous new powers, sexual stamina, and energy, but at a terrible price—the loss of his essential humanity, including his morality. And the twin doctors in *Dead Ringers* have no individual personal identity; they share in everything and are shown in one nightmare sequence to be connected by a huge umbilical cord. When Bev reconstructs his brother's body to try to "separate the Siamese twins," they both die.

These movies also exhibit the Cronenbergian attention to broad questions about the nature and significance of human embodiment, raising deep questions about identity and morality. *The Fly* is a film about embodiment in relation to having (and losing) some fundamental features of *humanity*. By contrast, *Dead Ringers* is about embodiment in its relation to personality and psychological *individuality*. In *The Fly*, Seth Brundle is fused with an insect to become Brundlefly; but in *Dead Ringers*, the Mantle twins are fused into each other and function as one dysfunctional whole. Beverly and Elliot, respected gynecologists and fertility researchers, cannot solve the problem of their own fertilization as identical twins who seem to share not only their mistresses but even their bloodstreams and nervous systems.

As we will also see, these films once again display the typical Cronenberg film style of cool horror. Like *Scanners* and *The Brood*, they are set in winter and shot with a kind of cool light. The tone is realistic; the settings include professional conferences, hospitals, urban apartments, or swanky high-rise offices. The films are also cool in the sense that they are cerebral and because their central characters reflect in unusual ways, with insightful yet alienated perspectives, on their own monstrousness. The comparison with Kafka's flat and yet surreal tone in

Metamorphosis is hard to avoid, especially given the insect theme in *The Fly*. In comparing these two films in my conclusion below, I will again discuss how their cool tones are interrupted by graphic displays of horror so as to highlight themes of performance and theatricality.

The Fly

In *The Fly*, the heroine, journalist Veronica Quaife (Geena Davis), is an ambitious, intelligent, pragmatic, and successful career woman. The opening credits play over kaleidoscopic movements of primary colors that gradually materialize into the bodies of people at a meeting—a visual foretaste of the actions of the telepod in this film, which dematerializes and reassembles the flesh. At the meeting, Veronica ("Ronnie") meets the brilliant but eccentric scientist Seth Brundle (Jeff Goldblum). He is a loner who gives her the chance to have an exclusive inside view of his world-shaking scientific invention, the telepod. This teleportation device will make transportation as we now know it obsolete by moving bodies across space—dematerializing and then reassembling them. While reporting the story, Veronica becomes romantically involved with the scientist (Photo 3.4). But when Seth is left alone one evening he gets drunk, upset, and jealous. He tries out his telepod but accidentally takes a fly along for the ride. His computer, confused, reassembles the two beings by genetically fusing their DNA. This leads to an eventual process of horrific degeneration and alteration in which Seth turns into a disgusting giant man-bug. In the final scenes of the film, Seth, now almost completely inhuman, tries to force Veronica to take a teleportation trip that will combine his DNA with hers and that of their yet-unborn child. Veronica is rescued at the last minute by her magazine editor, Stathis Borans (John Getz). He has lost limbs to "Brundlefly" in revolting fashion after the fly vomits acid onto him but still manages to blast apart Seth's equipment with a shotgun. Veronica escapes while Seth is accidentally fused with the telepod. In the final scene, the creature mutely pleads with a sobbing Veronica to shoot him and end his misery, and, breaking down, she does so.

In an initial feminist reading, we might note that there are some significant problems with Veronica's representation as a lead female character here. First, she behaves in unprofessional ways, having first slept with her college professor (now her editor) and later with the subject of her current research article. Furthermore, she seems to exist in the film primarily in her relationship to the male mad-scientist Brundle. The film is a narrative about his activities and their ramifications, not about hers. Veronica thus resembles Elizabeth in the *Frankenstein* narrative, a woman who exists as a foil to register and resist the man's descent into madness

PHOTO 3.4   *Veronica (Geena Davis) prepares to film Seth's experiment with the telepod in*
The Fly *(1986).*

and monstrosity. The film narrative takes a very traditional form: The scientist exceeds his role and must pay for it. The male acts, the woman feels. Her emotions and perceptions are clues to guide us, the film viewers, to regard the man, despite his hubris, with love, pity, and sympathy. Since the woman has to deal with the man's problem, love and empathy are key female traits. There is no real challenge to this gendered division of labor or to the idea that stories are primarily about men, secondarily about women.

Nevertheless, to counter this initial feminist critical reading, we could also say that Veronica is important in a more metaphysically complex construal of the story. She functions as the secondary character or the chorus of an ancient Greek tragedy. The film prompts viewers to adopt her viewpoint to observe, with horror, yet also with pity and fear, the transformations that occur as the fly takes over the scientist. Although the movie has been taken as a metaphor for cancer or even AIDS, Cronenberg sees *The Fly* as the story of a love relationship fraught with risks and losses, one facing all the pressures that time, jealousy, distrust, aging, and disease can bring. This might seem implausible concerning a story most would see in terms of its mad-science/science-fiction narrative (with often quite gross special effects), but I endorse Cronenberg's claim. The movie has a clear narrative arc: Boy meets girl, boy makes mistakes and runs risk of losing girl, girl returns but too late, and boy dies in the end. Of course this summary leaves out a lot—I omitted the part where "boy becomes fly." (No wonder he loses the girl!) A key point, though, is that when he has to die in the end, it is truly tragic. This downfall is necessary, but it evokes pity and fear regarding a good man who committed a mistake, not a venial sin.

Cronenberg's films are usually about horrors of embodiment. The particular horrific threat of this movie is an invasion by the other, alien, insect species of *both* the male and female body. This takes a specific turn against Veronica when she discovers that she is pregnant. Seth is already deteriorating, so she cannot be sure their child would be truly human. Undecided about having an abortion, she has a terrifying nightmare about the delivery room, in which she gives birth to a huge squirming white maggot. The scientist/fly demands to use and corrupt her reproductive abilities in his last-ditch effort to regain some humanity. Ultimately, it is hard to say which character suffers more. He is punished for his scientific hubris, but she must fulfill his request for a merciful death.

The true horror of this film involves not female reproductive power but the invasion of a male body, Seth's. The particular physicality of Jeff Goldblum as the actor playing Seth is crucial here. In the opening scenes, he appears to have frenetic moments and bulging eyes, hinting at the fly potential inside. He starts out as a geek in tweed jacket and white shirt (he has five sets of everything so that he can wear the same thing every day—imitating Einstein). But as he learns more about love, sex, and the body from Veronica, we begin to see him nearly naked, and in one scene, he runs on the streets with a leather jacket over his bare chest, looking for hookers. The actor's body in this film is *exposed*: the long legs, the well-developed chest, the muscular arms. The film is an effort to use cinematic magic, first by merging him with the stunt man who performs his amazing gymnastic feats early on, later to convince us that *this* body is decaying before our very eyes. His face becomes patchy, coarse hairs grow from his back, and he becomes preternaturally swift and strong. Things speed up when Brundle starts to lose his teeth, ears, and fingernails. Only at this stage does he start to admit that Veronica may be right about a flaw in the experiment (Photo 3.5). Until now, he has felt better, stronger, purer, more energetic, and more sexual. An especially horrific scene occurs when he examines himself in the bathroom mirror. His electric shaver fails to cut his new hairs. His fingernail squishes out with a pop of juicy white fluid. At last he, too, becomes horrified. This moment of realization is very disturbing. "Oh no," he says, "what's happening to me? Am I dying? Is this how it starts? My dying?"

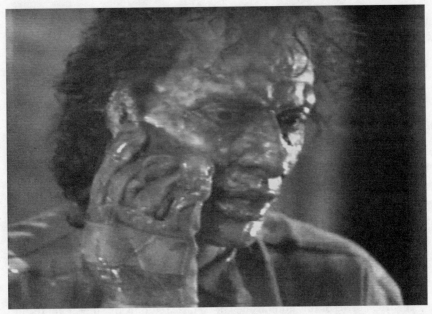

PHOTO 3.5   *Seth Brundle (Jeff Goldblum) is dismayed as he becomes transformed into a fly* in The Fly *(1986).*

Yet even this is not even the worst horror the man experiences. A more jolting moment comes when he goes to the computer to study the records of his teleportation trip. As the disks reveal genetic analyses of his companion, we see a sequence of images rebuilding the decomposed element on screen, moving upward from the molecular level to parts that look like mysterious bulging eyes, and then finally, we get an image of the whole being—a common housefly. Brundle asks the computer, "What happened to fly?" and gets the unbelievable result in one word: "Fusion." From this point on his transformations become more and more gross and horrific. Throughout the process, Brundle/Goldblum maintains his wit, his eccentric sense of humor, and his analytic scientific viewpoint. He loses external body parts like his ears but keeps a kind of archive of them in the bathroom cabinet. A pan of the assorted items in this cabinet is another freakish moment in the movie. We see teeth and an ear and something that may be a penis and scrotum. Their very unidentifiability makes them all the more disturbing. It is also worth noting that when I watched the film with closed captions on, there were a number of phrases on screen that were quite evocative and unusual: "nneogh," "bbluup," "squish," "kkkkt," and "grzugh." Seth demonstrates his disgusting flylike digestive system by vomiting on camera before Veronica, sarcastically describing this as a tape to educate children. He seems to observe with interest his own new ability to walk upside down on the ceiling. Finally, he warns Veronica she must never come back: "Have you ever heard of insect politics? Neither have I. They're very brutal, no compassion, no compromise. We can't trust the insect. I'm saying I'm an insect who dreamt he was a man and loved it. But now I'm saying the insect is awake. I'm saying I'll hurt you if you stay." After she rushes out sobbing, the fly-man, now nearly unrecognizable as human, pounds his own head in anguish like the Karloff Frankenstein monster, uttering nonverbal plaints "Nneogh! Nneogh!" We next see him, like Quasimodo atop Notre Dame, eyeing Veronica from above on the roof of his building as she prepares to leave.

One might maintain that our horror as Seth Brundle is transformed into the hideous gooey and amoral fly is a horror of what we all have come to regard as abject in infancy. But as I argued in Chapter 2, it could more plausibly be argued that there is a unique, sui generis, and in some instances reasonable human fear of things that are dead, cannibalistic, and disintegrating—especially insects. The thought of turning into an insect is in itself horrifying because of the loss of identity and fundamental humanity it entails. Surely Kafka knew this: Brundle's story is, like that of Gregor Samsa in *Metamorphosis*, a metaphysical tale about the loss of what it means to be human. This Kristevan line of interpretation ignores some important aspects of the film's narrative: its links to both the mad-science tradition of *Frankenstein* and to the plot patterns of classical tragedy.

To follow up on this last connection, we could try to identify Brundle's *hamartia*, or fatal mistake. Some of the deepest considerations advanced in this movie concern the nature of the flesh. To begin with, Brundle confides to Veronica that his teleportation system has one major limitation: It only works on inanimate objects. In the movie, this is presented as a probable consequence of his social and emotional isolation from other humans. As he struggles to improve his device, we witness a grisly failure when an experiment to transmit a baboon leaves only a quivering bloody mass of flesh. Seth explains in depression before Veronica's camera: It failed because "I must not know about the flesh myself. I'm gonna have to learn." Significantly, this is followed by the couple's first sex scene after she follows him to the bed where he has flopped down in despair. Later during a postcoital embrace, Veronica kisses him and declares jokingly that she wants to eat him up: "That's why old ladies pinch babies' cheeks. It's the flesh—it makes them crazy." Brundle suddenly realizes he has to teach the computer to "be made crazy" by the flesh. Somehow this enables him to perfect his system.

Brundle's major flaw is that he is too new to the flesh; as a novice, like any earnest first-time lover, he succumbs to weaknesses of the flesh. He transmits himself without being properly careful because he is drunk, upset, and jealous that Veronica has gone off to see her editor and former boyfriend Borans. He places a moral construal on the teleportation process since it seems to invigorate and improve him. He becomes frenetic, consumes cappuccino with seven packets of sugar, and wants to have nonstop sex. When Veronica refuses to join him in the "dynamic duo" by being teleported herself ("[D]on't give me that born-again teleportation crap!"), he declares angrily:

> You're a fucking drag, do you know that? I bet you think you woke me up about the flesh, don't you. You only know society's straight line about the flesh. You can't penetrate beyond society's sick gray fear of the flesh . . . I'm talking about penetration beyond the veil of the flesh . . . A deep penetrating dive into the plasma pool!

Because Seth sees the teleportation process in moral terms, he argues that it is a purification to have one's atoms dematerialized and then reassembled. Later, he explains to Veronica that what went wrong in the experiment was that he "was not pure." On the more obvious level, this means that the fly was in there with him. But it is also as if he takes on the responsibility for already being a creature who could harbor a fly inside himself. When awakened from his scientific isolation by love, romance, and sexuality, he begins to acquire darker elements that are now emerging as "the insect."

Horror here in *The Fly* is complex; in rewriting the original story to bring out its poignant emotional possibilities, Cronenberg made good use of the genre's open-ended possibilities. Horror is present to be sure, but it is tied in with such other genres as science fiction, romance, and tragedy. The movie was financially successful and its love story is no doubt central to the film's emotional impact, but these are not conventional because of the film's uncommon gross-out effects and thoughtfulness. Still, the depth of the characterizations is central because only if we believe in the love story does Brundle's demise become piteous, heart-rending, or even tragic.

Dead Ringers

Like *The Fly*, *Dead Ringers* is an unusual sort of horror movie that shows the genre's boundaries are very elastic. Here, horror is muted and transformed; there are fewer supernatural or science-fiction overtones, and it takes on darker psychological, even existential, nuances. The premise of the tale recapitulates *Frankenstein* as a story about a man (or men) who meddle with natural reproductive processes. The brilliant clinicians and researchers, Beverly and Elliot Mantle (twins both played by Jeremy Irons) focus on the insides of the female body in attempts to make infertile women conceive and bear children. Thus, they create births that are in some sense unnatural. While they were still in graduate school, they developed a device for surgery, the Mantle retractor, that has become the standard in the field. This device has made some professional colleagues jealous since it was considered too radical at the time of its invention: In a flashback to medical school, a professor warns the young men that it "might be fine for a cadaver, but it won't work for the living patient."

As researchers, the men's only focus is on women; they "don't do husbands or babies." Their research on fertility, displayed in various clinical and surgical displays, lectures, and articles, has brought them fame and prosperity. Fertility is also a central issue for the actress Claire Niveau (Genevieve Bujold), who comes to their clinic for diagnosis and treatment. It turns out she has no chance of having babies due to being a "trifurcate": She has three, not one, cervical openings. This abnormal multiplicity of anomalous female reproduction is an obsession for the Mantles and attracts them to her. Their mother's fertilization was also multiple, as it produced a splitting of the embryo that made them identical twins. As a result, they have very deep problems about identity and separation.

Much of the movie concerns the impact of the twins' work on female fertility in relation to their sexuality but also, and more important, to their twinship. A flashback at the film's start shows the twins as precocious boys discussing sex. When Elliot explains that fish don't need to touch to have sex, Beverly says, "I like that idea." As adults, the two men have maintained a "fishy" attitude toward sexual touching and closeness. Analytical and distanced, they are intimate only with each other as they cynically share women and report on their experiences. Their own relationship is all that matters and is their only emotional involvement, until Claire disrupts it and sets them on a spiraling downward path toward emotional anguish, drug abuse, separation, and death by murder/suicide.

Each of the lead characters in the film is a sort of reproductive mutant. In Claire's case, this is due to her rare cervical anomaly. After he has fallen in love with Claire, Bev feels jealous of a man who answers the phone in her hotel room and warns him that he is "fucking a mutant." And the twins consistently identify with the original Siamese twins, Chang and Eng, considering themselves to be almost literally connected in the same way. They view themselves as unique, freaks of nature, two humans whose borders are not clearly individuated. The *Frankenstein* dimensions of the story come from their inability, despite advanced scientific work on reproduction, to resolve these most basic issues of their own birth. They cannot accept facts about human physicality and identity, nor can they reach an emotional acceptance of life as it is.

Embodiment is once again a theme Cronenberg addresses in this film. Much of the movie revolves around the conflation of the inside and outside of the body.

Whereas Seth Brundle's telepod took bodies apart at the molecular level, the Mantles take them apart and reassemble them biologically in the surgery. When he examines Claire in the first scene in his clinic, Bev seems awed by her internal landscape. She is bemused at being taken as unique in this odd way—as a famous actress, she is more used to adulation for her exterior. Bev even says there should be beauty contests for the interior of the body. Obviously, Bev and Elliot have very odd views about their own bodies, both outside and inside. They believe that they are connected in their experiences, perceptions, and desires. Bev tells Elliot that he "was there" at a recognition dinner simply because Elly was present. Elly exclaims that Bev has not fucked a woman until he has told Elly about it. Bev worries that they lack independent nervous systems; Elly asserts that their bloodstreams are connected—"That is an objective medical observation."

There are other echoes of *Frankenstein* in this movie. Just as Victor Frankenstein gradually degenerates into a sort of madness and decay, so do the Mantle twins. Claire leads Bev into a cycle of drug abuse that moves from occasional use of uppers and sleepers to mainlining narcotics. In a kind of sympathy or synchronicity with Bev's addiction, Elliot becomes an addict as well. Mental decay prompts Bev to begin seeing all the women at his clinic as mutants: "The patients are getting strange. They look all right on the outside but their insides are deformed. Radical technology was required." Bev violates bodies, including female bodies and, in the end, his own and the feminized body of his brother. He ties Claire up (at her request) during sex; he abuses drugs; he uses a surgical retractor for a nonsurgical gynecological exam; he creates and employs experimental medical tools in surgery and almost kills a woman. Eventually, he uses his radical new tools to restructure Elly's body in order "to separate the Siamese twins." The surgery kills Elly, apparently by disembowelment. In the final scenes, both men's bodies are shown lying on the stirrup-equipped examination tables in their clinic—tables usually employed for women's pelvic exams. Although Bev tries to leave Elliot at the last, he is not able to abandon his brother's corpse. In the final scenes, we see the two brothers, embracing and half-nude, both dead on the floor of their clinic.

The female body is subjected to technical control by the Mantles; we actually witness pelvic examinations, on-camera shots of surgery on Fallopian tubes, and medical diagrams of leukorrhea. Thus, the usually eroticized spectacle of female genitalia is made distant and clinical.[28] Knowledge of the body takes on many forms in this movie. The two brothers manipulate women's bodies through their examinations, research, and surgeries. This knowledge seems to translate as well into terrific sexual prowess—at least if we take as evidence the magnificent orgasms Claire has ("Doctor, I'm cured" she says breathily after one of them). Cronenberg comments,

"Gynaecology is such a beautiful metaphor for the mind/body split. Here it is: the mind of men—or women—trying to understand sexual organs." He made the twins as boys very analytical: "They want to understand femaleness in a clinical way by dissection and analysis, not by experience, emotion or intuition."[29] This is the problem, in a nutshell, of the scientific standpoint.

There are clear disadvantages, then, to the erotic knowledge of the gynecologist: It is attained through a kind of clinical distancing. Cronenberg has written about how the gynecological theme of the film might seem to alienate or scare women but is actually more disturbing to men, who find the female plumbing system "icky." He thinks they also fear that this scientific figure might know the insides of "their" women's bodies in superior, more intimate ways. There are two scenes in the movie that show men who do perceive the details of gynecology as "icky." When Elly has his first dinner date with Claire and her business partner and inquires about her periods, the man at the table with them blanches and soon says he has to leave. And again, when Bev speaks in jealousy to Claire's male secretary on the phone, he says: "Lubricate the two prime fingers of your right hand and insert them in Claire Niveau's vagina. You will feel three and not one cervical heads." The young man gulps, hangs up, and then Claire explains later, "He's defiantly gay, and you managed to gross him out completely."

Cronenberg's characteristic style of cool horror reaches an extraordinary new plateau here in *Dead Ringers*. The movie has a visual theme about water that is introduced at the start when we see the twins as boys discussing why fish do not have sex by touching, since they live in water. These remarks, their virtual identity, their odd manner and their precociousness, set up a picture of them as not quite fully human that persists in the movie. The director comments about the set used for their apartment: "The feeling is that of an aquarium, as though these are strange exotic fish creatures. That's why I wanted their apartment to be purply and blue and submarine. It's very cool. People find it extremely disturbing. The fact that they can't exactly say why—there isn't much blood, etc.—makes it more so."[30]

Scenes in the twins' apartment or clinic are often shot at night with a lot of exterior light filtering in as floating blue patches that do indeed look watery. These are echoed in many other scenes such as the gray clinic with flourescent lighting and tasteful blue and white robes, the wintry light in the bathroom, or pale light seeping through venetian blinds. Such scenes stand out when compared with many external scenes with different color schemes. Claire's elegant apartment is all antiquey with polished white objects and wood with gilt touches. There are also several scenes set in a baroque restaurant or in a bar festooned with crystal chandeliers, with operatic arias in the background and rococo paintings of nude women(!) adorning the walls.

The coolness here is not simply a matter of the color scheme, however. It derives also from the attitude and atmosphere, the cerebral dialogues, the sheer elegance of all the sets. Also the music, again by Howard Shore, is especially crucial.[31] Right from the start, the credit sequence rolls over vivid red backgrounds while Howard Shore's lush romantic string music plays on the soundtrack. This might seem "hot" except that what we also see against the red backdrop are rows of mysterious, frightening-looking gynecological instruments. They resemble barbarous tools of torture. There are also old medical text illustrations of pregnancy (including diagrams of twins in fetal stages). The movie includes many scenes with professional settings where everyone is courteous and reserved; this is Canada at its most British, with polite audiences at formal dinners, massive podiums in stately university halls, and austere gray medical boardrooms peopled by disapproving silent judges. Jeremy Irons himself is an actor it would also be fair to describe as "cool"—in contrast, say, to Jeff Goldblum in *The Fly*. Where Goldblum is geekish and charmingly shifty even at his most intellectual, Irons is often languid and always elegant, with his thin mouth and sleek coiffed hair, dyed blondish in this film. He dresses with gorgeous style, appearing several times in a tux or in beautiful suits and cashmere overcoats. The women in Elly's life, whether Cary, his nurse-assistant, or the twins he requests from an escort service, are also cool, well-coiffed, soft-spoken, and elegant. Elly is shown several times watching *Lifestyles of the Rich and Famous*. He comments that it is his favorite show and that he is "into glamour."

These cool, upper-class settings contrast not with brutal scenes of gory horror like those we saw in *Scanners*, *The Brood*, or *The Fly* but rather with the implied horror of the stark stainless-steel instruments and with the hints of inner uprisings caused by slimy interior body tubes and organs. The underlying psychological horror builds unbearably as the two men decline into drug abuse, mental instability, and eventual murder/suicide. But the scene of Bev's final operation on his brother is treated in a very understated way (especially for Cronenberg). Shot at night in dim light, it shows us no actual rending of the flesh. Instead, we see Elly laid on the table. At first, we see what seems to be his unusually large head from a distorted angle, in a magnificent shot that pans up from below his feet, eerily separating the head against the nighttime skyscrapers lit behind him. This is the *Frankenstein* monster lab scene filmed in an utterly new way—it is after all the scene of an unnatural birth. Bev tells Elly that this is their birthday, meaning the day of their separation. In this very disturbing and yet sad scene, we see the following: first, a row of instruments; then a stabbing motion Bev makes, and Elly's grimace; next, a rivulet of dark red liquid running onto the white plastic surfaces of the examination table; and finally, Bev's tears as he wipes his eyes with a bloody surgical glove. The only other view we are shown of this grisly scene is discreetly distanced. Bev wakes up the next morning calling out to Elly about having had a nightmare. Both men are lying as mirror images on examination tables. Bev glimpses the desecrated body of his brother, which we can barely see with its red abdomen. He both recognizes it and avoids it. In a scene that is as heart-rending as Veronica's loss of Brundle at the close of *The Fly*, Bev begins to call out for Elly. He sidles along the room avoiding the corpse and eventually his cry degrades into a singsong repetitive chant, "Elllly, Elllly, Elllly," etc.

Theatricalization in *The Fly* and *Dead Ringers*

We can track in these two movies, *The Fly* and *Dead Ringers*, the start of a sort of transition in Cronenberg's oeuvre. With *The Fly*, his biggest financial success, Cronenberg began getting recognition for the emotional nuances of his work in the horror genre. And by the time of *Dead Ringers*, it seems clear he had moved on from being the "B-movie" or schlock director he was initially known as to achieving critical recognition as a bona fide auteur. The on-screen displays of horror are much more muted in *Dead Ringers*, but perhaps this makes them all the more intensely psychological and disturbing—preludes to the erotic violence, anomie, and voyeurism of *Crash*. And no doubt drug use as a theme in *Dead Ringers* helped pave the way for the more surreal kinds of visions Cronenberg would provide his viewers in *Naked Lunch*.

Again, as with *Scanners* and *The Brood*, theatricalization is significant, as scenes of horror erupt on-screen in shocking contrast to their cool cerebral surfaces. Both films emphasize the visual display of horror, in part by focusing on the physicality of their lead actors. The male body is very much at issue here. Seth Brundle (Jeff Goldblum) in *The Fly* changes gradually from within as his body takes on the fly's genetic composition. First he grows nasty metallic hairs, then he loses fingernails, teeth, and ears. He remains human even as inexorable processes lead to changes in his locomotion, diet, and even his digestive processes. Jeff Goldblum's body is foregrounded throughout these transitions as a site of physical eruptions and decay. He appears often on screen with his chest bare and is sometimes nearly nude. His physicality and acting ability are showcased as he manages to make humanity and his eccentric wit visible through layers of ghastly makeup. Part of what raises the movie well above the level of a gore fest involves the believable emotions relating its two main characters in the romantic couple. Goldblum and Davis were in fact romantically involved at the time of making the movie. Whether because of this or simply because of good acting, there is a definite chemistry on-screen between the two, apparent from their first meeting through to their on-screen sex and also evident in their conversations and happy shopping or eating interludes.

Dead Ringers is of course also a cinematic and acting tour de force in that one man, Jeremy Irons, performs and embodies on screen the role of two distinct individuals, through Cronenberg's innovative use of the motion-control camera. The fact that they are in the end not truly distinct reverberates with Irons's obvious, yet intermittently forgettable, singleness as an actor. Most striking perhaps in his achievement here are several scenes in which he plays one brother impersonating the other, where we can see the layering of roles at work in very subtle ways.[32] *Dead Ringers* is chock-full of allusions to performance, filming, acting, witnessing, and audience. It concerns not performance in the sense of the performance of a gender identity but performance at an existential level, the level of being human—something also dealt with by writers like Samuel Beckett, Luigi Pirandello, Franz Kafka, and Jean-Paul Sartre. The film asks, like plays or stories by those authors, what it means to *act* as a human and to achieve an identity through one's actions. Horror arises from the gap between role and person or the inability to find a real identity of one's own to enact.

We should also notice that Claire, the heroine and main romantic interest in this film, is a character who is an actress. Thus, we expect her to be a person playing at parts. We see bits and pieces of her professional life over the course of the movie: Bev rehearses scenes with her to help her memorize lines, Elly visits her in her makeup trailer on set (where she sports large, nasty but fake bruises), and we see her throwing a tantrum directed at the wardrobe person on her new film. Elly makes numerous disparaging remarks about Claire's profession that imply that it is a world dominated by faking and insincerity. She's just into games about sex, she's conning them for drugs, she's having an affair because "show-biz ladies are like that." Yet ironically, it is the actress Claire who is a genuine person in the movie. She displays emotions and admits to fears and needs, she has intuitions and perceptions about what is really going on with the twins.

By contrast, it is the twins in this film who are performers, fakes, failures at their parts. They enact life but do not live it. Bev performs at the clinic and surgery, while Elliot performs in giving lectures and speeches. These speeches are often shown and are staged as elaborate performances. Elliot's charm and insincerity suggest that he is always "on," and we have reason, given his promiscuity and cynicism, to be dubious about his officious speeches honoring medical ethics and respect for women as the source of life! We see no fewer than six occasions of Elliot's appearance at formal events with audiences in the film: at medical school when his retractor is honored, at the formal dinner, in a surgical theater, at a medical-school lecture, at the board hearing, in a scientific setting. The surgical theater scene is an especially striking one because both men are performing—Bev in the surgery and Elliot outside lecturing with two monitors of his brother's work

PHOTO 3.6   Elliot Mantle (Jeremy Irons) lectures while Beverly Mantle operates in Dead Ringers *(1988).*

on display (Photo 3.6). Bev is shown tending to women patients at the clinic in scenes that we may also infer are performances, given the cynicism he expresses about these "bimbos."

Behind all this play at identity is the deeper and more magical play of identity of the cinematography and acting in this film, which creates two men from one. There is an irony in the fact that one man, Jeremy Irons, plays two men who cannot really find their own individuality or separation. This sets up an odd and perplexing kind of metaphysical tension in the movie. Through an obvious tour de force of acting and cinematic production, the two men really do seem different to us, as they do to Claire—though there are moments of blurring or confusion. When Claire demands to see the two twins together, she could be said to express our own desire as curious filmgoers, and the scene teases us by continuing for some time to show each man in a single shot. The movie would take on a different meaning if the roles were played by actual twins (and there are in fact two sets of actual twins in the cast). Irons is acting the part of two men who to start with do manifest some fairly clear distinctions. They look slightly different, with minor variations in their clothes and hairstyle. Their expressions and attitudes are different, too: Elliot is urbane, extroverted, and snidely charming; Bev is serious, tired-looking, more fragile. Bev's physical appearance deteriorates much like Brundle's in *The Fly*, though without the sci-fi dimension, as the drugs leave him ghastly pale, with matted hair and great shadows under his eyes.

It is also very intriguing that in the movie each twin performs the part of the other. We see Bev imitating Elly when he goes to visit Claire the first time. (This is all the more ironic, given that she was first seduced by Elly in the opposite role, imitating Bev.) Meanwhile, Bev had taken on Elly's public relations role by dining out with a potential donor and his wife. He later imitates Elly, to the latter's dismay, to display how charming he, "Elly," has been to the hosts. We also see Bev claiming to be Elly at a formal recognition dinner, and we watch Elly pretending to be Bev before the medical board. Each man is not quite successful at portraying the other. "I don't think they bought it, Bev, I think they knew it was me," mourns Elly after the board dismisses them from the hospital.

Claire disrupts things for the two men because she is the first person who is dead-on at being able to distinguish between them. This may not be attributable so much to her having "woman's intuition" as to her expertise about acting. Elly wants her to love or become involved with them both, and when she says she cannot, he asks, "Are we really that different?" He seems dumbfounded when she replies, "You really are." In her first encounter with the twins together, angry at being duped into sleeping with them both, she cries: "Sweet little act you have. You [Bev] soften them up with all that smarmy concern and along comes Dracula here [Elliot] and polishes them off." She accuses Bev of merely acting in showing concern and care for his women patients at the clinic, something confirmed when Bev, drunk, complains at Elliot's recognition dinner: "I slave over the hot snatches while Elliot gives the speeches. I do everything for those bimbos except take them home and stick it in them."

Over the course of the film, the brothers become even more identical. In the final scenes, Irons plays them indistinguishably as corrupted, sad, and decayed. They pathetically revert to childhood by eating cake with orange pop, and Elly cries because he wants ice cream. The physicality of the male actor's body is just as important in its own way here as it was in *The Fly*—here, too, we are witness to a literal process of physical disintegration, only one accomplished with no (or few) special effects—apart from the one big cinematic trick of twinning a single individual. The actor's body is used especially well in the final scene, which showcases the two male bodies together, nearly nude (Photo 3.7). Their beautiful musculature and sculptural look make them resemble a perverse sort of *Pietà*, brought out by the fact that the scene is lit (unusually for this film) with golden morning light. This scene is at once very sad (we hear again the mournful and eerie music), beautiful, disturbing, and mysterious. Cronenberg leaves us with one last image composed by cinematic magic, as our eyes take in the doubleness of this one actor

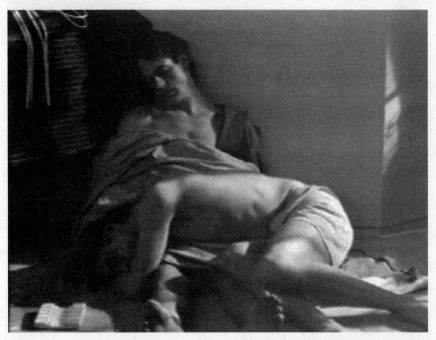

PHOTO 3.7   The Mantle twins dismantled (and Jeremy Irons doubled) in the final scene of
Dead Ringers *(1988).*

playing two distinct men who died because they could not love women or face the
mystery of their unnatural birth,[33] failing to live as truly separate individuals.

Conclusion

In his most recent and more "arty" films *(Crash, M Butterfly, Naked Lunch,*
Videodrome, eXistenZ), Cronenberg has extended some of the themes I have examined in the four films of this chapter. His work may seem to have become less
horrific, but he continues to pursue issues concerning the human body and the
risks of monstrous flesh, as well as his themes of artistic performance and theatricality. These come together in several of the more recent films' meditations on the
relation between embodiment and *desire.* Characters in these films flout the limits
of acceptable sexual behavior, usually with dire or bleak results. These new imagined worlds can be utopian, enticing and marvelous, but in these movies—which
are still in a sense horror movies—people can never advance to their wonderful
new powers without risk, pain, suffering, and, inevitably, horror. Max in

Videodrome wants to share in the dangerously stimulating pleasures of the Videodrome snuff-TV channel, but he can only do so at the cost of losing his normal perceptions when strange new openings appear in his body.

The role of the artist is a clear continuing theme in Cronenberg's films. No doubt it is in part his attention to artistry as a subject that has gradually permitted Cronenberg to evolve from a "B"-horror director known best for the exploding head in *Scanners* into a risk-taking auteur making art films like *Naked Lunch* and *Crash*. Cronenberg's recent films present work by literary artists whose writing is very self-referential and has a huge cult following. *Naked Lunch* features a writer (based on William Burroughs himself) who experiments with drugs and alternative sexual possibilities. *Crash* is about a character named James Ballard (after the author, as in the novel), who meets a man, Vaughan, who makes car crashes and ghastly wounds into a kind of erotic performance art. And *eXistenZ* is about an author of virtual-reality games who becomes trapped in her own latest and best game. It is perhaps more noticeable after these films how strikingly strong a presence of artists there is in the earlier movies. *Scanners* has powerful scenes set in an art gallery and in the studio of an artist/scanner. The man's life-size sculptures express the anguish of the scanner experience of life; he explains that only his art keeps him sane. In *Dead Ringers*, Bev commissions a sculptor as well to cast his bizarre designs for gynecological instruments and then steals them when the artist exhibits them at a gallery. (These instruments were based on a sculpture that Cronenberg once did himself.)[34] Scenes of artistry draw more attention to the filmmaker's art (and also to that of the set designers, special effects crews, and others). Horror filmmaking requires a delicate balance between the presentation of beauty and an utter disruption of the serenity of the image. In movies like Cronenberg's, this can contribute to the exquisite enjoyment of extremely painful and disturbing material.

PART TWO

From Vampires to Slashers

chapter four: Seductive Vampires

The Vampire's Unique Horror

Along with the werewolf and Frankenstein's monster, the vampire has become a staple of both literary and cinematic horror.[1] A villainous vampire stars in one of the earliest of all horror films, F. W. Murnau's *Nosferatu* (1922); they have continued to appear on the screen right through the 1990s with *Bram Stoker's Dracula*, *Interview with the Vampire*, *Blade*, and *Vampires*.[2] Literary vampires abound in Anne Rice's best-selling novels, and the bloodsucking Count Dracula has turned up in other art forms, like ballet, as well.[3] Dracula reaches new generations through new media: His lore is recounted on innumerable web sites, and his image has influenced the look and lyrics of contemporary rock bands.[4]

Fascination with vampires is so prevalent that in his recent book, *What Evil Means to Us*, C. Fred Alford observes that for the younger people he has interviewed, "the vampire has replaced Satan as the leading figure of evil."[5] Alford laments this as indicative of a cultural vacuum of symbolic resources for envisioning evil:

> Satan tempts your soul, corrupting you from inside out, exploiting your pride against your will. The vampire just wants to suck your blood; about your soul he knows and cares nothing. . . . Evil is no longer a force in the world, no longer about temptation of the soul. Instead, evil has lodged in the body, and has become weakness.[6]

Alford draws a strong contrast between vampires and the fictionalized Satan of Milton's *Paradise Lost*, a figure of evil who is allegedly more grand and subtle because he invites human collusion with his monstrous pride and rebellion. I will argue that Alford's dismissive treatment of the vampire is mistaken. Some of the films I discuss here use vampires to offer complex and nuanced visions of the fine shadings in between good and evil. Vampire evil, often shown as willed monstrousness, is similar to Satan's vow in *Paradise Lost*: "Evil be thou my good." Vampires can function more ambiguously than Alford allows: Although at times they are rather one-dimensional, at other times they exemplify our own human desires, some more complex and subtle than others.

In twisting values as they turn death to life, night to day, and evil to good, vampires manifest three fascinating features. First, the vampire violates the norms of femininity and masculinity, as allegedly directed through heterosexual desire to marriage and procreation. Sexuality is rife in the vampire genre, which is unusual in horror for its eroticism and beauty. Often vampires are wealthy, beautiful, and aristocratic, so that the vampire film may be decked out with trappings of ancient European nobility: cloaks, candles, chandeliers, chariots, castles. Vampires are polymorphously perverse: In their search for blood, they can find physical intimacy with a person of almost any gender, age, race, or social class. Sexuality is transmuted into a new kind of exchange of bodily fluids where reproduction, if it occurs at all, confers the "dark gift" of immortal undead existence rather than a natural birth. Transgressive and violent eroticism links the vampire's monstrousness to revolution against norms established by patriarchal institutions of religion, science, law, and the nuclear family.

Second, since vampires violate the boundaries between life and death, they prompt us to rethink our ordinary conceptions of good and evil. They violate natural laws and God's laws; as Van Helsing, the vampire tracker, says in the 1979 John Badham film version of *Dracula*, "[I]f we are defeated, then there is no God." Vampires pose a deep metaphysical puzzle about how to create new structures for meaning and value within the time scale of godless eternity. Like Nietzsche's Zarathustra, some vampires seek to create new ethical norms in a vacuum where traditional science and religion have lost their grip. However, as they seek a Nietzschean "transvaluation of values,"[7] do they perpetuate standard, familiar human values in a new context? Vampire values smack suspiciously of old Hollywood values in such examples as *The Hunger* or Francis Ford Coppola's *Bram Stoker's Dracula*, with its slogan "Love Never Dies." Perhaps vampire eternity, rather than being exhilaratingly open and free, is ultimately horrific, boring and repetitive.

Third, I will argue that Alford is wrong in his claim that vampires are poor figures of evil because of a paucity of symbolic or imaginative associations. The vampire genre is a gold mine of endlessly varied imaginative possibilities offering the pleasures of storytelling and fantasy. Vampire films afford very specific *aesthetic* or cinematic pleasures that accrue precisely because these monsters have become so popular and multifarious. Some of these pleasures attach to the special visual spectacles that vampires provide as they employ the persona and body of an actor in the fascinating role of a familiar villainous hero or heroine. From Bela Lugosi onward to Frank Langella, Louis Jordan, David Bowie, Brad Pitt, Tom Cruise, or Gary Oldman, vampires have been played by attractive, sexy, and prominent male actors. Female vampires lag somewhat behind in prevalence, but there are still some devastatingly beautiful ones such as Delphine Seyrig in *Daughters of Darkness* (1970) or the lesbian lovers played by Catherine Deneuve and Susan Sarandon in *The Hunger* (1983).

Genre familiarity means that we bring cognitive and emotional capacities to bear on the interpretation and assessment of films' narrative structures and resolutions. We are all familiar with the many rules that govern vampires, so we may greet familiar scenes with relish: the absence of reflections, the opening coffin, the bite on the neck, the howl of wolves, the opening of an antique authoritative leather-bound book.[8] Even though a given film might violate a few of the standard rules, deviations are allowed only within certain parameters. Some things remain as staples—blood, coffins, fangs, and crucifixes. The genre plays upon and rewards this sort of audience expectation and knowledge.[9]

In this chapter, I will examine these three basic themes of transgressive eroticism, the challenges of godless immortality, and the pleasures of genre. The first half of my chapter takes up the most famous vampire, Dracula, beginning with Bram Stoker's novel. This will orient my observations on how the monster has shapeshifted in three film versions: those directed by Tod Browning in 1931 (with Bela Lugosi), John Badham in 1979 (with Frank Langella), and Francis Ford Coppola in 1992 (with Gary Oldman). Then in the second half of the chapter, I will examine two non-Dracula vampire films, *The Hunger* (1983), whose lesbian vampire narrative has roots in another vampire classic tale, Sheridan Le Fanu's *Carmilla*, and *Interview with the Vampire* (1994), based on Anne Rice's hugely popular (and ongoing) series *The Vampire Chronicles*. Throughout the chapter, I will defend the vampire as symbol of evil against the challenge posed by Alford.

Bram Stoker's Novel

Bram Stoker's *Dracula* presents a vampire who is clearly evil, but Alford would be right to say that he lacks the tragic or epic grandeur of Milton's Satan. He appears only as a monstrous and evil man as seen by others. They all portray him as ugly and disgusting, with hairy palms, bad breath, distinct gleaming teeth, a skull-like ugly high forehead, and so forth. This Dracula is quite repulsive rather than handsome and appealing. Stoker does not imagine him from within as having any sort of tortured self; we do not hear of his search for meaning and value. *Dracula,* written in 1897, has been much discussed in the past few years since its centennial. Stoker's theme of blood pollution seems fresh in the AIDS era (and is a subtext of the most recent film versions). The novel's unusual eroticism and gender dynamics have also been foregrounded in recent critical analyses by feminists and queer theorists.[10]

Ironically, although the Frankenstein monster's trip from page to screen took him into greater dimensions of hideous and unsympathetic monstrousness, Dracula has become increasingly attractive and sympathetic.[11] Film versions recognize that a more multifaceted Dracula can become a fascinating figure poised between villain and tragic hero. He or she may be conscious of having monstrous status (like Gary Oldman's vampire in Coppola's film). Or the vampire may (like Louis in *Interview with the Vampire* or Miriam Blaylock in *The Hunger*) mourn his or her separation from mortals. Only occasionally is the vampire creative and happy to be bad when transvaluing values (like Frank Langella's feudal Prince Dracula in John Badham's movie, or Lestat in Anne Rice's *The Vampire Chronicles*).

Certain key elements of Stoker's novel are crucial for screen versions and pave the way for depictions of increasingly polymorphous vampire sexuality. In the book are seeds of the genre's gender revisionism; certain key scenes of erotic exchange are always enacted and reenacted on film, so that what is fun about filmic versions is the choreography of these familiar episodes. One of these three important moments is Jonathan Harker's seduction by Dracula's brides. This scene occurs quite early in the book, in chapter 3, shortly after Jonathan has glimpsed Dracula in his coffin, looking younger and "engorged with blood like a leech." It is narrated from Jonathan's overheated and ambivalently erotic point of view as he first hears one of the women comment, "He is young and strong; there are kisses for us all." He then continues:

> I lay quiet, looking out under my eyelashes in an agony of delightful anticipation . . . as she arched her neck she actually licked her lips like an animal, till I could see in the moonlight the moisture shining on the scarlet lips and on the red tongue as it lapped the white sharp teeth . . . I closed my eyes in a languorous ecstasy and waited—waited with beating heart.[12]

Jonathan obviously both desires and fears being made a sexual object at the hands of women. The homoerotic threat of an attack by the male vampire also gets raised as the real seducer/predator lurks behind the scenes. Dracula emerges to chase away his wives and insist that the victim belongs to him.

A second key scene of transgressive eroticism is Dracula's rape of Lucy on a bench by the sea in Whitby; this occurs roughly one-third of the way through the novel, in chapter 8. This scene, told from Mina's point of view, first registers her awareness of Dracula's presence.[13] Awakened in the night, Mina has the strong sense that something is wrong. Suspense builds and time is almost halted as Mina attempts to rush through the dark landscape, until finally she glimpses an appalling spectacle: "I could see the seat and the white figure . . . There was undoubtedly something, long and black, bending over the half-reclining white figure. I called in fright, 'Lucy! Lucy!' and something raised a head, and from where I was I could see a white face and red, gleaming eyes."[14]

Third and last is Dracula's seduction, or rather rape, of Mina in chapter 21 (after Lucy's death and ceremonial beheading). This scene is narrated by Dr. Seward, who sees Mina's head held against Dracula's bleeding chest:

> He held both Mrs. Harker's hands, keeping them away with her arms at full tension; his right hand gripped her by the back of the neck, forcing her face down on his bosom. Her white nightdress was smeared with blood, and a thin stream trickled down the man's bare breast which was shown by his torn-open dress. The attitude of the two had a terrible resemblance to a child forcing a kitten's nose into a saucer of milk to compel it to drink.[15]

Mina's contamination with the Count's bad blood in this scene was no doubt considered too racy and risqué to be shown directly in many film versions. And even in the 1979 *Dracula* with Kate Nelligan and Frank Langella, it was considerably revised (as in Coppola's later movie) by making the woman *choose* to drink, in an even and free exchange of vital fluids.

Stoker's novel ends oddly by describing itself as "just a story."[16] This device is a striking move, and I will refer to it below as we trace equivalents on film. Stoker releases us from the chilling grip of his tale, but he raises doubts about whom to trust: Is this admission itself just a ploy? After all, the book is scary in its evidentiary form, as evidence accumulates through a painstaking assembly of witness testimonials, recordings, diaries, newspaper clippings, scientific articles, weather reports, letters, and the like. If none of these can truly serve as "authentic documents," then whatever could? This same paradox is central to the vampire film, which invariably raises within it skeptical doubts about the existence of its monsters. Other horror films might also make the issues of discovery and confirmation central to the plot, but the vampire film is different because the vampire preys on our very skepticism and suspicion. Van Helsing says in the 1931 *Dracula*, "The strength of the vampire is that people will not believe in him." Failure to come to terms with the possibility of evil might itself endanger us.

In every version of the story, some characters are taken through an initial phase of skepticism into belief and then action by the leadership of a scientific-medical authority figure, Van Helsing or another.[17] And a huge old, authoritative leather-bound book becomes a key image that recurs in the film versions of this story. Ultimately, this trope of "the book" is so central that I propose we consider that Bram Stoker's novel itself is the book that sets up the parameters we must study to learn about vampires. What we come to "believe" is the fictive reality that has been recreated again and again and that has been kept alive—like Dracula himself—ever since its publication in 1897. Stories about vampires are stories about human choices, about our life and our death, about what counts as good or bad for us. Although a film about a fictional monster like a vampire is, of course, not credible if we take it as "evidence" that vampires really do exist, it may become real for us in other significant ways as a story about human evil that we tell ourselves and enjoy watching.

Tod Browning's *Dracula* (1931))

Bela Lugosi's performance in Tod Browning's film version of *Dracula* was crucial in transforming Bram Stoker's villain into an erotically compelling figure. Yet this Dracula is still depicted as evil and in some ways repulsive. In the end, the film asks us to celebrate Dracula's destruction as an act that restores the normal order: His death will release the romantic couple to walk up the stairs together, from darkness into light. Apart from Lugosi's sex appeal in the role, we can also see some of the first steps taken here toward a sympathetic portrayal of the vampire that acknowledges more tragic dimensions of being undead. This is briefly hinted at when Dracula comments in his first encounter with Dr. Seward, John, Lucy, and Mina: "[T]o die; to be really dead . . . that must be glorious. There are far worse things awaiting man . . . than death."

The duality of Gothic romance characterizes the two lead women's reactions to Lugosi's Dracula. After they meet at a concert, he becomes the subject of their discussion and fantasizing; they see him as a romantic foreign aristocrat living in a ruined castle. Lucy imitates his eccentric phrasings and imagines being "Countess Dracula." She says to Mina, "Laugh all you like. . . . I think he's fascinating." This vampire is the chief spectacle of the film, not only for the women but also for viewers. Lucy is right to emulate his accent because much of Lugosi's odd attractiveness stems from his unusual voice, with its exotic phrasing and alien inflection patterns. The allure of Lugosi's erotic Dracula works against his evil nature and nefarious activity; later films will make the erotic part of the monster's evil nature but perhaps in doing so will mitigate his evil. This is one case, then, where Alford's dismissal of the vampire as symbol is far too quick and crude. Like many film vampires, Lugosi in this movie is a parody of an attractive "foreign" woman, with his pale skin, eyeliner, and darkened lips. This vampire is above all a monster to be *looked at*, or gazed upon, with his slick black hair, eloquent hands, handsome top hat, dazzling shirt, and magnificent black cape.[18]

But the vampire's power is shown from the start to reside in his *own* possession of a remarkable, even hypnotic, gaze (Photo 4.1). He functions, then, both like a fascinating passive woman and like an active evil man. In one of our first glimpses of him, we see only blazing eyes that emerge from his disguise as the coach driver. (Lugosi's eyes are frequently lit with bright spots in this film, as they had been in the stage play.) Dracula's powerful look mesmerizes Renfield, the visiting English estate agent. The slight and effete Renfield becomes the vampire's first victim in a highly eroticized scene of attack, where Dracula leans down over the younger man's prone body on the bed. This attack is the first sign of the vampire's omni-sexuality. Dracula's femininity attracts us to look upon him and entices Renfield into a sort of trance in his chambers. Thus, his blood lust combines indeterminate female or homoerotic male powers of attracting and consuming.

Dracula's Medusa-like gaze mesmerizes more people, but from now on, only women: a flower vendor, a theater hostess, a maid, and, ultimately, the two mid-dle-class heroines of the film, Lucy and Mina. His power stops only with Professor Van Helsing—his anomalous male force is stopped by "proper" patriarchy. Even the wise Dutch doctor is drawn to the vampire before he can resist Dracula's hyp-notic power ("[Y]our will is strong, Van Helsing," Dracula says). We can see from this battle that to draw neat and simple links between the male viewer who "has the gaze" and the male agents acting in the film will not work. *Dracula* under-mines such links because the vampire is shown as both subject and object of the gaze, both agent and victim of the men in the film. He is complex enough, then, to begin suggesting ways we can respond to Alford's critique of the vampire as sym-bol, even if in this particular film these possibilities are not fully developed.

Browning's movie tones down some of the eroticism of Stoker's novel. We are shown a glimpse of Renfield (not Harker) meeting with Dracula's brides, but this scene is cut very short. Lucy's seduction by the vampire is not portrayed as a scene of unnatural mating in the dark by the sea, voyeuristically witnessed by Mina. Rather, Dracula flies in her window as a bat who materializes into human form and leans down over her. We do not even see him actually touching her body, and after a quick cut to the next scene, she is already dead and her corpse lies on the table in a

PHOTO 4.1   Bela Lugosi's hypnotic gaze as the Count in Dracula *(1931).*

surgical theater. There is no real development of Lucy's character, nor any suggestion that she has courted death by her flirtatious behavior with three suitors.

Dracula's conquest of Mina is the one moment from the book realized with
some real erotic flair in the film. First, Dracula flies in her window in the form of
a bat, while Renfield, watching from his cell window, screams, "No, not her, please
don't, please!" The next morning, a hysterical Mina babbles about dogs, mist, and
glowing red eyes. Dracula's next attack on Mina transpires in a sequence with the
surreal quietness of a dream. The vampire awaits her on the lawn, eyes glowing,
and she leaves the house in her flowing nightdress. The film cuts to a long shot
that shows him, waiting erect out on the lawn, clothed in his cape with only that
sleek dark head visible. Mina approaches to embrace him, and in a swift, silent
gesture, he wraps her within his dark cloak. Lugosi's Dracula seems a stealthy fe-
line predator, augmenting his association with furtive wolves and bats.

Unfortunately, the Mina of the movie (Helen Chandler) is rather pale, wan,
and nerveless—a far cry from Stoker's intrepid character. When Dracula appears,
Van Helsing orders Mina to her room like a child. After her first encounter with
Dracula as bat, Mina feels polluted and warns John tearfully that he can never kiss

her again, that their love is impossible. She later eyes his neck with a mad gleam but ultimately confesses that the Count has forced her to drink from his veins—notably, veins in his arm, not his breast. This scene is not shown, nor is it even described with anything like the physical intimacy of Stoker's novel.

Lugosi is indeterminately male in the film, an actor who wavers between matinee idol masculinity and overdone exotic femininity. He is physically dangerous, carrying an infection. He threatens the weak, small Renfield by looming over his bed or from behind him, just as he will later victimize women. Yet he is not simply a representative of normal patriarchy, since he is opposed to the male heroes of the film, who are Western, rational, and bourgeois, as an exotic "other" who is "Eastern," feudal, and aristocratic. He is marked as alien by his unusual accent, voice, and manners, as well as by his attire. Indeed, his sexual duality is contrasted in the film with a distinct and rigid patriarchal code, enforced by a clear ordering principle among the "Western" men. This film sets up a distinct patriarchal hierarchy to combat the vampire's hypnotic allure. The oldest, and presumably wisest, man in the film, Dr. Van Helsing must direct the young, handsome, and virile "John" Harker, and to do so, he temporarily assumes control over Mina's behavior and even her body. The hierarchy of male power and authority leads in a clear order from Van Helsing to Dr. Seward, here not a young man and Lucy's suitor but an older man and Mina's father, to boot. Next in line is the handsome but impetuous John; then the comic relief character, a Cockney asylum guard; and finally the slight, boyish, and effeminate Renfield, Dracula's first victim in the movie. Although Van Helsing is presented as "right" or genuinely authoritative in the movie, he is odd, arbitrary and eccentric—so alien that he is almost a match for Dracula himself. The other men, Harker in particular, find his belief in vampires and his plans to protect Mina with garlic and wolfbane irrational and superstitious. Yet Van Helsing, as the personification of the patriarchal order, is the one who protects the young hero's interests in the woman. He takes control, restricting the acts of the hero himself, though in the end he does relinquish the woman to her proper, and younger, mate.

Despite the fascination the vampire exercises on his victims and, by extension, on the audience, ultimately in Browning's film version, as in the novel, he is defeated. Dracula here is evil, but not in a very complex or interesting way—his motivations are not explored, nor do we learn much of his past, his views, or his values. Alford might be right about the actual role of the vampire here, if we confine our observations to the script and dialogue. Even acknowledging the subtlety, nuances, and complexity of Lugosi's performance in the role—with its suggestions of real menace combined with great allure—we can still complain that he is too easy to ridicule because of his foreign weirdness, stagy deliberateness, exaggerated accent, campiness, his masquerade of weird femininity, if you will. As in the novel, the narrative is carried to its perhaps simplistic resolution through the intrepid team of male investigators (a doctor, a professor, and a solicitor), led by Professor Van Helsing (who says at one point, "If I am to help I must be master here.") But even this apparently patriarchal resolution to the tale has intriguing aspects, because the science Van Helsing professes is a kind of necromancy, involving silver crosses, grotesque acts upon corpses, wolfbane, wreaths of smelly garlic blossoms, and so forth. Browning's film emphasizes the alterity of this science by including numerous comments comparing Van Helsing's weird views to those of the inhabitants of Dr. Seward's asylum. The guard says everyone in the house is crazy; Harker comments that one of Van Helsing's remarks sounds like something he would expect one of the patients to say; and Renfield, overhearing their conversation about stakes through the heart, remarks, "Isn't this a strange conversation for men who *aren't* crazy?"

As with Stoker's novel, then, Browning's movie makes much out of issues of credibility, evidence, and science. When Dr. Seward insists to Van Helsing that "the vampire is pure myth, superstition," Van Helsing responds that "the superstition of yesterday can become the scientific reality of today." Van Helsing offers "proof" here that gradually accumulates for both viewers of the film and for characters within it: bite marks on victims' necks, the absence of a reflection in mirrors, Lucy's walking the lanes and abducting small babies, and finally the presence of the vampire himself within his coffin.

Apart from Lugosi's performance, the most striking thing about Browning's movie is the look of the film. The sets enhance the movie's creepy and gloomy atmosphere, as does its unusual (for us) silence—the film has no musical sound track. Almost as much as the pleasures of viewing the vampire as an erotic male, these cinematic features of the 1931 film set the template for later versions that revel in pleasures specific to this genre—the pleasures of recognition and familiar repetition. The sets of Dracula's castle in Transylvania and then of his lair at Carfax Abbey are particularly striking. Although they are Gothic and shadowy, shot in something of the same way as Frankenstein's laboratory in the 1931 Universal Studios version of *Frankenstein*, they have a different feeling: not expressionist but truly Romantic. They possess a decayed and crumbling grandeur, a majestic yet dark beauty. The scenes of the climax in the crypt are superb, with three figures positioned across the sweep of a curved stone staircase and over a large Gothic arch. Juxtaposed by their shadings, these three figures are given a clear moral symbolism: the vampire clad in black, Mina floating in pure white, and Renfield already half-corrupted and wearing gray. The sinuosity of the stairs suits Dracula's lithe, predatory movements. His destruction occurs when he goes to ground in his coffin: He is earthy and evil, whereas Mina floats upward into her "natural" element of good pure white light, as church bells toll on the sound track to confirm that God's value system has been upheld.

Browning's and Lugosi's realization of Dracula modified the character permanently by adding an erotic charge that had not been present in Stoker's villainous and repulsive Count Dracula.[19] There are scenes of inherent eroticism in the book, to be sure, but they rely more upon the action than on the personality, looks, and character of the vampire. Lugosi's brilliance was to conceptualize an aura as he lent the vampire an association with Byronic or Romantic-satanic male figures that Stoker's Dracula lacked. We can find a hint in the 1931 movie of the vampire's weariness at his immortality, in his brief remarks that convey a longing to die. But the character is not shown as one who suffers bitter loneliness and metaphysical pain. At most, we can speculate that he is in search of a companion, but the film does not show anything specific about Mina that prompts him to choose her. It does not in the end complicate the clear-cut distinction between good and evil. Dracula's erotic attacks are deadly, not pleasant; and his gender transgression is not appealing but foul. His immaculate and unchanging appearance suggests that this vampire has no room to grow, alter, or develop. He is stuck, static. Thus, this Dracula is unlike many of the other vampires presented to filmgoers in subsequent years.

John Badham's *Dracula* (1979)

Other film versions of *Dracula* are more subversive of the classic thrust toward a narrative resolution that restores the patriarchal order. John Badham's *Dracula* (1979) presents its heroine, Lucy (Kate Nelligan), as a New Woman whose desire drives the story.[20] Apart from the unconventional treatment of the erotic angle, Badham's film subverts the original tale in a variety of other ways. It is visually disorienting: The camera often plunges viewers into scenes without warning or establishing shots. This is true right from the start, when suddenly we see huge waves washing over a ship about to founder, the slashed throats of its seamen garishly in focus. Later scenes shift the view provocatively into the maelstrom of Dr. Seward's insane asylum, where inmates rampage during a thunderstorm, and later to a close-up of the driving hooves of Dracula's black steeds.[21] The film's sound track is similarly disorienting because the sounds often precede visual cuts, providing a jarring link across scenes, as when a sudden sharp scream cuts across Lucy's romantic candlelit dinner with Dracula.

The Lucy character here is modeled on Stoker's Mina but also has some features of Stoker's original Lucy. Even more than Stoker's Mina, this Lucy is independent. Unafraid to push forward her own participation in a law firm, she reminds her friend Mina that, after all, "We are not chattel." She is also, like the original Lucy, sexually forward: She boldly kisses her fiancé and creeps downstairs for a midnight rendezvous with him. The film emphasizes the heroine's erotic desires by showing the male vampire (Frank Langella) as the sensuously beautiful object of her gaze. It also teases the viewers by revealing only parts of his body in a gradual process that builds anticipation. At first we glimpse only portions of the vampire's body as he sails through the sea to England. Then we see just his hair and elegant hand after he has been shipwrecked and found on the coast by Mina. We finally see Dracula full-view as Lucy does when he is announced at Dr. Seward's house. This film even exceeds its predecessor by making the vampire into a spectacle, permitting women characters (and the film's viewers) to glean certain pleasures of looking and fantasizing. Framed in a doorway, Dracula strides into the room and dashingly tosses away his long black cape. The film emphasizes its heroine's perceptions of this vampire as it immediately cuts to show Lucy's reaction shot—she takes him in with obvious admiration. And why not? Langella's Dracula is a playboy foreign aristocrat, immaculately dressed and exotic, with high cheekbones, sensuous lips, and soft styled hair. It is no surprise that Lucy chooses Langella over her plebeian boyfriend with his freckly-faced boyish looks.

Although Lucy immediately acts somewhat flirtatious, she is still a woman with a mind of her own. She says that she "likes to be frightened" but criticizes Dracula for hypnotizing Mina, saying "now she has no will of her own." But, clearly intrigued, she invites Dracula to dance, and the camera replicates their erotic plunge by its vertiginous movements. Although Dracula hypnotizes the weak and ailing Mina, he passively awaits the choices and declarations of the independent, powerful Lucy. Dracula comments to Harker that Lucy is stronger than most women, and this strength seems to draw him to her. She goes alone, against her father's and her fiancé's wishes, to dine at the vampire's castle, which is transformed for the occasion into a glittering candle-lit palace. The increasingly intense erotic relationship between Dracula and Lucy is depicted in a sequence of three scenes leading up to an elaborately staged bedroom seduction. In the first, the camera conveys their increasing intimacy by moving from an establishing shot that shows them separated by the distance of a formal dining table to a succession of closer-in views, until it has zeroed in on their faces. Dracula says: "I must warn you take care. . . . If at any time my company does not please you, you will have only yourself to blame for an acquaintance who seldom forces himself but is difficult to be rid of."

Next, the two step outside onto a terrace, and Lucy comments: "I love the night. . . . It's so exciting." "Yes, it was made to enjoy life and love," Dracula replies. Then, ever courteous, he says, "You must forgive me for intruding on your life." "I came of my own accord," she replies. They kiss. He eyes her neck, but bites her ear instead, waiting for her willing and informed commitment to this unnatural partnership. "You should perhaps go," he says, warning her again. "No, I'd rather stay," she insists.

Third is the bedroom scene, in which at least some of Stoker's original encounter finally reaches the screen. Lucy removes her cross and sits awaiting Dracula, who materializes from fog outside her window. The mist dissipates to reveal him standing there—tall, dark, and handsome, with a poetic white shirt open at the throat (Photo 4.2). The next sequence is pure Harlequin romance: He calls her his "best beloved one" and, as the music swells, picks her up to carry her onto the bed. There follows a somewhat impressionistic sex scene showing vortices of red light and silhouettes of bats. This Dracula actually makes love to his victim before telling her that he needs her blood. The exchange is mutual, as Dracula next gashes his chest and offers it to her (not forcing her head into it, as in Stoker's book). These "exchange of bodily fluid" scenes are handled by suggestion, as in elegant soft core. When Lucy moves toward his chest to drink, her face is hidden so that we see no actual blood; instead, we see him looking exhausted, even drained, by the woman's sexuality.

Lucy in Badham's *Dracula* is never afraid, does not hesitate about her decision, and chooses her own fate. Because she is so spirited and attractive, the film cannot manage to depict its central vampire as evil. He is rather at worst a Latin lover Dracula with a sophisticated kind of ennui. By contrast to this virile and suave Dracula, the authority figures of British or Northern European patriarchy in this film are all colorless, ineffective, or impotently comical. Lucy's father, Dr. Seward (Donald Pleasence), confesses that it has been a long time since he practiced "real" medicine—he prescribes laudanum for all ills. Plump and prone to fright, he is constantly shown stuffing himself with food. Van Helsing (Laurence Olivier) is elderly and feeble, with a cartoonish Dutch accent. His research into arcane books proves ineffective because Langella's Dracula is not bound by the familiar laws of vampires: He can move about in daylight and turn crosses into flaming torches. Eventually, Dracula even kills off the rather weak, elderly Van Helsing with a stake through the heart. Finally, Lucy's lover, the solicitor Jonathan Harker, is officious, bland, and openly jealous of his aristocratic rival.

At the culmination, even though Harker seems to destroy Dracula by forcing him up into the daylight, the movie's ending is ambiguous. It hints that the vampire has escaped another of the usual scientific rules of his species and flown away through the bright sunlight of the morning. His cloak, transformed into a dark bat shape, floats away as his theme music swells. Lucy watches and smiles, planting the definite suggestion that she anticipates further meetings with her handsome lover.

PHOTO 4.2   *Dracula as Latin lover: Frank Langella as the Count in* Dracula *(1979).*

From a feminist standpoint, Badham's film has numerous problems. It pays lip service to the Liberated Woman but subversively restores patriarchal values by showing her that she really just needs a properly masterful man—then she will live on, forever enslaved in passion to her master. Even given a more charitable interpretation that makes the lovers equal, the film is a farrago of romantic escapism. Lucy and Dracula may find romantic fulfillment in a world where they reign, but questions linger: What of *this* world? What of her ambition to participate in a law firm? What about all those sad patients in her father's asylum? Obviously such mundane matters will not distract the lovers from their higher plane of superhuman intimacy. The film has also been criticized for its fascism, as Dracula insists that he is a "king among his kind" and that he will make Lucy his queen: "I have had many brides, but I shall set Lucy above them all." He promises Lucy that they shall make more of their kind as they rule the earth—presumably preying upon the rest of an insignificant, proletarian population.[22]

Still, Badham's film version has its merits: It is visually striking; Nelligan is appealing; Langella creates a wonderful variation on Lugosi; and the movie affords a subtle reworking of the central figure of the vampire. Langella here is a weary and languid vampire. Instead of Lugosi's famous line about the wolves—"Children of the night; what sweet music they make"—we hear this Dracula say, "[W]hat *sad* music they make." He seeks Lucy for specific reasons that emphasize the great value of human existence: the warmth of her human emotions and the spontaneity of someone with warm blood running through her veins. He hopes to be revived by her life force and energy. He has a conscience and hesitates before enlisting Lucy to his cause, as he mulls over whether this decision is right for her. Another of Lugosi's lines is given a new reading when Langella says softly to Lucy, "There are worse things than death; you must believe me." Regrettably, Badham's movie does not consistently develop its glimpses into the vampire's tortured conscience. Lucy is not tempted so much by challenges of a new vampire morality as by ordinary sexual attraction. In Coppola's subsequent film version of the story, the cloying Harlequin-romance imagery will reappear. But it will be tempered by the vampire's acknowledgment of his own monstrousness, so the woman faces correspondingly more complex choices. Dracula and Mina must each struggle to renounce the other in order to save their love and their eternal souls.

Bram Stoker's Dracula: Love Never Dies (Coppola, 1992)

Francis Ford Coppola's film version of *Dracula*, based upon a screenplay by James V. Hart, purports to be true to the original—it is after all titled *"Bram Stoker's Dracula"*—but it falsifies Stoker's story narratively, intellectually, and emotionally.[23] Narratively, it adds a pre-story about how Dracula, a.k.a. Vlad Tepes or Vlad the Impaler, became a vampire in the first place. Intellectually, it frames this transformation as a tragic result of Vlad's passionate rejection of Christian faith. Emotionally, it traces the cause of Vlad's satanic rebellion to the loss of his wife, Elisabeta, whom he finds reincarnated in Mina (hence the movie's subtitle or slogan "Love Never Dies"). In this film, the vampire is presented as a tragic hero who has become monstrous through a sin or a mistake, a *hamartia*. His satanic rejection of the faith occurs in a moment of passion when he realizes that his princess is dead through human betrayal. Vlad blames God for making him who he is, but in the film's logic, he is redeemed by retrieving his love and this time sacrificing it willingly; he gets released from the curse of his undead immortality.

Christian themes and ceremonies abound in the film, so that at times it is not clear whether we are watching *Dracula*, *The Exorcist*, or yet another *Godfather* movie. As Van Helsing leads Lucy's three young suitors to cleanse her from her undead state, she writhes, hisses, and spits out gobs of blood just like Regan in *The Exorcist*—and Anthony Hopkins does a creditable imitation (in a Dutch accent) of Max von Sydow, proclaiming, "Christ compels you." Scenes of intense eroticism or violence are intercut here with scenes of stately religious ritual, like Mina's marriage to Jonathan (in Eastern Orthodox rites, no less!) or the men's cleansing of vampire coffins with holy wafers. Such juxtapositions recall famous examples of cross-cutting in the *Godfather* series, though what was innovative and brilliant there verges on imitative and formulaic here. Mina's role here is to be a female saint or Mary-like intercessor figure who enables Dracula to repent and attain Christian forgiveness. Despite this foregrounding of Christian themes, though, the movie has a larger moral, not just religious, framework concerning human sin, loss, and redemption. This is the kind of complexity that Alford does not seem to register when he finds the vampire genre lacking in symbolic and imaginative resources necessary to picture evil.

Coppola's film offers much of great interest; his is the first film version faithfully to portray on screen, with real emotional force, the three key scenes of erotic transgression in Stoker's novel. Jonathan's seduction by Dracula's brides is close to pornographic, with thinly veiled hints of fellatio and a lot of luscious female nudity. It is saved from being merely pretty and soft-core by macabre touches, such as the brides' snakelike hair and tongues and their abnormal frog-leg movements. Mina's voyeuristic view of Lucy's mating on the bench with Dracula as a wild beast is truly horrid yet still arousing: Lucy wafts down through a Cocteau-like misty landscape with loose tresses and floating red gown to meet up with the hideous red-eyed monster. And the bedroom scene of Dracula's mating with Mina is shown with more romance, though with dark overtones, since it involves her drinking blood straight from his chest.

Particularly in romantic interchanges like this one with Mina, Dracula is revealed as a complex and tortured figure. He longs to avenge himself on his long-ago betrayers and to prove he can violate divine law by claiming his bride in death throughout eternity. Yet he is also aware that this conversion will condemn Mina's soul to a foul and monstrous existence. Such a condemnation is evil religiously because it is a separation from God, but it is more mundanely evil because it would remove her from a mortal life she has every reason to find rewarding. Life offers Mina normal human fulfillment in connection with her work, husband, and family. Since this Mina is neither repressed nor surrounded by fools like Lucy in Badham's film, there is not such an evident reason for her to choose a vampire's existence.

Coppola's film provides perhaps the most intriguingly nuanced study of *Dracula* on screen. Gary Oldman's Dracula here is alternatively very evil and monstrous and yet appealing and sympathetic. The special effects and costumes depicting his physical transformations support these various moral shadings as he shape-shifts. He appears as an ugly and ancient schemer, a disgusting pile of rats, a monstrous bat, a beastly "wolfen" gargoyle, and a young and sensitive dandy who courts Mina in the absinthe bars of London.

But Coppola's film succeeds above all else as an exercise in the pleasures of the genre. Here is the vampire movie to end all vampire movies! It is visually gorgeous and endlessly creative, abounding in filmic and literary intertextuality. This film in effect reconceives the paradox of the novel's ending with the ploy or the twist of "believe me/don't believe me." The tension between good acting and storytelling and cinematic artifice is heightened by the film's many allusions to other movies, not only in its sets but also in its visual style.[24] Coppola uses engaging young actors but places them artificially in their exotic costumes amid obviously fake sets (Coppola instructed the set designer to build sets that "looked like any other Dracula movie").[25] He sees the beginning of the film in battle scenes with Turks in terms of Kurosawan filmic battles and refers to the ending of Stoker's novel as a "John Ford shoot-out," and he staged it just that way.[26] Scenes of the asylum here resemble those in Badham's film, and the green-lit mist may allude to green spots highlighting Lugosi's glare. Actor Gary Oldman also says that he was indebted to both earlier movies and to other vampire novels: He studied Bela Lugosi's performance ("[H]e was really onto something the way he spoke and moved")[27] and gives reprises of famous lines like "I never drink—wine" with obvious relish. Oldman also says he was inspired to capture the ambivalent spiritual essence of Dracula—his weary yet determined aspect—from the vampires in Anne Rice's novels.

Coppola's film makes numerous allusions to alternative modes of cinematic vision. These devices provide even more for the audience to observe and appreciate. The story's artificiality, genre conventions, and historical references are multiplied and highlighted by the director's use of large maps and texts, a keyhole opening or closing lens, overlays of Dracula's shadow or eye stalking Jonathan or Mina, or framed filmic inserts. For example, on her romantic date with Prince Vlad when Mina imagines his home and his princess, we actually see these inset into the frame beside her. The film thus invites us to both become involved and stay distant. It draws us into its lush spectacle—music plays a strong role in this—yet at the same time maintains a patent artificiality. Artifice is evident in its use of puppets and cutout silhouettes in the early scenes that pantomime Vlad's battle with the Turks. The exteriors of Dracula's castle or of Carfax Abbey are again both archetypal and yet fake; this is a story that is meant to be seen *as* a story, just as Dracula's clothes refer not to any historical period but to other artworks, whether the films of Kurosawa or the paintings of Gustav Klimt.[28]

Differential modes of vision emphasize the nature of stories told in the filmic medium. We notice this more, for instance, in scenes that present Dracula's move-

PHOTO 4.3   *Dracula (Gary Oldman) sits before the screen of the Cinematograph in* Bram Stoker's Dracula *(1992).*

ments in wolf form given his predatorial point-of-view in pixilated vision or in Coppola's use of the pathé camera to convey Dracula's movements in London—we see him as if experiencing an old movie. The puppets used in the "realistic" Turkish battle sequence are later shown *on a screen*—as artificial, that is—in an important self-referential scene when Vlad and Mina visit the Cinematograph of London (Photo 4.3). Vlad as foreigner is drawn to this display, even though Mina the proper English girl recommends a museum instead. Ken Gelder complains in *Reading the Vampire* that this scene places Mina in a passive and submissive role in relation to the cinema, a role unlike her usual adept mastery of new technologies in the Stoker novel.[29] He also complains that this shows us, the movie audience, as "feminised" or "primitive":

> Mina is in control of her own modernity in the novel, but in the film she is out of control—surrendering totally (and mysteriously) to an irresistible force . . . . Dracula, in Coppola's film, is a romantic and "naturally" cinematic hero who sweeps Mina off her feet: after just a little while, she simply cannot say no to him.[30]

PHOTO 4.4   Dracula (Gary Oldman) resists biting Mina (Winona Ryder) in Bram Stoker's Dracula *(1992).*

Gelder is not a good observer of the scene. Mina is compelled not by fascination with the screen images but by the sheer force of her attraction to Vlad/Dracula. Vlad speaks to Mina in Romanian and she *recognizes* him: "I know you. Who are you?" It is no accident that this crucial scene of recognition takes place within a movie theater. This setting suggests that we in the audience are also not merely passive before the screen but active—like Mina, we, too, engage in acts of memory and recognition in response to Vlad. We recognize him as the famous film character taking on a new shape and persona in this movie. One of the chief attractions of this film is the number of changes that we can observe in Vlad/Dracula. These are marvelous, and often novel, but always "recognizable," whether he appears as wolf, chrysalis in the coffin, old and ugly man, or—as here—medieval prince, in all his glamour, power, force, and potential brutality. True, the vampire has physically swept Mina away into the shadows and bent down over her; he must struggle with himself not to violate her, and his eyes glow red (Photo 4.4). He holds back because he wants Mina to succumb to him voluntarily, from recognition and desire. The same invitation or expectation extends to us. And so, like Milton's Satan, this vampire is a scary but subtle monster, a villain who asks us to join him. Neither we nor Mina are expected to be passive. Joining him means rethinking our usual assumptions about the nature of vampire evil.

Christian symbols accumulate in the Coppola film. There are many crosses, crypts, and holy wafers in evidence, as in other vampire films; but here the Christian theme is more central, as it grounds an alternative resolution of the story. These themes render the plot structure quite similar to *Paradise Lost*. This Dracula is evil, unlike the aristocratic lover in the Badham film. But he is far more interestingly evil and developed than Lugosi's monster, who was dispatched off-screen and with no psychological turmoil or tension. Rather, the final death scene of Vlad/Dracula here takes on Luciferian dimensions that would no doubt have appalled Stoker. Because Vlad has found romantic love, the plot implies, he has acquired some sort of new faith or hope in the possibility of goodness. This means that he can at last be freed from his cursed and monstrous form of existence. His death is represented as morally right because Vlad knows it is wrong to convert Mina to his form of life. She has pleaded with him to bring her back to his castle, but he is deeply regretful and suffers over her choice. When they can both be released from the curse of vampirism, it is represented as a victory wherein Christian love is transmuted into deep eternal romantic love.

The ending in the film changes the book dramatically. In Stoker's vision, patriarchy wins out as the four virile young men destroy the vampiric threat and win back "their" Madam Mina. But here, Jonathan Harker prevents his buddies from finishing off the prince and says: "Our work is finished here. Hers has only begun." Mina and Dracula escape into the chapel where Vlad literally expires on the steps of the very altar he had blasphemed at the start of the movie. As he waits for Mina to release him, in somewhat shocking parody or allusion to Christ's last words, Dracula complains first that God has forsaken him and then says, "It is finished." Resurrection and hope are clearly implied as Mina, sobbing, must do the only humane thing—kill the man she loves. Restored, he is young and handsome; Mina loses the burned brand on her forehead left by the holy wafer; and the pair are apotheosized in the film's final image, which shows the original prince and princess floating in the gold Byzantine sky of "Heaven" above. Their love has conquered death, just as good has conquered evil.

Summary

The topics of gender transgression and of Dracula's evil are treated very differently in Stoker's novel and in the three films I have discussed. In the novel, Dracula is unremittingly evil, as symbolized by his ugly, disgusting appearance (hairy palms and nostrils, bad breath). He is a nasty and metaphysically evil monster in Noël Carroll's sense: a violation of nature's categories, a thing that causes revulsion and disgust. Jonathan's picture of him lying in his coffin as an engorged leech conveys this perfectly. The threat of gender transgression lurks amid scenes of erotic abnormality and rape. When Dracula becomes a sort of sex icon with continental flair in Bela Lugosi's film performance, his evil is also transformed. He is now evil primarily as a sexual threat and a male predator. This film does not go much further than Stoker's novel in presenting any interior consciousness for the vampire, nor do we begin yet to get a sense of the vampire's loneliness and weariness over the centuries. Because he calls out for women to come to him and they imagine him as a romantic partner, a kind of internality is projected onto him. Here, as in Stoker's novel, the vampire must be vanquished in the narrative.

In the next two films, female sexuality and sometimes-perverse desires or attitudes reveal more about Dracula's moral status. The two later film versions, Badham's and Coppola's, are tales of female erotic perception and desire. There are hints in the Lugosi film that such female desire is illicit, a subversive force released threateningly by the vampire, hence in need of punishment. But ideologically, if the woman is shown as free and equal in adventurousness (Badham's) or as reciprocating the male's romantic passion (Coppola's), then the vampire's evil and monstrousness are diminished. Feminists might still condemn the films for perpetuating illusions about "true love" or promoting female submission to male forces of primal attraction. But by making the vampire someone who seeks an active female response, these films work against the grain and encourage women to explore and know their own desires for the kinds of partners depicted on-screen.

The vampire may or may not be evil as he helps the females in the story travel their course of gender transgression. This is partly because of his own dangerously "perverse" sexuality. Although male, he is often coded as female, in part because of his Medusa-like gaze, exotic otherness, and love of fancy dress, as well as his appearance and gesture (what feminist critics call the masquerade). Dracula has powers and goals that threaten to undermine patriarchy, but particularly significant is his threat to attract women away from the men who control them (fathers, husbands). He promises women to make them, like himself, immortal and powerful, creatures who feed on others, who turn against their stereotyped roles by killing grown men and devouring helpless babies. Against this power, the standard vampire narratives can provide only puny defenses, ultimately just the magic of garlic, wolfbane, crosses, and wafers (mystery, not science; folk remedies, not medicine; hope, not legal argument). The question is, does he simply take women from capitalist patriarchy back to feudal patriarchy, back into his medieval and "Eastern" harem? As a number of *Dracula* movies make clear, there is room for ambivalence in the audience's shifting identification with or critique of the monstrous vampire figure and his victims.[31] The vampire story permits plot variations that subvert audience expectations of narrative closure, in particular of the sort found in a standard detective story.

Since the character of Dracula has been so far extended and developed on film, the screen is the key place where we in the audience come to recognize and reflect upon him. In the Langella version, we hear of the vampire's loneliness and search for an immortal queen to match him. This world-weariness is shifted in Coppola's film to a rejection of faith, something deemed so "bad" in the course of the film that this Dracula cannot make a proper romantic partner for the heroine. He may "fit" in the sense of already knowing and belonging with her, yet he is "unfit" in the sense that he sees himself as monstrous; he tries to push her away before consummating his seduction. This is the only ending that can both sustain the romantic illusions of the film and still be "moral": to have the vampire cleansed in ritual fashion by the woman who loves him. With Coppola's version, then, the Dracula tale has become tragic in the epic style of Milton. This Dracula is not an evil man who must be stamped out but a mortal human man who grieved so fully that he made a mistake. He was evil, but evil can be forgiven; *katharsis* is possible.[32]

Two Non-Dracula Vampires

Vampires were never the sole province of Bram Stoker, nor is Dracula the only on-screen vampire. Other films that depict vampires offer variations on my three key themes of erotic transgression, moral transvaluation, and genre exploration. Next, I turn to two films with non-Dracula vampires, *The Hunger* and *Interview with the Vampire*, both focused on vampire eroticism and evil. Transgressive sexuality is very much in evidence in each film, both in the lesbian sex scenes of *The Hunger* and in the homoerotic (not to mention pedophiliac) relations in *Interview*. Although these movies depart from Stoker's story and characters and abandon many of the conventions that govern Dracula films—here, vampires might cast reflections in mirrors, go about in the day, or have no fear of crucifixes—there are other staples of the genre, especially the need for blood, that reappear to afford the audience familiar genre pleasures.

Both films are especially interesting because they compose meditations on vampire immortality in terms of the half-life of beautiful, yet fragile, images or illusions. Both movies offer a cinematic equivalent to the paradoxical ending of Stoker's novel. The book tries to appease readers by promising that its story cannot be proven, lacks evidence, and hence should not be believed. The films offer a visualization of characters who are only actors playing vampires and yet who as "stars" acquire their own shadowy half-life form of immortality on celluloid. They attain a desirable but vampiric, dependent, and fleshless immortality.

The Hunger (Tony Scott, 1983)

The Hunger is either a very stylish or a maddeningly mannered film, depending on your taste. It has been criticized for MTV-style editing that fragments and fetishizes (especially female) body parts. Nonetheless, it has pluses: a certain verve, an interesting musical score, and intriguing performances by strong actors. Its sexual adventurousness has made it celebrated by lesbians for its portrayal of the erotic relationship that develops between two women in a steamy sex scene.

The film's plot concerns Miriam Blaylock (Catherine Deneuve) and her vampire existence, which is fraught with loneliness. Her isolation is treated as a tragic inability to grant true immortality to her successive human lovers. At the start of the movie, Miriam and her husband, John (David Bowie), pick up two strangers at a disco and, after erotic foreplay, attack them to drink their blood. These scenes are crosscut with images of an American scientist, Sarah (Susan Sarandon) at work in her lab studying the aging process in monkeys. Vampirism is elegantly sanitized here; it is not until well into the film that we actually see anyone drink blood. John and Miriam Blaylock do not kill with their fangs; rather, they slash their victims' throats using chic Egyptian ankh jewelry. We see only the vaguest spurt of blood followed by the cleanup operations, the two ankhs rinsed clear in the sink and neat black plastic bags put into the incinerator. Murder only gets messy for John when he becomes old and weak, and the violence and repulsiveness of his attacks on young humans are depicted as a consequence of his aged ineptitude rather than as the usual nasty sordid business of the vampire.

The first half of the film concerns Miriam's loss of John, who suddenly begins to age, much to his shock and horror. Bowie's persona as glamour rock star reverberates in ironic ways here. At the film's opening, we see a Bowie-like rock singer with on-stage "Goth" persona. Bowie in the audience trumps the on-stage vampire because he is "the real thing"—despite his elegant suit and coiffed hair. As the aging process accelerates, John's skin wrinkles and sags, and his hair falls out in clumps. He complains that Miriam had promised their love would be "forever and ever," but she admits that she can neither rejuvenate nor kill and release him. John seeks help at Sarah's clinic, but he becomes increasingly decrepit and ultimately Miriam removes him, in sorrow, to her attic, where she sadly shelves him away alongside other coffins that contain, we infer, her previous lovers.

It is impossible to consider this movie without discussing the physical presence and beyond-screen personae of its three key actors: Deneuve, Bowie, and Sarandon.

Here are three movie stars who loom larger than life as they play vampires in situations that hint of their own more-than-human glamour and power.[33] The enacting of a vampire by a star can be distracting, as is the case with Tom Cruise playing the Vampire Lestat (I find myself wondering if his smile has always looked this toothy). But the connections between person and persona are especially salient in *The Hunger*. Each actor carries a national and cultural association that befits the part. Deneuve is perfect as an elegant and ancient vampire (flashbacks suggest her history extends at least back to ancient Egypt). She has a quiet grace and mature sensibility, and she is French—"European," as Sarah puts it after their first tryst. The actress's inimitable style, from her sleek blonde chignon right down to her impeccable suits and trim ankle boots, conveys superior cultural knowledge and sophistication in relation to Sarandon's casual American brashness.

Sarah will replace John for Miriam because she is a woman of the new age. John's status is, culturally and emotionally, in between the worlds occupied by Sarah and Miriam. Flashbacks indicate that when he was first seduced by Miriam, he was perhaps a young English dandy of the eighteenth century. Ironically, Bowie's elegant glam-rock persona suits his role here as John, a tired British relic whose cultured English accent, ennui, and cool manner contrast with Sarandon's fresh American energy and drive. Sarandon quickly moves from passivity to activity. Although at first she turns large luminous eyes to gaze upon Deneuve as if in response to a kind of subliminal call (signaled on the sound track by a high whistle), she becomes the sexual aggressor in their love scenes together. These sex scenes are treated as classic soft porn: gauzy curtains blow about, we hear a lovely operatic duet between two women, and the sex is conveyed salaciously by snippets of breasts, French kisses, glimpses of a bare leg or of Miriam's black corset. Sarandon's sexuality in this movie is foregrounded (Photo 4.5), Deneuve's carefully monitored. Sarah can be revealed because Sarandon typifies the smart, sexually assertive and pleasure-seeking American woman of the early 1980s (just before the dawning of AIDS awareness). Sarah, "of this era" right down to her smoking and brisk walk, is well enacted by Sarandon, an actress who occupies the role of mainstream film sexpot. She is an actress unafraid to reveal her breasts and body nude or to engage in protracted on-screen sex scenes in the role of sexual initiator.[34]

But Deneuve's character Miriam, the beautiful actress playing a beautiful vampire, is at the heart of this film. The remarkable appearance of this famous model (a Chanel "mannequin") enables her perfectly to portray a woman whose perpetual youth and beauty have become a sort of burden, though one she manages to carry with grace. Only at times of great emotional stress, as when John begins to decay and age, does her serene façade crumble. Even this is the groan of the tragic mask rather than real human emotion: Miriam's weary despair does not quite crack and ruin her beautiful face—she is too ancient, too classic.

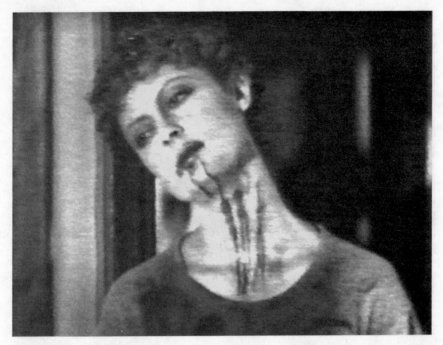

PHOTO 4.5   *The lusty Sarah (Susan Sarandon) gets a taste of vampire life in* The Hunger
(1983).

But there is finally an event that makes the vampire deteriorate: Sarah's rejection of the offer of a love that will last "forever and ever." Although already bitten and "turned" by Miriam, Sarah rejects vampire existence as repugnant and cuts her own throat with an ankh. Now Deneuve/Miriam falls apart (Photo 4.6). Suddenly, she appears disheveled, with stray hairs tumbling down, her bloody mouth smeared like a child's with chocolate, her eyes desolate—are those wrinkles we can spot there? In the film's narrative logic, Sarah's rejection of the principles that have guided Miriam's millennia of existence literally makes Miriam's world crumble to pieces. A cataclysmic earthquake brings all of her previous lovers out from their caskets in the attic. Decayed and hideous, they advance and demand her love until she is forced over a balcony and falls to her death. She writhes, decays, and crumbles into skeletal dust before our eyes.

The Hunger has a more cynical or negative ending than *Bram Stoker's Dracula*. Evil does not get vanquished but reappears. This is not surprising, since the film also lacks the Coppola movie's Christian context, with its promise of redemption to follow remorse. *The Hunger* concludes with a brief epilogue suggesting that Miriam has somehow lived on through the body of Sarah. Newly elegant and

PHOTO 4.6   *The elegant Miriam (Catherine Deneuve) about to crumble and decay at the end of* The Hunger *(1983).*

cool, Sarah (who now dresses in white and wears Miriam's earrings) kisses a lovely young girl in a chic high-rise and muses, viewing the distant horizon. Sarandon makes an intriguing successor to the ancient and classic vampire. The movie tells us that now it is time for the intelligent woman scientist who has studied death to take over and carry on the burden of evil vampire immortality.

Nina Auerbach in *Our Vampires, Ourselves* complains that *The Hunger* suffers by comparison with the novel upon which it is based. Part of her complaint is that in the film, Miriam's existence as a vampire becomes restricted to the pursuit and glorification of capitalist consumer goods: "Vampires in *The Hunger* are not their powers, but their assets."[35] Some of this is surely a matter of adherence to genre conventions, though. Miriam's mansion is just the modern-day equivalent of the Gothic castle in Transylvania. It has a guarded gate (with a closed-circuit security monitor) in place of a moat; vaulted Gothic ceilings; long, flowing white curtains rather than spiderwebs; a deep dark basement (with incinerator) instead of a crypt; and a lofty attic, like a castle tower, complete with literal skeletons in closets/caskets and fluttering doves. Such trappings of sinister elegance are common to many vampire movies—the vampire is, after all, often a count from an old family, with its associated host of treasures; it was not for nothing that Marx invoked this image in characterizing capitalists!

What is new in *The Hunger* is its *aesthetic* interpretation of vampire morality. Miriam's commodities are not so much an accumulation of wealth as an accumulation of *taste*. They suit this wise, learned woman who has devoted her particular immortality to the pursuit of art and beauty. Miriam has spent her eons on two primary projects: cultivating intense romance and pursuing her art collection and her music. She chose John Blaylock as partner because he was an especially promising music student, and she seems set on replacing him with her new prodigy violinist, Alice. *The Hunger* tries to present Miriam as tragic because she cannot maintain her quest: She fails to sustain an immortal romance and so her aesthetic façade crumbles as she dies in the end, more because the quest has made her weary than because she is inherently evil or tragic. And in any case there is no background story about her sin or mistake *(hamartia)* that would give this film the scope of tragedy.

What then of the significance of the film's ending, with one death and completion that leads on into another life with its own potentially tragic form of quasi-immortality? *The Hunger* presents a vision of vampire immortality as sustainable only through images. The young violinist Alice obsessively shoots Polaroids, and after Miriam has decayed before our eyes, we are shocked to see her fresh and pristine image on a snapshot one last time. We witness John's aging process as he compares his thinning hair or lined face to the younger Polaroid image he carries about with him. Bowie's face gets treated as a cinematic canvas written upon by special effects people with their own version of the aging process, until we wonder if that is still really Bowie whose sad eyes look out at us from within the ancient-man makeup.

Celluloid illusion and fame are just one version of a plastic, problematic immortality. Acting and taking on another's role are also shown as tissues of image construction, psychic takeovers, or vampiric emptying out of human souls. Thus, Sarandon as vampiric victim is treated as a kind of mirror image of both Bowie and Deneuve: of the former because they share the same gesture of pushing back their short hair, of the latter when Miriam recurs in Sarah's body at the end. Sarandon replaces Miriam as the actress and becomes an image of Deneuve—without any dialogue but simply through changes in her hairstyle, walk, and dress.

I find it hard to imagine an audience without a smidgen of regret at this replacement, however—at the loss of Deneuve's glorious even if highly artificial beauty. If vampiric immortality is sad in this movie, it is because our vision of *her* is sad. Can this marvelous woman be real? What did it cost to create and sustain such a vision—the makeup, clothes, hair, hats, underwear, and shoes? How was such beauty created, and how fragile is it in the end? Deneuve's face in this film makes the strongest case for seeing that vulnerability and mortality lurk just beneath the surface of ageless vampire perfection. The preservation of beauty on-screen becomes an issue for the viewer as we almost literally obsess over Deneuve's gorgeous face and body for signs of imminent collapse. No wonder that Andrea Weiss mentions that the lesbians fantasizing about the sex scene speculate (correctly) that there is a body double in Deneuve's place.[36] What I see when I look at Deneuve in her final scenes are the remnants of the fragile, demented pale beauty that she once was—almost twenty years earlier—in *Repulsion*.[37] The actress-as-vampire-as-film-star is simultaneously both a powerful, even immortal, queen and a frightened, decaying mad girl. She will wither away and die at the same time that she will be ageless; she will recur forever in both forms; her guise is her reality.

Interview with the Vampire (Neil Jordan, 1994)

Anne Rice's vampire stories develop the familiar genre themes and explore vampire good and evil as they depict the vampire's blood sucking as symbolically equivalent to deep erotic experimentation. Her vampires flirt with intense homoerotic relationships and even with pedophilia. Because Rice did not begin from the basic *Dracula* plot but created a new vampiric dynasty all her own, she can expand the scope of the vampire narrative and alter some of its parameters, while invoking and retaining many standard conventions of the genre. A dual familiarity then, both with her books *The Vampire Chronicles* and with previous vampire movies, informs many viewers of the film *Interview with the Vampire*, providing a series of quite complex pleasures. Genre experimentation and innovation here, as in *The Hunger*, take on a particular form that sets off vampire nature and values against the physicality and personae of the actors playing vampires.

Rice's vampires are erotic and metaphysical with a vengeance; they are not only beautiful and sexy but also thoughtful and "deep."[38] Her new figures of demonic agency reflect at great (and sometimes tedious) length on their unnatural existence as they seek to create new values to guide their immortal lives. Both the novel and the film of *Interview with the Vampire* foreground the figure of Louis (Brad Pitt) as narrator or storyteller. He is the vampire moralist who reluctantly accepts an invitation to join vampire life out of despair, as "a release from the pain of living." But once "turned," Louis's life as a vampire is filled with remorse. He resists having to kill and feed on humans because of his "lingering respect for life." Lestat (Tom Cruise), the vampire who created Louis, shocks his companion with the challenge: "What if there is no Hell? Ever think of that?" For Louis, this hell is his very nature, the truth of which Lestat keeps urging upon him: "[F]or do not doubt—you are a killer." The two men create a "daughter" vampire from a beautiful young girl, Claudia (Kirsten Dunst), who at first seems a better companion for Lestat than Louis because she is "an infant prodigy with a lust for killing that matched his own."

Lestat is also clear about the vampire's status vis-à-vis God. He sees vampires as rivals in a stronger sense even than Milton's Satan, who can never match his creator. Lestat tells Louis: "God kills indiscriminately and so shall we. For no other creatures under God are as we are; none so like Him as ourselves." Louis's view is quite different. After he seeks other vampires in Europe, he muses, "What would the damned have to say to the damned?" For a third major vampire character, Armand (Antonio Banderas), good and evil have been reduced to a simple formula: "Perhaps death is the only evil left. I know nothing of God or the devil." Despite the allure of both Armand and Lestat, Louis is meant to seem special because of his conscience and guilt about vampire existence. Claudia tells Louis, "Your evil is that you cannot be evil."

For Anne Rice's vampires, as for Miriam Blaylock in *The Hunger*, immortality is a heavy burden. Armand even comments to Louis, "Do you know how few vampires have the stamina for immortality?" Much of the interest of the series of novels lies in the different responses and meditations offered by various vampires concerning this problem, one that philosophers have called "the tedium of immortality."[39] Louis's response is passionate guilt and concern, which finally dwindle away to loneliness and cold regret about his evil condition. Armand says Louis is beautiful because he is "a vampire with a human soul, an immortal with a mortal's passion." Armand's own cool acceptance of vampire existence puts him in danger of such indifference that he may die. Lestat, the hero of *The Vampire Chronicles*, truly relishes vampire existence, and only he seems to want to transvalue values in the literal sense of making evil his good. As he takes over the narrative of the second book, he is portrayed as attractive because he expresses obvious relish for immortality. However, in the film version, Lestat's more perverse aims are not highlighted. Instead, if he seems appealing at all, it is for fairly typical human qualities such as his zest for novelty and power.[40]

Transgressive eroticism in *Interview with the Vampire* takes several forms. First, and most obvious, are the deep romantic and homoerotic links among Louis, Lestat, and Armand. As portrayed by three of the leading sex gods of the 1990s—Brad Pitt, Tom Cruise, and Antonio Banderas—each vampire is devastatingly attractive and charismatic (Photo 4.7).[41] They dress elegantly and frequent expensive hotels in fascinating cities (New Orleans, Paris, San Francisco). They can charm the

PHOTO 4.7   *Tom Cruise and Brad Pitt as sexy vampires in* Interview with the Vampire *(1994).*

most beautiful of women or boys. Given their superior powers and longer time frame, it is no surprise that vampires turn their desires away from mortals and toward one another. They may desire a human woman (and such scenes of eroticism are frequently depicted in the movie), but this is the desire for blood and the kill, not a truly erotic desire. Ordinary humans are so irrelevant that *Interview with the Vampire* includes several very disturbing scenes of male predation against women or helpless children, where, despite the violence, the vampires are not shown as deranged but as attractive and appealing.[42] I will suggest in my next chapter that such scenes link the vampire genre to the slasher film, where often-charismatic killers indulge their own blood lust. If this were all the film or books offered, Alford's criticism about the superficiality of the vampire, or about his sheer obviousness as emblem of evil, would be correct. But there is more.

The erotic gets redefined in *Interview with the Vampire* as something that goes beyond blood, flesh, and genitals, beyond norms of heterosexual attraction and marriage. Psychological intimacy is the need that compels Lestat to create his "family" and what drives Louis into Armand's den, where he feels he has at last found a mentor. In the Louis-Lestat-Claudia family nexus, we can see platonic love perversely transfigured. Whereas in Plato's account the two homosexual lovers pursue beauty and engage in a "higher" form of reproduction by giving

PHOTO 4.8   Louis (Brad Pitt) and Claudia (Kirsten Dunst) in an incest-laden scene from
Interview with the Vampire (1994).

birth to something immortal, here they devote themselves to a different kind of
immortal production by becoming the "parents" of the girl-child vampire
Claudia. This act of supreme male vampire power supplants the female role in reproduction, but it results in something monstrous (Photo 4.8). Although Louis
loves this daughter, none of them can forget that making her a vampire so young
was deeply wrong. Her ageless childhood is a curse that makes their relationship
inherently perverse, erotic yet filial, hence very unstable. Louis's inability to sustain this relationship or to save Claudia from the other vampires who destroy her
leaves him empty in the end: "All my passion went with her golden hair."

Louis's fate as a vampire is meant to seem tragic: He cannot be satisfied with his
child partner but finds the one mature person he seeks and can love, Armand, only
too late. Armand loves Louis for his human passion, something Louis loses when he
loses Claudia. Thus, when Armand offers to teach him the "first lesson of vampire
existence"—"We must be powerful, beautiful, and without regret"—Louis responds: "What if it's a lesson I don't want to learn? What if all I have is my suffering,
my regret? You regret nothing, you feel nothing. I can do that on my own."

The great and conscious irony of the film, of course, is that Louis wishes his
story to end up repelling the listener: "I'm a spirit of preternatural flesh.
Detached, unchangeable, empty." But his epic of despair, loss, and death becomes

for others—for Molloy the interviewer (Christian Slater) and for us in the audience—a fascinating tale of adventures we wish to share, and in a sense we *do* share it. The interviewer pleads with Louis not to let the story end here but to confer upon him the dark gift of immortality. Louis's response is to threaten violence and make the man think twice about his request. Like Molloy, we might be frightened by Louis's faster-than-light attack and baleful glare; but still, even after this, his story remains fascinating. The ending of the film shows Molloy leaving the scene of the narrative (as we will leave the movie theater), but this is not the actual ending. In a coda, the somewhat decrepit Lestat makes a sudden reappearance in the "outside" (i.e., "our") world. "I assume I need no introduction," says Tom Cruise (who of course doesn't need one), and then, after taking a drink of blood, he revels, "I feel better already." Lestat's humor is welcome after what he labels Louis's narrative "whining." Thus, the film plays a dual trick on the audience. Not only might we, like Molloy, remain fascinated by Louis's story and find what he regards as evil attractive but we also now have a quickening new interest in the ongoing adventures of the ever-charming and energetic Lestat, who could not disagree more with Louis about the virtues (or vices) of vampire life.

The most obvious explanation for our ongoing fascination with film vampires like these is that they are actually—surprise—movie stars! The star makes a perfect vampire, because (as Louis tells Madeleine) he seems unnervingly beautiful to (ordinary) humans: He has special eyes and flesh, wealth, experience, elegance, amazing powers, and a distinctive, quasi-immortal status.[43] This may also explain Anne Rice's about-face from her initial criticisms of the casting of Tom Cruise as Lestat. The short, dark Cruise did seem an odd choice for the tall, blond Lestat, but Rice realized after seeing him that a multimillionaire screen star like Cruise has exactly the on-screen persona to carry off the arrogance and compelling personality of a Lestat.[44] Lestat in the second book of her *Chronicles* series becomes a famous rock star, ironically reversing David Bowie's transition from rock star to (on-screen) vampire. But if he could only walk about comfortably in the daylight, Lestat would probably choose instead to be a wealthy and successful film star—perhaps someone like Tom Cruise, a top box-office attraction!

The most interesting thing about the Anne Rice vampires is that they exist in "chronicles": Their need from us humans, first and foremost, is to be listened to and understood. This layering of performance with reality is made evident in the vampire theater scene led by Armand (Photo 4.9), where, as Claudia puts it, we see "vampires who pretend to be people pretending to be vampires." In much the same way that the vampire needs a mortal, the star needs an audience: In the theater scene, these two needs coincide as the vampires get the blood they need while entertaining and titillating their audience. Having grand passions is not enough;

PHOTO 4.9   *The vampire Armand (Antonio Banderas) leads his troupe of vampire actors (with real victim) in* Interview with the Vampire *(1994).*

describing or enacting them is better.[45] Enacting them is preferable because it inspires admiration and perhaps even envy in us, the mortal audience for immortal beauty.

Cinematic Vampires and "Stars"

The paradox of Stoker's conclusion to *Dracula* is that it tells us not to believe the story that has just held us in its grip—that its seeming assemblage of evidence is not really "proof." This issue of the "real" existence of vampires is central in the two films I have just discussed, *The Hunger* and *Interview with the Vampire*. Often, vampire films present moments of critical doubt, when a "scientific" expert banishes skepticism and paves the way for belief by finding "proof." (Recall Van Helsing's claim in the 1931 *Dracula* that the vampire's strength is that people will not believe in him.) Movies, like Stoker's novel, give us proofs that they then say we probably cannot believe, and this is their seduction—this genre tempts belief by continually offering itself as unreal. What better way to carry off this sleight of hand than by offering us figures of movie stars as vampires? With Cruise, Pitt, and Banderas in their roles, or with Bowie, Sarandon, and Deneuve, we can actually "see" that these special beings are out there. Vampire existence gets translated into "real" images of glamorous stars on the screen, revealing their "preternatural" flesh and assuming their status as our ageless icons of immortality. They need us, the audience—they need us to be both frightened and fascinated by them.

Thus, vampires' transgressive eroticism in these two films is linked to their mode of existence as recurring icons, as familiar appearances *on film*. The erotic vampire as spectacle both haunts and attracts us, both desires and is desired by us. This is not simple predation; if it were, then Alford would be correct in asserting that the vampire has no real interest in intimacy or in the personhood of his or her victims. If vampires thought that humans were only there to be taken, used, spoiled, and abandoned, their evil would indeed be uninteresting. Someone who sees them this way might critique them as exemplifying a sort of life-sapping male aggression—and this is like the radical feminist view argued for by Andrea Dworkin in *Intercourse*, where she cites vampires' sexuality as exemplifying the worst features of males in sex.[46] Then we could say that even a strong female vampire like Miriam Blaylock exemplifies an approach to sexuality that is male, in the sense of being predatory, violent, and objectifying.

But this sort of picture is inadequate, in part wrong because it oversimplifies vampire *sex*. We have seen from Bela Lugosi onward that the male vampire's ex-oticism may brand him as "feminine," and we have also seen the homoerotic ties between male vampires or female vampires in movies like *Interview with the Vampire* and *The Hunger*. Recent accounts within queer theory celebrate this sub-versive eroticism of the vampire.[47] Since the erotic focus becomes the mouth on the neck rather than the penis in the vagina and since the vampire *receives* fluids (red blood) rather than *spending* fluids (white semen), there is a sort of feminized component even in their "masculine" aggression and violation. This kind of switching between activity and passivity also characterizes the screen audience's relation to the figures so familiar in this genre.

This means that vampire evil is not just about sex, masculine aggression, or even animal predation. Vampires may desire the blood of humans, but it is often not their literal blood that the vampire longs for so much as their very status as mortals. The vampires in *The Hunger* and *Interview with the Vampire* want what they cannot have: passion, limitation, mortality. Why else is there such emphasis in these films on grand epic passionate love? Dracula on screen also always loves the beautiful and human Mina. He may aim to make her his undead queen and companion (as in the John Badham 1979 *Dracula*), or he may ultimately be un-able to do so because he has been lost to life (as in Coppola's 1992 version). Miriam Blaylock longs for a human companion for her immortality, but she can-not secure this, so she grieves and dies. Anne Rice's vampires Louis, Lestat, and Armand cannot love mere mortals, and thus all their erotic intimacy is directed at

each other. The homoerotic nature of these desires is not a matter of being attracted to physical beauty (what, after all, does a vampire want from another vampire's body?) but to wisdom, spiritual characteristics, power, knowledge, attitudes.

I propose that *The Hunger* and *Interview with the Vampire* ask their audiences
to desire the vampire as a spectacle of seduction. The vampire in these films is always a "star," a fascinating exotic creature of multiple powers, circumscribed by a
fleeting and rule-bound existence when walking the earth. On-screen, we can see
this magical creature as a being who longs for and desires us. Vampires seek out
the mortal, not simply to drain our blood but because they need our energy,
drive, desire, and warm-blooded emotion. Vampires are, after all, cold and dead.
They are weak and pale creatures without us; they need our admiration and passion more than we in the end really need them.[48] They are images; we are flesh
and blood. The vampire is a creature of night, usually destroyed by the light.
Vampires' magical abilities are well suited to film: They can fly, practice time
travel, hear people's thoughts, shape-shift into fog or mist, run like a wolf, sneak
out of coffins and into crypts. Their age, exoticism, eccentricity, and aristocratic
nature may be conveyed by all the usual tricks of acting and sets. The film vampire, too, exists in the half-light of the projection on a screen. Neither being has
true flesh and blood. Each creature—the vampire and the screen star portraying a
vampire—attains a kind of immortality, but it is an odd, unreal kind of life. As
Louis tells Molloy at the start of the film version of *Interview with the Vampire*,
"I'm flesh and blood, but not human." The vampire, like the actor in a film, is a
simulation, both more and less than human.

Conclusion: Vampire Evil and the Pleasures of Genre

At the start of this chapter, I cited C. Fred Alford's critical remarks in *What Evil
Means to Us* about the shallowness of the vampire as symbol of evil. I said that
Alford betrays a limited understanding of the nature and appeal of contemporary
vampires. Alford sees vampires as sending a message that dependency is bad because it is equated with powerlessness and the loss of freedom. Young people thus
regard others who depend on them in any way as evil in the same sense as vampires, a view he considers immature and shallow. "The fictional vampires of infor-
mants are symbols of social isolation, not cultural integration."[49] This is mistaken,
because certainly the meditations of Coppola's Dracula or of Louis, Armand, and
Lestat in the Anne Rice novels are about vampire evil as a corruption and a threat
to the integrity of the soul. Anne Rice's vampires are obsessed with spiritual good
and evil. Furthermore, though they prey upon humans, they are lovers in the
truer sense only of one another. Psyches, not bodies, interest them.

Evil and monstrousness in classic horror films often have a paradoxical nature, one especially foregrounded in *Dracula* and the vampire genre. The monster is evil, yet he both attracts and repels; we in the audience want to look at the same time that we are afraid to look. What is evil is also interesting, what is ugly or distorted can be fascinating. In classic horror, there are usually male investigators who drive the narrative toward resolution by conquering the monster and banishing what is ugly, monstrous, or fearful. The fates of monsters and women get strangely paired on the side of the spectacle. Although monsters usually threaten a woman and we may be expected to approve her release, we may also want to sustain their threatening presence in order to know them. There is a tension between our desire to become acquainted with the horrific, disgusting monster by looking at the spectacle (for instance, at the monster biting the woman's neck) and our desire to restore the moral order by saving the woman and punishing the monster. In classic horror, then, spectacle and the narrative are in a very complex relation. Narrative, of course, may itself proceed on the visual level, since to follow the story requires interpreting, collating, and understanding images. As Noël Carroll's account of horror emphasizes, horror in general attracts us because we want to *understand* the monster. But film horror works because we *see* the monster and his victims. (In film, seeing is a kind of understanding.) And depending upon how attractive the monster is and how inept the closure provided by the investigator, the film ending may or may not be satisfactory when it finally puts a stop to our ambivalent desire for the spectacle of horror. In the vampire film as in most other horror films, the narrative focuses on the intellectual, fact-gathering activities of the male investigators; narrative closure is achieved by some device of incorporation within the patriarchal order. Thus, narrative puts an end to the spectacle (our vision of the monster and of the woman/victim).

In Stoker's *Dracula* and even more so in the vampire movies I have discussed here, there is a recognition that the monster can be sympathetic or even desirable. This is why, I suggest, there are recurring paradoxes in the story, such as Stoker's claim that the proofs assembled by the book cannot suffice as evidence or other filmic depictions of the vampire as simultaneously decayed and beautiful, a celluloid shape-shifter. Even a predatorial killer like Lugosi's Dracula can be fascinating, and all the more so a playboy like Langella or any of the others I have mentioned. As if to acknowledge the audience's interest in the monster, narrative closure is often threatened, and by a variety of means: Langella's Dracula escapes at the end; Oldman's corrupt and aged prince becomes young and pure; Miriam is reborn in the body of Sarah; Lestat is definitely "alive" and ready to rock 'n' roll. Some versions of *Dracula* hint at the vampire's continuing erotic alignment with the heroine, his (or her) victim/mate. Alternatively, even if the patriarchal order of law, justice, heterosexual marriage, and science is restored, it may be subverted within the narrative. This is what happens in Badham's or Browning's *Dracula*, with their intimations that the scientist/hero is insane or a fool.

This ambivalence about the monster carries over into complexities about vampire morality. Several of the vampire movies I discussed in this chapter show a vampire who copes with setting goals or values for a godless existence throughout all time, searching for ways to be sustained through a now interminable life. What is remarkable is that vampire evil so often amounts to something we can judge in our ordinary mortal terms. Vampire evil might just be killing and using, or it might mean selfish disregard for others. Only rarely does it become truly epic, like the evil of Satan. I find this hinted at most strongly in the characters who figure in Coppola's *Bram Stoker's Dracula* and *Interview with the Vampire*. Oldman's Dracula does aim at evil when he rejects God and faith, but he is redeemed, not just from the outside by the tired old formula of a woman's love but from the inside by a rediscovery of his own capacity for faith. Anne Rice's vampires differ. Louis is highly moral in a traditional sense of being loyal to friends and regretting past misdeeds; he aims at virtuous proselytizing by using his story as a cautionary tale. Lestat is meant to be the most Nietzschean of all vampires, but even he seems somewhat unoriginal in his goals of power, wealth, sex, and fame; his pursuit of rock-star fame and fans is a rather disappointing goal that we can scarcely imagine Nietzsche's Zarathustra would applaud.

In the end, then, the common dependency of vampires in their new form of "undeath" upon mortals goes along with a surprising dependence upon our familiar value schemes. It is also worth noting here at the end of this discussion that what the newest vampires seem to aspire to most of all is art: Miriam through compiling her collection and performing, Louis by telling his story, the story we can enjoy and find fascinating and seductive—even if sometimes also repulsive.

chapter five: The Slasher's Blood Lust

Slashers as New Monsters

In 1960, two films, *Psycho* (Alfred Hitchcock) and *Peeping Tom* (Michael Powell), permanently altered the face of the horror-film monster. They chillingly depicted "ordinary" men who were unable to connect with the reality around them.[1] These films not only naturalized the horror-movie monster by turning him into the boy next door, but they solicited audience sympathy and even invited voyeuristic participation in his gruesome murders as his blood lust drove him on to greater crimes. Due to traumas of childhood and sexual repression, so the story went, these men became mad slashers who murder women. This scenario has become formulaic and has been given numerous subsequent variations; the slasher subgenre became the dominant form of horror in the 1980s.[2]

In this chapter, I will discuss *Peeping Tom*, along with two of its slasher movie successors, *Frenzy* (Alfred Hitchcock, 1973), and *Henry: Portrait of a Serial Killer* (John McNaughton, produced 1986/released 1990). The latter is a movie loosely based on the story of real-life serial murderer Henry Lee Lucas.[3] These three important films feature as their monster an ordinary human man who murders women. I call all three films "slashers," although, strictly speaking, not all of the murders in them are committed using knives or blades; the killer may strangle his victims or even snap their necks. I use the term "slasher" as a generic label for a movie with a psychopathic killer, usually a male, whose assumed blood lust drives him to a sort of extreme violence against women. Such violence, often eroticized, is showcased by the camera in increasingly graphic and disturbing ways. We shall see that despite surface differences, slasher films can be considered heirs to the vampire movie: Erotic predation (or blood lust) is at the center of both genres; only the monsters are updated.

Realism is the key factor that differentiates slashers from their predecessors in horror. Here the monstrous killers are not undead, supernatural vampires or hairy hulking werewolves but living, breathing men. *Psycho* was based on a book by Robert Bloch about a real killer and corpse stealer named Ed Gein.[4] It is no news that horror fiction imitates real-life crime: Mary Shelley's monster was born out of Galvani's experiments on the publicly displayed bodies of executed criminals, and nineteenth-century newspapers inspired the more chilling episodes in Dickens, Poe, and Dostoyevsky.[5] But in slasher-film horror, the ties between fact and fiction have become increasingly intricate and ramified. The fictions of *The Silence of the Lambs*, a story about a cannibalistic killer also based partly on Ed Gein, permeated media coverage of the arrest of cannibalistic serial killer Jeffrey Dahmer; publicity over Dahmer's arrest in its turn threatened the box-office take and opening date of the horror film *Body Parts*. Like these movies, other horror-film stories may begin in the newspapers and then move swiftly on to Hollywood contracts and major motion pictures.[6]

In the three films I will discuss in this chapter, there is a common theme of male predation against women and of eroticized violence. I shall look especially at the scenes of attacks to consider how they offer up both a new kind of horror-film monster and a new conception of slasher evil. I want to consider several questions about the slasher genre. First, what happens to the monster as he becomes more naturalistic? To answer this will involve considering the nature and prominence of spectacles of violence and horror in this genre. And second, more deeply, what do these changes in monsters and spectacles tell us about the views of the nature of evil presented in such films?

The most obvious assumption is that the slasher killer is an evil man, a psychopath. However, some films in this genre, like *Psycho* and *Peeping Tom*, imply that the killer is a sympathetic, conflicted man who commits crimes against women because of a particularly abusive childhood. Thus, in asking us to question whether he is truly evil, they appear to perpetuate a conservative and troubling gender ideology that might excuse or explain his crimes against women. Even beyond this, many such movies convey the message that bad parenting was responsible for turning these men into monstrous killers who cannot help what they do. Ever since *Psycho,* this bad parenting is often held to be the particular fault of the mother. Thus, women get blamed as well as victimized in the slasher genre, making it seem particularly offensive to feminists. Surely these movies present very troubling depictions of women and of male violence; but the task of moral assessment is complex and demands more subtlety.

Much has been written about all three films, by feminists and other critics. By juxtaposing these particular movies, I will to trace some developments, connections, and contrasts within the genre. The slasher genre begins in *Peeping Tom* with a monster who is somewhat sympathetic and whose madness is plumbed and explained. We move on in *Frenzy* to a monster who is shown as repellent and whose motivations are just vaguely sketched—at best inferable only from the genre's key precedents like *Psycho*. Finally, in the most recent of the three films, *Henry*, we find a monster whose evil is banal and repetitive. Henry himself should be an uninteresting if monstrous killer, but he is made to seem interesting in two ways: first, the heroine of the film (perhaps a stand-in for us) projects a romantic façade onto him as she imagines his tragic childhood; and second, he is cast in the mold of the familiar Hollywood rebel. *Henry: Portrait of a Serial Killer* may come closest of any horror film I know to capturing what Hannah Arendt famously called the "banality of evil."[7] Yet even here, evil is not truly presented as banal; perhaps the horror film inevitably must make evil "interesting," even if the monster is ordinary. My project here is to see why and to offer critical discussion of this evolution.

Peeping Tom

Peeping Tom is a very self-consciously metafilmic movie. Right from the opening credits, it makes the violence of filming its central theme. In this movie, characters engage in explicit discussions about neurotic watching or "scoptophilia." The film almost offers itself up on a platter to feminist analysis since it draws its own connections between movie voyeurism and male violence. (In fact, the videotaped edition of it is now available, complete with commentary by feminist film theorist Laura Mulvey.)[8] But despite its textbook presentation of the risks and dangers allegedly inherent in "the male gaze," this film is far from formulaic. It can elicit substantial and subtle moral consideration (feminist and otherwise).

Peeping Tom offers a sympathetic depiction of the murderer in a film that many people may find repulsive. Mark Lewis (Carl Boehm) is a handsome, soft-spoken, and sensitive man, who, we learn, suffered extreme cruelty as a child when his father, a famous and brilliant biologist, made him a guinea pig in studies of fear and the nervous system. The elder Lewis turned a camera on his son and recorded his every experience, even designing experiments to terrify him. Mark now reviews all these tapes (both audio and video) compulsively, hoping that the records of his father's coldness and brutality may somehow serve some good. Mark's neighbor Helen (Anna Massey), a woman he comes to know and like, challenges this faith abruptly when she learns of the experiments, saying, "A scientist drops a lizard onto a child's bed and good comes of it?"

Mark, the film tells us, has dealt with his horrific childhood by taking over the role his father played with him. He uses his own camera to photograph women, especially aiming to capture their fear. Mark explains to Helen that he is making a documentary; it turns out to be the documentary of his own life—he is continuing his father's work. He keeps trying to capture "the perfect face of fear" as he kills women. Helen recognizes Mark's reliance on his camera as dangerous or sick, and she forces him to leave it behind when they go out on a date. Although he is reluctant to do so and obviously feels threatened, he enjoys their date and promises earnestly never to photograph her.

But the other women in Mark's life are not so lucky. We learn this right from the start of the film. We watch through the crosshairs of Mark's camera lens as he picks up a prostitute, goes to her room, and then approaches her with something that evokes sheer terror on her face. The film dissolves into a close-up of her screaming mouth. This sequence is first shown live and in full color—the prostitute's fur coat and flaming orange skirt attract attention—and it is then replayed during the credit sequence, this time shown in black and white on a screen that the young man watches in his dark, cloistered room. We proceed to see more of the man's life: He films the police investigation into the murder, shoots pictures of pornography models, and does his job as a focus puller at a movie studio. He also kills two more women, with the same view being offered to us of the camera zooming in to focus on their fearful screaming faces. One victim is a stand-in at the movie studio; the second is one of the pornography models. The film treats these women as pitiful creatures. Mark is drawn to their fear and even wants to photograph the bruises on another model's face.

As he gets to know Helen, Mark finds her interesting as a person; she invites him to collaborate on a children's book she is writing about a boy with a magic camera. He shows Helen the films his father made and confides his past. Meanwhile, Helen's blind mother is suspicious of Mark. She calls his footsteps "stealthy" and is sure that he is up to no good watching films night after night in the darkened room above her. She forbids their relationship to continue. In a fearful confrontation, the mother tries to force Mark's secret out of him by demanding to be "taken to his cinema." Mark actually does play the film of his latest murders for Helen's mother, but interestingly, neither person finds the movie viewable. Of course, the blind woman cannot see it, though she responds to its emotion. In an astonishing sequence, we watch as both of them are silhouetted against the large screen containing the terrified face of Mark's latest victim. Helen's mother raises her hands as if trying to use her sense of touch to feel the film (earlier, when she feels Mark's face, he asks, "[A]re you taking my picture?"). Mark approaches the screen too closely, so that the movie plays over his back—we see the woman's large face and startled eyes appear there. This movie fails to deliver catharsis to either character: Helen's mother is terrified and dismayed, and Mark flails against the screen in despair over not yet having captured the perfect expression of fear he seeks.

Finally, Helen herself learns what Mark has done when she pokes around in his room and plays his movie. We do not see this latest film as the reels rotate; we only see Helen's face. She starts out smiling and expecting to enjoy Mark's artwork. Her expression gradually changes until she runs to hide behind shelves, peeping out to watch in horror and screaming when Mark suddenly appears behind her. She accosts him, wanting reassurance that it is "only a movie." Mark confesses that he is a killer, warning Helen not to let him see her fear, demonstrating his technique (Photo 5.1). Just as the police are pulling up downstairs, Mark completes his documentary ("I've planned this for such a long time"). Racing over to set up the tripod leg of his camera—a knife blade extended neck-high and a reflector mirror in place at the top—he prepares to film and watch his own death. Tapes roll and flashbulbs pop in succession as he runs to impale himself (Photo 5.2). "Helen, I'm afraid," he says at the end, "and I'm glad I'm afraid." Mark runs the knife into his own throat, collapses, and dies. The last thing we see is Helen sobbing near his body, then the empty screen in his room, half-lit with the red light of the darkroom.

Feminist critics (notably Carol Clover, Laura Mulvey, and Linda Williams) have made many good observations about this film.[9] One thing they have not focused on, as I will, concerns what it says about the nature of evil. Whether Mark is evil, and if so, why or how he became so is one issue, of course. But to press this issue, we must think about ways in which evil in this film is intrinsically linked to our various human modes of knowledge. Mark's father was indubitably evil, a mad scientist in the *Frankenstein* tradition whose hubris offends nature. Mark explains to Helen: "He wanted a record of a growing child—complete, in every detail. He was interested in the reactions of the nervous system to fear." Mark's father made the obvious mistake of thinking that a filmic and scientific record, something "objective" and distanced, could capture a personal, subjective, and emotional phenomenon. He wanted only to study Mark coldly as a science project, not to be a father who would comfort him when he was frightened or sad at the death of his mother. If science in *Peeping Tom* is flawed, art fares little better. Both of the film projects we see in this movie, one documentary and one commercial ("artistic"), are disasters. Mark's own documentaries are obviously rooted in sadistic and evil violence; he only replicates the evil of his father. And he works on a movie set where the director barely restrains his contempt for the lead actress, a "bimbo"

PHOTO 5.1   *Mark Lewis (Carl Boehm) shows Helen (Anna Massey) how he films "the face of fear" in* Peeping Tom *(1960).*

who cannot manage to get her scenes right by fainting on cue in the proper way. When a trunk on the movie set is opened during filming and accidentally discloses the corpse of the stand-in whom Mark has murdered, the actress does faint; rather than showing sympathy or concern, the director yells: "That bitch! She fainted at the wrong scene!"

The men in the movie (Mark included) who use science or art to live by exemplify the wrong relationship to life and emotion. What then of the women? Helen and her blind mother in this movie are "good." They have the "right" relationship to life and emotion—and this is so even though Helen's mother is a cynical alcoholic. These two women see with their feelings, instinct, or intuition, especially the blind woman. She demands to "see Mark's movie," and when he pleads that he needs to finish it to show Helen, she replies, "She [Helen] sees enough without your photographs." There is a value system in this movie, summed up when the blind woman comments on her own relation to life: "Instinct's a wonderful thing, isn't it. A pity it can't be photographed. If I'd listened to it, I might have kept my sight. I wouldn't have let a man operate on my eyes I had no faith in." Here in a nutshell is the movie's philosophy. Seeing and photographing, in whatever mode—the studio motion picture, the scientific record, the psychological investi-

PHOTO 5.2   *Mark Lewis (Carl Boehm) cries, "I'm glad I'm afraid," before he kills himself*
in Peeping Tom *(1960).*

gation, the documentary, the pornographic photo, the police study—cannot substitute for instinct. Emotion is one thing, photography another.

This point is made again in the scene where Mark meets the psychiatrist who is
a consultant on the movie set. When Mark says that his job is to be the focus
puller, the doctor laughs and says, "So is mine in a way." But he then fails to "focus" on the anxious urgency in Mark's voice when Mark asks if he had known his
father. The doctor wants only to gain access to some important unpublished
manuscripts. The concluding words of the film, after Mark has died, with Helen
collapsed beside him on the floor, confirm this negative view of psychiatric science. We hear the taped voice of Mark's father saying distantly, "Don't be a silly
boy, there's nothing to be afraid of." Mark replies, in a small child's frightened
voice, "Good night Daddy . . . hold my hand." We must imagine that this never
happened: Real affection was always replaced by clinical study.

Peeping Tom forces us to get into Mark's head, at least to the extent of seeing
victims the way this murderer does.[10] The most problematic thing about this
movie is how attractive it makes the serial killer at its center. With his classic
blond good looks, neat clothes, polite phrasings and gentle manner, Carl Boehm
is one of the most engaging serial killers ever seen on screen. His quiet manner,

odd responses, and German accent link Boehm as Mark to Peter Lorre playing the repellent, yet still pitiful and sometimes sympathetic, child murderer in *M*. Yes, he is a madman, a psychopath, but he does not rave or foam at the mouth. Everything about him is explained so that we can understand his motives and see why he does what he does. He even knows this about himself and tells others he is a madman. He clearly expects to be tracked down and has planned suicide as an escape. So is he evil?

We wind up in a paradoxical position if we offer our own critical study of the film. By dichotomizing reason and feeling and by placing cinema on the side of reason, the movie appears to condemn us if we become overly analytic and judgmental. Reason tells us that Mark is an evil perverted killer, but our emotions might be guided by Helen's responses of sympathy and empathic interest. The film in effect forces us into a paradox if we try to form conclusions about this killer. As analytical investigators, we prove to be watchers in the very mode of Mark and his father, whom it criticizes. The analytical response is to infer that the film is a film about filming and to condemn such voyeurism. But emotional responses are another matter. We "can go to Mark's cinema" in the way Helen's mother does, through instinct. In this path, we start out as frightened viewers giving instinctive responses and recoiling from what we see, fear, and cannot comprehend.

Most important, as a monster Mark Lewis is *interesting*: The spectacles of violence in *Peeping Tom* are his spectacles, created by him and for us. To appreciate the film is in some sense to appreciate him and *his* spectacles of horror: He makes *himself* an ultimate spectacle of horror. We shall see whether this equation persists in the next two films.

Frenzy

Frenzy has been described as the filmic completion of a goal that Alfred Hitchcock could not consummate on the screen until relatively late in his life: *Frenzy* shows on-screen the murder that could only be hinted at in *Psycho*, due to prevailing censorship regulations.[11] Whereas *Psycho* conjured up a hideous crime by its now famous elaborate sequence of quick cuts, the horrific murder of a woman occurs before our very eyes in *Frenzy*, depicted on-screen with slow detail and in excruciating, graphic excess. *Frenzy* tells the story of a necktie murderer who strangles women; his serial crimes both haunt and titillate London in an old-fashioned Jack the Ripper fashion. We are set up at the start, by visual links from the tie around a victim's neck to the tie being donned by a young man, to expect that Richard Blaney (Jon Finch) is the necktie murderer. But soon we learn "firsthand," by watching the crime, that the killer is instead Blaney's friend, the charming greengrocer Bob Rusk (Barry Foster). Rusk visits the marriage bureau run by Blaney's ex-wife Brenda (Barbara Leigh-Hunt), but she recoils from him in disgust, insisting that her agency cannot provide for his peculiar and deviant sexual tastes. Rusk protests that people *like* him—he has good qualities and a lot to give. He then informs her that *she* is his kind of woman. As he sidles up to her, she becomes frightened; then he attacks, rapes, and strangles her.

This attack scene is extraordinary because it is so drawn out and anti-erotic. We watch as the charming and dapper Rusk becomes transformed into a crazed psychopath before our very eyes: here is a wolfman transformation with no makeup. His movements grow abrupt and violent: He opens drawers and slams them shut; he seizes Brenda's apple and takes a bite; he corners her and throws her down. She is no longer a capable businesswoman but a frightened-looking animal, rabbitlike with her large, soft brown eyes. When Rusk tears open her dress, one breast flops out into view—perhaps the most unerotic breast ever shown on screen in a rape or any other scene.[12] This breast is bare raw flesh, pinky-white and doughy as the man mauls her. He makes obscene pelvic thrusts just off camera and moans a refrain in crescendo, "Lovely . . . Lovely . . . *Lovely . . . Lovvvelly*!!" Then, suddenly enraged, he screams she is a "bitch" and strangles her (Photo 5.3). (We are later told by the police inspector that such men are impotent and become aroused only by violence.) The murder, like the rape, is shown as an uncommonly "fleshy" deed that requires sweat, grunts, and huge physical efforts. The camera alternates between the man's debased grimaces and the woman's desperate hands as she struggles to free her neck. This scene lasts for what seems a very extended time; when it is done, Rusk calmly steps back and resumes eating Brenda's apple. Her poor body lies, splayed and inert, before him. He shows no relish, regret, or triumph but simply walks away.

Apart from this familiar theme of sexualized violence, *Frenzy* focuses on another typical Hitchcock theme, the innocent man framed and trying to clear himself. Rusk sets Blaney up as the killer by stuffing a victim's clothes into Blaney's suitcase and calling the police. Blaney is arrested, convicted, and jailed in short order. This strikes viewers as wrong because Blaney is fairly sympathetic in the film. Down on his luck, the former Royal Air Force squadron leader is fired from his barman's job in the opening scenes and then wanders about looking lost. He visits his ex-wife Brenda, who takes him to dinner; he sleeps at a flophouse where he is nearly robbed; he finds money Brenda has left in his coat and spends it on a hotel room, to which he takes his barmaid girlfriend Babs Milligan (Anna Massey). Learning that he is under suspicion for the murder of Brenda, Blaney holes up with his friends Johnny and Hetty. Babs returns to work, then runs into Rusk, who seems the soul of kindness as he offers to help her hide out from the police—"no strings attached." The charming fellow leads Babs home. Suspense builds, and

PHOTO 5.3   *Brenda Blaney (Barbara Leigh-Hunt) is strangled in* Frenzy *(1973).*

then just as they are about to enter his door, he says insinuatingly, "Do you know, Babs, you're my kind of woman." This ominous phrase repeats the very words he has said to Brenda Blaney before killing her. He will, of course, proceed to murder Babs as well.

But the camera does something remarkable in this key scene: It withdraws. Instead of putting us through such torture again, Hitchcock ups the ante by requiring that we imagine and speculate about it. Rusk does kill Babs at this point, but we watch no other murders on the screen (seeing only hints of this one in a flashback and brief glimpses of Rusk's final victim). We do not accompany Babs into Rusk's room. Rather, the camera moves backward and silently reverses its path down the stairs, around a corner, out the building, and into the street. This reverse tracking shot takes several minutes. All is very silent in the hall; only gradually do we rejoin the outside world with its commotion and busy street noise. We can see Rusk's room with its neat flowers in the window boxes, but we cannot watch the murder taking place inside.

The camera withdraws from the spectacle at several other key scenes in *Frenzy* as well. After Rusk has murdered Brenda Blaney and left the scene, Blaney himself comes up to her office, perhaps to return the money she loaned him. Finding no one in, he leaves. Brenda's secretary, Monica Barling (Jean Marsh), sees him on the street. She goes inside, but the camera stays out in the street, which remains empty and quiet for the next few moments. Finally, two women come around the corner on-screen just as Monica's scream of discovery shocks the silence. Someone else has been tormented by this gory vision.

A similar withdrawal of the camera occurs at the climax of Blaney's trial for murder. The action has been telescoped: We cut instantly from Blaney's arrest to his trial. Our view is shared with a young constable who sits outside the courtroom; we only hear snippets as the door happens to open. We hear the judge reading the charge and asking the jury for their verdict. But the door swings closed, and we again watch the action within, silenced, from a distance. Finally, the curious constable cracks open the door, and we hear the judge intoning, "[Y]ou have been found guilty of a serious crime." Blaney is taken off to jail, screaming hysterically, "Rusk, Rusk did it!"

The plot of *Frenzy* sounds thoroughly grim. Not only is there a nasty psychopathic necktie strangler but an innocent, likable man is framed and convicted for his crimes. This is anything but a grim movie, however. Amazingly enough, it is funny, almost side-splitting at moments. Much of its persistent black humor concerns food. This humor somehow seems to associate women with food—often with bad, rotten, or even poisonous food—and has therefore been construed by feminists like Tania Modleski as adding to the disturbing misogynistic tone of the film.[13] As if the graphic murder of an innocent and helpless woman were not enough, the film hints that women are somehow at fault or to blame for male violence against them. This would be more disturbing even than the actual lurid nature of Brenda Blaney's murder.

There are almost too many examples of this black humor directed against women to mention. At the beginning, a fabulous airborne tracking shot takes us up along the Thames into the scene of a politician promising to clear up pollution of waterways. Meanwhile, the crowd spots a nude woman's body down in the muck—one of the necktie strangler's nude victims has been swept ashore as just one more piece of urban detritus. The "garbage" and not the litterer evokes the politician's disgust. Indeed, the killer is a figure of fascination. Two men in a pub gossip about him, commenting on how such serial murder is good for tourism. The woman serving the men comments salaciously, "I heard he rapes them," and one man winks and says, "Every cloud has a silver lining."

Brenda Blaney herself gets treated as both nurturer and food here. On the one hand, she takes her ex-husband to dinner and gives him money; on the other hand, she has served up some unhealthy recipes at her marriage service. We see that she has paired two seemingly mismatched individuals as we watch them leaving her office through Richard Blaney's mocking eyes. The woman, large and loud, towers over the small timid man, instructing him about how her first husband served breakfast in bed each day. Both Brenda and her secretary are depicted as prudish and yet prurient, disgusted but intrigued by talk of sex. Rusk wants to feed Brenda because her lunch is too frugal, but she smiles modestly at his talk of her opulent figure. Not only does Rusk, the greengrocer, associate her with the English apple he bites crisply into but he associates his own mother with the town she is from, Kent, "the garden of England." The large smiling mother is by implication the original nurturing figure, and now he craves more from Brenda's professional services.

Relationships are all awry in this film. Blaney's marriage to Brenda went badly wrong, perhaps because of his violence. When Babs is killed, Blaney seems upset, but less about her death than about being arrested for it. His friend Johnny, who promised him shelter and a job in Paris, is henpecked by his bitchy wife into reneging. Meanwhile, the policeman in charge of the necktie murder investigation, Inspector Oxford (Alex McCowen), suffers through a sequence of hilariously inedible dinners as he politely tries to eat the disgusting dishes with fancy French names that his wife (Vivien Merchant) cooks to show off after taking a course in gourmet cuisine (Photo 5.4).

But what is the real message of these scenes that associate women with flesh and food? Brenda's murder is sad and horrifying because her fleshy nature is so undeniable. Rusk's next murder, of Babs, takes this theme of women and food to yet another stage. The film deals not just with the fleshy nature of the woman being murdered but with the aftermath of murder, where she becomes even more firmly fleshy. In an amazing sequence in a potato truck, Hitchcock's black humor reaches its peak. Rusk realizes that he has made a mistake in hiding Babs's nude body in a potato sack when he finds his tiepin missing—the pin he always uses to clean his teeth. He runs to find it in the truck where the body is hidden; just as he begins his search, the truck takes off on its journey north. (Earlier we had seen Rusk discussing the vegetable business with a potato man, depressed that poor sales were forcing him to return a truckload of rotten potatoes.) Rusk must struggle now with Babs's body in full rigor mortis. Potatoes roll around, he sneezes from dust, the truck bounces along the highway; he even gets hit on the chin by a long leg and hard foot. Finally, when Rusk finds his tiepin, it is clutched in her tight grasp and to extricate it he must break her (dead) fingers one at a time. This horrific act against Babs's nude, defenseless, dead body is startling; it takes the black humor immediately into horror and offers at least an equal to his earlier disrespect of women when he murdered Brenda. My contention is that Hitchcock locates the association of women with food primarily in the flawed, even psychopathic, viewpoint of the male characters in the film (especially Rusk).

PHOTO 5.4   *Inspector Oxford's inedible fish soup in* Frenzy *(1973).*

What does this indicate about where Hitchcock himself is, here? Tania Modleski acknowledges that in part because the men's desires and characters are represented in the film as foul, the director shows sympathy to the plight of women in patriarchy.[14]

> [A]t the same time that *Frenzy* undoubtedly shares some of the contempt for and fear of women exhibited by the men in the film, it also portrays the main female characters more sympathetically than most of its male characters. Even more importantly, the film links the sexual violence it depicts to a system of male dominance rather than confining it to the inexplicable behavior of one lone psychopath.[15]

But even so, Modleski thinks that Hitchcock himself, not just the characters in the film, shows revulsion toward women. She writes:

> There is little doubt that part of what makes the crime Hitchcock depicts so repellent has to do with an underlying fear and loathing of femininity . . . In *Frenzy* ambivalence can be related to the polarity between woman as food vs. woman as poison (source of "pollution," "waste-product" of society, to use the politician's words).[16]

Modleski interprets the film as "a cultural response to women's demands for sexual and social liberation, demands that were, after all, at their height in 1972 when *Frenzy* was made."[17] Some of her evidence stems from other work in the director's oeuvre. But Modleski also thinks we need to consider "why women are the exclusive objects of rape and mutilation in the film or why it is their 'carcasses' that litter the film's landscape and not men's." Thus, she is critical of commentators who think that Hitchcock manifests equal disgust with both male appetites and female bodies.[18]

Modleski may be right: After all, Brenda's naked white flesh with that lolling breast does get compared to the delicious English apple that Rusk bites into both before and after killing her; Babs's dead flesh is depicted as dusty, foul, and browny-white, like the undesired and rotten potatoes that surround her body. Women are supposed to be nice, plump, and juicy—caretakers who nurture men. But is this Hitchcock's own view, or is it an ironic view he presents that is critical of the men in the film—particularly the repulsive killer Rusk? Rusk most clearly embodies this outlook. When Rusk learns that Blaney has been fired from his job, he gives Blaney a bunch of nice grapes and says, "Have Babs peel you one—at least you won't starve." It is quite possible logically to distinguish the director's viewpoint from one that he implies belongs to Rusk. Recall how Rusk shows off his own beaming mother by commenting that she is "from Kent, the garden of England." Hitchcock condescends to Rusk when he shows the greengrocer fantasizing about this motherly garden, or about visiting Spain or California, where his tropical fruits come from. Even more of this attitude is subtly present in how the film depicts Rusk's room décor: The man has pictures on his walls of stereotypical dusky-skinned romantic señoritas—presumably women he imagines as luscious because of their close acquaintance in his mind with sunny climes and exotic fruits.

I think it is similarly possible to see a duality in Hitchcock's treatment of the dinners shared by the police inspector and his wife. True, this woman is neither a tasty apple nor a rotten potato; she is instead a delicate and non-nourishing bird-like creature—she resembles the tiny quail she sets before her husband for dinner one night. Neither one can nourish the normal, pleasant inspector. But even though she seems to flutter about unable to tend to her husband's needs, Mrs. Oxford is far from birdbrained. She has insights that her husband lacks: He forces the course of Blaney's arrest as obvious and uncontroversial, whereas she immediately denies that Blaney could be the murderer of his wife, commenting that such a "crime de passion" would not likely occur after ten years of marriage. Later, she protests that woman's intuition tells her that certain things "stand to reason," such as Blaney's innocence. She even wants to invite Blaney over to dinner to make amends (her husband snidely replies, "Well, he's used to jail food, I suppose he'd eat anything").

PHOTO 5.5   Bob Rusk (Jon Finch) shows murderous rage in Frenzy (1973).

The real test of Modleski's thesis is to assess what the director's attitude is—as well as that which he invites viewers to share—during the crucial murder scene. Modleski thinks the scene is repellent because of how the female flesh in it is treated—"with an underlying fear and loathing of femininity." I disagree and find that this also fits poorly with Modleski's own claim that this breast is "infinitely sad" and "pathetic." The director presents a realistic picture of how a frenzied murderer sees female flesh; this does not mean that either he or we must share the view. Perhaps we can share it enough to imagine feeling that way, but this does not preclude the moral judgment that it is wrong, loathsome, or evil. It is perverse to insist on some form of a priori grounds, psychoanalytic or otherwise, that Brenda's body somehow is just more repellent than Rusk's murderous frenzy in this scene. The shots emphasize her fear, vulnerability, resignation, and soft flesh, in contrast to his strength, brutality, rage, and "frenzy" (Photo 5.5).

Another way to see this is to think about the striking contrasts between the murder scenes, and the depiction of the killer, in Frenzy and in Peeping Tom. Both films feature a killer who does violence against women. In Frenzy, Rusk is only superficially charming. He becomes revolting due to the way he kills. It is necessary to show the flesh in its fleshiness to show both how he feels and how difficult it is to take another person's life. These details make him out as more clearly, irrevocably, and also uninterestingly evil. Mark, by comparison, remains sympathetic right to the end in *Peeping Tom*. By creating sympathy for him, the earlier film is far more insidiously misogynistic. There is a deeper effort at psychological explanation in the earlier movie. We, like Helen, seek to understand what has gone wrong with Mark, what produced such a killer; female qualities are superficially praised by the film simply in order to absolve the murderous man. But Rusk in *Frenzy* is unexplained, apart from the brief picture we get of him with his beaming mother beside him in the window. To build a case of any proportions out of this—to presume that this alludes to a *Psycho*-style explanation of the pathogenic mother—is simply ungrounded in anything but film-theory logic. Rusk's murders make no sense: We do not see any rationale for his choices, except perhaps the fact that two of the women he targets are associated with Blaney; however, there is neither homoerotic attraction nor male rivalry to explain things in this way, either.

The scenes of spectacle in the two films present the most striking difference between them. *Peeping Tom* looks at the face of fear. The women's fears are what we ourselves must study as we watch the film. This need not mean feeling the fear or even empathizing with it. The film suggests that several of the women are not very appealing: They are not developed enough as personalities for us to care when they are killed. *Frenzy*, as its name suggests, looks at the woman's fear but also looks at the face of the killer while he kills Brenda, a decent woman who would feed and give money to her ex-husband. Murder is not a pretty sight; whereas *Peeping Tom* omits the blood and gore of deaths mediated by a weapon, as well as the aftermath of dealing with a heavy and recalcitrant body, the strangulations in *Frenzy* are immediate, personal, and flesh on flesh. We sympathize in this movie with the victim and not the killer. The killing is both more repulsive and more banal, precisely because it seems more random, mundane, and matter-of-fact. But killing in the real world is like that; monstrous killers in the real world may be banal, not psychologically deep, conflicted, or "interesting." *Frenzy* launches a new direction; it moves away from the explanations offered for Norman Bates or Mark Lewis. And the slasher killer will take on an even more extreme form as we witness the banality of his murders in the next movie I consider.

Henry: Portrait of a Serial Killer

Henry: Portrait of a Serial Killer is another story about a serial killer who targets women. The film flouts horror-movie conventions for suspenseful narrative.[19] Its opening scenes show an array of corpses accompanied by an eerie sound track, intercut with scenes of a young man (we infer he is the multiple murderer, Henry) talking to a waitress in a late-night diner. The film sets up the viewer to expect him to attack her, but nothing happens. Next, Henry follows a woman home from a shopping mall. Tension rises almost unbearably, but at the last moment as she arrives home, a man greets her, and Henry drives away. Even when Henry finally does kill, the film again flouts conventions by withholding the spectacle of the murder. Henry picks up a hitchhiker carrying a guitar and returns home later carrying her guitar. Then, in a long shot, we see a woman let Henry into her house with his exterminator's equipment. The audience is encouraged to expect to enter the house and witness a murder. Instead, the film cuts to a shot of a living room; a slow and impersonal pan reveals the woman, naked and dead. A third killing happens so fast and is so obscured that it barely has time to register. Henry snaps the necks of two prostitutes in his car, then goes with his friend Otis to buy a hamburger.

The plot of *Henry* seems flat and random. Certain events occur when Becky, the sister of Henry's roommate, Otis, moves into their small Chicago apartment and disrupts their somewhat repressed homosexual partnership. Victimized by incest, Becky has sought refuge with her brother, who also proves abusive. A parole violator and drug pusher, he repeatedly kisses Becky and demands to see her breasts, as her father had. Becky tries to normalize the household by getting a regular job and fixing meals, but her efforts fail. (At one point the film cuts from the corpse of the woman Henry has "exterminated" to a shot of a fish Becky is vigorously cleaning in the kitchen sink.)

Otis and Henry had met in prison, and when Becky asks Otis what Henry was in for, he at first refuses to say. "What did he do, kill his mama?" she asks. "Yes, he killed his mama with a baseball bat," Otis replies, as if it's a joke. Later, Becky pursues the subject with intense fascination. In the only scene in the film that tells us anything about Henry, the facts remain hazy. Henry says that he killed his mother, that he stabbed her to death. He tells Becky: "Daddy used to drive a truck before he got his legs cut off. My mama was a whore. But I don't fault her for that. She made me watch; she beat me; made me wear a dress and watch." Becky responds by confiding that she, too, was abused, by her father, then says gushingly, "I feel like I know you, have known you for a long time." Henry says, summing up, that yeah, he shot his mother on his fourteenth birthday. "Shot her?" Becky asks, "I thought you stabbed her." "Oh yeah," he says.

From this point on, the intensity of the killings in the film escalates. After a fight during a drug deal, Otis comments, "I'd like to kill somebody." Henry subsequently takes him out for sport to shoot a young man who stops to help with their car. Again, it is all over in a flash. Henry then murders a pawnshop owner

PHOTO 5.6   Otis (Tom Towles) and Henry (Michael Rooker) watch one of their murders on video in Henry: Portrait of a Serial Killer *(1986).*

after an argument over the purchase of a TV. He turns murder into a science, explaining to Otis how you must vary the method each time, switch guns so as not to be caught, and so forth. Henry remarks: "It's either you or them. Open your eyes, look at the world, Otis. You or them, you know what I mean."

The stage is now set for two especially gruesome final scenes of killing. First is the killing of a suburban family. In a long shot, the killers are shown approaching a house at night. Then the scene switches to a grainy, tilted home-video version of the family's murder. It will become apparent later that we are watching alongside the killers, who sit on their sofa reviewing this footage (recorded by their stolen camcorder) after the events (Photo 5.6). Point of view and real time are wrenched in a disconcerting way, with contradictory effects. On the one hand, the scene distances viewers and makes the murders seem less awful. The effect is as though we were just watching something on TV. The people in the family are already dead, depersonalized, not individuals. On the other hand, the amateur camera also makes the murders seem more real: Things happen unexpectedly; everything seems unplanned and awkward. The viewpoint is not standard, and the murders are not cleanly centered for our observation.

The most graphic and bloody of the murders in *Henry* is Henry's murder of Otis, whom he has caught raping Becky. Henry blinds Otis and then stabs him while lying atop his body in an orgiastic, sexualized attack. Henry chops up Otis's body and loads it into large garbage bags, which he packs into suitcases and dumps in the river. He leaves town with Becky, who looks at him and says, "I love you Henry." "I guess I love you, too," he responds. The car radio plays the song "Loving You Was My Mistake." They stop for the night at a motel room and get ready for bed. Becky looks trustingly up at Henry, who says it is time to turn in. The next morning we see Henry shaving with a straight razor, getting dressed, and leaving the motel room—alone. He piles suitcases into the car and later stops along the road to leave a large suitcase along the roadside. In close-up, we see blood seeping through the soft-sided case. That's it—she's dead. Inevitable. Henry drives on in his beat-up old Chevy. The movie ends.

What kind of monster is Henry in this movie? Is he an evil man? Is he a fascinating complex figure of evil like some vampires are? I would say that yes, he is evil, but his evil is neither fascinating nor complex. It is banal, summed up in his formulaic lesson to Otis: It is you or them. The character of Henry in this movie is unmotivated; he seeks neither intimacy in the seduction of souls nor the transvaluation of values. His only good point is that, at least temporarily, he is chivalrous to Becky. She responds by eroticizing him, and the film conspires in this as the camera lingers on the good-looking young actor, Michael Rooker, who plays Henry. He is treated throughout the movie iconographically as an angry young rebel in the Marlon Brando/James Dean mode, complete with his pout, mumbles, short curly hair, square jaw, and white T-shirt. What is most striking is that Becky begins to eroticize Henry just when she learns he is a killer—but isn't this the source of our fascination, too? Henry/Rooker's assimilation to the "angry young rebel" category is heightened by the film's promotional materials, which feature him scowling at himself in a mirror. (Indeed, when I watched the film on video, there were advertisements for Henry posters and T-shirts featuring the dark young man in a white T-shirt at the end of the tape.)

Henry provides a standard and clichéd psycho-film explanation for the behavior of its monster. When Henry was a child, his mother, who had a lot of lovers, symbolically castrated him by forcing him to wear a dress while watching her have sex. However, the fact that there are three different versions of this story marks it as a generic explanation and undermines its authenticity. The pathogenic role of the mother has become a familiar empty formula to us, a vague sort of hand-waving in the direction of "here's why he is the way he is." We notice this and then blithely move on, ready for the next murder or scene of mayhem.[20]

Another key feature of *Henry* is its displacement of interest from plot onto spectacle. *Henry* is not a narrative of discovery like *Peeping Tom* or *Frenzy*. Although those two films revealed the identity of the monster to us in the audience, they kept a narrative of unveiling in the foreground by focusing on the investigations and discoveries of a key figure, either Helen in *Peeping Tom* or Inspector Oxford in *Frenzy*. Spectacle does play a prominent role in those earlier films, but it is the very thing that structures the narrative of *Henry*. This film moves the viewer through a gradually intensified spectacle into climax and denouement. *Henry* shocks and announces its gory nature by its opening graphic sequence of nude corpses. But it reveals spectacle slowly, and the scenes that depict killings play with the viewer's emotions in nonstandard ways. When Henry and Otis kill the man in the pawnshop, the vicious and gruesome murder is rather comically cross-cut with a scene of Becky washing the hair of a large Chicago matron who spouts racist slogans. After this murder, the spectacles begin to crescendo through the murder of the family to climax in the particularly intense, brutal, and sexualized murder of Otis. Finally, as a diminuendo or anticlimax restoring symmetry with the opening sequences, *Henry* ends after implying the off-screen murder of Becky.

"Real" Monsters and Movie Spectacle

Henry: Portrait of a Serial Killer continues the direction launched in the slasher genre by *Peeping Tom* and *Frenzy* toward new forms of realistic or naturalistic horror. Based on a real serial murderer, *Henry* features a possible, hence a realistic, monster, a psychopathic serial killer. Henry represents a kind of reversal of both *Peeping Tom* and *Frenzy*. Whereas Mark kills with the eye of a documentary filmmaker and Rusk kills with frenzy, Henry kills for no particular reason, just on a whim. Like many of the more supernatural kinds of movie monsters, serial killers seem all-powerful, unpredictable, and, above all, sources of hideous violence. Their approach to some of their fellow humans is loathsome. We do not believe, while watching the movie, that this monster threatens us; and yet monsters like him *do* threaten us—there *are* men who kill others randomly on the streets, in stores, and in their homes. A monstrous killer like Henry is a possible being—the character is based, after all, upon a real Death Row killer, Henry Lee Lucas. What is monstrous about both versions of Henry, real-life and fictional, is not simply the deeds he has done but the attitudes he manifests toward them, especially the banality or the flatness of his affect. The real killer Henry Lee Lucas says: "It all seemed fun to start with, I should have my tail kicked for that. I just didn't have any willpower."[21] He is talking here about confessing, not about the murders themselves.

Many other horror films also feature a realistic or possible monster. As a new subgenre of horror, the slasher film would seem to be the antithesis of the vampire movie. Characters get less interesting and spectacles of violence become more graphic and prominent. Violence in the classic vampire film is often subtle and sanitized. Bites on the neck occur after the vampire has hypnotized his victim, so there is no struggle. Rather, the victim, usually a woman, simply swoons; she may even bare her neck as she passively awaits her undead lover. Blood, if shown at all, is a delicate dribble rather than a messy flow. As I showed in Chapter 4, vampire movies have increasingly focused on the psychology of either vampiric seduction or undead existence. But in the slasher film, the focus is on the weapon and on scenes of attack. We see blood and damage being done. Rather than focusing on how to combat an anomalous, unknown monster like a vampire, Alien creature, or mutant cockroach, we see the all-too-familiar "ordinary" human (a man) who commits "ordinary" (if newsworthy) violence. The film of this genre, as its name implies, highlights violent activities, often of repeated slashing, stabbing, or piercing. The primary link to the vampire genre is that this violent killing is lustful, sexualized, somehow driven by the monster's own nature. As we watch the killer deliver orgiastic thrusting motions, the knife or other weapon obviously functions as phallus. Everyone knows (like the teenagers in *Scream*) this is what such violence "means."

It is common for us to refer to contemporary serial killers and other "heroes" of realist horror films as monsters. Jeffrey Dahmer and Ed Gein, as much as "Buffalo Bill" and Hannibal Lecter in *The Silence of the Lambs*, are horrific, loathsome, disgusting creatures that skin, eat, or have sex with corpses and kill without remorse. Our interest in killers like Henry Lee Lucas or Dahmer—the basis on which they quickly achieve a certain celebrity status—seems to amount to a direct fascination with the sheer fact of their monstrousness. Movie or TV versions of their stories may surround their vile deeds with context by supplying an alleged meaning or motivation; but the manifestation of such fundamental human evil remains baffling. Symbolic enrichment on film often lends such evil (perhaps because of its mystery) an odd erotic edge—we see this in films like *Henry* or *The Silence of the Lambs*, films that pair the monster somehow with a sympathetic young woman.

The slasher subgenre of the horror film shifts emphasis away from plot to monstrous graphic spectacle. Some might consider the movement away from evil monsters like vampires and toward serial killers as a degradation of the horror genre. A theorist of evil like C. Fred Alford would see things in much the same way; the prevalence of slashers means that our culture fails to supply symbols that are sufficiently serious, complex, and interesting to help us face up to hard issues about evil. Alford does not even think that vampires are interestingly evil, let alone a slasher killer: Film slashers are too much like the real murderers whom Alford studied, whose conceptions of evil were shallow and bankrupt, like Henry's. As Alford sees it, the real-life killers enacted stories of evil in violence upon people's bodies due to their lack of richer imaginative resources to combat an inner emptiness or dread.[22]

The notable distinction between the slasher, a natural but banal human killer, and the vampire, an unnatural but interesting monster, has led Noël Carroll to deny that slasher killers should be counted as horror-movie monsters. Carroll argues in *The Philosophy of Horror* that men like Norman Bates in *Psycho* are not monsters because they can be given a naturalistic explanation—as indeed happens at the movie's conclusion. Carroll emphasizes the *fictitious* nature of the monster in horror by defining a monster as "any being not believed to exist according to reigning scientific notions."[23] He considers this restriction essential to keeping the emphasis on narrative or plot, thus to preserving the particular distanced and aesthetic response of art-horror. Carroll almost seems to see in the new monster of the slasher film, the psychotic killer, a sort of falling away from some kind of essence of horrific monstrousness. A film like *Psycho* is not horror because the monster in it, Norman Bates, is naturalized: "He is a schizophrenic, a type of being that science countenances."[24]

Movies like *Peeping Tom, Frenzy,* and *Henry: Portrait of a Serial Killer* are like *Psycho* in that they violate the definition of horror-film monsters laid out by Carroll. But I would insist that even if Mark Lewis, Bob Rusk, and Henry are true-to-life rather than supernatural beings, they *are* monsters. Further, the slasher film is such a prevalent and important subgenre that it obviously deserves consideration in any discussion of the nature of evil in horror films. My examples span three decades, and there are countless others. The exclusion of the slasher film from the horror genre reflects a larger issue about the role of spectacle in the horror film. We saw in the three examples I have discussed that the graphic spectacle of violence (usually directed against women) is at the forefront of the slasher genre. The killer's violence is something that really might happen, and the way it is shown on the screen sometimes makes it difficult to sustain an intellectual, aestheticized attitude toward it: The slasher gets us in the gut. But this does not fit with Carroll's deeper aims in his book. He in effect defends the status of the troubling genre of horror by denying that the audience's primary interest is in graphic spectacle. Instead, he argues that the enjoyment of horror is focused primarily on plot, which provides the cognitive pleasures of investigation and problem solving.

These are presumably higher and more worthy than a direct interest in spectacles of gross violence.

Carroll's view falls in with opinions advanced by a long line of philosophers who have displayed suspicions about the attractions of spectacle in art. An interest in spectacles was also seen as inhuman and demeaning in classical Greek attacks upon tragedy. Plato categorized our drive toward violent spectacle as lowest among his rank ordering of human desires.[25] Aristotle's *Poetics* defended tragedy by rejecting the notion that the audience responds with a direct, problematic interest in fearful violence; but even Aristotle argued that spectacle is the "least artistic" of tragedy's six parts.[26] He describes plot structures to explain that there were loftier audience interests in tragedy—that it can offer cognitive challenges leading to an emotional *katharsis*. Carroll similarly argues that the horror genre evokes a distinct aesthetic or distanced response, a response to fiction and not real life, which depends upon a cognitive interest in plot or artifice. Because we enjoy tracking the suspenseful narrative, we put up with the revulsion that Carroll calls "art-horror."[27] This is a distanced emotional response that refers to a representation, not a reality: Although monsters in horror are repellent and scary, they do not threaten us directly, and we are protected by knowing they are in fact impossible. They fascinate us because they violate our conceptual categories, arousing in us a strong desire to know something unknowable.

Carroll's concerns about the role of spectacle in slasher horror mirror feminist critiques of this subgenre. All the movies I have mentioned feature graphic representations of disturbing male violence against women. One natural feminist response is to decide not to watch them—even to protest or dismiss them from serious consideration. It is easy to argue that slasher movies, mostly directed by men, are simply manifestations of patriarchy's contempt or hatred for women. But I would respond that although the films do manifest disturbing and sexist ideology, they function in ways that are more complex—perhaps even more insidious— than might be first recognized. In fact, the films I have selected actually open a path toward critical reflection because they make an issue out of particular representations of sexualized violence against women. These are not just representations of violence but are films that ask us to reflect on the troubling messages that they present about the nature of evil—about its association with men (i.e., male humans in particular) and the possibilities of confronting it.[28]

We must go beyond the limitations of a somewhat immediate feminist condemnation or of Carroll's "Aristotelian," or classical, approach to horror to study violent spectacle and its role in the realist slasher horror film. Such films raise hard questions about the nature of audience interest in these new figures of monstrous evil. I would propose that even if we are interested in spectacles like those in the films we have considered, we do still see the films *as* representations; and their naturalistic monsters are still the creatures of artifice. Ambivalence about the immediate spectacle of violence is the theme of these movies. They are striking not just for their depiction of the killer at their center but for the way in which they link this monster to the horrific spectacle so as to *make an issue of* our interest in it. To look only at spectacle here and to denounce either its seeming direct appeal or its surface violence against women is to fail to respond to the complexity of these films as films. They foreground spectacle to evoke ambivalence, both interest and revulsion, prompting some form of moral analysis.

Let me expand on my claim that these films themselves make spectacle the issue. *Peeping Tom*'s killer is a voyeur who films the murders he commits. We watch the murders through his camera, and we see his victims' faces reflected in his mirror. The movie clearly involves us in his aggressive search to get the perfect picture of fear, pointing out alternatives to Helen's intuitions and emotions. It offers a sort of moral closure when the presumed perfection can only be found as he commits suicide. *Frenzy* shows an act of murder where the violence against the woman's body is very graphic, reaching a new level of on-screen, horrific violence. But *Frenzy*, too, provides a moral resolution when the innocent man is finally cleared and the guilty one is caught, in the last scene. *Henry: Portrait of a Serial Killer* is more disturbing both because of its realism of style and its amoral viewpoint. It violates the usual rules of both the horror genre in general and the slasher in particular: It offers no audience identification figure, nor does its plot depict any righting of wrongs.[29] *Henry* succeeds by creating terror and unease, both promising and withholding the spectacle of violence, as Henry also films and later watches his own murders—and we watch beside him. This film, like the other two, makes us contemplate our interest in the subject by forcing us to watch what the killer watches, his own crimes. A major problem I have pointed out with this film is that it takes the moral high ground in suggesting narratively that Henry is banal and uninteresting but undercuts this message through its visual depiction of an attractive, sexy, and "interesting" rebellious killer.

If slasher killers are not interestingly evil, as Alford would say, then why do they continue to populate the screen? But if they are interestingly evil—and I am afraid that they are—what does this tell us about ourselves? I maintain, contra Carroll, that our fascination with serial killer monsters persists in the face of a basic frustration of our desire to "understand" or explain them. If the serial killer monster is given any motives at all, they are empty formulaic sexual ones that play upon societal assumptions about aggressive male sexuality. Indeed, in a reversal of the usual relation of reality to representation, clichéd horror film "explanations" are now trotted out in news accounts of real cases and purported scientific explanations of violent sex crimes:

In sado-sexual killings, "the payoff is erection and orgasm," said forensic psychiatrist Park Dietz of Newport Beach, Calif. The highly popular "slasher" and horror movies incessantly exploit precisely that combination. On the screen, "the baby sitter starts to take off her bra," Dietz said, "which makes the kid in the audience get sexually excited. Then Jason comes in and decapitates her."[30]

Feminists are right to complain that the particular sort of graphic violence typical of the slasher killer film—as evidenced in the three I have examined in this chapter—targets women in reprehensible ways.[31] In the three films I have discussed, the monster is a male killer who targets women. But the sexism lies at levels beyond the screen violence: It resides in the "interest" of the monster, his sexiness, and in the implied moral analysis. Although all three men are clearly evil and loathsome, the films do not exactly treat them this way—at least, not consistently. The monster is at first shown as fascinating, sad, conflicted, and sympathetic *(Peeping Tom)*; then as a figure of certain comic and repulsive fascination, emblematic of man's inhumanity to man and of our lives in a world that is "not the Garden of Eden" *(Frenzy)*; and finally as an eroticized rebel, updated to the 1980s, a man out to get others before they get him *(Henry)*. It is women who cue our reactions to the killers; here, as in the mad-scientist movies I considered earlier, men *act* and women *react*. Helen cries over Mark's dead body, Becky pities and tries to love Henry, and before she dies, Brenda Blaney tries to appease Bob Rusk so as to suffer the least damage possible. But why are women forced to deal with these monstrous men in the first place? Some feminists would argue that the only way to deconstruct or undo the damaging myths of fascination of monstrous killers is to argue, persuasively and rationally, that they are not extraordinary or monstrous and deserve no particular attention.[32]

I think, perhaps cynically, that such a move is too utopian; it is impossible to undo the mechanisms that currently exist for making such evil male killers sympathetic, interesting, and famous (Mark Harmon, the actor portraying Ted Bundy, for instance, was once dubbed the "sexiest man alive" by *People Magazine*). A less utopian, but also less cynical, alternative is to maintain, as a cognitivist might, that audiences can enjoy a filmic spectacle in ways that are not simple and transparent. We may assess and read a slasher movie by seeing it *as* a hyperbolic charade as well as by directly critiquing it. Surely we have begun to take the spectacle to extreme forms that make it deconstruct itself when we find the repulsive one-eyed short and dumpy Henry Lucas recycled into the handsome Brandoesque Michael Rooker. Hitchcock's black humor maintains distanced and aesthetic responses to what is at the same time a disturbingly realistic movie. Can audiences really be duped into liking the cannibal killer Hannibal Lecter without being aware of how well this mad genius-villain is being played by the well-known and popular Anthony Hopkins (in an Oscar-winning performance)? To reflect here on a movie as a representation involves confronting real and disturbing issues along the way about our fascination with killers and with the very spectacle we are watching.

I have pointed out an insidiously troublesome feature of realist horror: the emotional burden these films bring to women. Such films often target and victimize viewers by playing on the fascination of the monster so as to eroticize him or to elicit sympathetic understanding. The killer is someone driven by blood lust like a vampire; he cannot help his nature. Male sexual desire in these films is a force easily channeled into destructive violence if its "natural" aims are blocked or thwarted. Furthermore, women often "ask for it": They place themselves knowingly into danger and behave seductively; by the films' logic, they "deserve" punishment for their sexual boldness, much like Lucy in *Dracula*. The vampire's predation and that of the slasher killer are depicted alike as the sexualized attack of a male human upon a woman, as even something that the woman longs for and enjoys. The woman fantasizes about the vampire or slasher, or she lures him from far distances; she is, then, the one "responsible" for his attack. Faced with either Lucy's bold innuendoes or Mina's purity and goodness, Dracula can scarcely resist. Like Frankenstein's monster, he is compelled by any vision of loveliness. Since slasher films typically depict an attractive woman as the killer's target, they perpetuate this sort of a view. *Psycho,* too, developed this theme and implicated the viewer, who voyeuristically watches the notorious shower scene where Norman Bates attacks the "nude" Janet Leigh.

In the slasher genre, as in some *Dracula* movies, women characters often fill in the gaps behind the inexpressive and unhappy man, making the banal killer like Henry into someone deep and interesting. This is as true in the presentation of "real" cases (Dahmer, the Menendez brothers, Bundy) as it is in the fictive examples of Henry or Mark Lewis. Even Bob Rusk asks for Brenda's sympathy by wheedling: "I have my good points. I like flowers and fruits." A film like *Henry* eroticizes the killer by linking him to traditional Hollywood film heroes like James Dean and Marlon Brando. Of course, from Gary Cooper to Clint Eastwood, this hero has been strong, potentially violent, inept at communicating, independent, and the rest. Significantly, although many real-life serial killers (like Dahmer) prey on young men or boys, this sort of killer has not been made the focus of major films, presumably because he violates the clichéd association between potent maleness and heterosexuality. In other words, realist horror creates links between the "dark side" of male traits (violence, uncontrolled sexuality) and the heroic side (power, independence, and so on). This means that realist horror legitimizes patriarchal privilege through the stereotyped and naturalized representation of male violence against women. These cultural narratives treat male violence as an inevitable concomitant of normal male sexuality:

> At a minimum, Dietz said, two conditions are necessary to produce a sexual serial killer: a psychopathic personality and a highly developed sadistic tendency. The former is in ample supply. According to studies done for NIMH [National Institute of Mental Health], about one in twenty urban males is psychopathic—that is, lacking normal inhibitory feelings of guilt or remorse and operating outside familiar social or moral constraints.[33]

In realist horror, male sexuality is a ticking time bomb, a natural force that must be released and will seek its outlet in violence if it is frustrated or repressed. Since women, and standardly the monster's mother (as in *Henry*, *Frenzy*, *Psycho*, or real-life accounts of criminals like John Hinckley Jr.), are scapegoated as sources of this repression, they are shown somehow to "deserve" the violence they evoke. The net effect is that we simply accept as a natural and inevitable reality that there will be vast amounts of male violence against women.[34]

Nevertheless, I believe that the formulaic depictions of violent male sexuality in realist horror can come to be seen *as* just that—formulas. Films like *Henry*, *Frenzy*, or *Peeping Tom* may actually lead audience members to question their own fascination with the monstrousness of the serial killer and to query such formulas and the associated icons of male heroism. This is a tricky point to demonstrate. Realist horror films like *Frenzy* may toy with or parody the standard *Psycho* explanations that scapegoat women, particularly mothers, for male violence. I have suggested that something like this occurs in *Henry*, a film that relies upon but simultaneously empties out the formula "he did it because of his mother." Similarly, in Chapter 6, we shall see that *The Silence of the Lambs* contrasts one stereotyped psycho killer whom the FBI can explain ("Buffalo Bill") with another whom they cannot begin to fathom. Although many news accounts struggled to attribute to the Luby's restaurant (Killeen, Texas) mass murderer George Hennard a motive stemming from his rejection by local women, others looked beyond this to discuss the man's work history, war record, and access to guns.[35]

The slasher horror film often involves very realistic depictions of ordinary men who become killers. It highlights spectacle over plot, and this means that one ideological effect of such narratives is to perpetuate a climate of fear and random violence where anyone is a potential victim. These films have messages that are troubling on grounds beyond feminist objections. They often obscure the truth about factors that produce a climate of violence: inequities in education, health care, social and economic status, and political power; urban blight and flight; racism; drug use; and gun laws. Thus, instead of the slasher horror film prompting action and resistance, it works to produce passivity and legitimize current social arrangements. Slasher horror even furthers a conservative agenda pushing for increased censorship in campaigns by targeting films and not actual social conditions.

A Final Word on Spectacle

Slasher horror offers itself as unusually realistic: It presents violent spectacles with an uncanny immediacy right before our eyes—reflecting the immediacy that the camera also facilitates on our nightly news. The play between fiction and reality about monsters is very complex. Numerous film characters (like Henry or Norman Bates or Hannibal Lecter) are based on real killers. There are also docudrama films about real killers (like Ted Bundy) and re-created "reality TV" shows enacting deeds of real killers (like George Hennard). In addition, real killers in the news (like Dahmer) may be described in terms of fictional killers (Lecter). Or real killers may have been inspired by fictional killers. John Hinckley Jr. committed his crime after obsessively identifying with film character Travis Bickle in *Taxi Driver*. Bickle's character was modeled on real attempted assassin Arthur Bremer, who was himself inspired by the film character Alex in *A Clockwork Orange*. Hinckley corresponded with serial killer Ted Bundy (before his execution)—subject of his own TV movie, *Deliberate Stranger*.[36] Other real killers or slashers in the news (the Menendez brothers, Lorena Bobbitt) become celebrities in trials that construct them in the media as alternative types of fictional characters (abused victims or vengeful villains).[37]

As news and reality interweave, there is a diminishing role for the constructedness of plot. Plots in the most recent examples of slasher films, such as *Henry*, become more like stories on the nightly news, which are dominated by the three "R's": random, reductive, repetitious. Both are about gruesome acts, spectacle, and aftermath more than about action, downfall, motives, mistakes, and justice. Thus, it becomes inappropriate to speak of any specifically aesthetic or distanced reaction of art-horror that is grounded in plot. Like the news, realist horror evokes real, albeit paradoxical, reactions. Such films are emotionally flattening (familiar, formulaic, and predictable in showcasing violence) and disturbing (immediate, real, gruesome, random).

The fact remains, of course, that films like *Peeping Tom*, *Frenzy*, and *Henry: Portrait of a Serial Killer* are films and not news programs. They are highly constructed artifacts, and they have merits as such. They are well-made constructions or representations that effectively carry out their aims of evoking suspense and horror; they are subtle and do not wear their "messages" on their surface. Such films force us to attend to the very problem of moral perverseness that we may prefer to avoid: We are somehow attracted to monsters and to the horrific spectacle itself. The orchestrated representation of violence evokes an ambivalent thrill as we react to realistic depictions of horrific events we know to be possible.[38] Standard critiques of our direct interest in such monsters and spectacles are often both simplistic and naive. A subtler sort of moral assessment recognizes the intricacy of interconnections between the news and film plots. We have also seen that some slasher movies themselves deal with the representational character of violence in realist horror.

The films I have discussed play a great deal not just upon reality but upon the new tradition to which they belong. They are films about films, in the sense of being about filmmaking (as we see obviously with the inclusion of the camera in two of them) or being about films in a vaguer sense (as we may infer by the ways in which *Frenzy* relates to *Psycho* and to Hitchcock's other movies). This means that in these films, an interest in spectacle need not be quite as disturbing as Carroll fears. When we watch the spectacle, our interest may not simply be in what is shown, a vision of suffering and traumatic violence, but also in how and why it is shown. These are the matters I have attended to in attempting to provide a subtler and more nuanced moral assessment of how evil is treated in these three different slasher films.[39] In a cognitivist framework, a "good" reading should say how a film is structured to elicit certain responses in the audience—judgments, hypotheses, and emotions; but we can also note that the audience may not exactly agree with or be unified in the reactions it has to the movie. Audiences may resist or even subvert ideological messages of slasher horror.

Even if we are members of the masses, we bear some responsibility for our participation in the spectacularization of violence.[40] The slasher horror film, by its very hyperbolic excess, may actively encourage the audience in its critical awareness of its own interest in spectacle. Recall that *Henry*, for example, is a particularly self-reflexive movie that forces viewers into the viewpoint of the murderers themselves as we become spectators, alongside Henry and Otis, watching their video-recorded home movies of murders. This naturally prompts audience unrest and questions, so I do not think it is sufficient to analyze it as an exercise in ideological control. Other horror films with naturalistic killers also allude to the use of surveillance devices in our culture to problematize the spectacle of violence. In *Menace II Society* the character O-Dog is criticized for repeatedly watching and screening a videotape that recorded his murder of a Korean store owner.

The slasher horror film may also be seen to use random, formulaic, or recycled, self-referential plots to challenge conservative, patriarchal social agendas. Despite the fact that the monsters in realist horror are typically men who exercise hideous

violence against women, they are also men who do not participate in the traditional patriarchal order (law, politics, the working world, medicine, religion,
morality, and so on). The killers in *Henry*, *Frenzy*, and *Peeping Tom* are men who
are "losers" in marginal jobs and have little social standing or political power.
Similarly, the psychotic assassin Lear in *In the Line of Fire* is clearly shown to be a
product of our government's, specifically the CIA's, training in assassination. The
film blithely depicts a situation in which key government agencies withhold secrets
and engage in subversive power plays against one another. Films like *Henry*, *Frenzy*,
and *Peeping Tom* actually do portray conditions of everyday violence in our culture: drifters living in poverty, jobless farmers, racist matrons in beauty shops,
Iowa farm girls who are victims of incest, bums mugging one another in city parks,
racist policemen, children raised in a drug culture, women making money by posing for pornographers, and so forth. Realist horror films with slasher killers can
raise disturbing problems because they present horrific events and focus on problematic spectacles of violence. Increasingly, slasher horror showcases spectacle,
downplays plot, and plays upon confusions between representations of fiction and
reality. But these movies do feature monsters and do function as filmic representations. They make us think more about evil as a depiction.

Slasher horror paves the way for even more graphically violent horror films like
some of the ones I will discuss in Chapter 8—*The Texas Chainsaw Massacre* and
the *Hellraiser* series. Such films go further in using visual excess as a mode of
structuring narrative; I will compare them to other genres of visual display, like
the musical and pornographic film, where minimal plots serve the "real thing"
that the film promises to deliver: scenes of tremendous visual spectacle.[41]

chapter
six: Feminist Slashers?

In this chapter, I will consider two films that foreground women as they focus on the peculiar evil of gruesome murders: *Repulsion* (Roman Polanski, 1965) and *The Silence of the Lambs* (Jonathan Demme, 1991). Each film tells the story of a horrific killer—a man in *The Silence of the Lambs* (two men, actually), and a woman in *Repulsion*. On the face of it, *The Silence of the Lambs* looks like an obvious candidate—if such a thing can be proposed—for a feminist slasher film. The movie was hailed by critics for its portrayal of a strong heroine, Clarice Starling (Jodie Foster, in an Academy Award–winning performance). She is a young FBI agent who not only tracks and kills the serial murderer "Buffalo Bill" but courageously faces off with the even worse cannibalistic killer, Dr. Hannibal Lecter (Anthony Hopkins, who also took home an Oscar). By contrast, *Repulsion* seems profoundly distinct, even antifeminist, for its depiction of a woman killer who murders men because of her extreme sexual repression and paranoia. Each film begins from a fundamental assumption about the existence of evil in our world, but they reach very different conclusions about its sources as well as about the possibilities of confronting it. In the end, *Repulsion* is more deeply probing in its explorations of both evil and gender ideology, despite the surface appearance of greater feminism in the more recent film.

Repulsion

Repulsion presents itself as a horror story in which a very beautiful and sexy woman, Carol Ledoux (Catherine Deneuve) becomes a mad slasher and villain who attacks and destroys men. We might now look back upon this movie as a sort of film noir that anticipated the recent spate of villainous females of the *Fatal Attraction* or *Basic Instinct* sort. Such a position is adopted, for example, by Andrew Tudor in his book *Monsters and Mad Scientists: A Cultural History of the Horror Movie*. Tudor comments that the film "traces a young woman's collapse into homicidal psychosis in almost documentary detail while implying some imprecise connection between sexuality, repression, and insanity."[1]

Carol, it might be said in Tudor's terms, is an alluring yet shy and inhibited femme fatale. Throughout the film, she seems unable to respond to men's advances. She does not reciprocate her handsome cousin Michael's attentions, and she languishes alone in bed in the apartment she shares with her sister, who vocally enjoys lovemaking with a boyfriend. When this sister goes off on vacation, Carol's repressions reach a peak (or nadir): She becomes too phobic to leave the apartment and so frightened of hallucinatory male attackers that she winds up killing two men (Michael and then the landlord) who come to see her. On this somewhat obvious line of interpretation, Carol is a woman whose repressed sexuality must unleash itself—and it does so ultimately in acts of horrific violence against the men she desires. This view of her as repressed and even voyeuristic might seem to be confirmed by various aspects of the plot and the filmic depiction of Carol: She dresses demurely, speaks in a low voice, walks down the street with her head down, bites her nails, hides behind her long pale blond hair, constantly peers with anxiety out the windows of her flat at a school run by nuns next door, listens intently to her sister's sexual moans and cries, and inspects and throws away the shaving glass used by her sister's lover in a fit of jealous pique.

However, this surface reading fails to capture what is of interest in *Repulsion*. Many of the point-of-view shots in the movie serve to identify us (as audience members) with men who leer at Carol, from her would-be boyfriend to her lusting landlord to the construction workers who jeer and whistle at her as she walks past them on the sidewalk (Photo 6.1). The camera is often positioned so as to spy on Carol as she walks along; it hovers just behind her hair or right at her cheek; it helps account for the anxious response she feels at being constantly the object of unwanted attention. By trying to glimpse her face as she hides, we also become intrusive spectators spying on her personal affairs (Photo 6.2).

There are also occasions when the film switches to adopt Carol's own viewpoint. (This ambiguity is signaled by the film's opening and closing shots, each of which are tight close-ups of her eyes: We both look at these eyes and have a sense of them looking out.) Since we share Carol's perceptions, we uncomfortably become even more aware of the reasons for her anxiety. We experience the world from her point of view as she is chased or visually assaulted by all the men in her immediate envi-

PHOTO 6.1   *A construction worker leers at Carol in* Repulsion *(1963).*

ronment—when a construction worker shouts propositions at her on the street or when she looks out the apartment peephole to find a huge man's head peering in at her. These point-of-view devices show Carol as a victim who merits our sympathy and empathy. Along these lines, we can reinterpret the feelings she has in the scene where she overhears her sister's lovemaking by examining her facial responses and behavior. These indicate less a feeling of jealousy and voyeurism than one of tormented embarrassment: Carol shows her desire to escape by pummeling her pillow and then burying her head in it to drown out the sounds.

In support of such a sympathetic reading, we should also note that the dialogue and narrative clearly indicate that Carol feels threatened by her sister's involvement with a lover: She fears abandonment, especially when her sister departs with the man for vacation (Carol repeatedly begs her not to go). Left alone in the flat, Carol becomes increasingly psychotic and delusional. As she goes mad, the audience's point of view is once again Carol's; we share her heightened perceptions, nightmares, and hallucinations. The sound track for *Repulsion* is very disruptive. It is unusually silent: Small noises loom large, like a dripping faucet, ticking clock, dogs barking, or someone playing piano scales in a nearby apartment. But there are also

PHOTO 6.2   *We relentlessly spy on Carol (Catherine Deneuve) as she begins to go crazy in* Repulsion *(1963).*

sudden assaults, both aural and visual. Polanski shocks and frightens us in parallel to Carol by, for example, depicting a crack in the wall that suddenly opens up and gapes wide with an earthquake's noisy rumble. Even worse, he shows faces that suddenly materialize from behind Carol in mirrors, hands that reach out from rubbery walls to grab and fondle her breasts, or menacing shadows that creep across her bedroom ceiling. All these visual assaults have unnerving aural accompaniment, whether shrieking sirens, loud drums, pulsing modern music, or weird and threatening grunts. Strange and unpredictable sounds enter abruptly from the outside world: clanging bells from the convent school next door, shrilling phone calls and doorbells, the odd music of a hurdy-gurdy band of elderly men on the streets below.

Given this increasingly deranged system of perceptions, we may reach the moral assessment that Carol's reaction when she kills the men who enter her apartment is a reasonable response to a genuine threat. After all, these men do literally break the door down to rush in upon her. Michael, who first knocks it down, apologizes but says he simply "had to see her." And then after Carol has nailed the door shut, her sleazy and lecherous landlord also breaks in. He forces his attentions on her, offering to accept something other than money for his rental payments: "You look after me and you can forget about the rent." "Repulsion" has a dual meaning here—it refers both to what Carol feels and to what she does. She dumps the first man's body in the bathroom and places it in the tub, as if to wash it clean. When she later visits the bathroom, the camera's lens offers a distorted image, suggesting her avoidance of vision by marginalizing the tub, pushing it off into the distance, as if visually signifying her attempts to deny its existence. (This scene is reminiscent of Beverly's avoidance of Elliot's disemboweled body at the conclusion of *Dead Ringers*, where the camera similarly conspires with the mad killer and averts its gaze.)

I would argue then that what is shown as evil in *Repulsion* is not the devious and sexually predatory woman killer, like the women in *Basic Instinct* or in *Fatal Attraction*; it is instead lechery or male attitudes of lust toward a beautiful woman who cannot escape the consequences of her objectification. The film highlights Carol's rough treatment by men and shows her inability to escape their threatening presence: She is never safe because she is constantly the target of men who wolf-whistle at her on the street, press her for dates, or attack her in her own apartment. Her cousin forces a kiss on her (encouraged by his lascivious friends from the bar); her landlord tries to rape her. She cannot escape even at home, where her sister's lover has carelessly scattered his personal hygiene items all around the bathroom—he has even put his toothbrush in her glass. He insists on his brute, hairy, male physicality in a way that disgusts Carol, especially when she finds his dirty undershirt on the floor. She is also trapped in her job as a manicurist as a cog in the wheels of the beauty industry, adorning women so that they may please men. Sequences at work show hilarious but grotesque matrons, masked in facials, their grimacing mouths huge on the screen as they complain that "there's only one thing they [men] care about—they're all the same." We also observe Carol's sobbing friend Bridget, who has been let down by her lover.

Repulsion strongly hints that Carol's psychosis and sexual repression stem from a history of child sexual abuse. Some disturbing sequences of the film convey Carol's nightmare memories of sexual assault. The film's naturalistic editing and conventional visual vocabulary alter in these scenes, which are disruptive and fragmentary: the sound track is quiet except for a loudly ticking clock. A man comes into the room and Carol screams silently as her hands grasp the bedclothes in distress. A face presses upon hers and someone grabs her hair. These nightmare sequences fit with and give us directions to understand the meaning of the family photograph that we are shown at several crucial points during the film. This photograph sits near a mantle covered with toys that are the remnants of Carol's childhood. At our first viewing, it seems a perfectly normal group, a middle-class

PHOTO 6.3   *The family photograph showing Carol as a young girl in* Repulsion *(1963).*

family that sits smiling on lawn chairs. We should be put off, though, by realizing that Carol seems to eye it from afar with fear. Then at the second viewing, the nasty landlord picks it up and comments, "Your family? How nice!" even taking it over to the light to examine, while Carol huddles fearfully on the sofa. In the closing sequence, after Carol has been carried away inert and catatonic, the camera pans again around her toys to linger on this photograph, now knocked onto the floor. We see it at the end of a very long slow sweep that takes in the apartment in disarray, with its debris from the murder, cracker crumbs scattered about, and so on. The focus zooms in very close to show a young blond girl we presume is Carol (Photo 6.3). She looks disturbed and frightened, her eyes turned fearfully to one side, looking at a man—perhaps the uncle who is "visiting her," as she told her landlord. This sequence returns us to the huge close-ups at the start of the film showing what we may now understand to be Carol's frightened and blinking eye. Ultimately, we move in so close to the image that it decomposes into a meaningless blur—like Carol's state of mind, we presume.

Perhaps the central and uniquely horrific image in this movie, however, involves not masculine aggression toward Carol, nor the murders she commits, nor yet again Carol's scary hallucinations. Rather, it resides in a series of shots depicting the carcass of a rabbit that Carol's sister has left in the refrigerator. We first hear about this rabbit when Carol refuses a date with Michael because her sister is planning to cook rabbit at home. "I thought they'd all been killed," says Michael, and Carol responds, "My sister has a friend—" "A rabbit?" he interrupts, laughingly, and she continues, "No, her friend has rabbits." "Poor bunny," says Michael. This brief conversation ties Carol in somehow to the "poor bunny" as a potential victim of masculine aggression—since the "friend with rabbits" proves to be her sister's married lover. When he arrives at the apartment, Carol's sister says to him, "I'm cooking your rabbit," and she even shows him a recipe. That meal gets postponed, though, when the lover decides to take her out, so his rabbit is left behind to haunt Carol. While she is left alone, Carol looks for food and removes the meat from the refrigerator. The skinned rabbit's entire body lies there raw, curled on a plate like a young human fetus. Suddenly, the phone rings, and after Carol carries the plate with her when she goes to answer it, she absently leaves it behind on the phone stand. In her increasingly deranged state she forgets it, nibbling instead on sugar cubes, crackers, and stale bread. The rabbit gradually decays in the heat and flies buzz around it. (These images are often juxtaposed to close-up shots of ugly, gnarly potatoes that are sprouting on the kitchen counter.) At some point, Carol places the lover's straight razor on the plate alongside the rabbit (Photo 6.4), and shots of this are followed up in another shocking scene at the beauty salon where Bridget finds the bloody rabbit head in Carol's purse. Finally, the landlord removes the nasty object. ("What the hell is this?" he asks, wrinkling his nose in disgust.) By repeated shots linking Carol to this stripped, rotting rabbit—which we perceive as tiny, pale, and naked, left all alone to rot on its plate—the film represents her as pathetic and vulnerable, yet at the same time somehow corrupted or decaying (Photo 6.5). The association is confirmed when the landlord sits near her and says, "Poor little girl, all by herself, shaking like a little frightened animal, alone."

By creating empathy with Carol, who is like a frightened rabbit, the overall narrative structure of *Repulsion* asks viewers to understand the logic of someone with the inability to make any real human response to generalized evil. This film presents the condition of horror as one of hopeless disruption and fragmentation rather than resolution; of suffering and reacting rather than acting. Evil is real here as a condition of existence for this woman. It lies in threats both from within and without; she cannot escape it even by locking her doors and hiding in her bed at night. Ultimately, Carol is vanquished and lies completely catatonic on the floor underneath her bed. She is once more the victim of a hostile world's stares as the entire apartment building—doddering old men and women bedecked with curlers—

PHOTO 6.4   *The rotting rabbit carcass in* Repulsion *(1963).*

troop in to stare at her and the scene of her crimes. Perhaps such evil had an original source in human men, but it has now become free-floating and externalized. Evil is "out there" in the world of apartments, city streets and school playgrounds or "in here" in Carol's apartment with its décor of dead rabbit. Such evil is not localized or related to one person, even to her uncle, the presumed abuser.

The story of *Repulsion* could not be said to be a tragedy in the classic sense. It occurs in a world that is overall less rational than the world of classical tragedy; it does not offer a narrative of a deed and its consequences, describing a heroine like Antigone, whose action or character is somehow flawed, precipitating her tragic downfall. At least in that sort of world, heroes defend some principles and assume responsibility for actions and their results. Instead, *Repulsion* presents a sort of anti-narrative about the inability to act, a continual waiting, passivity, and suffering that is like something out of Samuel Beckett rather than Sophocles (but without Beckett's humor). Even Carol's final acts of killing the two men seem to be reactions rather than genuinely intended deeds. Surely this woman does not "deserve" her suffering: she is not an evil *Fatal Attraction*–style femme fatale whose death we are invited to celebrate at the end of the story. Carol is more like the violated and damaged Blanche du Bois at the conclusion of *A Streetcar Named Desire.*

PHOTO 6.5   *Carol (Catherine Deneuve) lies dazed and nude on the floor in* Repulsion
(1963); note her resemblance to the naked rabbit in Photo 6.4.

Repulsion is not a visionary feminist tract; it does not offer up an alternative
model of gender roles that would prevent Carol's suffering and that of women like
her. Nevertheless, it certainly does call existing roles and attitudes into question in a
particularly interesting way by implicating the audience in watching this woman.
She is very beautiful, perhaps to many viewers desirable—this is, after all, the fabu-
lously unflawed Chanel model Catherine Deneuve, whose persona and façade I discussed in Chapter 4 while considering *The Hunger*. Here, too, her image is interestingly central to the film, and it can preoccupy viewers as the camera relentlessly
tracks her. We follow her as she walks down the street, we gaze at extreme close-ups
of her face and eyes—she begins to seem to want to hide from the camera's inspec-
tion behind her long pale hair. The camera lingers on her feet and long slim legs or
follows her around, focusing on her midriff as she wears only a slip. Or it jumps dis-
concertingly from behind to in front, examining this woman from all angles. At one
moment of her near-final disintegration, she is shown nude on the floor.

Repulsion constructs a surprisingly critical representation of male sexual desire
and the accompanying objectification of women, and it links this kind of visual

objectification to acts of violence and sexual abuse like incest. Moreover, it suggests that when women fight back against such violence and abuse, their actions may be reasonable and warranted as sheer self-defense. But it does *not* imply, as do so many movies in the recent "rape revenge" genre (or as my next film will), that the women who fight back against such abuse will achieve psychological satisfaction or be backed by a powerful judicial system.[2] To my mind, *Repulsion* would be less good if it did so—and that would also make it more problematic in its gender ideology—because it would misrepresent and gloss over existing power and dominance relations within patriarchy.

The Silence of the Lambs

There is another kind of representation of evil in relation to patriarchy and gender ideology in *The Silence of the Lambs* (Jonathan Demme, 1991). This recent thriller is an heir to classic early slasher films like *Psycho* and also to the vampire tradition. The male psychopath at its center is intensely compelling; Dr. Hannibal Lecter, "Hannibal the Cannibal," is a brilliant psychiatrist imprisoned for grisly serial murders in which he consumed his victims as part of gourmet meals. These acts place Lecter within the vampire tradition, as do scenes that show him with bloodied mouth. This link is highlighted when a frightened young police officer asks the heroine, "Is it true what they're saying, he's some kind of vampire?" The answer is both yes and no: "They don't have a name for what he is," she replies. Lecter also functions like a vampire because he is a figure on whom the camera lingers, a monster who can mesmerize by his intense gaze, a villain who seeks intimacy with the heroine (the audience's surrogate).

Because it places a female detective at its center, *The Silence of the Lambs* has been described as a feminist film—"deliberately, unabashedly, and uncompromisingly a feminist movie."[3] True, this film might seem to reverse some traditional assumptions about the slasher genre. Jodie Foster's Clarice Starling is a young woman in transition from adolescence into adulthood rather than a boy investigating the adult world, like the young man of David Lynch's *Blue Velvet*. Still, I would say that beneath its surface, the narrative logic of *The Silence of the Lambs* is traditional and patriarchal, parallel to stories from the original *Dracula* through to *Psycho* and *Blue Velvet*.[4] Like its predecessors, this film traces an investigation that successfully restores the normal order of law and justice. Clarice acts like a typical male hero who kills the monster (a male "psycho") and rescues the damsel, a young woman who functions like all her murdered forebears in slasher films as pure victim.

Thus, we cannot count the mere fact that its hero is female as the grounding for a feminist reading of *The Silence of the Lambs*. More important are some nonstandard features of this movie, or ways in which it thwarts usual detective-story expectations. The ending subverts narrative closure on some levels, and the film also affords a weird eroticism—making it resemble some of the *Dracula* movies I considered in Chapter 4. *The Silence of the Lambs* curiously lets the audience have its cake and eat it, too, by providing not one but *two* psycho killers. Only on the surface is it a detective thriller, as I have noted. The "outside" story of the film shows a heroine who makes her transition to full adulthood by triumphing over one killer, "Buffalo Bill." In this story, Clarice functions like the normal red-blooded male hero who saves the woman from the monster. She is strong and smart, so she grows up and wins her badge. But there is an "inside story" as well. Just as *Blue Velvet's* narrative depicts the boy's maturing through his strange alliance with the monstrous Frank Booth (who tells the boy, "You're just like me"), similarly, Clarice must get to know the horrifying Dr. Hannibal Lecter in order to get his help in catching Buffalo Bill. Like *Psycho's* psychiatrist, Dr. Lecter "has all the answers" from the start; he assists the detective in tracking Bill down. Clarice's oddly intimate relationship with Lecter, coupled with his escape at the end of the film, makes this movie less standard. We need to ask, though, whether these twists make the film feminist and if they provide a truly interesting picture of evil.

Each of the psychotic killers in *The Silence of the Lambs* is linked to numerous horror-film predecessors or monsters by certain not-so-subtle devices. I have already commented on Hannibal Lecter's resemblance to the typical film vampire. The first time we see "Buffalo Bill," he is wearing bizarre night-vision goggles, so that his face is masked and we hear his heavy breathing—à la Leatherface in *The Texas Chainsaw Massacre*, Jason in *Friday the 13th*, and Michael Myers in *Halloween*. Bill is thoroughly predictable, a standard "psycho killer" sort of movie villain, modeled after the cross-dressing Anthony Perkins in *Psycho* (and no doubt countless others). A full dossier is supplied to give a psychological explanation of his motives. Lecter, the expert whom the FBI consults about serial killers, explains about Bill: "He wasn't born a criminal. He was made one through years of abuse." Bill kills women because he "covets" what they have; he thinks he wants to be a woman. He is using their skins to sew himself a "dress." Obviously, his desire is perverted and he must be punished; he dies for it. In this inner story of *The Silence of the Lambs*, gender norms are upheld and Bill gets classified as evil because he transgresses them. The inner story with this formulaic evil killer also features a typical damsel in distress, one whose screams are largely ineffective. She exists only as someone to be saved by the hero(ine), so it is not surprising that she remains opaque and uninvestigated as a character.

In the outer story of the film, though, Lecter's evil is developed by showing his unfolding relationship to the heroine. Clarice Starling is not the usual strong silent hero who solves the problem, rescues the maiden, and dispatches the villain. She is a complex figure, fragile and vulnerable, a woman who needs the assistance of a male mentor in order to succeed. She gets this assistance from the unlikely quarter of the more "interesting" villain, Hannibal Lecter. Like Buffalo Bill, Lecter's character seems evil in part because his image resonates with previous filmic monsters. Even before our first view of him, we have been prepared to find here an ultimate horror-movie villain. Dr. Chilton, the prison psychiatrist, says simply, "He's a monster," and Starling's FBI mentor warns her, "You don't want him inside your head." The camera follows Clarice as she descends into Lecter's subterranean cell through a maze of halls, as if his prison is a classic dungeon in Transylvania. Thus, it is no surprise when we finally see him behind the special glass safety walls, standing up erectly at attention, like Lugosi's Dracula, in his neatly pressed blue jail suit, his dark hair slicked back over a high forehead. Throughout the film, Lecter manifests a vampirelike ability to violate, mesmerize, and suck away life and energy (Photo 6.6). All this is emphasized by the way he is lit and shot, especially in close-ups, where his blue eyes stare out with a fiercely hypnotic gaze. Lecter looks just like any movie vampire who lurks with glowing eyes outside a Victorian lady's bedroom. And later, Lecter also shows up in a Jason-like fashion statement, wearing a hockey mask when he is transferred from his glass security cell. This serves, of course, to make him look more menacing.

The Silence of the Lambs is an excellent film on many levels. It has a literate script, beautiful cinematography, crisp direction, suspenseful pacing, and a haunting score (by frequent David Cronenberg film composer Howard Shore). But perhaps paramount is the fact that its characters' juicy roles are occupied by talented actors. This film is most gripping when it depicts the powerful developing relationship between Lecter and Clarice, one in which Lecter "more than fulfills the gothic archetype of the charismatic suitor who may also be a crazed murderer."[5] Lecter becomes Clarice's intimate father-confessor, almost her lover. When she comes to visit him in his holding cell in Memphis and insists, "I came because I wanted to," he responds archly, "People will say we're in love." Lecter helps Clarice solve the case by passing her a clue hidden in her case notes. When he transfers these to her, we witness a forbidden touch between them: Lecter caresses one of her fingers with one of his—a tiny but obscenely erotic gesture that produced whoops in the audience where I watched the film.

Clarice's alliance with this frightening figure is at the center of the movie. She needs him to further her entry into a patriarchal world. To be successful, and for the narrative to be resolved satisfactorily, Clarice must carry out her own form of (gender) transgression to negotiate entry into the male-dominated world of the FBI. This is made even more difficult by her feelings of being orphaned when she

PHOTO 6.6   *A vampiric Hannibal Lecter (Anthony Hopkins) in* The Silence of the Lambs
(1991).

lost her father, the only parent she ever knew. At several points in the film, she has
flashbacks about him. The film's title alludes to Clarice's central psychological
motivation, her need to come to terms with disturbing memories of the lambs being slaughtered at her cousin's farm. These suffering lambs become a central image of the film (though they are not actually depicted until later in the plot when
Dr. Lecter consumes a dinner of "lamb chops, extra rare"). Lambs function in this
movie much like the rabbit carcass of *Repulsion*: They are central signs of the very
existence of evil and suffering in the world.

The Silence of the Lambs offers Clarice an alternative pair of father figures to aid
her in subduing her disturbing memories or in silencing the screams of the lambs
as she attempts to rescue a new "lamb," Buffalo Bill's current victim. The twist is
that the "good" father who actually helps her is the evil monster Dr. Lecter.
Clarice's FBI mentor Jack Crawford (Scott Glenn) promotes her career, but he is
emotionally distant and withholding. When he offers her a job, he downplays its
importance ("Well, not a job really, more of an interesting errand"), as if he is just
sending her out for coffee in asking her to get a profile from Dr. Hannibal Lecter.
Crawford uses Clarice as bait without confiding his real purpose, which is to get at
Lecter's expert advice about "Buffalo Bill." She realizes this and chides him for it
later, just as she rebukes him for excluding her from a meeting with a local sheriff
and detectives. Near the end of the film, Crawford puts Clarice at great risk when
he patronizingly dismisses her from the case, thinking he has himself found

Buffalo Bill. She is ordered to "clean things up" like a good little girl at a different crime site. Through Crawford's own hubris, Clarice is left alone and must meet Bill one-on-one in his darkened basement lair.

However, Clarice finds Hannibal Lecter a more emotionally demanding and involving father figure. Despite or perhaps through Lecter's perverse desire to torment her into confiding past secrets, he gets to know and understand her. He gives Clarice useful if challenging clues about her case so she can track Bill and "silence the lambs." Lecter is horrifyingly evil, but he is never evil to *her*, the heroine, the personification of goodness in the film. Rather, around Clarice he is downright chivalrous. He is intense, polite, brilliant, precise in his speech and manners, and he has a wonderful, if sick, sense of humor (commenting about a patient who had been murdered, "It was the best thing that could have happened to him; his therapy was going nowhere").

One of the most important facts about *The Silence of the Lambs* is the identity of the actress playing this young heroine, the heroic woman transgressing gender expectations, the experimenter who would enter into a dangerous, semi-erotic relationship with a mad killer like Lecter. The audience is prepared to accept all this because of who Jodie Foster is and what she brings to her cinematic role here. She is a "star" with an accumulation of previously known outsider personae. She is known for her on-screen association with danger and risk: child actress/prostitute from *Taxi Driver;* a psycho killer in *The Little Girl Who Lived down the Lane;* Academy Award–winning rape victim in *The Accused.* Perhaps even more significant, Foster is known for her off-screen risks as real-life Yale student who was object of a fanatical obsession by psycho gunman John Hinckley Jr.[6] Hinckley, too, was unable to separate Foster the real person from her on-screen image as the tiny fierce girl-woman endangered by psycho sex fiends and mad killers. Then there is also the alleged character of Jodie Foster, often rumored to be a closet lesbian, another real-life role that might buttress our expectations about Clarice's gender transgression. Our knowledge that all this is in *this actress's* past or present life falsifies the director Jonathan Demme's disingenuous claim that he will not put this heroine into any sexual danger.[7] This particular actress carries about with her a sort of cinematic *essence* of sexual danger. Foster has the irrevocable, if acquired, persona of a young woman known for her brave and unconventional psychosexual risk taking.

Because both Lecter and Clarice transgress usual social norms and collaborate on a task, an alliance between these two makes sense. They are Others who are outside the System, the male psycho killer and the female orphan, a "well-scrubbed hustling rube" trying to make it in a male-dominated world. In one early scene at the FBI Academy, Clarice's separation from her milieu is shown as

PHOTO 6.7   Clarice Starling (Jodie Foster) dwarfed by classmates at the FBI Academy in The Silence of the Lambs *(1991).*

she gets on an elevator and is surrounded by young men who tower over her (Photo 6.7). Her diminutive size is emphasized in other ways, as when Lecter tells her to "fly back to school, little starling." But Lecter seems to respect Clarice's ambition to create herself, disguise her class background, and to realize a world in which justice reigns so that she can put an end to the screaming of slaughtered lambs that so traumatized her in childhood. Lecter asks her if she thinks that saving the young Catherine Martin from Bill will finally silence the lambs and end her nightmares. Indeed, early on when a newscaster announces the name of the latest victim, it sounds like "Catherine Mutton."

Clarice's self-formation is comparable to what Lecter has also done (in a far more troubling and extreme way, and at the crucial cost of taking other human lives). Lecter is an aristocratic and selective murderer, much like the Dracula of many film versions. A *New York Times* reviewer wrote that this character "illuminates the appeal of profound evil": "[H]is personality is the source of the film's terror. Intellectually powerful, culturally refined, innately curious and possessed of exquisite manners, Lecter is an evil genius, the embodiment of mysterious, inexplicable and unmitigated perversity."[8]

This reviewer's claim about "Hannibal the Cannibal" is troubling. Lecter *exemplifies* the appeal of profound evil but without exactly "illuminating" it—discovering *why* his evil is appealing is precisely the task before us. I propose that there are three answers to this question. First, and most obviously, Lecter functions primarily as both a suitor and a mentor for Clarice. He appreciates her in much the way Dracula appreciates Mina, as a heroine who combines a "man's brain and a woman's heart." This side of Lecter is not disturbing because it shows that he, like we, appreciates something very fine, and in doing so he manifests just plain good taste. Beyond this, as a psychiatrist Dr. Lecter really does function to help Clarice grow up and reconcile herself to her bad childhood memories. He respects Clarice and pays her the ultimate compliment of saying, "I think it would be something to know you in private life."

Second, and also fairly obviously, Lecter can seem admirable because he bucks the system and refuses to be just another statistic in some study. In this movie, *Psycho*'s know-it-all psychiatrist has been supplanted by a mad and deviant psychiatrist—as if to say that these formulas will no longer suffice for horror films. This psychiatrist, knowing all the relevant rules about his monstrous species, is the expert whom even the FBI wants to consult. We have seen enough psychokiller slasher movies to know their formulas and to be bored by them. We want more, and here we get it, since, like Dracula, Lecter shows up in no mirrors—he resists categorization by "normal science." Think about the pattern behind Lecter's attacks: He has bitten out the eye of a nurse who attempted to *record* his EKG; he ate out the liver of a *census taker;* he plans to kill Dr. Chilton, who has made him the subject of a *psychiatric study;* and he contemptuously throws away the FBI *personality test* Starling hands him, asking, "Do you think you can dissect *me* with this blunt little tool?" Lecter's primary motivation throughout the film is to escape confinement, whether psychic or physical.

This second reason for Lecter's appeal, then, states that he is attractive because he is so exceptional—just like Clarice, the tiny brave woman learning the ropes of the big male world of the "Eff Bee Eye" (as Lecter derisively drawls it out). *The Silence of the Lambs* is thus in its own way a strange subversion of the narrative logic of films like the original *Dracula* or *Psycho*. At the conclusion of *Psycho*, there is a full restoration of order with a complete explanation of the psychopathic killer, since the psychiatrist "has all the answers." Similarly, in most versions of *Dracula*, the Dutch scientist Dr. Van Helsing knows the rules that govern vampires and has the strength of will and tools that enable him to defeat the monster. Lecter remains a cipher, someone who understands the rules that govern psycho killers but refuses to conform to any of these rules.

This brings me to the third and final reason that Lecter's evil has appeal. He is, quite simply, an interesting *film monster*. He is complex, unconventional, unpredictable, eloquent, and intelligent, but above all, he is cinematic: He is *visually* interesting and creative. Lecter has consciously formed himself and aimed to transvalue values in a Nietzschean sense, putting himself outside conventional morality with a kind of omnivorous aesthetic all his own. He has developed his own kind of refined standards of taste to lead life by, like the elegant vampire Miriam Blaylock in *The Hunger*. Lecter describes the macabre murder of one of his victims as a gourmet experience of consuming the man's liver with "with fava beans and a nice Chianti."

We actually witness one of Hannibal the Cannibal's grotesque aesthetic acts, a deed that affords the film's director Demme the chance to create a bizarre and hideous, but compelling and stunning, on-screen horror spectacle. Lecter's murder of his two prison guards is presented as a piece of performance art: The killer, like the movie director, orchestrates the murder as part of a seamless whole. First, the camera pans slowly across Lecter's beautiful drawings of the Duomo in Florence and of Clarice with lambs, to show his dinner of "extra-rare" lamb chops lying next to *Gourmet* and *Poetry* magazines. The sound track plays Bach's peaceful and analytical *Goldberg Variations*. Lecter calmly plots and enacts the murders as the music plays on, and even after the grisly deed is done, he pauses and gazes upward, enraptured by Bach. This murder is not simply bloody (it is that); it is "artistic": Lecter leaves one man's body stretched high across his prison cage as a sort of disemboweled Leonardo angel (Photo 6.8) and skins off the other man's face to provide a disguise. Lecter's means of attacking, with his teeth, and his bloodied yet coolly smiling face, reinforce his links to the vampire monster in film tradition. He resembles the aristocratic Count Dracula, who believes ordinary human lives have no consequence.

I suggest, then, that Demme, like the novel's author Thomas Harris, is partly gripped by a vision of Lecter as creative artist or entertainer, who, like a horror filmmaker or writer, sets the audience up for suspense and grisly spectacles. Demme makes sure that we see and share the expectations of the local police, who have been duped by Lecter into thinking that one of the crime victims is in desperate need of rescue, when this is Lecter himself wearing the man's face. Lecter fools the police, just as Demme has fooled us.

But this third kind of aesthetic rationale for Lecter's appeal is very disturbing. Although this moral outlook is different from, and perhaps subversive of, the more conventional patriarchal moral messages of films seen as heroic or epic narratives, it is hardly feminist, either. To understand why, we need to think back to the crucial theme of the slaughtered lambs and meditate on how these lambs both do and do not resemble the central symbol of *Repulsion*, the slaughtered rabbit. Clarice finds even the treatment of animals as meat too horrifying to accept, so of course she is committed to seeing humans as more than "meat" (or "skins," as Bill does). Lecter's choice of lamb chops—rare and bloody ones—for dinner on the evening he plans his grisly escape underlines his indifference to the suffering of

PHOTO 6.8   An example of Hannibal Lecter's grisly "art" in The Silence of the Lambs *(1991).*

others. Also, his skinning the face of one jailer links Lecter with Buffalo Bill. Bill, too, after all, is an aesthetic murderer, a creator who loves costume design and the unusual moths he collects. Lecter is just more interesting than Bill because he has worked his consumption of others into a more elaborate code, a more refined taste. His code is that of the Outsider who obeys only his own rules, and he respects Clarice because she is equally capable of molding herself into an individual character. Lecter particularly admires Clarice's frankness, since he insists he has the power to tell when people are lying. One is almost left with the feeling that he eats other people because he considers them liars, discourteous, or not worth getting to know! They are not truly human but mere "meat" in his value schema.

The film's ambiguous moral message rests on this point, as we can see all three reasons for Lecter's evil appeal come together. If we admire Clarice, as we seem expected to do, then we are drawn to the very quality about her that she shares with Lecter and that he also recognizes and admires in her. For Lecter, the code of individual self-creation and "bucking the system" includes a commitment of politeness and respect for those few others who do the same and who hence "count": He says, "[D]iscourtesy is what I hate most." This is why Clarice is not afraid of him when he escapes. She explains to her friend and FBI Academy roommate: "He won't come after me. He'd think it was, well, rude." And indeed, when he phones Clarice at the end of the film, Lecter says: "The world is more interesting with you in it. Extend me the same courtesy." Predictably, she tells him that she cannot make that promise. But *The Silence of the Lambs* leaves both characters alive at the end, able to pursue their creation of self. "Good" does not combat "evil" here because they are in effect mirror images of one another, not polar opposites.

The Silence of the Lambs seems similar to *Psycho* and *Blue Velvet* in that the narrative requires completion by an investigator who acts on behalf of the patriarchal order—the FBI and law enforcement—to rescue the damsel in distress and destroy the monster. Clarice gets recognized as brave and is rewarded by winning her badge at the end. Crawford even tells her (as if we needed one more paternalistic flourish), "Your father [a policeman] would be proud of you today." But the film is extremely subversive of the genre in many respects. The head of the FBI Academy, shown in the film's concluding ceremony of initiation, is none other than Roger Corman, the famous Hollywood producer-director of "B" horror movies. This film's depiction of the villainous Lecter reflects an attitude of complete moral ambiguity, so that ultimately his escape and planned revenge against his warden, the incompetent psychiatrist Dr. Chilton, threatens any full sense of narrative closure or restoration of the order and security of the status quo. This film is significant and disturbing because of the way it makes viewers root for Lecter even after his horrific murders of his guards, perhaps because Lecter seems almost benign compared with his own psychiatrist/nemesis Dr. Chilton, a monster of insensitivity, egomania, and gross ambition. Chilton is slimy and deceptive, punishing Lecter with loud gospel TV; and he even hits on Clarice at the start with the corny line "Baltimore can be quite a fun town if you have the right guide." So there is a delicious thrill in Lecter's plans at the end to "have an old friend for dinner." It is revealing in this regard that the two audiences with whom I watched the film in dollar-cinema theaters were clearly and vocally on Lecter's side in this conclusion, where he ambles off down a street in the Bahamas in casual pursuit of his nemesis.

Conclusion: Heroines in Evil Worlds

Significantly, Demme makes choices in his film that are quite unlike Polanski's in *Repulsion*. *The Silence of the Lambs* never takes us into Lecter's point of view; this is someone whose head we, too, would rather not get into. But even so, the movie in effect celebrates Lecter as a creative, artistic, and interesting figure; one might even guess that he escapes in the end almost as a reward for the filmmaker's identification with him. Lecter is really not appealing because of his evil but rather because of his artistry. We do not sympathize with his desire to kill—or share his point of view to see that his victims somehow deserve to be killed, as we share

Carol's in *Repulsion*. We do not occupy Lecter's visual awareness any more than his psychic states. Still, and despite this, Demme conspires with Lecter so that the movie's ending rather famously prompts cheers from the audience when he escapes and sets his digestive sights on the prison psychiatrist Dr. Chilton.

Despite the fact that the moral ambiguity of *The Silence of the Lambs* is disturbing, *Repulsion* is a more deeply unsettling film. It shows evil to be evil, rather than papering it over with cinematic allusions and toying with the attractions of Nietzschean amorality. The difference rests on two factors. First, as I have noted, Polanski's movie invites us as viewers into a closer identification with the point of view of its central "psychotic" character. Many of the visual and emotional experiences of *Repulsion* are depicted from Carol's own point of view, whereas the point of view of *The Silence of the Lambs* is usually Clarice's and not Lecter's. This is never more evident than in the central murder scenes: We witness what Carol does (and the reasons for her actions) largely from her viewpoint, but we learn mostly of Lecter's crimes by report, witnessing the aftermath when he escapes. His murders are spectacle on film, not real; they are orchestrated precisely to be filmed. Her murders are accidents that the camera seeks to avoid.

And second, as I have also noted, *Repulsion* depicts a world that has gone badly awry, where even if we can tell the difference between good and evil, human action cannot succeed in removing the overall atmosphere of evil. This film ends in despair. In contrast to Carol, Clarice occupies a more standard (male) heroic role within a narrative arc that presents a solution to the evil of at least the inner story of *The Silence of the Lambs*: she kills off the "bad guy" and rescues the "damsel." Thus, this film suggests that a woman can become victorious over evil by taking on stereotypically male attributes and insignia. Not only is she rewarded for her actions by external recognition and initiation, but she has an internal psychological victory as well. She has now fought off the demon memories of screaming lambs—ironically, the psychiatric administrations of Dr. Lecter have helped her do this. He asks when he phones at the end, "Well, Clarice, have your lambs stopped screaming?" Despite Lecter's escape, he does not threaten her. Good wins out, so the film can be seen as upholding the traditional patriarchal values of initiative, intelligence, and independence. Whereas Clarice's lambs are laid to rest, Carol's future of disintegration and ultimate decay is forecast by the rotting rabbit flesh on her kitchen table. *Repulsion* ends in despair, *The Silence of the Lambs* with both a banal formula and a cynical cinematic thrill.

Repulsion puts us in the head of the murderer and shows that this is an unbearable place to be, that she ended up there because of an unbearable world. *The Silence of the Lambs* holds us back from the head of its primary killer, but it slyly implies that this would be an interesting place to be and that he got there through creative resistance against a mediocre and boring world. This is a nasty, brutish message, even when sugar-coated with the surface morality tale of a detective story that rewards the persistence of an attractive and spirited heroine.

My readings of *The Silence of the Lambs* and *Repulsion* have been structured by my philosophical approach to horror. I have suggested how our critical readings can be feminist without psychoanalytic underpinnings, and I have highlighted these films' intellectual engagement with themes of evil. Both films are complex and well-designed artistic artifacts, and I have emphasized that the audience's critical readings of them are crucial for emotional response. Critical readings may be individualized, though they do need to recognize what is actually there on the screen, and I have tried to point to evidence in the films to support my interpretations. I have not invoked any purportedly universal or totalizing psychological responses; audience members will bring their own knowledge and attitudes to horror films. In my view, a number of feminist readings might be possible for each film. Feminist film readings interpret how films function as artifacts, and to do this, they must explore such diverse aspects of a film as its plot, editing, sound track, point of view, dialogue, character representations, use of rhetoric, and narrative structures. But film artifacts function within a context, and the context is constantly changing. I do not contend, for example, that the sort of reading I have offered here of *Repulsion* would have leapt so naturally to mind in 1965 when the movie was released. We see this film differently in retrospect against the contemporary background of *Fatal Attraction* and *Basic Instinct* and by comparison with the recently emerging genre of the rape revenge movie. Further, and this is important, there is far greater social awareness in 1999 than in 1965 of problems of incest and child sexual abuse, and such awareness coupled with our exposure to ongoing publicity about the murder of the little blond beauty queen JonBenet Ramsey might significantly affect how a feminist of today reads certain allusions in the film such as the family photo focused on at the end.[9]

I have discussed *Repulsion* and *The Silence of the Lambs* within my recommended cognitivist framework, focusing on the depiction of evil and the gender ideology of each film. I said in the Introduction to this book that horror films may solicit a kind of cynical and subversive audience response. *The Silence of the Lambs* is a case in point. When people cheer Hannibal Lecter's line at the end about "having an old friend for dinner," this might reflect not so much endorsement of his cruel cannibalism as appreciation for an interesting character and a desire to see an outsider beat the system. The prison psychiatrist really is a despicable person in that movie, and many of us might share Hannibal's resistance to being pigeonholed by an incompetent and smarmy bureaucratic shrink. We can applaud Lecter for many of the same reasons that we applaud Clarice in this movie. She breaks into the male world of the FBI—another bureaucracy, which the movie also pokes its own sly fun at through positioning Roger Corman as its head. Although their messages are very different, both *The Silence of the Lambs* and *Repulsion* depict a gender ideology that they simultaneously undermine through subtle critical devices.[10]

PART THREE

Sublime Spectacles of Disaster

CHAPTER
SEVEN: Uncanny
Horror

This chapter is about two films that are uncanny, where evil is a disembodied, vague state of cosmic affairs: *The Shining* (Stanley Kubrick, 1980) and *Eraserhead* (David Lynch, 1978). Both directors—Kubrick and Lynch—have inspired fanatic devotion and a plethora of critical studies. Rather than delve into their styles, techniques, themes, or other works, I will focus on how each film presents a picture of the world as an evil and forbidding place. Using narrative and cinematic features, they in a sense *argue* that the world is uncanny and hence horrifying: They create a convincing vision of an uncanny world parallel to, perhaps congruent with, our own. My aim is to understand how they do this and why such uncanny horror is enjoyable. Since each film personalizes the uncanny by focusing on the experiences of a man who becomes a murderous father, we can also trace an evolution in horror's depictions of male sexuality, heroism, and the father's role within the family. The defeat of the male in his traditional heroic role seems associated with uncanny evil. Is this defeat itself what makes the world so deplorable? Does the uncanny here *cause* or rather *result from* the man's displacement from his traditional positions of authority and privilege?

The Shining and *Eraserhead* share a number of features. Each is the story of a father threatened by an uncanny or monstrous child. Because he attempts to destroy this child, the father himself must die. Conditions surrounding this family melodrama make father and child seem as much victims as they are monsters. Although the children here are unusual or even freakish, they are innocent—not like the nasty girl in *The Bad Seed* or the demonic Regan in *The Exorcist*. And though at times in these films the evil is localized in the father as a murderous agent—either the inept Henry in *Eraserhead* or the ax-wielding Jack in *The Shining*—I would contend that neither man is a true horror-film monster. Rather, they are signs and perhaps even victims of the vague yet powerful cosmic evil that the movie posits. These films describe a world dominated by a foreboding of fate or doom that has no clear, obvious explanation. In keeping with the dislocated force of evil here, much of the violence in these movies is implied rather than literal, anticipated rather than shown.

Although the plot of each film exhibits a structure and forward trajectory, their narratives are illogical and unpredictable, emphasizing the characters' inability to take meaningful action. Disruptions of time block orderly cause-and-effect narration. In *The Shining*, the little boy, the hotel's cook, and the hotel itself are all assumed to have an ability to "shine," to reveal evils both past and future. In *Eraserhead*, our earthly landscape has become eerily threatening. Both films end with several deaths. Whatever the evil is due to, it has neither been dispatched nor dealt with, only (at best) fled from.

The evil that dominates the worldview of these films is not just a product of literary elements; its evocation fundamentally involves the filmic medium as a whole. *The Shining* and *Eraserhead* are films of mood and atmosphere. Music and sound (or noise) combine with visual effects, lighting, dialogue, and characterization to conjure up a pervasive aura of evil and dread. Ominous sounds accumulate: strange music, heartbeats, and the noise of the little boy's tricycle in *The Shining*; eerie songs, wails, and hissing and industrial sounds in *Eraserhead*. Striking visual images reinforce the films' perspectives on evil. Viewers, like characters, can *see* an evil here that cannot be named or dealt with. As a whole, the films afford a kind of "proof" or "evidence" of things that evoke dread in unspecified ways. One of the most chilling scenes of *The Shining* (it was used in trailers to promote the movie) shows elevator doors that open to release an ocean of dark blood; it sets furniture afloat and ultimately splashes up to cover the camera. Our whole view of the world has been almost literally bloodied. *Eraserhead* includes numerous surreal sequences: small bird torsos dance on a dinner plate; wormlike creatures somersault across the carpet; a distorted woman sings happily in a tiny theater in the radiator tubes of the hero's apartment. This film at moments turns not red but black or blindingly white, as if it must stretch the conditions of cinema beyond their limits to convey that certain sights cannot really be shown.

I will discuss these movies in turn to describe their complex and synoptic visions of the horror of uncanny evil. I will then trace the uncanny as an aesthetic category related to the sublime. Freud, too, wrote about the uncanny, but I disagree with his diagnosis and assessment, so I will offer my own account of its appeal. These films suggest that uncanny evil arises in part from threats to our paradigms of masculine activity and heroism.

The Shining

The Shining vacillates between realism and the supernatural. Kubrick was attracted to the film's source, a Stephen King novel, because it "seemed to strike an extraordinary balance between the psychological and the supernatural."[1] Both novel and film offer an undecidable account of uncanny evil that may stem from a psychotic man or from more unearthly sources within the remote and eerie Overlook Hotel. Jack Torrance (Jack Nicholson) is hired as winter caretaker to cope with the hotel's "damage and deterioration," but instead *he* is the one who gets damaged and deteriorates. He becomes a mad ax murderer and tries to kill his wife and son—either because he is "psychotic" or because he becomes possessed by the evil spirits of the hotel. ("Cabin fever" supposedly led the previous caretaker, Charles Grady, to "run amok" and slaughter his family.) The movie maintains this essential ambiguity as it switches from images of the murderous and crazed Jack (a wildly overacting Nicholson) to stranger, more surreal depictions that conjure up ghostly presences. We see the insides or backs of mirrors, a beautiful woman whose flesh suddenly decays, skeletal ball-goers in evening costume, and more.

The opening credits set up a tension between realistic depiction of the landscape and an uncanny evocation of supernatural presences. The camera glides across vast beautiful, empty Alpine scenery; we follow a tiny car down the highway through disorienting swooping motions.[2] That the atmosphere is threatening, not bucolic, is also suggested by the camera's vertiginous dive into forest and trees and by strange music that shifts from the sounds of grandiose horns to the eerie wailing tones of a primeval voice.[3] This opening suggests that it may not be simply the Overlook Hotel that is a locus of evil here but Nature itself—at least, this entire region of nature, which indeed has a bizarre and threatening history. We hear later about the faded glory days of the hotel's "illustrious past," the ill-fated cannibalistic Donner party, an Indian burial ground on the hotel site, and new disasters like a missing woman mentioned on the TV news.

The camera in *The Shining* is a particularly eerie and disorienting force. One reviewer commented, "Most of the film feels like an endless subjective shot: we appear to be watching the hotel and its occupants through the eyes of an unearthly prowler, someone who sees very differently from the way we see."[4] Even the more straightforward passages that represent dialogue or lay out the hotel's rooms and corridors become uncanny through unusual camera motions or per-

PHOTO 7.1   *The elevator of blood in* The Shining *(1980)*.

spectives. Kubrick's well-known penchant for tracking shots was taken to an exalted level in this film by his early and extensive uses of the Steadicam camera.[5]
Mounted just below the level of a Big Wheels tricycle, the camera tracks Jack's son
Danny (Danny Lloyd) as he races around corners and down the hotel's long corridors. We come close to occupying Danny's point of view in terms of both position
and motion, but our perspective is not quite identified with his in these scenes.
Instead, we follow behind him like a force that keeps him in view for unknown,
perhaps nefarious, ends.

    The camera in this movie also has a tendency to watch scenes from a distance.
This conveys the feeling that we cannot see exactly what is going on and must
creep forward to find out.[6] Numerous sequences in the film are shot down the hotel's long passageways, including a very frightening scene where Danny sees the
two little Grady girls down a hall that looks like a fun-house distortion. The girls
plead with Danny to come and play, but he suddenly sees their bodies lying
bloody and lifeless. A similar device is used when we first learn about Danny's in-
visible friend, Tony, who lives in his mouth and "tells him things." As we look
down a hallway, we hear Danny talking to someone. Gradually, we advance and

turn to look into the bathroom; he is talking to his own face in the mirror. He asks Tony about what is wrong at the Overlook Hotel and then becomes frightened. We move into a close-up of Danny's face as his eyes open wide, and by implication, we next proceed "inside" his mind to see the vision he has of the elevator filled with blood (Photo 7.1). This sequence is cross-cut twice, first with brief static images of the two (now dead) Grady girls, who are standing silently and staring like the weird twins in a famous Diane Arbus photograph,[7] and then with a shot of Danny hiding his eyes in fright. The sequence concludes with a blackout on-screen that is literally Danny's own blackout. After a cut, light seeps in and the next thing we see is (again from Danny's point of view) a concerned doctor bending over him.

The camera is dislocated from its normal vantage point in many other ways and scenes in *The Shining*. It almost acts as if it has a will of its own, conjuring up the independent evil forces that reside in the Overlook Hotel. As the Torrances tour the hotel's vast lobby, the camera glides sideways, moving as if it were able to pass through walls to follow and watch them. (Kubrick was especially pleased with the Steadicam's ability to pass within an inch of door frames.[8] This same technique is used again as they tour the great cavernous kitchen.) Gradually, the camera's odd perspective indicates that the hotel's evil forces are joining Jack to prompt his ultimate acts of mayhem. A fusion occurs just after his wife Wendy (Shelley Duvall) discovers that Jack has not been typing the novel he is supposed to be working on. First, we watch Wendy's face from below as she reacts in horror to her discovery. Then we switch to her point of view as she fumbles through his "manuscript" to find page after page covered with the same nonsense line. At this point, the camera shifts and glides in from the side along a dark hallway. What first seems to be an objective long shot showing Wendy's distress is slightly repositioned to reveal the back of Jack's head as he watches her (Photo 7.2). Since his head also looks dark and shadowy, it is as if Jack has blended physically with the hotel's dark spaces, from which he just mysteriously emerged. He has become one with the hotel's ominous watchers.

Other scenes invite us to experience—to literally see—a reality that exists only in Jack's mad mind; here the movie recalls Carol's hallucinations in Polanski's *Repulsion*. Often, these scenes play on the ambiguous space of mirrors, suggesting that we have crossed into another reality that does not perfectly correspond to the one we think we live in. These include scenes where Jack orders drinks from the satanically red-lit bartender Lloyd or where he bumps into the former caretaker Grady, who spills wine on him and leads him into an extraordinary bathroom to clean off his clothes.[9] This scene is especially eerie not just because of the bizarre design of the bathroom—with Art Deco styling in brilliant red and white, with

PHOTO 7.2   Jack (Jack Nicholson) emerges from the hotel's dark shadows to threaten
Wendy (Shelley Duvall) in The Shining (1980).

repeated red sinks—but because of odd lighting and shifts in the point of view.
We watch their conversation at the start from a middle distance, with both figures
centrally framed; but the visual logic of the sequence as it continues is unnerving
(Photo 7.3). At one moment, Jack is in the foreground, so we see Grady's face;
then we suddenly switch to the opposite perspective to see Jack's face. These
switches occur randomly rather than being structured to create a "rational" dialogue through the usual visual logic of shot-reaction shot. Jack insists that Grady
was the murderer of his own wife and child, but Grady denies this. By undermining conventions for dialogue depiction, Kubrick hints that this conversation may
just be Jack's delusion. In particular, once Jack has begun to doubt his own point
of view, we shift to a closer perspective that no longer provides two-shots. Instead,
the film cuts sharply between Grady's face, elegant and normally lit (implying he
is the orderly rational one), and Jack's face, bizarrely lit so that he looks mad, un-
shaven, Neanderthal. The "message" Jack acquires from Grady in this scene is that
his son Danny is dangerous and must be "corrected." Jack is convinced by the tact-

PHOTO 7.3   Jack (Jack Nicholson) becomes demonic in his imagined conversation with
Grady (Philip Stone) in the red bathroom in The Shining (1980).

ful butler that this is the "proper" thing to do, and he departs to do it. We have actually watched him become more demonic.

Other scenes that use mirrors similarly evoke weird doubling or a second reality that is different from our own. For example, in the notorious Room 237, Jack
sees a beautiful woman whose flesh decays, but only in the mirror; and as I mentioned above, Danny is looking at himself in a mirror when he sees the elevator of
blood. A particularly ominous scene with a mirror shows Jack talking to Danny in
their bedroom at the hotel. Although Jack caresses Danny's hair and assures him
that he loves him, the dialogue has an ambiguous tone, and Jack's duality is hinted
at because we see Danny situated between the real Jack on the bed and a kind of
evil twin image shown in the mirror.[10]

The camera is also used to convey the power of things that can "shine." On
Danny's first day at the hotel, he has another vision of the two Grady girls. He also
realizes that the cook has established a mental link to him. Both these moments are
represented through a kind of frozen "looking," intensified by a loud humming or

electronic buzzing sound. The cook, Hallorann (Scatman Crothers), explains "shining" to Danny: Some people can communicate telepathically and "see" things, just as some places reveal traces of what has been left behind—like the smell of burned toast. The camera reveals many instances of how the Overlook Hotel "shines": Danny's visions, Jack's view of the beautiful nude woman, a ballroom full of people where Lloyd is tending the bar. Once we witness a vision that Hallorann has of the hotel from across the country as he lies in his room in Florida. The movie cuts from Danny shivering in fright on his bed to a close-up of Hallorann's eyes staring fixedly and with great concern at something. We zoom down on these eyes from straight above as he lies in bed, then cut back to Danny.

Some particularly remarkable scenes of *The Shining* locate a special uncanniness in the hotel's famous garden maze.[11] The tracking shots here are also spectacular, as we whiz along following Danny down its long corridors. Positioned at Danny's low angle, the camera emphasizes the maze's height (thirteen feet), complexity, and density. One especially ominous scene cross-cuts from Danny and his mother playing in the maze to the increasingly deranged Jack. He rises from his "work" at the typewriter to look down upon a model of the maze that sits on a table in the lobby.[12] The camera zooms slowly down on the model until its edges disappear. Because its focus is on the center and we begin to hear voices of the woman and child, it becomes difficult to say whether we are still looking at the model or at the actual maze itself. Although the child and woman are not directly visible, they seem subject to Jack's godlike or demonic agency. The maze is also uncanny because Jack will die there. In an extended climactic sequence, he chases Danny murderously through this space in a snowstorm. It is impossible to tell where we are or where he is, so we, too, experience the maze as utterly confusing. The camera twists and turns; disorientation is increased by the blinding backlit snow. Danny escapes, but Jack is lost in the maze and freezes to death. In the last shots, the camera cuts away from one frozen image of him to another. We see first the frosted and silenced Jack and then, after a very slow tracking shot down the hallway into the Gold Ballroom, a photograph of what looks like a young and handsome Jack at a party scene dated July 4, 1921. Now he is frozen in time.

The effectiveness of *The Shining*'s depiction of the uncanny depends not just on the story, plot, characters, and acting but also, as I have suggested, on nonnarrative aspects of the filmic medium. The camera's unusual movements and angles contribute to an irrational narration. Although this is not the complete irrationality of avant-garde cinema, it is enough to become disorienting. The film's use of music and sound are equally relevant to this process. The music, which includes modern classical music by Krzysztof Penderecki and György Lygeti, often melds into strange electronic noises or music, contributed by Wendy Carlos and Rachel

Elkind.[13] We hear shrieking or wailing violins, eerie choruses, or ominous hums on the sound track. Occasionally, the music transports us in time, as when we hear old Victrola waltz music. Danny's visions are accompanied by an electronic humming sound, to suggest that reality itself is throbbing in an aural equivalent to his visual "shining." The sound becomes especially loud and intense in the vision of the elevator, a kind of thrumming that seems to stop the action or time of normal reality.

Another narrative sequence that is woven together across time and space by the loud sound of a heartbeat starts after the boy, using Tony's voice, tells his mother that Danny "can't wake up" and has "gone away." We begin hearing a heartbeat as Wendy paces anxiously and talks to herself about how to get away. It continues as she talks to Danny and then as Jack walks along the hall to disable the radio when he hears forest rangers calling to check in with them. The sound persists as Hallorann calls the rangers from Florida to ask whether the Torrances are safe. Worried, he boards a plane, and we *still* hear the regular heartbeats as we watch him on the plane the next morning, about to land in Denver. This long sequence suggests that Hallorann can directly hear Danny's frightened heartbeats and is responding to his summons across the miles.

Even the on-screen titles in this movie enhance its horror. Displayed at intervals as small white Helvetica all-cap letters against a black background, they seem unremarkable at the beginning, e.g., "THE INTERVIEW" and "OPENING DAY." But their function and impact gradually shift as they become more random. First we see "A MONTH LATER" and then "TUESDAY" or "SATURDAY," until finally we are shown only dislocated times like "8 A.M." The later titles are slammed onto the screen suddenly, often with a noise, so that even they acquire the power to shock. They enhance the eerie, dislocated atmosphere of the Overlook Hotel, where time has become disoriented or dislocated.[14]

I have described various features of *The Shining* that make this film a persuasive presentation of something uncanny. Despite the fact that Danny and Wendy escape at the end, the film's vision is dark and bleak. Evil was "always there" at that hotel, and we see in the concluding shot of the young and handsome Jack (in a tux at the July 4th ball, 1921) that Grady was right to say to Jack, "You have always been the caretaker." This was foreshadowed earlier in the film when Jack tells Wendy that he "fell in love with the place right away," adding: "It was almost as if I'd been here before. It was almost as if I knew what was around every corner." The place creates its own continuity of caretakers, its own legacy of evil. This is confirmed by Wendy's sudden visions at the end of the film, as she, too, becomes able to "see" the hotel's "shining."[15] The hotel reveals more and more of itself, perhaps "thinking" that Wendy will not escape but will join its history of ghosts and memories of atrocities that linger (like the smell of burned toast). She, too, sees the blood coming out of the elevator and the skeletal remains of ball-goers, and in one truly bizarre vision, she glimpses two men through an open door engaging in an act of fellatio, one in tux and the other in animal costume. Nightmares accumulate and Wendy's status as "seer" is elevated along with our own—but this is not at all a moral or welcome kind of elevation.

The film does not convey an uplifting message, despite the fact that the woman and child escape (or do they?—all we know is that they drive off on a twenty-four-mile-long dangerous road in the middle of a bad blizzard). In *The Shining*, nature is ominous, not simply an indifferent force that will suck things up and leave no sign behind. It is a dark force of evil that can be reflected in but is not confined to human nature. The hotel is left standing in Kubrick's version, and with Jack's photo on the wall among the other memorabilia, it presents a continuing threat to "shine," to reveal its evil power to haunt subsequent caretakers during lonely desolate winters.

What is the source of evil in this film? It is unexplained, disembodied and floating yet somehow localized in this place.[16] The hotel at its center somehow enhances powers of evil that enter from without. Remember that Jack came into the Overlook already belonging there in a sense, as an ill-fated and pathetic man—alcoholic, child abuser, disaffected teacher, failed writer, unsympathetic husband. The place works subtly on Jack's latent evil to turn him into a crazed and violent ax murderer.[17] The movie is built on frightening intimations of violence, but its actual scenes of violence are surprisingly limited and quick. We see only brief flashes of the two dead girls' bodies on screen and only the briefest view of Jack striking Hallorann's chest with the ax. Again, when Wendy sees the cook's body, it is (just as when Danny sees the girls) from a distance. Blood is not lovingly studied here, as in other horror films, while it oozes or pours out of human bodies. Rather, it is disembodied, almost an evil natural force that builds up, pools, and forces the floodgates open.[18] It attacks the camera with a dark power that obscures vision. This suggests that blood here is not so much that of a single person as it is symbolic of the accumulated death force of the Overlook Hotel itself, a hallmark of the violence and evil that occupy it.

Critics of *The Shining* who feel it departed too much from the Stephen King novel (including King himself) say that Kubrick does not understand the horror genre, but I disagree.[19] He is taking horror beyond its usual formulas into something more metaphysical. King's novel features a large topiary animal instead of the maze; at the end, it comes to life to attack Jack, and the boiler that he has left unattended blows up, destroying the hotel. The novel thus provides a sort of just revenge and polishes off evil at the conclusion. This is utterly unlike the film, which kills Jack only to hint that he is a continuing presence in the still-standing hotel. It seems hard to deny that the film's vision is far more horrific![20] Kubrick clearly wanted to make a film with an unremitting sense of evil and horror; he and cowriter Diane Johnson worked by steeping themselves in horror classics of Poe and H. P. Lovecraft and also by reading Bruno Bettelheim, Kafka, and classic Gothic tales like *Jane Eyre* and *Wuthering Heights*.[21] Kubrick has said that the film is about an evil he understands in terms of Carl Jung's notion of "the Shadow," an archetype that is associated with humans but transcends any one individual human (like Jack in the movie).[22] This seems to fit also with a similarly dark vision Kubrick manifested in other films such as *Dr. Strangelove, Full Metal Jacket*, and even *Lolita*.

Other horror movies also depict uncanny evil through an emphasis on claustrophobia, suffering, eerie attacks, and the passivity of the characters in the face of larger mysterious evil forces. *Repulsion*, which I discussed earlier, Hitchcock's *The Birds,* and Romero's *Night of the Living Dead* also present a kind of uncanny threat and have a dominantly bleak point of view; escape may be impossible or only temporary and illusory. It is interesting to compare the male hero in *The Birds* or *Night of the Living Dead* to Jack in *The Shining*. People in the two earlier films were also isolated and shut off from the outside world; they quarreled, but the men were heroic and took steps to fight off the menace. Jack, instead, himself becomes the menace. Instead of this man protecting the women and children, it is Jack they must run from. The traditional masculine virtues have been perverted into abusive power as Jack merges with evil. He loses his reason, control, ability to work, and (apparently) sexuality. Only through his murderous behavior will he come to "belong" in the company of the hotel's past clientele, its wealthy and elite white pleasure seekers. He becomes a parody of the traditional masculine role as he comes to believe Grady, who tells him that his son is a "naughty boy," his wife is "more resourceful than we anticipated," and that "the nigger" is planning a rescue. All of these people "need correcting." Jack gives an ironic twist to the paternal role with his famous line, "Wendy, I'm home!" (as he comes wielding the ax). Although the movie offers a promise of hope for Danny and Wendy, it is significant that their "delivery from evil" is not shown; and we should keep in mind that the sympathetic and wise elderly black man has been slaughtered like an animal. For this movie (also unlike the novel), the *hotel*'s survival is what counts—not theirs. The ending photo of Jack "frozen" in time suggests that he, too, will survive now that he has proven through his violence that he belongs. We can see that in a real sense, he "has always been there" or "has always been the caretaker." There is a sort of victory to the paternal order, but it is dreadful; the ending mitigates any sense that the film has shown Jack being punished while the innocent Danny escapes. Jack is still alive, beaming, happy, partying. Evil flourishes.

Eraserhead

I turn now to *Eraserhead,* another film that presents visions of uncanny horror. Like Kubrick in *The Shining,* director David Lynch has made a film that treats the monstrously evil as a fundamental mode of human experience. Again we see how the evil plays out by affecting a man in the context of family life. The uncanny of Lynch's *Eraserhead* is remarkably sustained throughout the entire film. Although other horror films (like *The Shining* itself) present uncanny horror, I can think of no others where horror is so relentless.[23] I will examine how the film uses narration along with aural and visual spectacle to achieve its effects.

To recite merely the "story" or unfolding of events will produce an inadequate sense of this film because many of its important elements appear through its distinctive style, sounds, and visions. The "story" merges inescapably here with the strange way it is told. As J. Hoberman and Jonathan Rosenbaum say, "Defying standard synopsis, *Eraserhead* drifts like a troubled dream through relative degrees of lucidity around the figure of Henry Spencer (John Nance)."[24] The film is a meditation on textures and sounds, many of them hard to identify. Even if familiar, they are distorted and made strange. Still, the plot is straightforward in its own odd way. As Michel Chion remarks, "Despite its gaps and incoherences, *Eraserhead* is a narrative film with dialogue, a hero, and a linear story."[25] The movie can be read as the story of a man's birth, romance, marriage, fatherhood, desires, fears, suffering, and eventual death.

Eraserhead opens with a cosmic prologue that shows a young man floating in outer space before a huge rough-textured planet. He has round cheeks, innocent worried eyes, and floating fuzzy hair. The next sequences show a sweating muscular man with a hideously scarred face who toils like a cosmic Vulcan at the levers of a huge machine. An umbilical-like cord appears alongside the first man, and he is expelled from space—perhaps thus born, or "fallen" down onto Earth.[26] This prologue is very dark. The screen goes entirely black several times; we see scenes of unidentifiable objects and spaces, and the camera zooms in to look at odd textures as loud clangs sound. During what may be the hero's birth scene, a volcano-like hole appears and turns into a puddle. Positive and negative images shift, rendering foreground and background spaces unstable and the spaces we see ambiguous. It is hard to know whether the man is emerging or submerging.

Henry Spencer, the hero, is next seen in nerdlike attire: suit and tie, pens in pocket guard, white socks with black shoes. Walking through a desolate urban industrial landscape, he traverses puddles and abandoned streets, climbs mounds of earth, passes metal doors and boarded-up windows, and finally arrives home, where he crosses a weirdly decorated lobby and takes an interminable elevator ride. At his door, a sexy neighbor lady tells him that someone named Mary has called on the pay phone to invite him for dinner. This first moment of dialogue occurs more than ten minutes after the film begins.

The next sequences represent Henry's ill-fated dinner with Mary's family. His evening with the X family is a disaster; the dinner scene (one of the longer sequences of the film) is torturous to endure. It has become a famous set piece in this cult movie. Henry meets Mary's macabre parents and grandmother, and various strange things happen: Both Mary and her mother have teeth-chattering convulsions; Mary's father grins maniacally and rants about "man-made chickens"; the inert Grandma is kept in the kitchen and fed a cigarette. As for the dinner itself: a teensy (presumably "man-made") chicken that is brought on a platter for Henry to carve thrusts its legs disturbingly and leaks a huge puddle of goopy blood. It is almost a welcome distraction when Mrs. X draws Henry aside. She confronts him about getting Mary pregnant, whereupon the anxious Mary says, "Mom, they're still not sure it *is* a baby."

The subsequent sequences take place back in Henry's apartment and depict family life of the not-so-happy young couple with child. Their premature "baby" is monstrous, with a bulbous slimy head and a mysterious body swathed in bandages. It cries and mewls and spits back its food. Mary "can't take it" and leaves. Henry, too, ponders escape and has encounters with other women—a dalliance with his sexy neighbor lady and meetings with a pretty but deformed blond woman who performs on a tiny stage set within his radiator tubes. She appears to Henry at his moments of despair, when magical white lights shine out of her theater and she sings about heaven where "everything is fine." Although she beckons to him, he cannot seem to join her.

In the final sequences, the baby becomes violently ill and wails when Henry tries to leave. He first cares for it but finally—just why is unclear—cuts into its bandages with scissors. The baby's unidentifiable body opens up to disgorge roiling organs and mountains of bile (Photo 7.4). Electricity goes berserk: Lights flicker and sparks shoot out from sockets. As the screen goes light and dark, we see intermittent visions of the baby's ugly fetal head, threatening and ballooned hugely to fill Henry's entire apartment. Everything goes haywire in this extended sequence, and the baby's death throes are so violent that they extinguish the frightened Henry as well. Emerging from this chaos, we shift back to see the man in the planet once more, trying to move a lever as if to apply some brakes. Henry gets propelled once again out in space (he "dies" as I understand it). For a moment the screen goes white, and in the bright mist, we can barely make out the lady from the radiator. She runs to him, and they embrace in bliss. Henry has at last joined the woman of his dreams in "heaven." The screen goes black and credits roll, accompanied by peppy organ music.

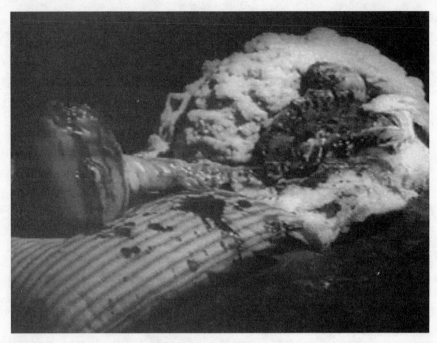

PHOTO 7.4   *The goopy and repulsive dying baby in* Eraserhead *(1978).*

   This summary, as strange as it may seem, still omits a good deal of the startling visions that make this film truly uncanny. *Eraserhead*, shot at night in 35 mm. black-and-white film and made over a period of five years, is unusually dark and textured-looking, as it dwells on the surfaces of things like mud puddles, twigs, hair, carpets, wet bricks, or the gooier fluids that ooze from bodies.[27] Lynch screened *Sunset Boulevard* for the actors and crew before the filming because he loved its dark, claustrophobic intensity of tone. Chion comments that *Eraserhead* "offers something archaic, stiff, and frontal which is close to early silent film."[28] This seems right, particularly since the dialogue is very limited. The sounds and visual linkages are so strange that they really do defy description. Some sequences seem to represent some of Henry's dreams, and there is a recurring motif of small spermatic or cordlike creatures.

   The strange mood of this film depends perhaps even more on sound than on the striking visuals. *Eraserhead* has a distinctive, eerie, and influential soundtrack. Lynch and Alan R. Splet, his sound man and former art-school friend, are perfectionists who took sound in this film to an extreme degree in their search for uncanny effects. There are *always* odd noises in the background. These vary from

low continuous sounds (the whoosh of steam in the radiator, the hum of electrical devices) to loud sudden or annoying ones such as thunder and lightning. We
also hear an almost nuclear wind, the incessant bleating-lamb cries of the baby,
dripping, ticking, bells chiming, sustained organ notes, and the rumble of trains.
In the early scene where Henry walks home, we hear foghorns, clanging ma-
chines, and an organ. There are many background sounds of hissing and grinding; when interviewed, Lynch emphasized that the inside-outside distinction
would be blurred by some of these devices, and he also talked about "room
tone."[29] Music is often put to odd use, especially organ music reminiscent of a
fairground calliope. There are also blendings between music and other sounds
(between, say, organ music and hissing tones).[30] Some sounds, like those from the
crying baby or the barking dogs, are sustained to the point where they become
maddening. Sounds also accompany visual cuts for strong effects, most notably
when Henry is trying to sneak out. The baby wails and a sudden loud chord accompanies the jump cut to a close-up of its face, now hideously blistered, gasping,
and feverish.

Even the most ordinary events seem strange in this movie, such as Henry's riding up in the elevator that takes forever to arrive or getting a small box in his mail
with a tiny larvalike creature that he seems to treasure. The nerdy Henry manifests many oddities. He keeps a bowl of water in the top drawer of his chest, places
a worm in a cupboard in his room, and has a stick of a plant growing from a rock
right behind the bed. Throughout the story, the remarkable actor Jack Nance
maintains a sort of Buster Keaton face, worried but long-suffering and patient.
His hair, which rises in an electrified six-inch pile of wild disorder over his head,
conveys that he is always astonished at what is going on.[31] Nance's flat voice and
speech style are also essential to Henry's character; despite his trials and tribula-
tions, he remains even-keeled except for a few scenes of whining or complain-
ing.[32] His suit, white socks with black shoes, and waddling walk recall Charlie
Chaplin's Little Tramp.

Undeniably, the horror in *Eraserhead* is centered upon the monstrous baby. It is
uncanny, frightening, disgusting, and yet pitiable. Lynch has kept the technical details about the baby a secret. It was probably created using the head of an animal
fetus, perhaps that of a calf or large dog. Its crying is also animal-like. Although it
looks remarkably alive and semihuman, it is truly repulsive—reminiscent of the
skinned and rotting rabbit carcass in *Repulsion*.[33] The sequence that leads up to its
death is truly horrific.

Many construals of *Eraserhead* treat it as a tale about a man unable to deal with
the horrors of parenting (some point out that Lynch was himself a new father at the
time of making the movie).[34] It is true that Henry's action was planned by Lynch as

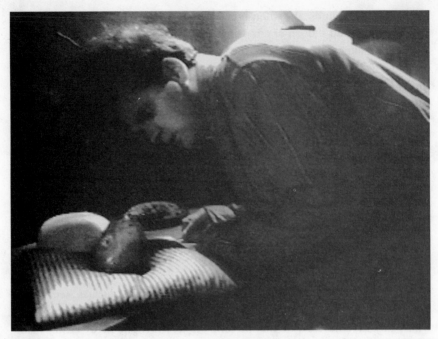

PHOTO 7.5   *Henry (Jack Nance) expresses concern for his freakish baby in* Eraserhead *(1978).*

a murder and that his cutting open the baby results in its death. But as I watch the movie, the tone seems different, sadder, the deed unintentional—a matter less of revenge than of consuming curiosity or even mercy. Henry *does* want to leave to go visit the sexy lady across the hall, and the baby *has* seemed to cackle over this, so he glares across at it. We view it from underneath, and it seems large and dominating. But the look on Henry's face might express not just resentment but also pity and a desire to clear up the mystery of this monstrous body. After all, Henry seems to care for the baby—at least, he has not left it, as his wife has (Photo 7.5). He smiles and touches it with some tenderness; he takes its temperature and runs a vaporizer for it. After the scene when he sees that it is suddenly worse off, covered by pustules and blisters, Henry says feelingly, "Oh, you *are* sick!" and returns to sit with it. When he has cut through the baby's bandagelike clothes, Henry is as shocked and horrified as we might be to discover that it does not seem to have a normal body with a clearly defined boundary. Since by now the baby seems in pain, shudders, and chatters its teeth, it may be a kind of hopeless desire to end its misery that prompts Henry to poke scissors into its swollen-looking organs. He (and we) recoil, and at this point things go completely out of control.

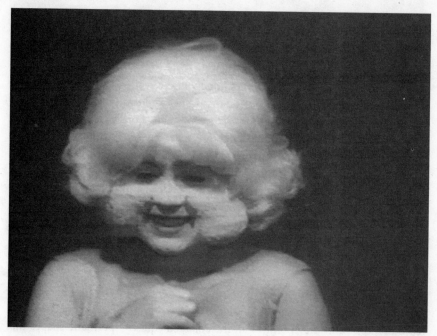

PHOTO 7.6   *Henry's dream woman: the Lady in the Radiator in* Eraserhead *(1978).*

Lynch's vision in this movie has been compared to Kafka's, and this seems appropriate.[35] I think not so much of Henry's resemblance to the hapless K of *The Trial* and *The Castle* as of the repulsive baby's resemblance to the sorry and disgusting Gregor Samsa at the end of *Metamorphosis*.[36] A second comparison I find natural to draw is with another commonly cited absurdist, Beckett, especially his *Endgame* and *Waiting for Godot*.[37] The weird relation to parents, suspicions about sex and reproduction, barely suppressed sadism, and apocalyptic tone of *Endgame* are all akin to the mood of *Eraserhead*. Similarly, the label "tragicomedy" for *Godot* (remember its leafless tree on the stage) could have been created to describe *Eraserhead*. Henry is like a Beckett hero in his escapist fantasies that revolve around art: Ham in *Endgame* whiles away his time and provides himself with glimmerings of meaning by telling his little story to himself, just as Henry loses his worries by looking to the artificial, brightly lit, and happy world of the little Lady in the Radiator (Photo 7.6).[38]

There are, of course, numerous suggestions in this film that Henry has problems with women and sexuality. But to say that sexuality is threatening in *Eraserhead* is to state something so obvious that it is unilluminating. It is too dismissive of the film's more cosmic observations about the strangeness and incivility of the universe. In fact, sex is shown as wonderful and desirable in one of the film's most gorgeous sequences, Henry's sexual escapade with his sirenlike neighbor. As they make love, they literally melt together in desire on the bed—that is, they sink into a pool and their bodies liquefy into a white haze, leaving only the woman's hair floating on top. (During this scene, we hear a noise that gradually modulates from a loud ringing tone to a strong cello chord to a bubbling sound, appropriate for the liquidity.) The delightful coalescence here is illicit, which perhaps explains why it is followed by Henry's disturbing nightmare, where his head plops off and is displaced by the fetus head emerging hideously from his suit. Thus, despite the allure, we can grant that sex is indeed a "problem" in this movie: It seems to suggest that just as sex with your wife leads to a monstrous baby, so sex with the neighbor lady may lead to punishment by decapitation.

But it may be not so much sexuality that is the issue or source of horror in *Eraserhead* as reproduction, considered not just as a consequence of sex but as a facet of life. The film shows that being born, or cycling between birth and death, is in itself uncanny and often horrific. Some critics write that the film draws nasty associations between sex and the limitations on freedom posed by marriage and reproduction—and they point to all the enlarged squishy spermatic shapes that squiggle onto the screen. George Godwin has written an extensive interpretation of the baby as an externalized partial object, Henry's vision of his own phallus, which he proceeds to castrate.[39] Along this line, Henry punishes the innocent but harassing and demanding baby by eviscerating it. I think that this sort of Oedipal line gets things wrong. It is again too reductive, treating the film's cosmic or metaphysical themes about life and death, meaning and meaninglessness, as rather commonplace observations about the difficulties of daily domestic life. In *Eraserhead*, it is not simply human sexuality that is at issue. The film seems to show all birth as troubling, part of an unhappy larger-than-human condition. Why else does the film begin and end with the literally cosmic outer-space sequences? I take the film to be in part "about" cycles of life and death, meaning and meaninglessness—where death and meaninglessness are real contenders in the struggle!

In this film, all forms of growth and reproduction—not just Henry's—go awry and become uncanny.[40] Women's bodies excrete growths: Weird spermlike things are expelled from Mary's body while she sleeps, and more squirmy nasties drop from the sky to be squished on-stage by the Lady in the Radiator. Plants grow from dry rocks and larvae are kept in boxes; water for nourishment is precious and kept hidden away in drawers. At the dinner scene at the X's home, a mother dog who has too many tiny squealing puppies looks disgusting but also pathetic.

This is not just a world where bodies can dissolve unpredictably and disappear; it is also one where they can flow and grow unpredictably. Growth may not be promising, either, but may be threatening. The plant imagery shows this, as does the depiction of the growing baby in the last sequence, which is similar to a time-lapse film showing the growth of a sunflower. The electrical explosions, shorts, and sparks at the end could also be associated in Lynch's mind with this fusion or indeterminacy between solid and fluid.[41] This fits with Lynch's aesthetic absorption with textures. Several interviews bring this out, as he refers to his experiments in dissecting creatures like mice or cats and his finding their insides very beautiful (even upon decomposition!).[42] In some sense, the uncanniness here is that even death and ugly dissolution can afford a kind of beautiful fascination.

Eraserhead is about dualities and oppositions: life/death, male/female, reality/fantasy, wife/mistress, dark/light, and good/evil. A major source of uncanniness in the film concerns the duality of solid/fluid, which takes on metaphysical and moral overtones. The spatial or physical world of *Eraserhead* is not dependably well organized: The film's physical reality does not pigeonhole objects into their usual categories. As we saw, sexual intercourse is shown as a literal dissolving of physical boundaries.[43] Seemingly solid bodies can dissolve upon contact, like those of the squab or the baby. Women's bodies are particularly prone to "leakage," as we see from the spermatic excretions that float around Mary and the Lady in the Radiator. Henry's solidity is threatened at the start when he splashes into a large puddle, soaking his foot and leg. Henry has a nosebleed at the dinner scene when he learns about the baby. His hair, always flying and floating, suggests that his head itself might simply flake away like the eraser tip of a pencil. In fact, the film's title derives from just such a specter in one of Henry's nightmare visions.[44] After his head is knocked off his neck and is replaced by the fetus head, it rolls in his own blood and plops outdoors into a puddle. A small boy scoops it up and takes it away to a sort of nineteenth-century factory, where it will be chopped up and made into erasers. We then see a vision of Henry in space ("dead"?) surrounded by the floating dust of pencil erasers. In short, something solid can dissolve and disappear; the living can liquefy and die. The undecidability here implies a difficulty in distinguishing between self/others, life/death, and good/evil.

Cinematically, the contrast between dark and light is the most significant duality in the movie; it pushes the boundaries of what can be represented. At moments in *Eraserhead*, the camera seems to follow an object into darkness or lightness, and at other moments, it emerges up out of something or to show something that "swallows" its vision. The darkness is worst in the outer-space scenes (perhaps this is a womblike darkness), and the brightness at its most extreme in the scenes in radiator heaven. When Henry "visits" the Lady in the

Radiator in a dream sequence, he appears on her stage as if he has materialized from a white mist. But reaching out to touch her, he makes her disappear—she is clearly anxious and dubious. He has tried to cross a line between his ordinary reality and the imaginations of art; he can only escape or get to another level of reality at the end, after his death, in "heaven."

There are moments of near-to-complete blackness on the screen and also of complete bright whiteness. If darkness is evil because it is linked to grainy, mundane, and exhausting urban alienation, then brightness is good since it is a feature of art, theatrical performance, escapism, romance, and "heaven." But neither of these conditions is stable, as manifested by the frequent transposition of positive into negative images. Since the film draws such attention to itself, it forces us to realize that each quality—total blackness or total whiteness—puts an end to filmic representation by closing off the narrative and blocking our ability to see. If light and dark represent good and evil, then their shifts and blending suggest we cannot always tell the difference between them. The uncanny in *Eraserhead* is what literally exceeds the limits of representation by disappearing from view. But despite its sustained uncanniness, I am not sure that *Eraserhead* ends as negatively as *The Shining*. It holds out the possibility of a kind of escape through the combination of romance and art. Henry must suffer and die in order to realize his sublime romantic escape into the arms of his beloved "Radiator Lady" in "heaven" where "everything is fine." Good does exist, although to get there you must endure the great evil of life, with all its dark uncanniness.

Conclusion

I now want to compare the two uncanny movies I have discussed in this chapter. *The Shining* is about disorientations—not simply problems among people but disorientations in time. Human identity is threatened less by people's confused minds than by the blurred boundaries between past/present, vision/reality, and physical or spatial parameters. The central metaphors in *The Shining* involve the distorted and scary spaces of mirrors and mazes—not just the actual outdoor maze, but also the mazes of highways, hallways, and the hotel itself. People rush about like small rats in a glass cage. Mirrors present visions of reversals, inside/outside, here/there. A similar disorientation of thinking as well as of space and time is also at work in *Eraserhead*. Henry has several doubles in his dreams; there are double women representing opposing aspects of femininity; and the baby itself is doubled, at least in size, by the end of the movie. *The Shining*'s ending is ominous; it suggests that Jack survives by joining in with the hotel's mysteriously evil forces. By comparison, *Eraserhead* offers a positive vision of an escape into romance and art, though life itself in its everydayness is permeated with evil and suffering. The bright white light seems good, but we should remember that in this film darkness and light are intertwined, and either one, taken to the extreme, will obliterate cinematic vision.

I have called these films uncanny and will now say more about the history of this term. In part I borrow it from Freud, who developed his account of the uncanny *(unheimlich)* in 1919 while he was working out the concept of the death instinct.[45] He traces the etymology of the term used to designate this concept in various languages; it always involves notions of what is familiar yet foreign, gruesome, ghastly, or concealed. Freud's essay "The 'Uncanny'" discusses one of the *Tales of Hoffmann*, "The Sandman," as its chief example of the uncanny. Hoffmann's tales are similar to Poe's and depend very much on an atmosphere of mysterious, implied evil rather than on any specific monster or scenes of violence. What is threatening here, as in *Eraserhead* and *The Shining*, is something from ordinary life that has a mysterious and familiar feel yet becomes alien and frightening. In "The Sandman," a young boy is haunted by the fear that an evil sandman (modeled upon a sinister visitor to his father's house) will snatch out his eyes. Not surprisingly, Freud interprets this as fear of castration due to Oedipal conflict and the repression of childhood libido. He therefore generalizes to say the uncanny refers to "the child's dread in relation to its castration-complex."[46] Later in life, the youth encounters the same evil man. It turns out that he has used his stolen eyes in the creation of a mechanical doll-woman, Olympia—but it also happens that our hero has fallen in love with Olympia. He experiences this man as "uncanny," very frightening yet familiar, and a block to his love. Again, Freud interprets all this by noting that the sandman serves as Oedipal barrier or threat to the youth's libidinal satisfaction. Freud diagnoses the uncanniness that the hero experiences at each of three encounters with the sandman as involving a "repetition compulsion"; it reflects the forced need to repeat a critical early trauma and "whatever reminds us of this inner repetition-compulsion is perceived as uncanny."[47] Freud is saying that when we enjoy a story that is uncanny, *we too* are going through this repetition-compulsion, and we somehow enjoy being forced to revisit the threatening psychic arena of the Oedipus complex.

However, there is a complication that Freud introduces into his account of the uncanny, which is potentially of interest because it concerns other sorts of uncanny stories and experiences. The castration complex cannot cover all cases, because some types of the uncanny have to do with other phenomena, for example, feelings of magical power, doubling, or helplessness. Freud comments, "The sources of the feeling of an uncanny thing would not, therefore, be an infantile fear in this case, but rather an infantile wish or even only an infantile belief."[48] This is a matter of "primary narcissism of the earliest period of all" that escapes the ego's capacity of self-observation or self-criticizing, and thus it signals "a regression to a time when the ego was not yet sharply differentiated from the external world and from other persons."[49] It also has to do with "effacing the distinction between imagination and reality."[50] We could call this, if we were sticking to psychoanalytic vocabulary, a pre-Oedipal uncanny, one that expresses depths of conflicted feelings about separation and loss or differentiation from the maternal body.[51]

Freud's notion of the uncanny is related to an important aesthetic concept that preceded it, the Kantian sublime, though it in effect reverses the feeling-tone of this earlier concept. The two notions are similar in that both the sublime and the uncanny are described as resulting from intense internal psychological conflicts. As Kant described the sublime, it involves a very strong tension that occurs when our mental faculties are confronted with something grand and massive or powerful like a mountain range or fantastic storm.[52] On the one hand, our sensibility and imagination become awed, overwhelmed, and even terrified because we cannot take in the vastness of this object. On the other hand, our reason feels exaltation at being uplifted by the experience of such vast natural powers. Reason somehow identifies with vastness, at least insofar as we sense our own superior moral powers.[53] In Freud's account, by contrast, the libido and infantile desires are threatened with destruction by a more powerful force imposing limitations: not the "law" of morality as Kant sees it but rather the force of the paternal law restricting desire's satisfactions, or more primitively, the extension of the vast maternal body preventing personal identity and separation. The uncanny in this case is something that engulfs the person who aspires to rise to the occasion; it threatens to obliterate the distinction between reality and imagination. This kind of uncanny feeling is like an antisublime.

Since both *Eraserhead* and *The Shining* do seem to concern paternal impositions of "the law" upon a freakish and demanding child, there is a natural temptation to draw on psychoanalysis to discuss the uncanniness in each film, as I have just sketched. I resist this temptation for a number of reasons, but mainly because horror of the uncanny in these movies (as in the stories of Poe and Hoffmann) extends beyond individual psychology. Freudian analysis reduces moral and metaphysical fears to psychological abnormalities. Why not equally diagnose this as a metaphysical neurosis—as a fear of dark metaphysics! Freud's account in terms of psychological theory reduces human concerns about ethics, aesthetics, religion, or metaphysics to neuroses or fears from the self or ego. The uncanny is made smaller and becomes human scale rather than being cosmic and metaphysical.

I propose that films like *The Shining* or *Eraserhead* that present a strong sense of the horrific uncanny are engaging us with an *antisublime*. They present a kind of inverse or variant of the more traditional aesthetic notion of the sublime, understood as an encounter with awe-inspiring power and grandeur. The sublime was said to characterize our response to natural forces of supreme power and grandeur—to objects so vast or powerful that they are overwhelming and terrifying. The uncanny, too, in both Kubrick's and Lynch's films, involves an experience of something that is excessive and grand, almost beyond cinema's abilities to represent. Historically, the concept of the sublime was developed as a comparison or complement to theories of the beautiful. Unlike the beautiful, which involves enjoyment of features of proportion and form, the sublime was seen as a paradoxical response, as aesthetic appreciation of something huge, formless, threatening, disproportionate, or disorderly. Yet in sublime nature or art, such forces are not threatening but energizing, dynamic, uplifting, or elevating. Like the uncanny, the sublime was described in eighteenth-century aesthetic theories as able to dwarf the self or ego. Whereas the forces of the uncanny are terrifying, the forces of the sublime can be exhilarating. For example, our sense of personhood may be threatened when we gaze out upon the Grand Canyon or feel the rumble and hear the gush of Niagara Falls. Yet somehow this threat is pleasurable, since our reflections on the power of nature show us our own powers and reinforce our sense of being human. Our physical powers may be puny and our size tiny, but we, unlike the waterfall or canyon, are able to reflect on this very fact! At the heart of the concept of the sublime is a nest of paradoxes. In the sublime, we gain humanity through loss of the self; we can conceptualize something inconceivable, we enjoy something terrifying.

By contrast, the forces of the uncanny dwarf us in a way that simply threatens a dissolution of the self, meaning, and morality. The uncanny as an *antisublime* involves the opposite outcome of these paradoxes or a failure to disarm them: We cannot adequately conceptualize a representation, we lose our sense of self, we are frightened by something unexplained, and we feel the loss of morality or death of the self in the face of a very great evil. Thus, whereas the experience of the sublime as traditionally defined was morally elevating because it prompted awareness of our own powers (particularly the powers of reflection and moral reasoning), the antisublime carries the opposite message. Films like *The Shining* and *Eraserhead* are morally deflationary, raising real questions about the limits of our human powers. No matter how much we reason about an uncanny overwhelming object, we are stumped. We feel puny in relation to a force with which we cannot identify because it is too strange, vague, alien, or evil. The message is a cautionary one. In *The Shining*, evil wins out, in the sense I have described. *Eraserhead* may end on a brighter note, but the world as described by that film is an even more thoroughly uncanny, evil, and forbidding place.

Like the sublime, the uncanny or antisublime can be frightening and yet pleasurable. Even a profound vision of evil can be appreciated if we come up against it
carefully presented in a persuasive form. Perhaps that vision will be expressed in a
work of philosophy—I am thinking here of some works by Kierkegaard and that
great philosophical pessimist Schopenhauer. Dark and pessimistic metaphysical
visions are also to be found in great works of poetry, fiction, or drama (think of
King Lear)—and also, I have argued here, in certain films. As readers or viewers,
we can enjoy such visions of evil, despite—perhaps partly because of—the ways
they challenge us to think of them as true. We find it interesting to conceptualize
the basically inexplicable evils shown in these movies. Most of us have encountered a brute and immovable power of evil at some point in our lives.[54] Uncanny
works encourage not elevation but an opposite emotional and cognitive effect
that I can best label "dread"; but such dread is a powerful emotion relevant to our
lives. Dread is a sense of something evil, something out there as a threat in a distinctive and stronger sense, different from the threat of sheer power. It is different
from fear because it is looser and less focused on an object. Kant's vast waterfalls,
mountains, or landscapes may astonish by their force or scope, but they just do
not attain the kind of threatening, destructive status of the monstrous nature
shown in the movies I have discussed here (recall how nature is shown at the beginning of The Shining, or space at the start of Eraserhead). Dread occurs if we
have an encounter not just with a natural disaster like a tornado but with a more
"biblical" phenomenon, such as a plague of locusts. There is a real power of en-
mity that threatens to erase the self in a serious and irrevocable way, and it goes
beyond the scope of a single father, as described in Freud's view of the Oedipus
complex—even if it is manifested by fathers like Henry or Jack.

The paradox of the uncanny or antisublime is that we can enjoy even the depiction of such a world if it is offered in a complex and persuasive enough aesthetic
form. Uncanny films like The Shining and Eraserhead are not enjoyable for their
presentation of interesting monsters, as some other horror movies are. I have suggested that the horror here goes beyond, or lies behind, the men who seem to be
monsters in them, so we cannot invoke Noël Carroll's views to explain their appeal.
Recall that Carroll argued that an interest in horror fundamentally involves learning
about monsters and the possibility of confronting them and that this process challenges our intellectual comprehension in a pleasurable way.[55] Other explanations
from cognitive psychology, such as Torben Grodal's proposal that the experience of
horror can be "ego strengthening," are also implausible in relation to uncanny horror: I have argued that these movies are "ego weakening," if anything![56] A simpler
explanation, such as Ed S. Tan's claim that there are specific fans of horror who relish predictable genre effects like being scared, may work better here, but that also
seems too reductive.[57] To pinpoint a fairly uniform and reliable genre response is

possible, but this resists or discounts the complex intellectual and aesthetic interest of films like the two I have discussed here. *The Shining* and *Eraserhead* are uncanny: Like the very best stories by Hoffmann, Poe, Lovecraft, and Clive Barker, they offer complex and intriguing visions of an evil cosmos.

My cognitivist approach explains that films like *Eraserhead* and *The Shining* are enjoyable because they stimulate a variety of interests and abilities in their audiences. These interests and abilities—cognitive, aesthetic, emotional, metaphysical—are focused on the film and on its presentation of the uncanny. We can have a complex appreciation of the film's plot and characters, point of view, moral attitudes, and cinematic features—particularly when the film is as good as these films are: complex, beautifully shot and edited, mysterious, with sympathetic central characters and challenging intellectual content. Films of uncanny horror prompt a complex cognitive and emotional response of appreciation for the kind of worldview they present. We may not endorse or accept their message, but we can find it worth considering and responding to. Uncanny films include elements that are repulsive and dreadful, but also intriguing. As a whole, the uncanny object, if it is an artwork like a film, can have an aesthetic power in the way it requires us to feel repulsion or dread, to "see" and reflect about the horrors it so evocatively presents. We could not think seriously about such a worldview if we did not picture it and respond to that image so thoroughly.

As it happens, the uncanny evil in each of the movies I have discussed is manifested through problems of sexuality and family relationships. The treatment of gender is very subtle in these movies. Since they depict such a vague kind of threat, we cannot locate an actual gendered monster in them, such as a giant queen ant or a suave Count Dracula. Still, sexuality and eroticism are significant factors, as the films suggest links between thwarted sexuality and cosmic unrest. The women in these films suffer in specific ways, and both films present a father in relation to a frightened yet freakish child.

Unlike the earlier films I have discussed in this book that highlight women and female reproductive powers, here the uncanny seems to center upon a man, a male parent. Threatened with evil and suffering, he is unlike his male predecessors in horror, whether mad scientist, slasher killer, or predatorial vampire. The uncanny is manifested in a set of concerns about masculinity, its powers, expectations, and limitations, all of which are heightened by the experience of fatherhood. In *Eraserhead* and *The Shining*, the uncanny seems to show up in a perversion of the paternal figure, now become villain. Only an unnatural and evil father threatens to kill his child. Henry Spencer's infanticide may seem destined, part of his overall cosmic suffering or symbolic of his general lack of control; Henry is almost literally swept along by events. By comparison, Jack Torrance is an all too realistic villain, the sort of abusive spouse and father we read about in the daily news. Both Henry and Jack

are failures in other areas of male expectations: They are not successful breadwin-
ners, are unable to connect with their wives, and cannot express love for their freakish offspring. Jack is a failed artist, an alcoholic willing to sell his soul for a drink,
and so on. He responds to Grady's admonitions that all his subordinates must be
"corrected" in a desperate attempt to salvage some power for himself.

Thus, on the surface both films present the uncanny as linked to significant
challenges to patriarchal heroism and power. But we need to go a step further to
question the underlying gender ideology of these movies. The loss of patriarchal
power is bad, but does cosmic uncanniness *cause* or *result from* the threat to male
heroism? A little of both. Jack Torrance seems evil to start with, yet he has moments of appeal or sympathy as a poor man who cannot live up to expected standards; this is why he cracks and breaks down. Perhaps no one could be expected
to fight off the forces of the Overlook Hotel. Jack, like Henry, is an agent only in a
limited sense, since he can be seen as a victim of larger forces. The defeat of masculinity here is a sign of the real power of evil in the cosmos: Even heroes will be
helpless. Humans may be overcome and turned against their own offspring. We
cannot assert that these movies promote a sexist gender ideology by suggesting
that the loss of male heroes is what accounts for horror. The evil here is too strong
and cosmic, the uncanny too overwhelming. There is no nostalgia here for a return to the days of *Bonanza, The Untouchables,* and *Father Knows Best.*

In my feminist analysis, then, it is possible to read each film as a critique of the
ideologies associated with patriarchy. They reveal the emptiness of traditional values and their inapplicability in the modern world. *The Shining* shows some things
from Jack's viewpoint, but it primarily encourages empathetic identification with
the wife, the young child, and the African-American cook, who all suffer at the
hands of this berserk and authoritarian father. His abuse of power and inability to
live up to patriarchal values combine to require that he be punished by death—
though this death has not clearly erased his evil force. *Eraserhead* also details the
failure of a father, and it, too, seems to suggest that he must die. It is overly simple,
though, to describe this film as a morality tale about how the hapless Henry must
"pay" for his negligent sex and reproduction. The film empathizes throughout
with Henry, and we see many scenes from his point of view. It is more metaphysically disturbing in some ways than *The Shining* because the horror of *Eraserhead*
concerns life, death, physicality, and the fluid boundaries of things. The outside
comes inside, living things grow out of control, dead foodstuffs become alive, and
the boundaries between the solid and the fluid get blurred. Henry also survives,
though this ending may be a kind of escapism. At any rate, his joy in "heaven"
does not cancel out the evil that *Eraserhead* has so relentlessly depicted as an inte-
gral part of life in the universe.

chapter
eight: Graphic Horror

Many of the best-known recent horror movies do not feature a mad scientist, monstrous mother, or uncanny sense of evil as the two films discussed in Chapter 7 do. In this chapter, I will look at another category of horror film: those that blast the viewer with graphic gory visual excess. Even in the earliest days of silent horror, films like Murnau's *Nosferatu* (1922) used special effects to startle and shock audiences. We might date the onset of horror gore back to the late 1950s. The trend developed in the 1960s and 1970s and reached new heights (or depths) in various long-running and well-known horror series of the 1980s and 1990s. Certain directors and studios were especially important to this progression. Hammer Studios in England, along with Roger Corman in Hollywood, effected the transition from black-and-white horror to Technicolor, done in the lurid tones of what has been called "color Gothic." John McCarty says that *Blood Feast* by Herschel Gordon Lewis (1963) was the "first of the gore films"—and he should know, since he coined the term "splatter film" and is the author of *The Official Splatter Movie Guide*.[1] The titles of films made by these directors are indicative: *Blood Feast, Bucket of Blood, Blood and Black Lace, Hatchet for a Honeymoon.*

Another gore landmark was George Romero's *Night of the Living Dead* (1968), which became a hit on the midnight cult film circuit.[2] Gore crossed over into mainstream cinema in 1973 with *The Exorcist*, a film with notorious scenes of pea-soup vomit and Regan's revolving head. Other infamous scenes of spatter include the famous exploding head in *Scanners* (1981), Leatherface wielding his sledgehammer and chain saw in *The Texas Chainsaw Massacre* (1974), and the huge shark chewing up Robert Shaw in *Jaws* (1975). We should also not forget related developments such as *The Rocky Horror Picture Show* phenomenon (1975), the tacky grossness of John Waters's movies, Italian art horror cinema by directors like Mario Bava and Dario Argento, or the ventures of Andy Warhol and Paul Morrisey like *Bad*, *Frankenstein*, and *Blood for Dracula*.

The genre of graphic horror seems to have reached self-perpetuating heights in three famous and long-running horror series that began in the late 1970s to early 1980s: *Halloween* (1978), *Friday the 13th* (1980), and *A Nightmare on Elm Street* (1984). They introduced, respectively, the unstoppable slasher-killers Michael Myers, Jason, and Freddy Krueger, all of whom are by now as well known and popular as Frankenstein or Dracula were to earlier generations. As of this writing, all three series are continuing and there is even a special meeting planned between two of their villains in the forthcoming *Freddy Meets Jason: A Nightmare on Friday the 13th*.[3] It would be hard to discuss the modern horror film without talking about scenes in these films (or their many imitators) of over-the-top, ever-escalating graphic violence and gore (or "FX" [effects] as the fans say). It is common to witness gross bloody dismemberments, piles of internal organs, numerous corpses in stages of decay, headless bodies, knives or chain saws slashing away at flesh, and general orgies of mayhem. In these films, flesh becomes meat, the inside becomes outside, blood pours out, skin is stripped off, viscera exposed, heads detached. People die in any number of creatively disgusting ways.

In this chapter, I will discuss important examples of the graphic horror genre (or subgenre). As with uncanny horror, I will ask some basic questions: Why do audiences enjoy such films? What do these films say about the nature of good and evil? And how do they present gender ideologies: Is it true that they endorse the mutilation of female flesh? What do psychological studies tell us about their effects or about the reasons audiences attend them? Horror in these movies is mainly physical and not psychological. If perhaps I have relied on a certain sort of intellectual appeal to explain our enjoyment of *Eraserhead* or *The Shining*, this option does not seem viable for *The Texas Chainsaw Massacre*!

We should remember that gore is not a new phenomenon in the art or entertainment of the twentieth century. Blood and gore are common to almost all cultures' literatures of wars and ancestral battles and heroes, and the West is no exception. Considerable gore is present even in the high art tradition. There is plenty, for example, in the *Iliad* or Euripides' *The Bacchae* and even more so in Roman tragedy and drama by Seneca and Tacitus. Roman works of literature include many scenes that would rival almost anything in modern horror.[4] Even so, one might point out that the excessive, over-the-top graphic visual gore in splatter horror films—particularly when shown on the large screen with Dolby sound— makes for new and truly remarkable spectacles of horrific force and power.

In graphic horror films, the spectacle becomes so vast and overwhelming that it makes sense to consider again how such visual spectacles can be related to the concept of the sublime. That is, perhaps the nonstop visions of blood and gore in these films work like a sublime artwork or natural force, something so huge and vast that it overwhelms the rational self. When this happened in the traditional sublime, the self supposedly felt threatened and yet also morally elevated. Graphic spectacular horror seems unlikely to provide moral elevation. To the contrary, it almost solicits identification with powerful forces of destruction. Appreciation of the traditional sublime required a certain aesthetic distance, but pleasure in the graphic sublime is *participatory*. And such participatory pleasure seems disturbing. When fans say that Leatherface's use of a chain saw on human bodies is "cool" or that *Hellraiser*'s Pinhead "rules" because of his violence, it seems fair to say that they relish, celebrate, and identify with these agents of bloody havoc.[5]

If the uncanny as I wrote about it in the last chapter is an *anti*sublime because of its moral negativity, perhaps we should say that movies of graphic excess constitute a kind of *perverse* sublime. They do not counsel despair in the face of great mysterious evil, but rather, they celebrate evil. A surface analysis would say that by reveling in dismemberment or terror and identifying with cosmic forces of amoral destruction, audiences reject all traditional moral values and endorse a kind of Nietzschean "Superman" who is "beyond good and evil." Such a diagnosis is tempting, but I disagree with it. We will see that some movies of graphic horror, surprisingly, endorse very conservative value systems. And further, I will argue that graphic horror movies with over-the-top excessive visual spectacles provide certain aesthetic pleasures to devoted fans of the genre.

The growth of gore in horror is obviously tied to the development of new methods and technologies for creating special effects in film. Hitchcock's *The Birds* (1963) made advances in special effects with optical printing and combined negatives; the film was three years in production. Specialty books about horror masters emphasize the industrywide effect of advances made in particular films, such as the Oscar-winning special effects by Rick Baker depicting David's transformation into a werewolf in *An American Werewolf in London* (1981).[6] Latex facilitated significant advances in creating realistic deformations of faces and bodies. Of course, another huge development was the onset of digital imaging, which was central to films such as *Jurassic Park, Terminator 2, Independence Day*, and *Godzilla*. Here, I will be looking at more typical spatter movies where the monsters are humans and the mayhem is exercised not so much on urban skyscrapers as on the human body.

There are far too many horror films that revel in visual excess for me to be able to discuss them all. Films of spectacular or splatter horror are not all alike, either in their functions and effects or in their moral viewpoints. I will therefore focus on several examples here that I consider good in some significant sense. These will not include some of the more long-running and famous horror series like *Halloween* or *Nightmare on Elm Street*, with their seemingly endless sequels. They simply do not interest me very much, for reasons I will try to explain further below.

I will begin with one of the most notorious (and notoriously titled) horror films of the last three decades, *The Texas Chainsaw Massacre*. This film will help me describe a transition from uncanny horror to graphic horror that often occurs in horror-film series of recent decades. I will then switch from Leatherface to another recent inductee into the Horror Hall of Fame, Pinhead from the *Hellraiser* series, one of my own favorites. Using these examples, I will show that, perhaps surprisingly, graphic spectacular horror can uphold a very traditional and conservative moral viewpoint. If there is any moral ambiguity in *Hellraiser*, it involves the appeal of the lead villain, Pinhead, but I will argue that this appeal is linked to a very specific sort of aesthetic pleasure. Horror audiences appreciate spatter films as created and skillful artifacts and accordingly appreciate their villains as types of creative entertainers. Since wit and parody are common elements in this kind of creative display in graphic horror, such horror often turns into comedy. I will close by discussing comedic elements in some extremely graphic horror films. This last point about the humorous side of graphic spectacular horror will help me conclude my comparison between the perverse sublime of these movies and other varieties of the sublime.

The Texas Chainsaw Massacre

The Texas Chainsaw Massacre (Tobe Hooper, 1974; hereafter *TCM 1*) has, surprisingly enough, few scenes of actual gore. (It is strange to view it now and to realize how little blood and gore it shows.) The original film, despite its notorious and suggestive title, is *not* a visual bloodbath (though its sequels most certainly are). Rather, *TCM 1* offers a clear example of what I have called uncanny horror: a disturbing and relentless vision of evil "out there" in the world. As with Jack in *The Shining*, the evil is localized in human form, but somehow it exceeds human instantiation and haunts the entire landscape. Significantly, this uncanny dark presence is not a factor in the second film (made twelve years later). Instead, *TCM 2* (also directed by Tobe Hooper, 1986) revels in excesses of gore as it presents a cartoonlike sketch of good and evil. Good clearly triumphs; the sequel banishes the original's moral ambiguity.

The contrast between the two films also involves remarkable changes in gender ideology. Whereas *TCM 1* centers on the traditional screaming damsel in distress,

TCM 2 offers a typical 1980s horror heroine, the resourceful Stretch, with her gutsy air and gravelly voice, who combats and defeats the monsters. Carol Clover has suggested in *Men, Women, and Chain Saws* that in such movies, the heroine succeeds by adapting the values and tools of patriarchy.[7] This seems so here: The final shots of the movie show Stretch standing atop a small mountain, triumphantly waving a chain saw over her head. *TCM 2* fulfills several laws of horror sequels: Spectacle is always more extreme and prevalent, and greater spectacle leads to more parody or comedy.[8]

TCM 1, framed with an ominous announcement that "you are about to witness a true story," adopts a semirealistic style to depict an encounter between five youths traveling in a van in South Texas and a cannibalistic, primitive family (father, grandfather, and two sons). Leatherface, one of the sons (so named for his macabre leather mask), kills four of the youths as his father plans to make human barbecue from their flesh. Only one girl, Sally, escapes. The chain-saw family lives miles from anywhere, isolated redneck manifestations of the bleak, forbidding Texas landscape. This flat prairie landscape shimmers with heat and becomes an inimical background presence reminiscent of the fiercely burning deserts of classic Westerns. Occasional "arty" shots show images of death or strange sunspots (with links to dialogue about bad astrological forecasts).

This movie implies more grotesque and extreme horror than it depicts. The opening shots are among the bloodiest in the film, but they do not showcase a murder. We first see a close-up of the grisly face of a corpse, lit by sudden flashes of (we presume) a police camera. The camera slowly backs away, and we then hear radio news reports about a grave desecration that has left body parts arranged as a macabre scarecrow atop a grave—almost, the commentator says, "like a grisly work of art." (As I noted in Chapter 1, this "arranged" scene is oddly reminiscent of the opening grave sequence of James Whale's 1931 *Frankenstein*.) The movie provides other hints of primitive evil, such as a mojo tree hung with bottles, various fetishes of bones and feathers, and a dead armadillo inverted on the road. When violence strikes, it is brutally quick. Leatherface clobbers two of the young men from the van on the head with a sledgehammer. They die after brief violent convulsions but with little blood. The first female victim is hanged from a meat hook. These first murders are shocking because they occur quickly with so little visual exhibitionism. We see too little to know what is happening. Nor do we get a good view of their murderer, Leatherface, except to see that he is hideous, hairy, and awkward, garbed in butcher's apron and crude leather mask. All we see of him are wild eyes and ugly stubby teeth; he communicates in animal-like grunts.

The film's emphasis on eerie intimations of horror rather than on actual violence may be seen in the sequence leading up to the first girl's death, when she looks for her boyfriend. Alone, she trips and falls into a bizarre room, its floor covered with feathers, bones, teeth, and other grisly remainders of bodies. The soundtrack includes unnerving noises that sound like a rhythmic rattling of bones. There are sudden cuts in both sight and sound; for instance, the one that cuts abruptly to the oddly out of place chicken clucking disapprovingly from a tiny cage overhead. In more cuts from odd angles, we see morbid arrangements of bones placed as if seated on the sofa (Photo 8.1), skulls arranged atop a bureau, lightbulbs gripped by dangling skeletal hands, and so forth. Suddenly, Leatherface finds the girl, hauls her into the kitchen, and hangs her on the meat hook (Photo 8.2), immediately returning to his perfunctory butchering of her boyfriend. Mayhem is matter-of-fact to him. The camera lingers on her screams, and her awareness of her situation is truly horrible, but we do not actually see the hook pierce her flesh or any of her spurting blood (as we would in a more recent film). In the only scene in the movie with an actual chain-saw murder, again no details are shown. Leatherface attacks the fourth victim, Franklin, who is confined to a wheelchair. Because he is helpless, his murder seems particularly heinous, but it is not visually displayed for the audience's titillation. Rather, we see the scene at night in dim light, watching from behind Franklin's chair. Hideous violence is implied as we see the wildly swinging saw and the young man's flailing arms, but once more we do not see any blood.

The rest of the "plot" of the film revolves around the family's pursuit of Franklin's sister, Sally, whom they chase, trap, and offer up to Grandpa to dispatch with feeble strokes of his formerly famous sledgehammer. (Perhaps this is poetic justice in some bizarre sense, because we learned earlier that Sally's grandfather owned the slaughterhouse nearby and that automation has displaced Grandpa and the old methods of "handwork.") Finally, Sally escapes, bruised and bloodied, and flags down a truck on the road. When Leatherface attacks the truck door with his saw, she and the driver leap out and run away. Ultimately, she escapes in the flatbed of another truck. In the final sequence of the film, as the truck drives away into the sunrise, we see Sally's image gradually receding as she laughs hysterically.

TCM 1 presents ambiguous views on gender. There is no hero to protect the young damsel in distress. Instead, the chief patriarchal figure is mad and abusive. The cannibal family includes only men. Given the entirely decrepit Grandpa, we could conclude that patriarchy has run aground. Yet the apparent heroine (or chief victim), Sally, has almost no personality other than wanting to be with her boyfriend. Her only merit is sympathy for her brother Franklin. She is not especially strong, brave, or resourceful: She runs around and screams. We sympathize with her only because she is a "victim." Although the film lingers on the suffering of this one female victim, the body count is actually higher for males than

PHOTO 8.1 *The artful arrangement of death: bones on a sofa at the cannibal family's house in* The Texas Chainsaw Massacre *(1974).*

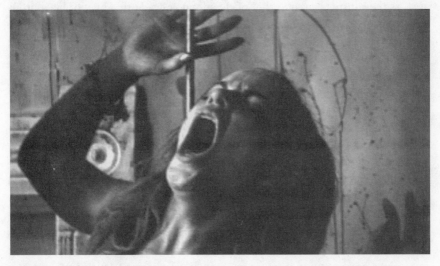

PHOTO 8.2 *The notorious "girl on a meat hook" scene in* The Texas Chainsaw Massacre *(1974).*

females.[9] There is no sexuality associated with the murders or violence in this movie. Sally is attractive, but Leatherface treats all of the youths alike as mere "meat." Even when the three men in the chain-saw family jeer at her at dinner, there are no hints of sexual threats, no come-ons or implications that they might rape her. Their only interest in her is as a sort of cow to be slaughtered, efficiently if possible by Grandpa, who has allegedly not "lost his touch."

In *TCM 1* there is an obvious way in which the crazy family seems evil and the teenagers innocent. But to be fair, the chain-saw family members have been displaced from their jobs and role in life. By contrast, the young people with leisure and funds to travel seem privileged, shallow, and vapidly pleasure-seeking as they squabble or giggle among themselves. Franklin, the invalid with whom we might expect to sympathize, is spoiled, self-pitying, and an obnoxious whiner. He even expresses admiration for Leatherface's nasty self-mutilating brother by saying, "It takes something to do that."

Some of the scenes of horror in *TCM 1* serve to advance the plot. But many bloody or gruesome scenes in this movie are static and call attention to themselves as "arty." These include, for example, the scenes that *arrange* the detritus of murder for visual display: the corpse in the cemetery; the room with bones, skulls, and fetishes; the macabre dining room and creepy Grandpa. The horror of most of these scenes fits with other devices that draw attention to the filmmaker's art, such as the sunspots, an odd shot of the moon, a dead armadillo, or languorous depictions of the Texas landscape. Together these make the film another example of uncanny horror, evoking a sort of nameless dread about the vague evil that abides in this desolate and hostile landscape.

TCM 2 is an altogether different movie. Like the first film, it opens with a grim announcement that "this film is based on a true story"; but the realism of *TCM 1* vanishes in *TCM 2* to be replaced by hyperbolic violence, violence as visual excess. The sequel is dominated by more active and dynamic scenes of hideous gore, but its whole tone is comedic rather than uncanny. "Texasisms" abound, making the place that was so singular in the first film—Texas as the Wild West, linked cinematically to the hardships of the desert and frontier—now the site only of clichéd references to a chili cook-off, college football, the Alamo, Texas Rangers, and six-shooters. Rather than the oppressive and isolated landscape of *TCM 1*, the setting is now an underground burrow beneath an abandoned "Battles of Texas" amusement park. And in place of the shivering and screaming Sally, we now have the gumptious and ambitious disc jockey Stretch, who wants to turn her accidental knowledge of the chain-saw family into a news story that will catapult her to fame. The two key settings here, amusement park and radio station, firmly indicate that our story will transpire within the realm of entertainment.

TCM 2 begins with several none-too-subtle pokes at Texas stereotypes. Two boys drive their Mercedez convertible from Oklahoma to Texas for a big football game. From the highway, they maniacally shoot at signs for the now defunct Texas Battleground Amusement Park. These obnoxious and spoiled boys use their car phone to pester Stretch on her dial-up radio request line. During one of their nuisance calls, they are suddenly attacked by the sons of the cannibal family. Leatherface saws off the top of both their car and the driver's head, which we and his buddy see split in two, still sitting uneasily atop his body. Within the first five minutes of this film, we can see that we are in a whole different world of horror.

Further graphic, tasteless scenes ensue at the radio station where Stretch works. Since she has captured the murder on tape during the boys' call, she plays the tape on air to flush the killers out. This is the strategy urged on her by the lone Texas Ranger, Lefty (Dennis Hopper), who is on an obsessive fifteen-year quest to bring justice to the men who killed his nephew Franklin. Stretch is convinced that this tape may be her avenue to radio-career success. Obligingly, the chain-saw sons show up. First, Stretch encounters the truly disgusting Chop Top, Leatherface's older brother. He wears a mangy black wig to hide the metal plate in his head, which we presume was inserted after his accident with a truck in *TCM 1.* Apparently his head itches, because he uses a nasty hook to dig something, presumably lice, out of his hair. He then eats them, displaying a rotten set of teeth in grimacing smiles.

Stretch is then attacked and chased upstairs by Leatherface, wielding his chain saw. Meanwhile, her sidekick, L.C., is bludgeoned to death by Chop Top with vicious blows to the head that go on endlessly. Poor L.C. (who was already fairly lumpen) quivers on the floor as the scene is extended past all bounds of taste and believability. Stretch's encounter with Leatherface sets up a new gender dynamic (Photo 8.3). He is clearly aroused by the sight of her long bare legs, spread-eagled over an ice bin where he has cornered her. She sees this and actually toys with him, trying to disarm him by asking, "How good *are* you?" His hips gyrate but he seems frustrated and impotent; his chain saw shorts out in the ice bucket. She escapes because Leatherface takes a shine to her. The sequence, like other ones later in the film, treat the saw-as-phallus so overtly that they veer from the horrific into the comedic or parodic.

Later, Stretch follows the cannibal boys to their underground catacombs beneath the amusement park. The last half of the film, which takes place there, abounds in nonstop scenes of visual excess. There is a tour de force sequence where Stretch runs along an endless maze of hallways lit by Christmas lights and decorated by tableaux of corpses and other body parts. The swift tracking shots are brilliantly executed (they are particularly stunning on the big screen). The sta-

PHOTO 8.3   Leatherface (Bill Johnson) attacks Stretch (Caroline Williams) with a chain saw in The Texas Chainsaw Massacre, Part 2 *(1986).*

tic and eerie visual displays of *TCM 1* are replaced in the sequel by a completely over-the-top (and appropriate) amusement-park style of dynamic filmmaking. Just as the (defunct) amusement park recreated scenes of past glory (and blood) at the Alamo, so this movie recreates the scenes of *TCM 1* as demonstrable fakes through the use of grotesque parody.

The parodic scenes in *TCM 2* are too numerous to mention. They include some spectacularly gross subsequences, such as a scene of Stretch watching Leatherface strip off sections of L.C.'s flesh. Although we assume he is dead, L.C. later stands up, briefly and amazingly, to help Stretch out of a pinch. This, even though he is hideously injured and badly skinned. In fact, Leatherface has helped disguise Stretch by making her don the skin of L.C.'s face. Touchingly, she restores it after his last chivalric gesture. Later, we see another macabre dinner-table scene where Grandpa tries but fails to clobber Stretch with the sledgehammer, just as he failed with Sally in *TCM 1*. Further parody involves an extended sequence when Dennis Hopper as the Texas Ranger visits a used-chain-saw supply store to purchase new weapons. He selects two, swings them wildly through the air, tests them in a display of virtuoso chain-saw skill, and then slings them onto his belt like ersatz guns. Throughout the whole sequence of Stretch's attempts to flee the family underground, Hopper is shown flailing away at the structures upholding the park. His manner and expressions become more crazed and lunatic until, wielding the chain saw, he becomes as berserk a figure as Leatherface himself (Photo 8.4). He

PHOTO 8.4   Lefty (Dennis Hopper) goes berserk with his chain saw in The Texas Chainsaw Massacre, Part 2 (1986).

sobs loudly and sentimentally when he discovers the skeleton of poor Franklin, festooned with feathers and twinkly lights, still sitting in his wheelchair. Lefty obviously cannot be relied on to rescue Stretch; she is on her own.

Because the scenes of gore and violence are so extreme, they become ridiculous. The atmosphere is comedic, not horrific, especially in the last half of the movie. Surprisingly few scenes here actually function to set up a mood of horror; the sequel is almost an inverse of TCM 1. Here horror is not hidden and uncanny, it is all on the surface. The gruesome scenes again call attention to the film's artiness, but it is extended way beyond that of TCM 1 in order to showcase the skills of the director, cinematographer, and special-effects guru Tom Savini.

As I noted earlier, the gender ideology of TCM 2 is also utterly different from the original. Key scenes in this film play with the sex/slash formula in perversely hilarious ways. The unforgettably frightening Leatherface of the first film has here become a rather pitiful younger sibling who gets a crush on the heroine and is teased about it by his brother. The notion of chain saw as phallic substitute is driven home (as if it needed to be) when the patriarch of the cannibalistic family tells Leatherface sternly, "Sex or the saw, son, you have to choose!" Although neither film shows any belief in the traditional male hero, it is also worth noting that TCM 2 goes so far as to depict the male rescuer as a loony Lone Ranger with chain saws instead of six-shooters in his gun belt. At least he does manage to "unman" the patriarch by a particularly well-aimed stroke of the saw. One final macabre twist is that in TCM 2, we

PHOTO 8.5   *Stretch (Caroline Williams) about to assume the dead matriarch's saw at the conclusion of* The Texas Chainsaw Massacre, Part 2 *(1986).*

learn that the cannibal family has a *matriarch*, albeit one who is dead (Photo 8.5). She is kept stuffed or mummified atop the battleground's fake mountain with a chain saw ceremoniously laid in her arms like a weird baby. Chop Top chases Stretch up to this aerie at the conclusion of the film and becomes frantic when Stretch threatens to "bother Mama." Thinking quickly, she grabs the saw, and thus, significantly, it is Mama's chain saw that Stretch uses to win her own victory as she becomes "Queen of the Mountain" at the film's conclusion.

Hellraiser: An Overview

My next example of graphic horror is the *Hellraiser* series, launched in 1987 with a film directed by the popular horror author Clive Barker, based on his own story "The Hellbound Heart."[10] There have been (thus far) three sequels: *Hellbound: Hellraiser II* (Tony Randel, 1988); *Hellraiser III: Hell on Earth* (Anthony Hickox, 1992); and *Hellraiser: Bloodline* (Alan Smithee/Kevin Yagher, 1996) (which I refer to here as *Hellraiser IV*).[11] This series resembles many others of the 1980s and 1990s: It has an indestructible central (male) monster, a female protagonist who combats the monster, and violence tinged with sexual overtones. Although the monster seems defeated in every film, a coda of some sort hints at his escape (allowing for sequels). Each series also manifests a trend toward greater excess and over-the-top spectacle. There are a myriad of gross-out special effects in the

Hellraiser sequels, but as in *TCM 2*, they are accompanied by dark humor and deepening parody. There are also increasing numbers of intertextual or inter-filmic references.

I find the *Hellraiser* series better, both conceptually and cinematically, than many of its better-known and longer-running rivals such as *Halloween*, *Nightmare on Elm Street*, and *Friday the 13th*. As in these other series, the makeup and special effects are inventive, gory, and spectacular. The *Hellraiser* movies are generally well made, with high production values, good acting, and literate scripts. The good characters are sympathetic and the plots are complex, so the series is also less formulaic than its rivals; that is, there is a lot to figure out, not just a sequence of slash scenes strung together like beads on a string. Finally, *Hellraiser*'s central monster, Pinhead, is more complex and interesting than Freddy Krueger, Jason, or Michael Myers. He is a true monster, yet elegant and eloquent.

In *Hellraiser,* the monsters are Cenobites—vampirelike creatures with white skin, S&M black-leather garb, and unusual wounds or deformities. They use cruel chains that drag their victims into Hell, where they are pierced, skinned, bled, and eventually transformed into fellow monsters. The Cenobites are said to take you "beyond the limits: pain and pleasure, indivisible." Pinhead, lord of the Cenobites, is named for his bald head studded with nails. His torso is pierced to reveal glimpses of interior organs, and he wears a sinister long black-leather robe, in the style of the Spanish Inquisition (Photo 8.6). I call Pinhead interesting as compared with the monsters of the other film series of the 1980s and 1990s for several reasons. Many other recent horror monsters are not even human: We could list the house with its demons in *Amityville Horror*, the mysterious ghosts of *Poltergeist*, Chucky the doll in *Child's Play*, or the wolves in *The Howling*. And even some of the prominent human monsters are mutely mysterious: Both Jason of *Friday the 13th* and Michael Myers of *Halloween* are (like Leatherface) masked and silent (if you don't count heavy breathing or grunting). They have no real identity and are not even played by the same actor in different films. Pinhead's only real contemporary rival is Freddy Krueger from *A Nightmare on Elm Street*. I do not want to take anything away from Robert Englund's Freddy, but I find him undeveloped and lacking in complexity. Whereas Pinhead and some of the female Cenobites are weirdly sexy (like some vampires), Freddy is just a pervert—a child molester whose interests in sex lack the subtle sophistication of a Cenobite. Pinhead savors victims' flesh salaciously, whereas Freddy just gobbles them down.[12] The Cenobite offers victims "a key to dark wonder, unknown pleasures."

An even more serious problem with Freddy is that the *Nightmare* series descended too fast into wisecracks and parody. Freddy is now famous for his

PHOTO 8.6   Pinhead (Doug Bradley), with his studded head and S&M garb, in Hellraiser
III: Hell on Earth *(1992).*

"Kruegerisms," no more than adolescent one-liners. By contrast, the dignified and
elegant Pinhead has almost Shakespearean scope, expressivity, and depth. As played
by British actor Doug Bradley, Pinhead speaks in a mellifluous deep (mechanically
altered) voice, which adds considerably to his threatening charm. He is clever at his
line readings and fond of alliteration, uttering sentences such as "Down the dark
decades of your pain you will think of *this* as a memory of heaven" and "The time
for trickery and temptation is past. It is now time for terror." Pinhead recalls
Milton's Satan in his devotion to evil and nihilism. In *Hellraiser IV,* when asked
where he places his faith, he responds: "I have no faith. I am *so exquisitely empty.*"
Pinhead especially recalls this figure when we learn about his "fall" and possible redemption in *Hellraiser II* and *Hellraiser III.* He became a Cenobite at some time after World War I, and in *Hellraiser III,* he is split into good human and evil Cenobite
halves at war with each other. True, in *Hellraiser III,* Pinhead comes close to undig-
nified Freddy-like levels of excess and parody, but even so the film presents an intriguing portrayal of this monster as the antichrist. Pinhead thus works well on several levels. As a demon he punishes the wicked, but as a charismatic cinematic
character he also entertains with his amazing spectacles. Even for the innocent,
these visions can be fascinating—an encounter with Pinhead is never dull.

To see how evil is represented in this series, we must look to its central image or
device. In a nutshell, the evil that befalls characters in *Hellraiser* emerges from a

metallic puzzle box, a magical Rubik's cube that some people open because they are searching for extreme stimulation, unearthly pleasure, or illicit knowledge. Opening the box, though, proves to open the gateway to Hell and to lead the pleasure seeker to the Cenobites and their maze of torture, destruction, and transformation—all with sadomasochistic overtones. Only the innocent can escape. I want to suggest that this box functions as a metaphor for the movie camera itself: Like the camera, it is another magical metallic device with complex parts and whirring gears. If you know how to operate it and push the right buttons, it will open up and emit delightful musical sounds and flashes of light. Like the horror-film camera, the key function of the puzzle box is to conjure up monsters. Initially, when the Cenobites are summoned we see only droplets or streaks of light, then great laserlike flashes that finally coalesce into the "physical form" of monsters who walk in to "visit" us from their other world, a world materialized from dazzling white light. The box is like the film camera that projects images of a world that will attract you, repulse you, and drag you in, a whole magical show made out of light and sound. Thus, it is fitting that one of Pinhead's more famous lines is "We have such sights to show you."[13]

We who watch these movies are thus parallel to the characters in them who want to open the puzzle box. There are two levels of interaction with the box. On the surface, certain evil people who succumb to the box's temptations enter a somewhat conventional hell peopled by demons who will punish them. But on a second level, we viewers are like the films' more innocent protagonists who accidentally open the box: They must confront and master its scary spectacles. Viewers can simultaneously relish punishment of the "bad" characters who have illicit desires, cheer on the more innocent characters, and enjoy a peek at the horrific sights of Hell. Nevertheless, like the heroines, our goal is to close the box back up. Ultimately, this will make the projected visions come to an end, locking all the horror and the evil denizens of Hell back within the box/movie where they belong.

By tracking developments in this series, I hope to illuminate the sensibility that governs the creation and appreciation of graphic spectacular horror. I will scrutinize scenes of violence from the *Hellraiser* series more closely here by describing and studying various "numbers." This is a term I borrow from the analysis of parallel genres of cinematic display, including the musical and pornography. I will keep in mind also the two basic assumptions I have used throughout this book: We should not separate form from content in analyzing horror films, nor should we separate the parts of the self—emotions and thought—that come into play in watching a film.

Number and Narrative

In films like *The Texas Chainsaw Massacre, Part 2* or *Hellraiser* that are so dominated by graphic spectacle, we have to explain how aesthetic pleasure in horror
may be bound up with gory scenes that ordinarily seem painful and disgusting.
Pleasure for fans is twofold. First, despite what might seem a mere vulgar emotional kick, the graphic spectacles contribute to the plot and to the cognitive-
emotional content of horror films. And second, for real genre (or subgenre) fans,
the pleasures of graphic visual spectacle are associated with delight in a certain
sort of cinematic creativity. To locate these different kinds of pleasures and interests in relation to *Hellraiser*, I propose to consider how "numbers" function in
these films.

Numbers are sequences of heightened spectacle and emotion. They appear to
be interruptions of plot—scenes that stop the action and introduce another sort
of element, capitalizing on the power of the cinema to produce visual and aural
spectacles of beauty or stunning power. Other genres featuring numbers include
the musical, Western, gangster film, and melodrama. Numbers in these genres
would be the musical selections with song and dance, the gunfights and shoot-
outs, or the scenes that portray overwhelming sadness and weeping. Linda
Williams employs this notion of "numbers" in her very interesting feminist discussion of pornography, *Hard Core: Power, Pleasure, and the "Frenzy of the
Visible."*[14] The numbers in pornography are, of course, scenes depicting sexual activity. Williams somewhat humorously applies this notion from the musical to the
pornography film, where we can also identify certain scenes as solos, duets, trios,
or (in orgy scenes) even choruses. Numbers function as the point of the film, as in
most pornography.

Much the same is true in horror. Visions of monsters and their behavior or
scenes of exaggerated violence are the numbers in horror: what the audience goes
to the films for and expects, what delivers the thrills they want to experience. To
overlook or downgrade these numbers is a mistake. But it is also a mistake to contrast numbers too strongly with the plot, narrative, or form of the film. We need
to realize that instead of being interruptions as they might seem, the numbers in
horror may actually further the plot and must therefore be considered part of the
form of the particular genre in question. As Williams puts it, "Narrative informs
number, and number, in turn, informs narrative."[15] She argues that in certain
cases, problems in the narrative cannot be resolved through the narrative but only
through the numbers: "The resolution of these problems comes about not
through the narrative, or through any one number, but through the relation of
number to narrative and number to number."[16]

I want to describe some numbers from the *Hellraiser* series and analyze the role they play in evoking horror. The task seems daunting: Doesn't their very nature as exemplars of visual excess preclude verbal labeling or discussion? In a sense, yes, the nature of the imagery in horror (as in pornography) must be seen for itself and cannot be captured in words. (This is part of the point of *Hellraiser*'s metaphor of the camera as magical puzzle box.) But still, numbers usually function in a movie in particular ways. The numbers in a musical may enhance the romance; gunfights in a Western advance the plot by depicting the confrontation of good and evil; numbers in pornography primarily aim at arousing the audience, and so on. Numbers in graphic spectacular horror function in at least three ways: (1) they further the narrative, so are part of a film's form or structure; (2) they produce its central emotional and cognitive effects: dread, fear, empathy, awareness of the monster or of evil; and (3) they provide certain aesthetic pleasures that have to do with the audience's knowledge and appreciation of the genre. With *Hellraiser*, as with any other horror series, it is a mistake to separate form (plot or narrative) from content (the spectacle of horror and violence). I want to suggest how films of graphic or excessive horror can produce a fused emotional and cognitive response that prompts us to ponder themes about the nature of good and evil. Numbers in these movies are also visual and creative displays that fans can appreciate for their own sake. Let us now look at some numbers from the *Hellraiser* movies.

Numbers in *Hellraiser I*

In *Hellraiser I,* the numbers or scenes of gore and visual spectacle serve primarily to advance the plot and heighten emotional effects. The movie is well paced, with very little excessive visual display. This will contrast strongly with the film's sequels, where (as in *TCM 2*) extended sequences of very graphic and gory numbers predominate and serve the purpose of cinematic display for its own sake. Accordingly, in my view, the monstrous Cenobites are more frightening in *Hellraiser I* than in the sequels, and its treatment of themes of good and evil is more subtle and ambiguous.

Numbers in the first film fit into a very clear narrative sequence: the film presents graphic, visually extreme numbers primarily to set up and then exhibit the basic confrontations between good and bad characters. None of the numbers in *Hellraiser I* is excessive, and in fact, many of them are surprisingly short—taking a minute or even less. They are more effective and sinister for this. *Hellraiser I,* like *TCM 1,* can be better described as a film about uncanny horror than as a true film of graphic excess (as are the sequels to both movies). Let me describe examples that fulfill the three kinds of functions I have listed.

Several numbers in *Hellraiser* serve the first function: They provide visual plot exposition by depicting the grotesque human monster Frank Cotton (Oliver Smith). These include an initial showpiece sequence where Frank emerges as a skinless man regenerated from drops of blood on the attic floor. The blood is from Frank's brother, Larry (Andrew Robinson), who has accidentally wounded his thumb while moving into the ancestral family house with his new wife, Julia (Clare Higgins). There are a few more short numbers that show glimpses of the hideous Frank as he makes himself known to Julia; these two had a tempestuous fling on the very day of her marriage to Larry. Flashbacks depict their coupling as heated and illicit, making it plain that Frank and Julia are evil, while poor deceived Larry is good and innocent. Frank persuades Julia to help reconstitute him by bringing him fresh blood, and she brings home men she has picked up in bars to murder for him. Then, in short but gross sequences, the vampirelike Frank sucks victims' blood and gets gradually restored, but the scenes are not dwelled upon as visual excess, so I would not quite call them numbers. What is actually more macabre is the sexual attraction between Julia and the deformed and still-skinless Frank.

Most of the early numbers in *Hellraiser* fulfill function 1 of numbers: They advance the narrative. But there are also a few short "teaser" numbers that serve what I have called function 2, heightening emotional effects. Such mood-setting numbers are typically very short; they create an enhanced sense of dread and hint at further gory spectacles to come. One example is a sequence where Frank first shows Julia the magic box and describes how it led him to the Cenobites and Hell. Told in flashbacks, it is elliptical and presents quick flashes of the evil-looking monsters at work torturing Frank. This sequence lasts just one minute. Another mood-creating number is a nightmare that Larry's daughter Kirsty (Ashley Lawrence) has, in which she sees her father's coffin. The scene foreshadows his death at the hands of his evil brother. Kirsty's nightmare is brilliantly filmed: She walks slowly toward a bier surrounded by candles in a dark room while white feathers softly fall like snow. We hear a child wailing. The bier contains a body covered by a shroud. Blood seeps out and wells up to soak the white cloth, and then suddenly the corpse sits up as the shroud slips off to reveal her father. This image is terrifying, so much so that Kirsty screams in her sleep, waking up bathed in sweat when her boyfriend shakes her.

Even the more major and extended numbers in the film, depicting Kirsty's encounters and battles with the Cenobites, combine the same two functions of plot exposition and heightened emotional effects. Scenes of Kirsty's initial meeting with the monsters are especially effective because the film, in effect, packs two different sorts of horror numbers back to back. First there is a three-minute sequence as she follows the sound of a child's cries down a long narrow corridor that has opened up in the wall of her hospital room. She meets a terrifying huge monster that chases her in a heart-pounding sequence. Scenes of this gross monster snapping its rancid jaws are intercut with her racing down the long corridor back to safety. However, she finds no safety in her room because this number leads directly without relief into another three-minute number with a different, slower, and much more ominous tone. It is also terrifying but uses quite different visual and aural effects, launched by a tolling bell. This is Kirsty's first encounter with the Cenobites, who emerge and announce plans to take her to Hell with them. They appear from a blinding white light amid swirling fog. Garbed in black leather, they have ghastly wounds and sport bizarre bondage devices. Some speak with mechanical or whispery voices; one viciously chatters his teeth at her. They appear emotionless and powerful as they inform her that anyone who opens the box *must* return with them to Hell. Despite her fear, the brave Kirsty bargains with them to release her if she will lead them to her evil Uncle Frank, who had escaped them.

The final number or spectacle in this film is its climactic depiction of Kirsty's last battle with and defeat of the Cenobites. Still relentless and calm, the stunningly scary Cenobites impale Frank's flesh with their weapons—chains with hooks at their ends. Although, along with Kirsty, we initially see the weapons gouging his flesh and blood soaking through his shirt, Pinhead tells her, "This is not for your eyes." And the camera shifts away obligingly, shielding us along with her. Soon, however, the Cenobites are finished with Frank and move on to pursue Kirsty, who finally stops them, one by one, by zapping them with the box. As she does so, it produces sort of lightninglike discharges. Thus, in just the way they emerged from light, so the evil Cenobites dissolve away into sizzles of light (Photo 8.7).

The film has a coda depicting a mysterious derelict who walks into a fire to retrieve the box Kirsty has thrown there. He burns but then rises as a huge skeletal bird and flies off carrying the box. This ending supports my interpretation of the puzzle box as metaphor for the camera, because we zoom closely into one panel of the box as it flies through the air. We then look into this circular, lenslike panel, and through it, we see a framed view of Kirsty and her boyfriend on the ground below, which recedes as the film ends (Photo 8.8).

I have said that the numbers in *Hellraiser* primarily serve the first two functions I listed, advancing the plot and heightening the emotional effects. But it would be unfair to deny that they also serve the third function, providing certain aesthetic pleasures of cinematic display. Devotees of horror appreciate the niceties of costumes, makeup, and special effects, and they consider how scenes have been made at the same time that they react to them. These are pleasures of what psychologist

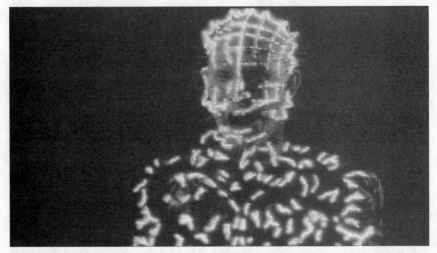

PHOTO 8.7   *Pinhead (Doug Bradley) is "zapped" by the box and vanishes into the light in* Hellraiser *(1987).*

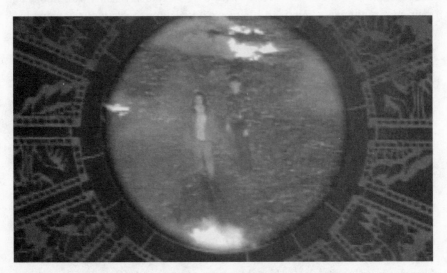

PHOTO 8.8   *Our view of Kirsty (Ashley Lawrence) and her boyfriend (Sean Chapman) through the "lens" in the puzzle box at the conclusion of* Hellraiser *(1987).*

Ed S. Tan, in his book *Emotion and the Structure of Narrative Film: Film as an Emotion Machine*, calls "cinephiles."[17] As Tan notes, cinephiles may have preferences for different genres. Much of the *Hellraiser* films' success depends on special effects by Barker's frequent collaborator Bob Keen, and horror fans will find these effects in themselves interesting and entertaining.

For example, the first number in the film, Frank's return from Hell as a skinless man, is quite spectacular. Larry's drops of blood have fizzed on the attic floor, and we see a mysterious acidic hissing and coagulation. Stringy bands emerge from the goopy mess, eventually blending into an exoskeleton that struggles to arise. The horror cinephile will appreciate this sequence as illustrating the masterful art of the horror "FX" crew. We will be interested in how effects man Bob Keen and his crew made this sequence as well as in its references to other classic scenes in the horror canon. Clearly, the sequence pays some homage to the inevitable filmic recreations of Frankenstein's monster from the spark of electricity. As we saw in Chapter 1, it seems to be a given that every *Frankenstein* film will feature as one of its numbers a painful birth scene of the monster who screams upon his awakening. We might note other things about this rebirth *Hellraiser* scene, such as whether the film has used models, animations, or digital enhancement or whether perhaps certain parts of the sequence were made by running film backward. This kind of observation of details about numbers tends to come much more to the forefront in horror-film sequels, so I turn next to that topic.

The Shifting Function of Numbers in *Hellraiser* Sequels

The role of numbers in *Hellraiser* that I have just summarized is typical of traditional horror, where numbers are effective in presenting monstrous evil but do not dominate the film. They are used sparingly and enhance our desire to see and know more, especially about the monsters. Numbers are interspersed with narrative so that certain scenes require the numbers to advance the narrative, and of course, they also heighten emotional effects of fear and dread. The third function of numbers—generating spectacles that reward special kinds of aesthetic interest—is not paramount. But it becomes so in sequels, as is evident in the *Hellraiser*, *TCM*, and other horror series of the 1980s and 1990s. Sequels exhibit a clear trend toward graphic spectacular horror or toward the use of numbers for their own sake. In sequels, since the numbers are usually not as well integrated with the film's plot or narrative, they primarily serve the third purpose I listed above. That is, they provide pleasures specific to the genre for fans, as they become more a matter of pure entertainment. This makes it appear as though sequels are orgies of visual violence. But I think to say that is too simple.

Sequels have a special appeal to the fans of a genre. They often prompt a switch from involvement in a film's plot to a metalevel sort of aesthetic appreciation based on special knowledge and interests.[18] Graphic horror sequels enable fans to study and comment upon cinematic techniques: plot variations, allusions, style, effects (FX) wizardry, parody, and "in-jokes." This trend toward in-jokes and witty visual excess holds true of the *Hellraiser* series. Successive films become more and more parodic and extreme. As the numbers take over, narrative and emotions are subordinated to spectacle as a goal in its own right. Sequels may try to develop the monster so as to take the story in new directions, but in essence, they are forced to rely on small variations in the human protagonists or villains and to offer new confrontations where the heroes or heroines can win out. Even if sequels showcase the monster and provide more explanatory or visual detail, this can only be interesting to the extent that the monster is interesting. Usually, sequels offer little further insight into the nature of the relevant kind of evil. Despite all the gore and violence, then, the evil that is depicted in sequels shifts from being threatening or mysterious and uncanny to something more cartoonlike. This actually makes evil in sequels less potent even as the violence is increased. In sequels, heroes or heroines become more insipidly virtuous and preternaturally strong. Since the battle's outcome becomes more foreordained, the audience's involvement can shift to sheer appreciation of the graphic spectacle as visual display.

Whereas in *Hellraiser I* the numbers are usually very brief and are interspersed among more ordinary narrative sequences, in *Hellraiser II* and *III*, the numbers take over. They *become* the narrative, so much so that there are vast twenty-minute sequences of nothing but spectacle, mayhem, destruction, and disaster: blood, nightmare scenes, explosions, attacks, and the like. For *Hellraiser II*, such numbers include horrific scenes of the regeneration of a skinless yet still sexy Julia from the bloody mattress on which she allegedly died in *Hellraiser I* or the transformation of the evil psychiatrist Dr. Channard (Kenneth Cranham) into a preposterously hideous Cenobite with a dozen snaky arms capped by nasty sharp medical instrument "hands." *Hellraiser III* features a set of creatively transformed-by-technology Cenobites, Pinhead slurping the skin off a woman, and a true bloodbath that slaughters dozens of victims in an S&M bar. The body count in *Hellraiser IV* may be lower, but the film still has its share of visually extreme numbers, such as a sequence where two frightened twin cops are transformed by torture into a new merged Cenobite with gruesomely deformed head and body.

Moments of spectacular horror in *Hellraiser I* worked to enhance the overall story line and atmosphere, but in the sequels, numbers are for visual display, an end in themselves. But I propose that audiences do not simply relish the sorts of spectacles I have just described as a kind of vicarious violence. Rather, fans often look for the way that the numbers employ wit, parody, intertextuality, and cross-references to earlier films. Cinephiles of horror follow not just the spectacles themselves but the intertextual references. Are they derivative and imitative or clever readaptations?

For example, in *Hellraiser III's* first number, a man who has opened the box is brought into a quiet emergency room. Disaster strikes spectacularly and suddenly, with bolts of blue light, chains out of nowhere, screams, and blood; the patient's head suddenly explodes (a clear reference to *Scanners*). In another scene at the S&M club where much of the action in *Hellraiser III* takes place, metal doors are bolted shut on victims trying to escape Pinhead's orgy of violence. Our view switches to the outside, and blood seeps or wells out on the floor from behind the metal doors. This sequence is a clear reference to the blood behind the elevator in *The Shining*. The conclusion, where Pinhead's two sides fight one another and blend together again, recalls *Scanners* and its concluding epic battle between good and bad telepathic brothers. And of course it is hard to forget various *Exorcist* scenes when Pinhead defeats the priest and forces him to "eat of my body." The film is even brazen enough to incorporate interfilmic reference to its own precursor: The evil J. P. tells Terri, his intended victim, to "come to Daddy," using the same gestures and tone of voice used by the evil and skinless Frank in the first *Hellraiser*.

In the *Hellraiser* sequels, Pinhead is brought more into focus as we are given an elaborate explanation of his origins. Another typical sequel effect here is the parodic nature of his accompanying band of Cenobites. Whereas in the first film these creatures were mysteriously medieval, slow, and silent, they subsequently become more like a combination of zombies, vampires, and punkish drug addicts, chattering mindlessly away in today's casual vernacular as they go about their evil business ("Relax baby, this is better than sex"). In *Hellraiser II,* the perverse psychiatrist, Dr. Channard, after his transformation, makes humorous "Kruegeresque" remarks, such as (appearing in ghastly form to the hospital) "The doctor is in" and "I'm taking over this operation, and you girls are my first patients." The Cenobites in *Hellraiser III* are all rather funny combinations of humans with technology: a disc jockey now has CDs impaled in his head, which he can fling like murderous Frisbees; a TV cameraman becomes a monster with a telephoto lens eye with which he can impale his victims. After he kills one man, he "focuses" on the heroine and says "Ready for your close-up?" and after another kill, "That's a wrap." There were no suggestions that Hell included similar dark humor in the original *Hellraiser*.

"Hell" and Evil in the *Hellraiser* Films

I have suggested that the numbers in sequels, which are often orgies of graphic visual excess, provide genre fans with specific kinds of aesthetic pleasures. I have also said that we need not assume that people who enjoy such films thereby endorse evil and cruelty. Instead, they enjoy the creativity of the cinematic visions behind the monsters. In fact, the graphic horror of the *Hellraiser* movies actually reinforces conservative conceptions of good and evil. The horror here is in fact very much in keeping with Judeo-Christian assumptions about Hell as a region transcending space and time, peopled by monsters, where horrific tortures are visited upon people who are in some significant sense bad ("sinners") and *deserve* it. We can see this by summarizing how the films portray their villains and heroes.

The villains of these films follow a transparent logic. In keeping with the two levels I have described, there are both stereotypical human and also creative cinematic personifications of good and evil. Each film juxtaposes the visually stunning Pinhead and the Cenobites, conjured up out of the box, to a human villain, the person whose sins launch the action by opening the gateway to Hell. Pinhead's evil exists on a whole different level from that of the human villains, not so much because he is supernatural (he is not, given his origins) as because he serves the spectacle in a way they do not. Their concern is with pleasure; his concern is with controlling the magic box. In the first film, Frank Cotton is a sexy ne'er-do-well, someone capable of seducing his brother's fiancée just hours before the wedding, killing this lover along with his own brother, and raping his own niece, the heroine, Kirsty. In the second film, the evil psychiatrist, Dr. Channard, violates patients' rights, searches for illicit knowledge of the paranormal, and performs unscrupulous and painful experiments on people's brains; he killed the mother of the heroine, Tiffany, just in order to study her brain.

In the third film, the villainous J. P. Monroe is a wealthy, narcissistic, and hedonistic owner of an S&M bar in New York who acquired his wealth after he shot and killed his parents for their fortune. He seduces women and casts them aside in such a crude fashion that he invites Pinhead's comparison of their behavior as equally vile consumers of female flesh. Pinhead tells J. P., "There is a place at my right hand for a man of your tastes—tastes I can help you indulge: power, dominion." Pinhead's attack and murder of all the many people at the S&M club the "Boiler Room" is an extended and very Bosch-like scene where all the people are killed by implements of their own pleasure, whether by CDs slicing their skull or by pool balls jammed into their mouths. This sequence piles up murder and mayhem in a really incredible way (impressive partly because each death is different). Finally, in *Hellraiser IV*, the sin is again that of excessive and illicit desires for sexual pleasure and power, now painted as emblematic of the decay of the French aristocracy.

Let us now turn to the protagonists. Typically, they are again young females. The first film is about family relations, and the setting is a suburban house. The heroine, Kirsty, is very sympathetic. She seeks adult sexuality, independence, and a happy relationship with her father. She desires just enough sexual knowledge that she opens the box and must pay the price, but she escapes in the end because her desires are not perverse. The second film is also about family, but now so disrupted that its setting is a psychiatric institution or asylum. In this film, Kirsty grows up and assumes a mothering role in relation to the younger asylum inmate Tiffany (Imogen Boorman) as they confront their evil psychiatrist and his attempts to win the pleasures of Hell.

The third film's heroine, Joey (Paula Marshall), encounters Pinhead only by doing her job of good investigative reporting. She is also motivated by a desire to know more about her dead father. Hell is treated here as having a religious significance that is very traditional. When a priest tells Joey, "There are no demons, those are only metaphors and parables," Pinhead quickly arrives on the scene to prove him wrong in the most vivid ways possible. He melts the silver cross, shatters the stained-glass windows, desecrates the altar, and acts the part of the antichrist by performing a black mass sharing out his own internal organs. The "sin" of this film is primarily hedonism. The film concludes with intimations of generic doom by showing businessmen rushing around a busy corporation lobby in a building decorated with patterns of the puzzle box.

The fourth film ranges among settings in three centuries: eighteenth-century France, twentieth-century America, and a twenty-second-century space station. It thus careens dizzily among the previous films and other genre films like *Interview with the Vampire* and *Alien*. We learn that the puzzle box was initially created in 1784 to whet the appetites—for both sex and black magic—of an evil Marquis de Sade–like French aristocrat, the Duc de L'Isle. Once again, the sin here is pleasure/hedonism. (Pinhead comments, "The Garden of Eden is a garden of flesh.") The film reinforces the importance of a belief or faith in good and evil that transcends rationality or scientific knowledge. In the antique French setting, a doctor performing an autopsy says to the young hero LeMarchand: "There is no hell. This is a modern scientific age." *Hellraiser IV* is especially significant because it shows that neither religion nor science can solve the problem of evil. What is needed instead is, almost unbelievably, *art!*—or more precisely, art combined with technology in the new geeky and technique-driven kind of creativity typical of the cinema itself.[19] Scientific rationality denies the existence of hell and demons, religion does not even seem a contender—but art recognizes there are demons and provides the means of banishing them. The young artist/scientist creates the box anew on a gigantic scale out in space so that it makes a cosmic laser light show to trap the lead Cenobite for all time (allegedly).[20] Once again, the box has become a clear metaphor for the movie camera.

It is interesting to speculate about why the fourth film breaks the usual pattern of exhibiting a heroine who combats Pinhead. The hero of *Hellraiser IV*, played in three time periods by the same actor, is a young male artist: a puzzle-box maker, an architect, or a space-station scientist who designs a light box to trap the demons his ancestor evoked. I think that the gender of the protagonist/chief victim changes in the fourth film because of stereotypical expectations about the "normal" gender role of geeky techno-computer artists. In the first film, the victim is coded as a family member who can be targeted by the villainous sexually predatory adult: She must be female to enhance her victim status. In the second film, the femaleness of the two protagonists again makes them better victims. Although they are orphans, they resolve their problems by creating a synthetic mother-daughter bond. In the third film, the victim is a young woman who is coded as "good" because she values work, friendship, and family over entertainment and sex. But in the fourth film, the victim/hero is an artist with technological skills. As someone able to use computers to create designs in light, he was presumably made male because he evoked echoes (whether acknowledged or not) of the all-male filmmaking team of writers, effects men, and directors. My suggestion is that since these craftsmen identified with the role, they chose to embody it in a male hero who would be a worthy antagonist of Pinhead.

Conclusion: Spectacular Destruction—and Creation

Some people would say that the numbers in graphic spectacular horror are sheer pyrotechnical displays of monstrousness that serve only the end of meaningless violence. I admit this may be true in some cases, but not all. Nor do psychological studies really support such a conclusion.[21] In graphic spectacular horror films, the role of numbers is more complicated. I think that this is so even though the horror films of recent decades have tended to have more and more gruesome and excessive sequences—what William Paul labels "gross-out" horror in his book *Laughing Screaming: Modern Hollywood Horror and Comedy*.[22] These post-1970s films employ brilliant special effects, but the numbers in them are not just there as spectacles of mindless gore. They convey information about the monster, its nature and its desires, and who it will attack and why. As we watch the numbers, we can try to learn the laws about these monsters, so as to classify them and address the evil that they represent. Also, the numbers provide the specialized aesthetic pleasures for fans that I have described above.

For example, I argued that the numbers in the *Hellraiser* series offer pleasures to fans on two levels, a filmic level of plot and a metalevel (or, as Ed S. Tan would say, an artifact level) of cinematic creativity. Accordingly, the moral theories they present are also dual—even often at tension with one another, a point that also applies to their gender ideologies. On the surface level of the plot or narrative, conventional morality reigns. Wicked people (or monsters) are punished and their evils are defeated, satisfying the superficial desire for justice to prevail. This level often features a human villain, usually a man who is overflowing with greed, lust, or mad desires for illicit knowledge and power. The story then puts him into conflict with a strong, virtuous, rather pure young woman who emerges victorious. The *Hellraiser* movies are typical in this regard, with their classical presentation of evil as a kind of human sin and of good as innocence that wins out and survives (after a certain amount of suffering). But on the metalevel, the audience here (as in other films like *Nightmare on Elm Street*) is emotionally invested in and desires the survival of the *monster*. And in the major horror series of recent years, this monster is invariably a male: Leatherface, Pinhead, Freddy, Jason, Michael Myers. What are we to make of this fact?

My reading of the monster's maleness is that he represents certain powers that are still regarded as virtues and that are stereotypically coded as male. In particular, the monster is male because he is like the filmmakers, a magician who makes the visual spectacles possible. The monster is associated with the creativity behind the numbers that constitute the aesthetic pleasures of graphic horror. I have suggested, by reading the central metaphor of the puzzle box as camera in *Hellraiser*, that the monster is valued so that our entertaining spectacles may continue. Pinhead arrives on the scene as a cue that the box has been opened and that amazing visual spectacles are about to begin. Similarly, Freddy Krueger arrives on the scene as characters begin their "dreaming." Dreams in the *Nightmare* series are analogous to the box in *Hellraiser*, a cue that visual pleasures are about to unfold. To say this leaves open the question of whether the audience that enjoys graphic spectacular horror thereby endorses or identifies with the amorality and cruelty of the monster. I myself doubt that this is true, since fans claim to find the numbers or visual spectacles of gore here entertaining and funny rather than seductive and alluring.

Each monster is different, however, and to prove my thesis in general would require the study and analysis of more films. The deviousness of Freddy, the single-mindedness of Leatherface, and the inexorability of Jason are distinct features that appeal to specific audiences. The Cenobites are almost unique among monsters, except for vampires, in that they are alluring. Their black leather clothes and "Goth" makeup are currently trendy and coded as sexy, and even "normal" people might wonder what it feels like to go "beyond the limits of pleasure and pain." But there are other factors at play here, including the use of wit, parody, and interfilmic reference in graphic horror numbers, along with Pinhead's refined use of language and his unique nihilism. I focused on the *Hellraiser* series because these movies so interestingly split the human villains from the supernatural ones. I find Pinhead a more interesting monster than Freddy because although he is disgusting and scary, yet we can sympathize with him—especially once we see that he has both good and evil halves. He is "one of us," a person who crossed over to the other side through temptation when he was bored and tired of living. His good half, Captain Spenser, describes himself as having been a lost soul who explored forbidden pleasures. The fact is, Pinhead is smart. He is just about the only person who has managed to get away with sin and enjoy "Hellish life." He is also truthful, even insightful—not just an agent of evil but an informant about it. As Spenser, he confides to Joey: "My evil was too strong. It lived . . . waited. What I was is out there in your world, unbound, unstoppable." Yet he is also cynical; as Pinhead, he comments to Joey in *Hellraiser III:* "Unbearable, isn't it, the suffering of strangers, the agony of friends. There is a secret song at the center of the world, Joey, and its sound is like razors through flesh." "I don't believe you," she replies, and he retorts: "Oh, come. Oh, you can hear its faint echo right now. I'm here to turn up the volume, to press the stinking face of humanity into the dark blood of its own secret heart." In sum, fans like Pinhead because of the very particular role he plays in the graphic spectacles of *Hellraiser*, a role that can be played only by good monsters in horror: He both reveals and punishes human monsters or evildoers. What we like about him is the very quality Spenser warns Joey about: "[H]e can be very persuasive . . . and very inventive." He only *threatens* to punish the innocent, since they eventually defeat him. In *Hellraiser II*, he cautions his band against taking the young box-opener Tiffany because "[i]t is not hands that summon us, it is *desire*." Perhaps the two levels I have described come together here: "Evil" humans are those with illicit and extreme desires, but even we, mostly innocent viewers, must also "suffer" the pains of Pinhead's gory spectacles as the price of our own somewhat illicit pleasure and desire to enjoy the forbidden spectacles of his (and Clive Barker's) "Hell."

Despite their individual differences, monsters like Pinhead, Freddy, Leatherface, and Jason function alike in one key way—they take graphic visual spectacle to new extremes. They figure in films whose numbers are given over to what I called function 3, display for its own sake. Their presence is linked to frightening displays of forces of destruction that can simultaneously be disgusting yet enjoyable. I have suggested that their maleness is emblematic of the creativity of horror filmmakers. Part of the pleasure they facilitate is, I have argued, pleasure in the sheer cinematic skill of these filmmakers, special-effects artists, and so on. In the end, I would say that the creativity and entertainment they bring are not perverse or disturbing, because the surface gore in graphic spectacular horror is mitigated by the simplistic and cartoonlike treatment of evil in these films. This makes graphic horror-film villains quite different from Hannibal Lecter. In graphic horror films, the directors expect audiences to recognize extreme graphic effects as fake and entertaining; in *The Silence of the Lambs*, as I suggested in Chapter 5, director Demme is more sneaky or underhanded in aligning himself with the artistry of Lecter's crimes. Graphic horror films like *Hellraiser* or *TCM 2* do not invite audiences to take evil seriously or to identify with it any more than with brutes in cartoons that routinely "blam" and "zap" their victims.

In many ways, graphic horror films are far less troubling than uncanny films like *The Shining* or *Eraserhead* that do hint or argue that there are powerful forces of evil in the cosmos. I called those two films cases of the *anti*sublime in Chapter 7 because they depict a world that overwhelms the self and undermines possibilities of moral action. Such uncanny evil flattens and narrows human possibilities. Despite their surface violence, the films of graphic spectacular horror are less unsettling and negative because their celebration of the monster's evil as creativity is joyous and affirmative. Each monster serves only a kind of formulaic and meaningless evil, one that we need not take seriously. The scenes of graphic horror are so far-fetched that they obviously present a kind of cinematic creativity to be relished.

I would relate this combining of playful creativity and destruction to another kind of sublime, which we could call the "Nietzschean sublime" as a tribute to Nietzsche's *The Birth of Tragedy*.[23] Nietzsche's celebration of the Dionysian in that work is often misrepresented. His book is subtitled *Hellenism Versus Pessimism*, and he contrasts Greek tragedy as optimistic to a sort of Schopenhauerian pessimism. Nietzsche traces the origins of ancient Greek tragedy to the suffering of Dionysus as a subject. Dionysus, in true horror-film fashion, was torn limb from limb; he suffered the extremes of violence but was continually reborn. Like the horror movie villain who continually reemerges from the dead, human counterparts who represented Dionysus on the stage were also destroyed and yet somehow exalted in tragedy. Nietzsche thus considered the plots of tragedies "optimistic" because they testified to this basic human resilience even in the face of an acknowledgment of evil and destruction. He made this point by saying that the Dionysian artist shows a primal unity of good with evil, of pain and contradiction.

But of course in Nietzsche's view, *creation* was equally important as destruction, and he had in mind the creative spirit behind the plays themselves. Nietzsche emphasized the optimism of this sort of creativity in tragedy by noting that the tragic Dionysian power of destruction was always presented or accompanied and complemented by an Apollonian structure and beauty in the plot and poetry of drama. The highly regulated structures of tragedy were necessary to enable audiences to view its horrific visions without despair. Thus, Nietzsche says such things as "without images there would be pure primordial pain."[24] The Apollonian elements of order and rhythm provided for a way to sustain individuality in the face of the cosmos's indifferent force of destruction or loss of self.

Of course, tragedy in Nietzsche's sense, at least on the surface, seems quite different from films of graphic horror. It might seem preposterous to maintain that films like *Hellraiser* or *The Texas Chainsaw Massacre* feature an Apollonian quality of beautifully ordered structure, since that would seem to put them on a par with the works of Sophocles and Aeschylus. Nevertheless, the principle is the same. Although it may seem to the uninitiated and squeamish viewer that there is little Apollonian structure and order in films of graphic horror, I have tried to show that a key thing fans like about the graphic and gory numbers on display in these movies is that they are highly structured. Fans recognize their creativity as artifacts and their intelligence or wit in making interfilmic references. Thus, surprisingly, an element of aesthetic distance does figure into the appreciation of graphic spectacular horror films, despite their orgies of destruction. Fans appreciate how well made these films are (if they are) *as* movies depicting destruction. This sort of amorality has an innocence to it and is not pessimistic, as the dark visions of uncanny horror films are. It is here, as Nietzsche said of tragedy, that "the existence of the world seems justified only as an aesthetic phenomenon."

In more traditional horror films, we almost never see quite enough of the monster to know him (or her or it). This suggests that evil is elusive and hard to pin down. The more we see evil, and the more numbers that put it on display, the more shallow its depiction usually becomes. It is treated more simplistically and is easier to make fun of and wipe out. This is why the Leatherface of *TCM 1* is much more frightening (and uncanny) than the more lovesick and silly version we see a lot of in *TCM 2*. In an odd way, then, the monster is almost more desirable the less we see of him—perhaps unlike (or maybe, like!) the genitals we can observe in pornography. Linda Williams in *Hard Core* emphasizes the fact that pornography focuses on the "money shot" or male "come shot" as visible "proof" of pleasure, but she notes that there is no symmetrical proof of female pleasure. Female pleasure is thus a "problem" that requires elaborate representation through facial gestures, sounds, and so forth. But Williams says these sorts of sounds may be inserted at the cost of the usual blending or seamless suture between sound and image. They end up being somewhat vague, indefinite, or dislocated indications of "pleasure" in the abstract.[25] In much the same way, I would argue that in horror, visual spectacle functions to provide a "proof" of pain. However, excessive, cartoonlike horror provides so many cries, moans, and screams that there is a similar dislocation of pain from the image. In the end, this makes the pain unreal since there is no "proof" of it— even and perhaps especially when we witness a lot of blood and gore.

Traditional horror films use blood and gore as part of their demonstration that evil exists, that it confronts us as mortal, fragile creatures whose bodies can be pierced and can bleed and come apart. Again, horror films traditionally reject evil in the sense that they depict its sources as monstrous, something that good humans must combat. Although evil is shown as a significant force, it is usually one that should and can be defeated. But as I have argued here, when the numbers in horror films become excessive, parodic, or comedic, as in *TCM 2* and the *Hellraiser* sequels, then the presentation of evil becomes much more cartoon-like—and the more extreme it is, the less believable and convincing. Graphic horror shares not just its penchant for numbers with pornography. Both genres are about the *embodiment* of humans or about intimacies of the flesh, but I find that both somewhat paradoxically make this embodiment unreal through their graphic excess and visual multiplication of details. Pornography makes breasts, buttocks, penises, and vaginas more beautiful (more large or hard or soft or juicy) than the best sex in real life. There is so much mounting, pleasure, moaning, coming, and semen it is impossible to believe in it all. Similarly, graphic horror shows more pain, screams, blood, wounds, and gore than is really possible or believable. Hence, the numbers in graphic horror movies are not really celebrating pain. Nor are they reinforcing the need to defeat monstrous evil. Rather, they are poking fun at it, denying its power and permanence. This, too, is why we desire the survival of the monster. After all, in graphic horror it is always the monster in the end who understands the humor behind the whole process and also accepts the fact that he himself must suffer the most violence—like Dionysus.

In moving from Chapter 7 to this chapter, I have described a kind of progression—or a falling away perhaps—in treatments of the sublime. For Kant, the sublime was a magnificent and awesome force of nature that overwhelmed and yet elevated us. But in uncanny horror, the message is about an antisublime, a superior force of evil that cannot be addressed and that will defeat us. Now in this chapter, in linking graphic spectacular horror to Nietzsche's particular view of ancient Greek tragedy, we encounter a kind of amoral sublime, an enjoyment of cosmic combined forces of creation and destruction. Evil is taken seriously in this subgenre of horror only in the sense that it is combined with powers that enable us to laugh at it and deny it.

epilogue: The Appeal of Horror

In *Nosferatu* (F. W. Murnau, 1922), among the first horror films ever made, the vampire Count Orlok (Max Schreck) is a creature of light and shadows, born of cinematic magic. He floats straight up from his dark coffin, materializes in gothic arches, passes invisibly through stone walls, and eventually pursues the heroine into a room where she waits alone, terrified, ready to sacrifice herself to save her husband. The most chilling sequence in this still-scary movie is Orlok's ascent up the stairs, shown largely through his hideous shadow, great clawlike fingers extended (Photo E.1). In this movie, all my themes come together: a repulsive figure in a beautiful film, the victimization of a woman by a monstrous man, his evil versus her purity and moral strength—a patriarchal picture that paints her as worthy because she will die for the man she loves. Her heroism does succeed in the sense that she detains the vampire until, in this movie, he is destroyed by a device Bram Stoker did not invent—the light that enters her room at dawn. Sunlight magically banishes him into a screen-magic puff of disappearing smoke. Similar tricks of cinematic magic abound in the films I have discussed.

I have argued in this book that horror films may present subtle, nuanced, and interesting symbolic visions of evil—that they need not be "stupid" or "juvenile," to quote again the pejorative terms director David Cronenberg also rejects. Horror films have appeal because they continue a lengthy tradition of making art, addressing human fears and limitations, forcing confrontations with monsters who overturn the natural order—of life and death, natural/-supernatural, or human/nonhuman. They depict vivid threats to our values and concepts, our very bodily and mental integrity. As a cognitivist, I hold that such films, like other cultural artifacts, engage many of our intertwined human abilities. Horror films may aim at producing gut-level reactions such as fear, revulsion, anxiety, or disgust, but they also stimulate more complex emotional and

PHOTO E.1   Orlok creeps up the stairs to attack the heroine in Nosferatu *(1922).*

intellectual responses. They provide visions of a world where action may or may not have meaning, where a monster may or may not be sympathetic, where evil people may or may not win out in the end.

Nosferatu provided a moral resolution at the cost of the heroine's life and so does *Alien³* many years later. But sometimes horror subverts standard gender ideologies; the sources of evil are unstable and shifting and often lie hidden beneath the surface. In *Frankenstein* and all its many successors, men (or women) who meddle with nature must pay the price. Horror films like *Frenzy* or *Repulsion* depict male violence against women so as to condemn it and make plain its monstrosity. In "women-and-bugs" movies, heroines help to restore order and justice, often by bringing intellect, strength, and intuition, in addition to emotions like maternal caring, into the picture. Vampire movies may loosen strict gender-role expectations by exhibiting attractive figures of polymorphous perversity. In uncanny films like *The Shining* or *Eraserhead,* men become evil destructive fathers as signs of a universe run amok. Even graphic horror movies with superhumanly violent male monsters like the *Texas Chainsaw* family can highlight female heroes who help set the moral order straight again in the end—and this time not by sacrificing themselves.

PHOTO E.2   *Orlok about to vanish from the sunlight of dawn in* Nosferatu *(1922).*

And what of evil? Evil was obvious in Murnau's *Nosferatu*. It dwelled in the vampire who brought plague wherever he went. It was simply death, but not conversion or seduction. By contrast, the vampires in Anne Rice's stories are seducers seeking partners in a shared life that "transvalues values." Pinhead's evil is instructively different: He offers people their due rewards, pain justly deserved for transgressive behavior. Pinhead sees himself as the antichrist; he is a Lucifer with the role of punisher rather than seducer into sin. He is always defeated, but "the box" that calls him survives—and so will human evil. This may seem simplistic; many horror films offer subtler but equally grim verdicts about human nature and the predominance of evil. We have seen movies with dire messages like *The Shining, Dead Ringers, Henry: Portrait of a Serial Killer,* and *Repulsion,* as well as more seductively cynical ones like *The Hunger* and *The Silence of the Lambs.* Still others offer up charms against evil—perhaps "female" values as in the *Frankenstein* tradition, the romantic love and repentance showcased in *Bram Stoker's Dracula,* or even "Art" itself, as at the end of *Eraserhead.*

Most of all, horror movies are about the very picturing of evil. Monsters in horror are, like Count Orlok, made of light and shadow, creatures born of film.

There are recurring allusions in horror films to the nature of our very fascination with horror—allusions to the processes of cinematic depiction, to the pleasures of spectacle, and to traditions of symbolic representations of evil and monsters. These show up in the formulas repeated in certain genres (the laboratory birth scenes of *Frankenstein*, the scenes of "the book" or "the bite" in Dracula movies). Francis Ford Coppola's Dracula is someone we, like Mina, recognize in the Cinematograph as a character we already know and love. Movies in the slasher tradition foreground the watching and filming of the atrocities they picture, inviting us into or excluding us from their villainous characters' perspectives. By "picturing" I mean the whole of cinematic art: special effects, sound, and music, as well as images, plot, and acting. We saw in such different movies as *The Shining*, *Eraserhead*, *Repulsion*, and *Scanners* that uncanny watchers are central, present not just in the unsettling scenes we view but also in what we hear—eerie heartbeats, echoes, ticks, clangs, and hisses. Orlok's evil has been updated and revamped in Pinhead, one of our newest movie monsters. *Hellraiser* gives us a new-yet-old version of the same cinematic monster magic, the creation of an evil creature who lives only on film and dies in the light. Pinhead materializes from and dematerializes back into the light, just like Orlok (Photo E.2). Pinhead and monsters like him will come to anyone operating the magic camera–like box, with its gleams of light and tinkling sounds. The allure of horror is that such monsters come out of their box to entertain, perplex, disturb, and provoke us, as they confront us with a multitude of visions of evil.

NOTES

Introduction

1. David Cronenberg, *Cronenberg on Cronenberg*, rev. ed., ed. Chris Rodley (London and Boston: Faber and Faber, 1997), 59.

2. C. Fred Alford, *What Evil Means to Us* (Ithaca and London: Cornell University Press, 1997).

3. Hannah Arendt, *Eichmann in Jerusalem: A Report on the Banality of Evil*, rev. and enl. ed. (New York: Viking Press, 1965).

4. Such audience activity is also a major theme in Noël Carroll's recent book, *A Philosophy of Mass Art* (Oxford: Clarendon Press, 1998); see especially 360–412.

5. See Martha C. Nussbaum, *The Fragility of Goodness: Luck and Ethics in Greek Tragedy and Philosophy* (Cambridge: Cambridge University Press, 1986).

6. Kendall Walton, *Mimesis as Make-Believe: On the Foundations of the Representational Arts* (Cambridge, Mass. and London: Harvard University Press, 1990).

7. I have offered an overview and defense of cognitivism in aesthetics, illustrated by examples of a variety of adherents from both the Aristotelian and the pragmatist tradition, in my article "Art and Moral Knowledge," *Philosophical Topics* 25 (1) (Spring 1997):11–36.

8. David Bordwell and Noël Carroll, eds., introduction to *Post-Theory: Reconstructing Film Studies* (Madison: University of Wisconsin Press, 1997), xvi. In that volume, Bordwell also explains in his essay "Film Studies and Grand Theory" that cognitivism "advocates the exploration of hypotheses about film reception in terms of the cognitive and perceptual processes of spectators, rather than in terms of the unconscious processes and syndromes favored by Theory" (p. 48). The editors emphasize the diversity and disagreement among cognitivists; see p. xvi. Two other recent volumes that include numerous essays that exemplify the cognitivist position are Richard Allen and Murray Smith, eds., *Film Theory and Philosophy* (Oxford: Clarendon Press, 1997), and Carl Plantinga and Greg M. Smith, eds., *Passionate Views: Film, Cognition, and Emotion* (Baltimore and London: Johns Hopkins University Press, 1999).

9. Ed S. Tan, *Emotion and the Structure of Narrative Film: Film as an Emotion Machine*, trans. Barbara Fasting (Mahwah, N.J.: Lawrence Erlbaum Associates, 1996).

10. Ibid., 34.

11. For recent audience research, see James B. Weaver III and Ron Tamborini, eds., *Horror Films: Current Research on Audience Preferences and Reactions* (Mahwah, N.J.: Lawrence Erlbaum Associates, 1996). My primary criticism of this text is that it does not attend enough to *aesthetic* features of films—or to audience interest in such features.

12. Noël Carroll, *The Philosophy of Horror, or Paradoxes of the Heart* (New York and London: Routledge, 1990).

13. Torben Grodal, *Moving Pictures: A New Theory of Film Genres, Feelings, and Cognition* (Oxford: Clarendon Press, 1997).

14. Ibid., 249.

15. Ibid.

16. Ibid., 252.

17. For an excellent discussion, see Peter A. French, *Cowboy Metaphysics: Ethics and Death in Westerns* (London and Boulder: Rowman and Littlefield, 1997).

18. My approach thus falls in with the anti-big-theory approach recommended by Karen Hanson in "Provocations and Justifications of Film," in Cynthia A. Freeland and Thomas E. Wartenberg, eds., *Philosophy and Film* (New York: Routledge, 1995), 33–48.

19. See Eugenia de la Motte, *Perils of the Night: A Feminist Study of Nineteenth-Century Gothic* (New York and Oxford: Oxford University Press, 1990). Much the same point is made by James Twitchell in *Dreadful Pleasures: An Anatomy of Modern Horror* (Oxford: Oxford University Press, 1985).

20. For discussion of this approach, see Noël Carroll, "The Image of Women in Film: A Defense of a Paradigm," *Journal of Aesthetics and Art Criticism* 48 (4) (Fall 1990):349–360. Carroll also emphasizes that cognitivism is compatible with ideology critique in his essay "Prospects for Film Theory," in Bordwell and Carroll, *Post-Theory*. He writes, "[I]deology might engage cognitive processes" (p. 49) and "cognitivists have attempted to model some cognitive mechanisms that might be important to understanding the operation of ideology in film" (p. 51).

21. I discuss a very important exception, *Eraserhead*, in Chapter 8, within a section of this book focusing on the role of visual spectacle in horror. Actually, *Eraserhead* is structured and unified by aural as well as visual spectacle and is almost unique in this regard.

22. Carroll discusses how "rhetorical strategies may be implemented in narrative film" (p. 223) in his article, "Film, Rhetoric, and Ideology," in Salim Kemal and Ivan Gaskell, eds., *Explanation and Value in the Arts* (Cambridge: Cambridge University Press, 1973), 215–237.

23. Carolyn Korsmeyer, "Gendered Concepts and Hume's Standard of Taste," in Peggy Zeglin Brand and Carolyn Korsmeyer, eds., *Feminism and Tradition in Aesthetics* (University Park: Pennsylvania State University Press, 1995), 49.

24. Luce Irigaray, "The Power of Discourse," in Irigaray, *This Sex Which Is Not One*, trans. Catherine Porter (Ithaca: Cornell University Press, 1985), 78.

25. Ibid.

26. Carol J. Clover. *Men, Women, and Chain Saws: Gender in the Modern Horror Film* (Princeton: Princeton University Press, 1992).

27. I part ways with Clover because I reject the assumptions grounding her readings in the truth of a given psychosexual model, Thomas Laqueur's "one sex" hypothesis. See my review of *Men, Women, and Chain Saws*, by Carol Clover, *Afterimage* 20 (8) (March 1993):12–13, and also my "Feminist Frameworks for Horror Films," in Bordwell and Carroll, *Post-Theory*, 195–218.

28. For a more extended illustration, see my discussion of *Henry: Portrait of a Serial Killer* in "Realist Horror," in Freeland and Wartenberg, *Philosophy and Film*, 126–142; also see Chapter 5 herein.

29. Noël Carroll discusses this point in relation to the "Althusserian model" of the ideological effects of cinema. Carroll argues for an alternative rhetorical analysis that draws upon Aristotle's in "Film, Rhetoric, and Ideology"; see also his *Mystifying Movies: Fads and Fallacies in Contemporary Film Theory* (New York: Columbia University Press, 1988), especially 84–88.

30. Michael Ryan and Douglas Kellner, *Camera Politica: The Politics and Ideology of Contemporary Hollywood Film* (Indiana: Indiana University Press, 1988), 136–167.

31. This genre is discussed by Nickolas Pappas in his article "Failure of Marriage in *A Sea of Love*: The Love of Men, the Respect of Women," in Freeland and Wartenberg, *Philosophy and Film*, 109–125.

32. Laura Mulvey, "Visual Pleasure and Narrative Cinema," originally published in *Screen* 16 (1975); reprinted in Mulvey, *Visual and Other Pleasures* (Indianapolis: Indiana University Press, 1990); my page references are to the reprinted version in Patricia Erens, ed., *Issues in Feminist Film Criticism* (Indianapolis: Indiana University Press, 1990), 28–40.

33. Feminist critics have argued against Mulvey on various grounds, particularly that she ignores the social and historical conditions of gendered subjects and oversimplifies the role of the viewer/director/camera (so that, for example, a subtler view may be necessary to account for the ambivalence of certain film directors like Hitchcock—as I suggest in Chapter 5). See Mary Ann Doane, "Film and the Masquerade: Theorizing the Female Spectator," in Erens, *Issues in Feminist Film Criticism*, 41–57; Jane Gaines, "Women and Representation: Can We Enjoy Alternative Pleasure?" in Erens, *Issues in Feminist Film Criticism*, 75–92; Marian Keane, "A Closer Look at Scopophilia: Mulvey, Hitchcock, and Vertigo," in Marshall Dentelbaum and Leland Poaque, eds., *The Hitchcock Reader* (Ames: Iowa State University Press, 1986), 231–249; and Naomi Scheman, "Missing Mothers/Desiring Daughters: Framing the Sight of Women," *Critical Inquiry* 15 (Autumn 1988):62–89. Mulvey's revisions of her view may be found in "Afterthoughts on Visual Pleasure and Narrative Cinema" in *Visual and Other Pleasures*; but also see my critical review in the *APA Newsletter on Feminism and Philosophy* 89 (2) (Winter 1990):52–55.

34. Linda Williams, "When the Woman Looks," in Mary Ann Doane, Patricia Mellencamp, and Linda Williams, eds., *Re-Vision: Essays in Feminist Film Criticism* (Los Angeles: American Film Institute Monograph Series, University Publications of America, Frederick, Md., 1984), 83–99; and Linda Williams, "Film Bodies: Gender, Genre, and Excess," *Film Quarterly* 44 (Summer 1991):2–13.

35. Julia Kristeva, *Powers of Horror: An Essay on Abjection*, trans. Leon Roudiez (New York: Columbia University Press, 1982).

36. Barbara Creed, *The Monstrous-Feminine: Film, Feminism, Psychoanalysis* (London and New York: Routledge, 1993).

37. Ibid., 10.

38. Ibid., 42.

39. See Frederick Crews, "The Unknown Freud," *New York Review of Books* 11 (19) (November 18, 1993):55–66; Adolf Grünbaum, *The Philosophical Foundations of Psychoanalysis* (Berkeley: University of California Press, 1984); Gilles Deleuze and Felix Guattari, *Anti-Oedipus: Capitalism and Schizophrenia*, trans. Robert Hurley, Mark Seem, and H. R. Lane (Minneapolis: University of Minnesota Press, 1983); Luce Irigaray, *Speculum of the Other Woman*, trans. by Gillian C. Gill (Ithaca: Cornell University Press, 1985); and Geoffrey Moussaieff Masson, *The Assault on Truth: Freud's Suppression of the Seduction Theory* (New York: Farrar, Straus and Giroux, 1984).

40. Researchers in contemporary cognitive science sometimes cite Freud as a precedent but emphasize that his knowledge of neurobiology was so limited as to be virtually negligible today. See, for example, the comment made by Antonio Damasio in *Descartes' Error: Emotion, Reason, and the Human Brain* (New York: Avon Books, 1994), 124: "The creation of a superego which would accommodate instincts to social dictates was Freud's formulation . . . which was stripped of Cartesian dualism but was nowhere explicit in neural terms."

41. See Chapter 2.

42. See Judith Butler, *Gender Trouble: Feminism and the Subversion of Identity* (New York: Routledge, 1990), and Eve Kosofsky Sedgwick, *Epistemology of the Closet* (Berkeley: University of California Press, 1990).

43. Of course, certain of Aristotle's sexist assumptions may have had an impact on his evaluational schema for tragedies; for more on this, see my "Plot Imitates Action: Aesthetic Evaluation and Moral Realism in Aristotle's *Poetics*," esp. 126–128 in Amélie Oksenberg Rorty, ed., *Essays on Aristotle's Poetics* (Princeton: Princeton University Press, 1992).

44. See Carroll, *Philosophy of Horror*.

Chapter One

1. Actually, we hear his words as reported to Victor Frankenstein and recorded by Walton. Although his voice is doubly mediated, he is a strong and distinct presence in the book.

2. My text is Mary Shelley, *Frankenstein* (New York: Dover Publications, 1994).

3. Fred Botting notes that *Frankenstein* "entangle[s] Gothic and Romantic forms to suggest that there is no absolute distinction to be made between them" in his *Making Monstrous: Frankenstein, Criticism, Theory* (Manchester and New York: Manchester University Press, 1991), 37.

4. Anne K. Mellor, in *Romanticism and Gender* (London and New York: Routledge, 1993), explains that the fearsome aspects of the sublime had been emphasized more by earlier theorists than by the Romantic poets (p. 89).

5. Ibid., 101.

6. Literary theorists describe female Romantic writers as responding to the "male empowerment" conception of the sublime in several ways; see ibid., 85–106.

7. See Susan Gilbert and Susan Gubar, *The Madwoman in the Attic: The Woman Writer and the Nineteenth-Century Literary Imagination* (New Haven: Yale University Press, 1979), 215.

8. For more on Mary Shelley's responses to her father and to her unusual intellectual milieu, see Mary K. Patterson Thornburg, *The Monster in the Mirror: Gender and the Sentimental/Gothic Myth in Frankenstein* (Ann Arbor, Mich.: UMI Research Press, 1987), 8–9.

9. Julie K. Schuetz writes, "During the past decade, Mary Shelley's novel *Frankenstein* has been established within the canon of British Romanticism as a critique of masculine Romantic idealism and imagination"; "Mary Shelley's *The Last Man*: Monstrous Worlds, Domestic Communities, and Masculine Romantic Ideology," web site at <http://prometheus.cc.emory.edu/panels/4A/J.Schuetz.html>. See also Audrey Fisch, Anne K. Mellor, and Esther H. Schor, eds., *The Other Mary Shelley: Beyond Frankenstein* (New York: Oxford University Press, 1993).

10. See, for example, Alicia Renfroe, "Defining Romanticism: The Implications of Nature Personified as Female in Mary Shelley's *Frankenstein* and Charlotte Bronte's *Jane Eyre*"; web

site at <http://prometheus.cc.emory.edu/panels/2D/A.Renfroe.html>. See also Mellor, *Romanticism and Gender* and her "Possessing Nature: The Female in *Frankenstein*," in Mellor, ed., *Romanticism and Feminism* (Bloomington: Indiana University Press, 1988), 220–232.

11. Muriel Spark, *Mary Shelley: A Biography* (New York: New American Library, 1987), 154.

12. See Anne K. Mellor, *Mary Shelley: Her Life, Her Fiction, Her Monsters* (New York and London: Methuen, 1988), 92, 105–106.

13. Humphry Davy wrote, "[I]n leading to the discovery of gunpowder, [chemistry] has changed the institutions of society, and rendered war more independent of brutal strength, less personal, and less barbarous." Quoted in ibid., 95.

14. Ludmilla Jordanova, *Sexual Visions: Images of Gender in Science and Medicine Between the Eighteenth and Twentieth Centuries* (Madison: University of Wisconsin Press, 1989), 111. This is also the theme of Chris Baldick's book, *In Frankenstein's Shadow: Myth, Monstrosity, and Nineteenth-Century Writing* (Oxford: Clarendon Press, 1987). Baldick mentions writers like Carlyle, Dickens, Haskell, Melville, and Marx.

15. Jordanova, *Sexual Visions*, 124.

16. Ibid., 125.

17. See Carolyn Merchant, *The Death of Nature: Women, Ecology, and the Scientific Revolution* (San Francisco: Harper and Row Publishers, 1980), 164, 181, 189–190.

18. Evelyn Fox Keller, *Reflections on Gender and Science* (New Haven and London: Yale University Press, 1985), 43. See also 53–54.

19. See Keller, *Reflections on Gender and Science*, 54, n. 20.

20. Shelley, *Frankenstein*, 102.

21. Val Plumwood, *Feminism and the Mastery of Nature* (London and New York: Routledge, 1993).

22. Ibid., 43.

23. Ibid.

24. This raises the issue of homoerotic bonds between Victor and the monster. These are mentioned by Mellor in "Possessing Nature," where she refers to other discussions; see 226 and 231–232, n. 7.

25. Shelley, *Frankenstein*, 191.

26. Mellor, *Mary Shelley*, 40.

27. Mary Shelley, author's introduction to the Standard Novels edition (1831), *Frankenstein*, 55, 60.

28. The first, from July 1814 to February 1815, when she was seventeen, resulted in a premature baby who died, and she reported having dreams about it. The next, from April 1815 to January 24, 1816, when she was eighteen, resulted in the birth of her son William. The third, from December 1816 through September 5, 1817, resulted in the birth of her daughter Clara. See Mellor, *Mary Shelley*, 54–55.

29. See ibid.

30. Shelley, *Frankenstein*, 246.

31. All the quotations in this paragraph are from ibid., 259–263.

32. See Mellor, *Mary Shelley*, 219–224.

33. See also on this Anne K. Mellor, "Possessing Nature" and "*Frankenstein*: A Feminist Critique of Science," in George Levine, ed., *One Culture: Essays on Literature and Science* (Madison: University of Wisconsin Press, 1988), 287–312.

34. Shelley, *Frankenstein*, 102; see Gilbert and Gubar, *The Madwoman in the Attic*, 232–233.

35. Shelley, *Frankenstein*, 91.

36. Mellor, "Possessing Nature," 227.

37. Shelley, *Frankenstein*, 146.

38. Ibid., 248.

39. Mellor, "Possessing Nature," 227.

40. Doubling and the difficulty of establishing a clear male-female distinction between Victor and his monster are treated at some length by Thornburg in *The Monster in the Mirror*, 9ff.

41. For feminist readings of these narrative strategies, see works cited above by Mellor and those by Gilbert and Gubar, Thornburg, and Botting.

42. The Edison film is briefly discussed in James B. Twitchell, *Dreadful Pleasures: An Anatomy of Modern Horror* (New York and Oxford: Oxford University Press, 1985), 178.

43. A wonderful source of information about the making of Whale's movie is Gregory William Mank, *It's Alive! The Classic Cinema Saga of Frankenstein* (San Diego and New York: A. S. Barnes and Company, 1981).

44. This framing device is discussed as exemplary of common devices for horror film promotion at the time; see Rhona Berenstein, "'It Will Thrill You, It May Shock You, It Might Even Horrify You': Gender, Reception, and Classic Horror Cinema," in Barry Keith Grant, ed., *The Dread of Difference: Gender and the Horror Film* (Austin: University of Texas Press, 1996), 117–142.

45. Twitchell considers this a major point in the film tradition of *Frankenstein*, arguing that Victor has been cast ("I suspect quite unconsciously, until recently at least") as bisexual (p. 179). The qualifier "until recently" refers to the *Rocky Horror Picture Show*; see Twitchell, *Dreadful Pleasures*, 196–203.

46. Shelley, *Frankenstein*, 99.

47. Shelley, author's introduction to the Standard Novels edition (1831), *Frankenstein*, 59.

48. Pierce, quoted in Mank, *It's Alive!*, 25.

49. Mank, *It's Alive!*, 27.

50. Edwin Jahiel, movie review of *Mary Shelley's Frankenstein*; web site at <http://www.prairienet.org/~ejahiel/maryshel.htm>.

51. Twitchell says that Whale was forced by the studio to change the original ending, where both Elizabeth and Frankenstein were killed: "No monster could touch a Hollywood heroine in 1931 and get away with it." Also, "Frankenstein's death . . . was to be the end of the movie, but once again Universal insisted that no hero of theirs was going to be so short-lived." (*Dreadful Pleasures*, 182).

Chapter Two

1. This is a key thesis in Barbara Creed's *The Monstrous-Feminine: Film, Feminism, Psychoanalysis* (London and New York: Routledge, 1993). Creed describes seven variations of the monstrous-feminine in horror films and notes that the prominence of female monsters in horror has been neglected by film theorists and historians; even those accounts that take gender seriously tend to assume that woman is, by nature, a victim (p. 7).

2. Carol J. Clover, *Men, Women, and Chain Saws: Gender in the Modern Horror Film* (Princeton: Princeton University Press, 1992). Clover treats *Alien* as part of her "Final Girl" series of modern horror films (p. 16).

3. I discuss these and other examples of graphic spectacular horror films in Chapter 8.

4. Also, the *Alien* story may have been based on a story by A. E. Van Vogt in *The Voyage of the Spaceship Beagle*, which featured a giant female wasp. It is, after all, wasps that cocoon animals as prey to feed "babies" once they hatch. Van Vogt won some damages in his suit against the first film. (I am grateful to Justin Leiber for this information.)

5. I will not address films in which female monsters confront *male* heroes, such as *Independence Day* or *Star Trek: First Contact*, though the buglike monsters in them definitely have a female construction. There are more buglike monsters of indeterminate gender in recent movies like *Starship Troopers* and *Naked Lunch*. Another recent film with a significant treatment of women and bugs is *Angels and Insects*, based on A. S. Byatt's acclaimed *Angels and Insects: Two Novellas* (first published 1992; New York: Vintage Books International, 1994).

6. My approach here is somewhat similar to one advocated by Noël Carroll in "The Image of Women in Film: A Defense of a Paradigm," in Peggy Zeglin Brand and Carolyn Korsmeyer, eds., *Feminism and Tradition in Aesthetics* (University Park: Pennsylvania State University Press, 1995), 371–391, originally published in *The Journal of Aesthetics and Art Criticism* 48 (4) (Fall 1990):349–360. Carroll writes, "The study of the image of women in film might be viewed as the search for paradigm scenarios that are available in our culture and that, by being available, may come to shape emotional responses to women" (p. 386). He refers here to Ronald de Sousa, *The Rationality of Emotions* (Cambridge: MIT Press, 1987), and to Robert Solomon, "Emotion and Choice," in Amélie Oksenberg Rorty, ed., *Explaining Emotions* (Berkeley and Los Angeles: University of California Press, 1980), 251–281.

7. See Creed, *The Monstrous-Feminine*, 16–30. Other films Creed discusses in her book are *The Exorcist, The Brood, The Hunger, Psycho, Sisters, I Spit on Your Grave,* and *Carrie*. The earliest of these movies is *Psycho*, from 1960, thus one complaint I have about her book is its neglect of the horror tradition; but there are other problems with her explanations, as I shall explain further below.

8. Ibid., 18.

9. Ibid., 19.

10. Ibid., 27.

11. Ibid., 29.

12. Ibid.

13. Ibid., 27.

14. Ibid., 28.

15. Ibid., 27–28.

16. Jonathan Lake Crane says that "to characterize Kristeva's summation as reductionistic is to miss the point of structural/psychoanalytic criticism." Still, he criticizes such approaches for failing to grasp changes in the very nature and operation of the unconscious: "[M]ight terror work on planes other than the extraordinarily vast territory claimed for the unconscious?" I believe there are serious problems with psychoanalytic reductionism, as I explain further here. See Crane, *Terror and Everyday Life: Singular Moments in the History of the Horror Film* (Thousand Oaks, Calif., London, and New Delhi: Sage Publications, 1994), 35.

17. Creed, *The Monstrous-Feminine*, 23; she is alluding to answers given by others to the question of why Ripley strips at the end of the film. Creed says questions are also asked about why Ripley saves the cat and risks violating quarantine laws. This is absurd, since the

quarantine laws apply to alien species or microbes only! The cat has a name and has clearly been on board all along as a crew pet. The psychoanalytic account is that Ripley saves it as substitute child (or phallus substitute); I would submit that she saves it because otherwise she would be utterly alone in a vast dark universe.

18. Thomas Doherty comments, "*Vagina dentata* and phallic drill, the alien is a cross-dressing monster from the id whose sexual confusion mirrors the shifting gender dynamics of the series." See Doherty, "Genre, Gender, and the *Aliens* Trilogy," in Barry Keith Grant, ed., *The Dread of Difference: Gender and the Horror Film* (Austin: University of Texas Press, 1996), 196.

19. I am thinking of stories like that of the female Christian martyr Perpetua, who was thrown to the beasts in the Roman Circus. See Perpetua, "A Christian Woman's Account of Her Persecution," in Ross S. Kraemer, ed., *Maenads, Martyrs, Matrons, Monastics: Sourcebook on Women's Religions in the Greco-Roman World* (Philadelphia: Fortress Press, 1988), 96–107. (I am grateful to Leslie Marenchin for bringing this text to my attention.) Female martyrs in literature and film often die as male warriors. We can think also of Greek heroines such as Iphigeneia in Euripides' *Iphigenia in Aulis* or of Joan of Arc. Creed notes, brilliantly, Ripley's similarity to Maria Falconetti in Carl Dreyer's film *The Passion of Joan of Arc*, when she appears with her head shorn and dies in the flames at the end of *Alien*[3]; see Creed, *The Monstrous-Feminine*, 52–53.

20. Effects and artist credits on these movies are lengthy, but to give partial credit where credit is due: *Alien* (1979), directed by Ridley Scott, special effects by Carlo Rambaldi, H. R. Giger, Brian Johnson, Rick Allder, Denys Aling; with Bolaji Badejo as the Alien. *Aliens* (1986), directed by James Cameron, special effects by Robert Soktak, Stan Winston, John Richardson, Suzanne Benson. *Alien*[3] (1992), directed by David Fincher (after Vincent Ward, original director), special effects by George Gibbs and Richard Edlund, Alien effects by Alec Gillis and Tom Woodruff Jr. *Alien Resurrection* (1997), directed by Jean-Pierre Jenet, visual effects supervisors Pitof and Erik Henry, alien effects designed and created by Alec Gillis and Tom Woodruff Jr.

21. Creed, *The Monstrous-Feminine*, 51.

22. Ibid., 53.

23. I prefer a reading of the films like that offered by Valerie Gray Hardcastle in "Changing Perspectives of Motherhood: Images from the *Aliens* Trilogy," *Film and Philosophy* 3 (1996):167–175.

24. Even if they are beautiful, like moths or butterflies, bugs can take on other complex metaphorical connotations, as A. S. Byatt's *Angels and Insects* demonstrates.

25. Fears of bugs might be irrational for reasons having nothing to do with the abject or the archaic mother. (1) Some cases of insect phobias have been cured by antipsychotic medications like Risperidone (see Gerard Gallucci and Gary Beard, "Risperidone and the Treatment of Delusions of Parasitosis in an Elderly Patient," *Psychosomatics* 36 (6) (November–December 1995):578–580. (2) Socialization may teach children to fear bugs through confusions that arise as they learn about illness and germs (Simon R. Wilkinson, *The Child's World of Illness: The Development of Health and Illness Behaviour* [Cambridge, England: Cambridge University Press, 1988]). (3) Delusions and fears of bugs are common effects of alcohol or other drug abuse; see Jerry Mitchell and Arlyn D. Vierkant, "Delusions and Hallucinations of Cocaine Abusers and Paranoid Schizophrenics: A Comparative Study," *Journal of Psychology* 125 (3) (1991):301–310. And (4) for an alternative psychoan-

alytic account of fear of bugs, see Michael Eigen, "A Bug-Free Universe," *Contemporary Psychoanalysis* 33 (1) (1997):19–41. (I am grateful to Anne Jacobson for research providing all these references.)

26. These points are noted by some (nonpsychoanalytic) critics. See especially Mark Jancovich, *Rational Fears: American Horror in the 1950s* (Manchester and New York: Manchester University Press, 1996), 58–61 (on *Them!*) and 176–188 (on *Creature from the Black Lagoon* and its sequel); also Peter Biskind, *Seeing Is Believing: How Hollywood Taught Us to Stop Worrying and Love the Fifties* (London: Pluto, 1983).

27. My reading of *Them!* is much indebted to the account offered by Jonathan Lake Crane in *Terror and Everyday Life*.

28. This is a crude summary; for an account that interestingly argues that there are certain feminist dimensions of the film, see Jancovich, *Rational Fears*, 176–184. He points out that the Creature is shown with sympathy and dignity, that Kay and the Creature share the "pre-phallic pleasures of the watery zone" where they swim, and that Kay keeps insisting on the fact that the Creature has not harmed her and that it should be left alone.

29. Here I am indebted to Jancovich's readings of both films in *Rational Fears*. He mentions yet another interesting female investigator in a 1950s horror film, *It Came From Beneath the Sea* (1955); see 61.

30. Jancovich notes the remarkable treatment of Pat Medford in this film ("*She* controls the gaze") and mentions that "it's the men who have problems"; *Rational Fears*, 61.

31. See Crane, *Terror and Everyday Life*, 100–131; he also points out that this movie was a real shocker at the time with its emphatic threat to children.

32. Crane comments: "*Them!* cannot go so far as to have the children eaten or trampled by the beast. As a compromise measure, the film will threaten children but not kill them" (*Terror and Everyday Life*, 126). Crane also comments, "The end of the crew is really extraordinary: in *Them!*, more people die than were probably killed in all horror films preceding the arrival of nuclear power" (p. 124).

33. Crane says that *Them!* "rapidly devolves from a relatively innovative horror picture into a routine war movie" (*Terror and Everyday Life*, 127).

34. Jancovich, *Rational Fears*, 28.

35. Per Schelde in *Androids, Humanoids, and Other Science Fiction Monsters: Science and Soul in Science Fiction Films* (New York and London: New York University Press, 1993) notes it is common for women in science fiction films to exemplify one or more of five key stereotypes: nurturers, producers of children, sex objects, earthy and homebound beings, and socializers; see 71–76.

36. Something should be said about the presence of large, emotionally expressive, and self-sacrificing black men in these movies: Parker (Yaphet Kotto) in *Alien*; Dillon (Charles S. Dutton) in *Alien³*; Leonard (Charles S. Dutton once more) in *Mimic*; and Dan Smithson (Forrest Whittaker) as the psychic in *Species* (1995). These men pose no sexual threats or erotic attraction to the (white) heroine; they die for or serve others; and there are no black women in the movies. I am not sure what to make of these facts, beyond the obvious stereotyping. Perhaps these heroic black men, like the strong white women in the films, reinforce the message that something has gone wrong with white masculinity. We might also note that the black character Dennis Gamble (Mykelti Williamson) in *Species II* (1998) is the one member of the crew on the Mars voyage who does not become infected by the alien parasite—due to, of all things, his carrying the sickle-cell trait! This proves the key to

killing the alien, and he, too, must shed his blood (a lot of it, painfully!) to destroy the monster. (*Them!* of course, as a typical example of 1950s representation of the U.S. citizenry, had no black people in it at all.)

37. For a far more negative assessment, see Thomas Doherty, "Genre, Gender, and the *Aliens* Trilogy": "Her alert intelligence and active initiative cannot be contained in marriage, the conventional wrap-up for female-centered narratives, yet neither can she be unleashed to roam free in an uncharted feminist galaxy" (p. 198). It is possible that some of my own assessment stems from the fact that I am writing after the release of *Alien Resurrection*, so I "know" that Ripley is not truly dead and perhaps is now roaming free in a far more uncharted galaxy with her new half-Alien DNA—not to mention her new inhuman daughter, Call (Winona Ryder), a pleasant enough substitute for the lost Newt. Even without knowing of this later "resurrection," I would be tempted to point out that martyrdom is, after all, a strong criticism of the status quo rather than an endorsement of it.

38. Noël Carroll, *The Philosophy of Horror, or Paradoxes of the Heart* (New York and London: Routledge, 1990).

39. I would except the monster in *Alien³* from this claim; to make it mobile, the artistic designer and special effects director have placed its familiar outsized head on a scrawny body. This results in a disproportionate and almost gawky beast rather than the elegant, massively impressive one of the earlier films. This is "Teen Alien," with disgusting table manners as it smacks while consuming its ghastly meals of human flesh.

Chapter Three

1. Cronenberg considered directing a new version of *Frankenstein*, but it was never done. See David Cronenberg, *Cronenberg on Cronenberg*, rev. ed., ed. Chris Rodley (London and Boston: Faber and Faber, 1997), 92. His earlier movies *Shivers* and *Rabid* also explore the horrific consequences of a mad scientist or corporation.

2. Cronenberg speaks of his fascination with the cell-like existence of people in institutions in *Cronenberg on Cronenberg*, 29.

3. I disagree with Tania Modleski's verdict that Cronenberg's films are antifeminist. There are more nuances to his films and their treatment of gender, as I try to show in this chapter. See Tania Modleski, "The Terror of Pleasure: The Contemporary Horror Film and Postmodern Theory," in Modleski, ed., *Studies in Entertainment: Critical Approaches to Mass Culture* (Madison: University of Wisconsin Press, 1986), 155–166.

4. Cronenberg disagrees with the basic premise of the *Frankenstein* plot: "You have to believe in God before you can say there are things that man was not meant to know. I don't think there's anything that man wasn't meant to know." *Cronenberg on Cronenberg*, 5–7.

5. "It has to do with this ineffable sadness that is an element of human existence." *Cronenberg on Cronenberg*, 149. The director especially credits Howard Shore's music for setting the mood of the film.

6. See *Cronenberg on Cronenberg*, 58.

7. I disagree with Lianne McLarty, who describes a "shift in Cronenberg's films from a horror of the (female) body to one of the male mind"; see "'Beyond the Veil of the Flesh': Cronenberg and the Disembodiment of Horror," in Barry Keith Grant, ed., *The Dread of Difference: Gender and the Horror Film* (Austin: University of Texas Press, 1996), 247. I view

all his movies as concerned with mind-body relations, which arise often in relation to male bodies. Cronenberg sees the mind-body problem as intricately linked to the problem of death, which is at the root of all horror; *Cronenberg on Cronenberg*, 58 and 79. For another account of the film, see Daniel Shaw, "*Dead Ringers*: Horror and the Problem of Personal Identity," in *Film and Philosophy* 3 (1996):14–23.

8. See *Cronenberg on Cronenberg*, 79–84.

9. Ibid., 80–82.

10. Ibid., 80.

11. For information about his crew, see ibid., 72 and 123. Regulars include Mark Irwin (cinematographer), Carol Spier (production designer), Bryan Day (sound recorder), Ron Sanders (editor), and often also Howard Shore (music) and Chris Walas (who has done special effects for several of the films).

12. Cronenberg asks: "Can you see *Scanners* shot in the lushness of summer? It was meant to be very deadly—a cold, harsh, nasty film . . . . And for *The Brood*, too. I loved it in the winter" (ibid., 87). There may be ties between Cronenberg's measured style and his "Canadianness," a feature he often mentions; see ibid., 118. For a more elaborate account of the director's Canadianness, see also Bart Testa, "Technology's Body: Cronenberg, Genre, and the Canadian Ethos," web site at <http://www.netlink.co.uk/users/zappa/cr testa.html>.

13. See *Cronenberg on Cronenberg*, 144.

14. "One of the things that I did in my own small way was to be part of bringing horror into the twentieth century. At the time I started to make *Shivers*, there was already *Night of the Living Dead*. But for the most part horror was gothic, distant, not here." *Cronenberg on Cronenberg*, 60.

15. Ibid., 43; he is discussing *Shivers* here, but the point seems generalizable. Cronenberg also says: "I'm presenting audiences with imagery and with possibilities that have to be shown. There is no other way to do it. It's not done for shock value." *Cronenberg on Cronenberg*, 41.

16. I found Kimberly Tyrrell's discussion of Cronenberg's use of special effects especially insightful; see Kimberly Tyrrell, "Special Effects and Gender in the Films of David Cronenberg," B.A. (honours) thesis in women's studies, Australian National University, August 1995.

17. Cronenberg discusses his use of test audiences to help decide whether to include two rather graphic dream sequences in *Dead Ringers*; see *Cronenberg on Cronenberg*, 150.

18. Cronenberg comments: "It's an incredible shot. Incredibly gruesome, but also quite beautiful. It's so surreal that it's also quite lovely in its own way." *Cronenberg on Cronenberg*, 90.

19. Cronenberg seems to feel there were actually pluses in being considered a "schlock" director early on; see *Cronenberg on Cronenberg*, 58–59.

20. See Barbara Creed, *Horror: The Monstrous-Feminine: Film, Feminism, Psychoanalysis* (London and New York, Routledge, 1993), 43–58.

21. See Marcie Frank, "The Camera and the Speculum: David Cronenberg's *Dead Ringers*," *Proceedings of the Modern Language Association of America (PMLA)* 106 (3) (May 1991):459–470.

22. Cronenberg admits that in a film like *Naked Lunch*, he may be expressing some sort of fear of women, but he comments sardonically: "If you were to find by analysing my films, for example, that I'm afraid of women, unconsciously that is, I would say, 'OK, so

what? What's wrong with that?' If I am an example of the North American male, and my films are showing that I'm afraid of women, then that's something which could perhaps be discussed, perhaps even decried. But where do you really go from there?" *Cronenberg on Cronenberg*, 99.

23. Ibid., 76.

24. Creed, *The Monstrous-Feminine*, 45.

25. *Cronenberg on Cronenberg*, 84.

26. "Kristeva's theory of the abject provides us with at least three ways of understanding the nature of Nola's monstrousness." Barbara Creed, *Horror: The Monstrous-Feminine*, 46.

27. He even says this about *The Dead Zone:* It is about God as a scientist, and "the Johnny Smith character is one of his failed experiments." *Cronenberg on Cronenberg*, 113.

28. Cronenberg says: "People who find gynaecology icky say, 'I don't find sex icky.' They've never gone into why . . . . That's one of the things I wanted to look at . . . . The other reason gynaecology weirds men out is that they are jealous." *Cronenberg on Cronenberg*, 145.

29. Ibid., 145.

30. Ibid., 144.

31. Cronenberg discusses his working relationship with Shore in the film and says they got down to the level of frames; ibid., 149.

32. Perhaps there is something similarly "real" or transparent about the coupling of Veronica and Seth in *The Fly*, given that the actors in lead roles were a couple at the time of making the film; Cronenberg felt this brought both pluses and minuses to the set; ibid., 129–131.

33. I don't mean to imply that twins are unnatural, only that the twinning process is biologically rare and raises some of the same perplexing and fascinating issues that cloning does.

34. *Cronenberg on Cronenberg*, 34.

Chapter Four

1. The list under "Dracula" in Howard Maxford's book *The A-Z of Horror Films* (Bloomington and Indianapolis: Indiana University Press, 1997) runs to four columns of fine-print titles.

2. This is not to mention television shows like *Buffy the Vampire Slayer* or *Knight Rider;* there are also endless pornographic vampire variations, such as *Ejacula, Dracula Sucks, Buffy the Vampire Layer, Intercourse with the Vampire*, and so forth.

3. Anne Rice's initial set of three novels in the series includes *Interview with the Vampire* (1976), *The Vampire Lestat* (1985), and *The Queen of the Damned: Book III of The Vampire Chronicles* (1988), all published by Ballantine Books, New York; the series has subsequently been expanded. Major full-length ballet versions of *Dracula* were performed in Houston in 1997 and in Winnipeg in 1998; both ballets have traveled to other cities or companies.

4. Marduk, a Dutch Black Metal band, cites Transylvania and Vlad Tepes in perverse idylls about Satan worship and lustful killing. (I am indebted to my student Brian Lacher for information about these bands.) Vlad's existence as Stoker's source is disputed by Stoker scholars; see Elizabeth Miller, *Reflections on Dracula: Ten Essays* (White Rock, British Columbia: Transylvania Press, 1997), 1–24.

5. C. Fred Alford, *What Evil Means to Us* (Ithaca: Cornell University Press, 1997), 13.

6. Alford writes: "The difference between the vampire and Satan is analogous to the difference between violence and more subtle ways of victimizing others. Vampires suck the life out of you when you least expect it, and there is nothing you can do. Satan requires your cooperation, your will." *What Evil Means to Us*, 95; see also 13, 89.

7. Friedrich Nietzsche, *Beyond Good and Evil: Prelude to a Philosophy of the Future*, trans. R. J. Hollingdale (New York: Penguin Books, 1973/1990), sec. 230, 160–162.

8. Norine Dresser has studied genre familiarity among young students in *American Vampires: Fans, Victims, Practitioners* (New York: Vintage Books, 1989), 114–116. For example, only 7 percent of the students did *not* know how vampires dress.

9. On destruction by light, see David J. Skal, *Hollywood Gothic: The Tangled Web of Dracula from Novel to Stage to Screen* (New York and London: W. W. Norton and Company, 1990), 226, n. 13; on the cape and other attire, see Norine Dresser, *American Vampires*, 79–119.

10. Feminists find *Dracula* interesting, for example, for its dual Victorian stereotypes of good and bad women through its contrast between the sexually adventurous Lucy and the pure, strong Mina; see Bram Stoker, *Dracula* (New York: Bantam Books, 1989), 62–64. Queer theorists have also found much to discuss here; see Bonnie Zimmerman, "Daughters of Darkness: The Lesbian Vampire on Film," in Barry Keith Grant, ed., *The Dread of Difference: Gender and the Horror Film* (Austin: University of Texas Press, 1996), 379–387; also see Vera Dika, "From Dracula—with Love," in Grant, *The Dread of Difference*, 388–400.

11. Elizabeth Miller notes that there are some—though few—grounds in the Stoker *Dracula* itself for holding that Mina feels moments of pity and sympathy for the Count; see *Reflections on Dracula*, 25–46. See also Elizabeth Miller, ed., *Dracula: The Shade and the Shadow, a Critical Anthology* (Westcliff-on-Sea, Essex, U.K.: Desert Island Books, 1998).

12. Stoker, *Dracula*, 39.

13. Mina does not actually see Dracula until several chapters later, Chapter 13—and even then is not sure whom she sees.

14. Stoker, *Dracula*, 96.

15. Ibid., 298.

16. Ibid., 400.

17. Noël Carroll's *The Philosophy of Horror, or Paradoxes of the Heart* (New York and London: Routledge, 1990) discusses the role of "proof" in the "complex discovery plot" as having four key phases: onset, discovery, confirmation, and confrontation; see 97–108.

18. It is also hard to avoid the crude psychoanalytic observation of another salient characteristic of Lugosi's, namely, his posture and its consistent rigidity or *erectness* as he rises from the coffin. See Roger Dadoun's similar comments on F. W. Murnau's *Nosferatu* and on Christopher Lee's erectness in the Dracula role, in "Fetishism in the Horror Film," in James Donald, ed., *Fantasy and the Cinema* (London: BFI Publishing, 1989).

19. David J. Skal's *Hollywood Gothic* contains excellent histories of the novel's gradual transition from stage play to screen and on Lugosi's ultimately tragic and inescapable association with the part.

20. Confusingly, the two women's names are reversed in this version.

21. Nina Auerbach comments: "The immobility of Bela Lugosi, star of the original play and film, dissolves in the incessant motion of Frank Langella, who is always touching, moving, dancing, climbing, or riding horses. Langella's graceful hands replace Lugosi's transfixing eyes . . . ." Auerbach, *Our Vampires, Ourselves* (Chicago and London: University of Chicago Press, 1995), 141. Browning's film *as a whole* is more stately and grandly Gothic; Badham's film *as a whole* moves much more in its cuts, sound, and narrative pacing.

22. Robin Wood, "Burying the Undead: The Use and Obsolescence of Count Dracula," in Grant, *The Dread of Difference*, 377–378.

23. The complete shooting script is included in Francis Ford Coppola and James V. Hart, *Bram Stoker's Dracula: The Film and the Legend* (New York: Newmarket Press, 1992).

24. For more examples, see ibid., 52.

25. Ibid., 42–43.

26. Ibid., 13; ironically perhaps, costume designer Eiko Ishioka refers to the fighters at the end as "the five samurai," 161.

27. Ibid., 162.

28. Ibid., 70.

29. Ken Gelder, *Reading the Vampire* (London and New York: Routledge, 1994), 88–90.

30. Ibid., 90.

31. In *The Return of the Vampire* (1943), Lugosi again plays a vampire who is ultimately defeated by a German bomb dropped on English soil!

32. Recent discussions of *katharsis* include Richard Janko, "From Catharsis to the Aristotelian Mean," 341–358, and Alexander Nehamas, "Pity and Fear in the *Poetics*," 291–314, both in Amélie Oksenberg Rorty, ed., *Essays on Aristotle's Poetics* (Princeton: Princeton University Press, 1992).

33. I am indebted to Stanley Cavell's reflections on the meaning of the "star" in "Audience, Actor, and Star" (pp. 25–29) and "The World as Mortal: Absolute Age and Youth" (pp. 74–80), both in *The World Viewed: Reflections on the Ontology of Film*, enl. ed. (Cambridge and London: Harvard University Press, 1979).

34. See Thomas Wartenberg's discussion of Sarandon's film persona in the role of Nora in *White Palace*, in "An Unlikely Couple: The Significance of Difference in *White Palace*," in Cynthia A. Freeland and Thomas E. Wartenberg, eds., *Philosophy and Film* (New York: Routledge, 1995), 166–167.

35. Auerbach, *Our Vampires, Ourselves*, 58.

36. Andrea Weiss, *Vampires and Violets: Lesbians in Film* (New York: Penguin Books, 1993), 98.

37. Deneuve was born in 1943; hence, she was twenty-two when *Repulsion* came out and forty when *The Hunger* was released; see John Parker, *Polanski* (London: Victor Gollancz, 1993), 85.

38. Ken Gelder's discussion of Anne Rice's vampires in *Reading the Vampire* is particularly insightful (pp. 108–123).

39. Bernard Williams poses the issue this way in discussing a play by Karel Čapek about a woman, now aged 342: "Her unending life has come to a state of boredom, indifference, and coldness." Williams comments, "[D]eath is not necessarily an evil . . . it can be a good thing not to live too long"; see Williams, "The Makropulos Case: Reflections on the Tedium of Immortality," in his *Problems of the Self: Philosophical Papers 1956–1972* (Cambridge: Cambridge University Press, 1973), 82–83. Of course, vampire immortality might be importantly distinct from human immortality.

40. In the novels, Lestat is more of a Nietzschean "over-man." In the film, he is just not developed enough to judge this. Mary Midgley makes a similar case that Satan's appeal in *Paradise Lost* is not actually because he is evil but because he has many qualities that are traditionally admirable, such as loyalty, courage, and devotion to liberty; *Wickedness: A Philosophical Essay* (London, Boston, Melbourne, Henley: Routledge and Kegan Paul, 1984), 132–138 and 151.

41. Anne Rice concurs about the actors' beauty: "These actors and actresses shape their own physical appearance with their educated brains and hearts. Beauty surrounds them and emanates from them. They walk in it, to quote Byron. If they had not expressed depth of soul in every word or gesture, their 'beauty' would have been brittle, and not beautiful at all." See Anne Rice, "From Anne Rice on the Film, *Interview with the Vampire*"; web site at <http://www.maths.tcd.ie/pub/vampire/morecomments.html>.

42. Anne Rice finds the movie's violence is untrue to her vision; see ibid.

43. Molloy's fascination is all the more poignant coming out of Christian Slater's mouth because (1) he has a bit part in a film glorifying male sexuality, and (2) he was a replacement for River Phoenix, who died just before filming was to begin (and to whom the movie is dedicated).

44. Rice explains: "That Tom *did* make Lestat work was something I could not see in a crystal ball. It's to his credit that he proved me wrong . . . . Tom has now transcended the label of biggest box office star in the world. He's better." Anne Rice, "From Anne Rice on the Film, *Interview with the Vampire*"; web site at <http://www.maths.tcd.ie/pub/vampire/morecomments.html>.

45. Gelder comments interestingly on this aspect of Rice's novel *Interview with the Vampire* in *Reading the Vampire*, 112, but he does not comment on the parallel I am making here between Rice's ploys and Stoker's at the end of *Dracula*.

46. Andrea Dworkin, *Intercourse* (New York: Free Press, 1987), 113–119.

47. Several prominent discussions in queer theory are summarized and discussed by Auerbach, *Our Vampires, Ourselves*, 181–186.

48. Gelder comments on Anne Rice's vampires: "Louis, Lestat and the other vampires do not work, although they do have investments and, with the help of financial advisers, are able to accumulate large amounts of capital. Their 'job' is, instead, to find out who they are and where they came from. In *Interview with the Vampire*, this is an entirely recreational procedure." Gelder, *Reading the Vampire*, 119–120.

49. Alford, *What Evil Means to Us*, 90.

Chapter Five

1. There are rare female counterparts in horror films, for example, in Roman Polanski's *Repulsion* (1965), which I discuss below.

2. The prevalence of realist horror featuring psycho killers is confirmed in James B. Twitchell, *Dreadful Pleasures: An Anatomy of Modern Horror* (New York and Oxford: Oxford University Press, 1985), and Andrew Tudor, *Monsters and Mad Scientists: A Cultural History of the Horror Movie* (London: Basil Blackwell, 1989). The definition of a slasher is up for discussion; one prominent account is Vera Dika's "The Stalker Cycle, 1978–81," in Greg Waller, ed., *American Horrors: Essays on the Modern American Horror Film* (Chicago: University of Illinois Press, 1987), 86–101; see also Isabel Cristina Pinedo, *Recreational Terror: Women and the Pleasures of Horror Film Viewing* (Albany: State University of New York Press, 1997).

3. Michael Graczyk, "Odyssey of Henry Lee Lucas," *Houston Chronicle*, August 15, 1993.

4. See Mark Jancovich, *Rational Fears: American Horror in the 1950s* (Manchester and New York: Manchester University Press, 1996), 235–260.

5. See Anne K. Mellor, *Mary Shelley: Her Life, Her Fiction, Her Monsters* (New York: Methuen, 1988), 98–100 and 105–106; and Thomas Boyle, *Black Swine in the Sewers of Hempstead: Beneath the Surface of Victorian Sensationalism* (New York: Viking, 1989).

6. See Lisa W. Foderaro, "Crimes of Passion, Deals of a Lifetime," *New York Times*, February 10, 1991.

7. Hannah Arendt, *Eichmann in Jerusalem: A Report on the Banality of Evil*, rev. and enl. ed. (New York: Viking Press, 1965).

8. Laura Mulvey, "Visual Pleasure and Narrative Cinema," in *Visual and Other Pleasures* (Indianapolis: Indiana University Press, 1990), 14–26, originally published in *Screen* 16 (Autumn 1975); Carol Clover, *Men, Women, and Chain Saws* (Princeton: Princeton University Press, 1992), 168–181; Linda Williams, "When the Woman Looks," in Mary Ann Doane, Patricia Mellencamp, and Linda Williams, eds., *Re-Vision: Essays in Feminist Film Criticism* (Los Angeles: American Film Institute Monograph Series, University Publications of America, Frederick, Md., 1984), 83–99.

9. See citations in previous note.

10. I do not think, however, that the film takes us as far as *Repulsion* does; as I argue in the next chapter, Polanski takes us further into the delusional world of Carol by subjecting us to her hallucinations and paranoia, even suggesting that her murders are rational.

11. Donald Spoto, *The Art of Alfred Hitchcock: Fifty Years of His Motion Pictures*, 2d ed. (New York and London: Anchor Doubleday, 1992), 370–376: "Pretty it isn't; morally savage, certainly. Everyone in the modern, bustling world of *Frenzy* is hungry indeed, despite the glut of food in this fallen 'garden,' Covent Garden . . . . *Frenzy* describes, in its brilliantly icy, angry moral outrage, a world in which Hitchcock has apparently lost hope" (pp. 375–376). For a criticism of this view that relates the movie to *Psycho*, see Tania Modleski, *The Women Who Knew Too Much: Hitchcock and Feminist Theory* (New York and London: Routledge, 1989), 101–114. See also François Truffaut, with the collaboration of Helen Scott, *Hitchcock* (New York and London: Simon and Schuster, 1985), 333–339.

12. Modleski comments on how this scene is the antithesis of the attack scene in *Psycho*, where the film toyed with an audience's salacious desire to see Janet Leigh's breasts: "In contrast to *Psycho*, which . . . had titillated spectators with hopes of seeing Janet Leigh's breasts but which had withheld the full sight of the desired objects, *Frenzy* shows an extreme closeup of the woman's breast as she struggles to pull her bra back over it, all the while murmuring the words of the psalm. It is anything but lovely; it is infinitely sad, pathetic, among the most disturbing scenes cinema has to offer." Modleski, *The Women Who Knew Too Much*, 113.

13. Ibid., 114

14. Ibid., 112.

15. Ibid., 112.

16. Ibid., 105.

17. Ibid., 111.

18. Modleski writes: "This cynicism seems to provide some critics with a convenient excuse for not dealing with the issue of misogyny at all: the logic seems to be that since Hitchcock shows contempt for women *and* men, there is no reason to single out his treatment of women for special discussion . . . . For feminists there is an obvious need to keep the problem of violence against women at the center of the analysis (as it is at the center of the film); nevertheless, we cannot afford to ignore the full complexity of the film and its attitude toward women." Ibid., 114.

19. Critical response was extremely negative, and the film earned an "X" rating. For discussion, see Pinedo, *Recreational Terror*, 97–105; also see my article, "Realist Horror" in Cynthia A. Freeland and Thomas E. Wartenberg, eds., *Philosophy and Film* (New York and London: Routledge, 1995), 126–142.

20. Modleski finds that a similar gesture toward the direction of the pathogenic "devouring" mother is made in *Frenzy*, but she does not seem critical of it—that is, she takes it on face value—the devouring mother is "a familiar figure in Hitchcock"; see Modleski, *The Women Who Knew Too Much*, 106–108.

21. Graczyk, "Odyssey of Henry Lee Lucas"; since the movie was made, Lucas's death sentence has been commuted to life imprisonment.

22. Alford, *What Evil Means to Us* (Ithaca and London: Cornell University Press, 1997), 13, 89, and 94.

23. Noël Carroll, *The Philosophy of Horror, or Paradoxes of the Heart* (New York and London: Routledge, 1990), 35.

24. Ibid., 38.

25. Plato, *Republic*, 439e–440a.

26. Aristotle, *Poetics*, 50b16–17.

27. Art horror is a complex aesthetic and emotional response; see Carroll, *The Philosophy of Horror*, 179–182.

28. This is a particular theme of Pinedo's *Recreational Terror*.

29. Clover argues in *Men, Women, and Chain Saws* that slashers usually do obey a certain moral code.

30. See Curt Suplee, "Serial Killers May Be Closer to Normal Than We'd Like to Believe," *Washington Post*; reprinted in *Houston Chronicle*, August 7, 1991.

31. See Tania Modleski, "The Terror of Pleasure: The Contemporary Horror Film and Postmodern Theory," in Modleski, ed., *Studies in Entertainment: Critical Approaches to Mass Culture* (Bloomington: University of Indiana Press, 1986), 155–166; and Linda Williams, "When the Woman Looks."

32. See Mary Lou Dietz, "Killing Sequentially: Expanding the Parameters of the Conceptualization of Serial and Mass Killers," paper presented at the First International Conference on "Serial and Mass Murder . . . Theory, Research, and Policy," April 3–5, 1992, at the University of Windsor, Windsor, Canada.

33. Suplee, "Serial Killers."

34. See, for example, R. Emerson Dobash and Russell Dobash, *Violence Against Wives: A Case Against the Patriarchy* (New York: Free Press, 1979).

35. Jim Phillips, "Killeen Quiet, but Questions Are Disquieting," *Austin American-Statesman*, October 18, 1991.

36. On Hinckley, see James W. Clarke, *On Being Mad or Merely Angry: John W. Hinckley, Jr., and Other Dangerous People* (Princeton: Princeton University Press, 1990).

37. "Potential Dahmer Jurors Asked If They Can Handle Gory Details," *Houston Chronicle*, January 29, 1992; "Menendez Mania," *Houston Chronicle*, October 13, 1993.

38. For a similar objection, see Robert Solomon, review of *The Philosophy of Horror, or Paradoxes of the Heart*, by Noël Carroll, *Philosophy and Literature* 16 (1992):163–173 (with reply by Carroll).

39. An example of an ideological analysis of horror is offered in Michael Ryan and Douglas Kellner's *Camera Politica: The Politics and Ideology of Contemporary Hollywood Film* (Indianapolis: Indiana University Press, 1988).

40. Jean Baudrillard is, of course, the contemporary philosopher who focuses most on this problem of spectacles of violence; but even he (in all his cynicism) suggests at some times that the masses have responsibility for their own "self-seduction." See Baudrillard, "The Masses: The Implosion of the Social in the Media," in Baudrillard, *Selected Writings*

(Stanford: Stanford University Press, 1988), edited and introduced by Mark Poster, trans. Jacques Mourrain, 207–219.

41. See Linda Williams, *Hard Core: Power, Pleasure, and the "Frenzy of the Visible"* (Berkeley and Los Angeles: University of California Press, 1989), 131–134.

Chapter Six

1. Andrew Tudor, *Monsters and Mad Scientists: A Cultural History of the Horror Movie* (London: Basil Blackwell, 1989).

2. On the rape revenge genre, see Carol J. Clover, *Men, Women, and Chain Saws: Gender in the Modern Horror Film* (Princeton: Princeton University Press, 1992), 114–165.

3. Amy Taubin, "Demme's Monde," *Village Voice*, February 19, 1991, 64; see also Demme, quoted on 64.

4. Noël Carroll describes and comments upon the components of the characteristic horror plot in *The Philosophy of Horror, or Paradoxes of the Heart* (New York and London: Routledge, 1990), 97–128.

5. J. Hoberman, review of *The Silence of the Lambs*, *Village Voice*, February 19, 1991, 61.

6. Stanley Cavell discusses the way in which the actor or "star" inhabits the character on the screen in "Audience, Actor, Star," in his *The World Viewed: Reflections on the Ontology of Film*, enl. ed. (Cambridge and London: Harvard University Press, 1979), 25–29.

7. Demme, quoted in Taubin, "Demme's Monde," 64.

8. Bruce Weber, *New York Times*, February 10, 1991.

9. For example, in a discussion of *Repulsion* written closer to the time of the film's release, T. J. Ross commented that "we are offered no explanations, by way of flashback or other means of diagnostic interlude, about the shaping traumas of her character." See T. J. Ross, "Polanski, *Repulsion*, and the New Mythology," in Roy Huss and T. J. Ross, eds., *Focus on the Horror Film* (Englewood Cliffs, N.J.: Prentice-Hall, 1972), 159, originally published in *Film Heritage* 4 (2) (Winter 1968–1969):1–10.

10. Tania Modleski offers a feminist discussion of ideology in horror films that takes a different approach from mine in her "The Terror of Pleasure: The Contemporary Horror Film and Postmodern Theory," in Modleski, ed., *Studies in Entertainment: Critical Approaches to Mass Culture* (Bloomington: University of Indiana Press, 1986), 155–166. Modleski challenges certain postmodern theorists who have championed some horror films, noting that these films attack the feminine through their attacks on representatives of the family or consumer culture. I still believe that horror films like *Repulsion* or *Silence of the Lambs* can support a more positive feminist construal.

Chapter Seven

1. See Vincent Lo Brutto, *Stanley Kubrick: A Biography* (New York: Penguin Books, 1997), 411.

2. Thomas Allen Nelson comments, "The opening camera movements swoop through the Rocky Mountains and pass over Jack's yellow VW like a bird of prey." *Kubrick: Inside a Film Artist's Maze* (Bloomington: Indiana University Press, 1982), 203.

3. Accounts of this music differ, and it seems worthwhile to get things right here, since this music sets the tone of the whole film and (like the rest of the music in the movie) is

essential to its uncanny effects. John Baxter, in *Stanley Kubrick: A Biography* (New York: Carroll and Graf Publishers, 1997), says that the music for the opening scene is by Penderecki: "He also contributed the music for the opening sequence of sweeping helicopter shots over still lakes and lonely mountain highways. Blaring electronic chords are interwoven with what sound like wordless cries, perhaps of animals, perhaps of local Native Americans dispossessed by the Overlook's builders" (pp. 324–325). Vincent Lo Brutto, in *Stanley Kubrick*, says, "The opening of the film features sounds created by [Rachel] Elkind's voice and [Wendy] Carlos's realizations. Many of the wind effects come out of sound-design elements created by them. Elkind's deep contralto voice has extraordinary range, and when combined with Carlos's processing, synthesizer, and multitrack wizardry, the sounds were transformed into ethereal moments of nonverbal sounds that sent a shudder through the airwaves" (p. 439). A third suggestion that strikes a compromise between these two (Penderecki revised by Carlos and Elkind) is made by Nelson in *Kubrick*. Nelson says that the music for the theme (credit) and Rocky Mountain section "*recalls* Penderecki's apocalyptic *Dies Irae Oratorium ob Memoriam*" (emphasis mine; p. 218, unnumbered footnote). The right answer seems to be, however, that the music begins with a synthesized tuba sound playing a variation on the *Dies Irae*, which is originally from the Gregorian mass for the dead but has been used repeatedly by composers throughout the centuries; the version here is close to that of Berlioz. "After this, the notes are gradually sustained so as to create some bleeding over of pitches, and pedal tones work their way under the melody. The interrupting gestures include synthesized voicelike screams with delay (to create an echo effect) and the percussive sounds that bend pitch after the initial attack. As the music goes along, the low, growling pedal tone gains prominence to create a sinister undercurrent." There is no Penderecki in the opening. For additional information, with a scene-by-scene musical description, see Shawn C. Martin, "The Shining Score," web site at <http://crash.simplenet.com/shining/>. (The parts of the preceding description in unattributed quotes are from University of Houston doctoral music student Eric McIntyre, whom I thank for helping me research this issue so as to describe the music correctly.)

4. Steven Shiff, review of *The Shining, Boston Phoenix*, June 17, 1980; quoted in Norman Kagan, *The Cinema of Stanley Kubrick* (New York: Continuum, 1995), 205.

5. For further discussion of Kubrick's work on this film with the Steadicam and its inventor, Garrett Brown, see Lo Brutto, *Stanley Kubrick*, 435–436, and Baxter, *Stanley Kubrick*, 318–320.

6. William Paul writes, "[A] central paradox in the film: forward movement (a necessary part of growing up in the film's terms) must lead you to disturbing sights that make you want to regress." *Laughing Screaming: Modern Hollywood Horror and Comedy* (New York: Columbia University Press, 1994), 339.

7. Kubrick knew and was influenced by Arbus; see Lo Brutto, *Stanley Kubrick*, 444.

8. Ibid., 425–426.

9. On the design for the bathroom, see ibid., 417.

10. Paul also emphasizes this scene in *Laughing Screaming*, 349. Nelson's *Kubrick* (pp. 207–209) actually lists twelve examples or cases of doubling in the film!

11. Given the subtitle of his book ("Inside a Film Artist's Maze"), it is no surprise that Nelson has a good deal to say about mazes and labyrinths; see *Kubrick*, 206–207.

12. Paul emphasizes that different senses of "overlook" that become relevant here; see *Laughing Screaming*, 347–348.

13. The film credits list original music by Wendy Carlos, Rachel Elkind, György Ligeti, Krzysztof Penderecki, with additional music by Béla Bartók; for more discussion of details about the music, see Lo Brutto, *Stanley Kubrick*, 446–448 and Baxter, *Stanley Kubrick*, 323–324.

14. Nelson comments about the titles, "the progression of events goes from months to days to hours, a process of reduction and intensification which moves toward a single moment in time when insanity breaks loose from the bounds of rational order." *Kubrick*, 211.

15. According to Kagan, Pauline Kael complained that it was inconsistent for Wendy to suddenly acquire this ability; but the film is showing that the hotel can wreak its ill effects on anyone. See Kagan, *The Cinema of Stanley Kubrick*, 213.

16. Many critics, dissatisfied with this understanding, either forced a more realistic interpretation of evil onto the film in terms of Jack's madness or called the film confused and confusing. See the overviews provided by Kagan in ibid., 212–215. Shiff wrote, "*The Shining* is a sadistically directed movie, not because it tortures us with fear, but because it refuses us pleasure—the cathartic pleasure of a real confrontation with the terrors it promises" (quoted in Kagan, *The Cinema of Stanley Kubrick*, 214).

17. On Nicholson's "craziness" at the time of making the movie (and Stephen King's complaints about it), see Baxter, *Stanley Kubrick*, 308, 313.

18. On Kubrick's obsession with getting the blood right, see Lo Brutto, *Stanley Kubrick*, 444.

19. For King's critique, see Baxter, *Stanley Kubrick*, 313–314.

20. King also reports on a debate he had with Kubrick, where the latter held that a belief in ghosts is optimistic, since they at least imply an afterlife (King disagreed and asked him, "What about Hell?"); see Lo Brutto, *Stanley Kubrick*, 414.

21. This is described by Baxter, *Stanley Kubrick*, 310; and by Lo Brutto, *Stanley Kubrick*, 413, 419.

22. Kubrick said: "There's something inherently wrong with the human personality. There's an evil side to it. One of the things that horror stories can do is to show us the archetypes of the unconscious; we can see the dark side without having to confront it directly." Kubrick, quoted in Norman Kagan, *The Cinema of Stanley Kubrick*, 203. See also Lo Brutto, *Stanley Kubrick*, 412, and Paul, *Laughing Screaming*, 340–341.

23. I discuss *Eraserhead* second, though it was made earlier than *The Shining*, for just this reason, that its vision of horror is more intense and sustained. Lynch, who is younger than Kubrick, says, "I think Kubrick's one of the all-time greats"; but he also says that he heard that Kubrick admired *Eraserhead* a great deal. See Chris Rodley, ed., *Lynch on Lynch* (London and Boston: Faber and Faber, 1997), 77.

24. J. Hoberman and Jonathan Rosenbaum, *Midnight Movies* (New York: Harper and Row, 1983), 214.

25. See Michel Chion, *David Lynch* (London: British Film Institute Publishing, 1995; translated by Robert Julian from the French edition, 1992), 41. But even the outline of the plot he offers takes four pages (see 30–34). There is a similarly extensive plot description in Hoberman and Rosenbaum, *Midnight Movies*, beginning at 214.

26. On the prologue, see Rodley, *Lynch on Lynch*, 462–463.

27. For more details on the filming, printing, and dark optical effects, see Chion, *David Lynch*, 35; on the comparison with *Sunset Boulevard*, see Rodley, *Lynch on Lynch*, 71.

28. Chion, *David Lynch*, 42.

29. See Rodley, *Lynch on Lynch*, 72–73.

30. Chion has a good discussion of the film's sound and music; see *David Lynch*, 38 and 43 (especially on its mixture of religious and profane music); see also Hoberman and Rosenbaum, *Midnight Movies*, 234.

31. Hoberman and Rosenbaum compare Henry to Harry Langdon; see their *Midnight Movies*, 236.

32. For more on Henry's walk and appearance, see Rodley, *Lynch on Lynch*, 70; and on his speech rhythms, see Chion, *David Lynch*, 35. There is also more on the unnatural pace of the dialogue at dinner (p. 36).

33. Hoberman and Rosenbaum refer to the baby as "a mewling, eye-rolling first cousin to the skinned-rabbit centerpiece of Roman Polanski's *Repulsion*" (*Midnight Movies*, 214). (I have not seen any actual direct references by Lynch to *Repulsion*, though he does refer to Polanski as a great director.)

34. His own daughter, Jennifer Lynch, makes this point; see Rodley, *Lynch on Lynch*, 78; and also Toby Keeler, *Pretty as a Picture: The Art of David Lynch* (Calabasas, Calif.: Fine Cuts Video Production, 1997).

35. See Rodley, *Lynch on Lynch*, 56; Lynch speaks of this kinship, comparing Henry to Joseph K in *The Trial*.

36. Another comparison can be drawn between *Eraserhead* and the final sequence of Kubrick's *2001* (1968). At the end of his psychedelic light-show time travel through space, Bowman the astronaut (Keir Dullea) experiences a relation to space and time that is utterly disorienting. The scene where he, and we along with him, see another man who turns out to be himself is very much like the scene of Henry's nightmare when he sees a man from behind with the sexy neighbor who turns out to be himself. And of course the huge floating fetus at the end of *2001* has its eerie echo in this movie, though it has a different sort of feeling tone. Chion reports that Lynch admired *2001*; see *David Lynch*, 27–28.

37. See Hoberman and Rosenbaum, *Midnight Movies*, 234; they mention that Henry Bromell draws a comparison between *Eraserhead* and Beckett's *Malone*.

38. See Rodley for more on this radiator theater and its importance; *Lynch on Lynch*, 64–66.

39. As reported in Chion, *David Lynch*, 45.

40. See Hoberman and Rosenbaum: "The horror at the heart of *Eraserhead* ... is the horror of procreation, esthetic and otherwise." *Midnight Movies*, 242.

41. See Rodley, *Lynch on Lynch*, 73.

42. See Hoberman and Rosenbaum, *Midnight Movies*, 229 and footnote; see also Rodley, *Lynch on Lynch*, 78. Keeler's film *Pretty as a Picture* also displays some of Lynch's paintings, which include rotting meat or rat carcasses.

43. Chion refers to it as a "bathtub full of milk" in *David Lynch*, 33.

44. See Hoberman and Rosenbaum for more on Henry's "electrified" hair in *Midnight Movies* 231. And on the meaning of the eraser motif, see 228.

45. Freud, "The 'Uncanny,'" in Sigmund Freud, *On Creativity and the Unconscious: Papers on the Psychology of Art, Literature, Love, Religion* (New York: Harper and Row, 1958), 122–161.

46. Ibid., 139.

47. Ibid., 145. Neil Hertz speculates that Freud found the repetition compulsion *itself* somewhat uncanny; see *The End of the Line* (New York: Columbia University Press, 1985), 102.

48. Freud, "The Uncanny," 140.

49. Ibid., 142–143.

50. Ibid., 152.

51. Thomas Weiskel links both sorts of Freudian uncanny to concepts of the sublime in *The Romantic Sublime: Studies in the Structure and Psychology of Transcendence* (Baltimore: Johns Hopkins University Press, 1976).

52. Immanuel Kant, *The Critique of Judgement*, trans. with analytical indexes by James Creed Meredith (Oxford: Clarendon Press, 1957).

53. For further discussion and applications to film, see my article, "The Sublime in Cinema," in Carl Plantinga and Greg M. Smith, eds., *Passionate Views* (Baltimore and London: Johns Hopkins University Press, 1999), 65–83.

54. See C. Fred Alford, *What Evil Means to Us* (Ithaca and London: Cornell University Press, 1997).

55. Noël Carroll, *The Philosophy of Horror, or Paradoxes of the Heart* (New York and London: Routledge, 1990).

56. See Torben Grodal, *Moving Pictures: A New Theory of Film Genres, Feelings, and Cognition* (Oxford: Clarendon Press, 1997).

57. See Ed S. Tan, *Emotion and the Structure of Narrative Film: Film as an Emotion Machine*, trans. Barbara Fasting (Mahwah, N.J.: Lawrence Erlbaum Associates, 1996).

Chapter Eight

1. John McCarty, *The Official Splatter Movie Guide* (New York: St. Martin's Press, 1989), 14–15. McCarty cites Lewis's film as the "debut" of the genre in his preface, x.

2. On this phenomenon, see J. Hoberman and Jonathan Rosenbaum, *Midnight Movies* (New York: Harper and Row, 1983).

3. Similar crossovers were made in the early days of horror: Think of *Frankenstein Meets the Wolf Man* (1943) or *Abbott and Costello Meet Frankenstein* (1948).

4. See Glenn W. Most, "*Disjecti membra poetae*: The Rhetoric of Dismemberment in Neronian Poetry," in Ralph Hexter and Daniel Selden, eds., *Innovations of Antiquity* (New York and London: Routledge, 1992), 391–419. (I am grateful to Richard Armstrong for bringing this article to my attention.) Most makes an acute summary at the close of his article: "Every represented torment of the human body implies a reflection on what it means to be a human being: and the more radical the former, the more urgent the latter. Pain, for all its private intensity, is a social construct, like the body itself" (409–410).

5. Various kinds of psychological studies are included and discussed in James B. Weaver III and Ron Tamborini, eds., *Horror Films: Current Research on Audience Preferences and Reactions* (Mahwah, N.J.: Lawrence Erlbaum Associates, 1996). Specific articles of interest in this volume include Dolf Zillmann and James B. Weaver III, "Gender-Socialization Theory of Reactions to Horror," 81–101; and Dolf Zillmann and Rhonda Bigson, "Evolution of the Horror Genre," 15–31. This last-mentioned article summarizes gender role socialization theories in contrast to rivals including the catharsis view, or views that emphasize the audience's hidden anxieties and urges, its need for vicarious experience, and so on; see especially 26–28.

6. Rick Baker has done many films' ape makeup as well as famous scenes such as that of the aliens at the bar in *Star Wars*; see Anthony Timpone, *Men, Makeup, and Monsters: Hollywood's Masters of Illusion and FX* (New York: St. Martin's Press, 1996), especially 23–37.

7. Carol J. Clover, *Men, Women, and Chain Saws: Gender in the Modern Horror Film* (Princeton: Princeton University Press, 1992).

8. This is generally true of related genres as well. See Scott Stossel, "The Man Who Counts the Killings," *Atlantic Monthly* 279 (5) (May 1997):86–104, where he describes studies that body counts always rise in action sequels: The first *Die Hard* movie had eighteen deaths, and the second had 264; the first *Robocop* movie had thirty-two deaths, and the second had eighty-one; and the three *Godfather* movies piled up twelve, eighteen, and fifty-three corpses, respectively.

9. See Barry S. Sapolsky and Fred Molitor, "Content Trends in Contemporary Horror Films," in Weaver and Tamborini, *Horror Films: Current Research*, 33–48. This article presents tables summarizing body counts in a number of slasher films in given years and shows that body counts for males are *higher* than for females in slasher films, contrary to popular belief.

10. Clive Barker, *The Hellbound Heart* (New York: Harper Mass Market Paperbacks, 1995), originally published in October 1986 as a part of George R.R. Martin, ed., *Night Visions 3* (Niles, Ill.: Dark Harvest).

11. This well-known Hollywood pseudonym is used by directors who disown a film due to loss of control to a studio. Here, the actual director was special effects wizard Kevin Yagher. See Timpone, *Men, Makeup, and Monsters*: "Due to squabbles with his producers, Yagher took his name off the trouble-plagued sequel" (p. 141).

12. Matt Rexer told me that "Neil Gaiman (who wrote the *Sandman* comics) said it best when he commented that at a formal dinner of movie monsters, Pinhead would be the only one who knew what fork to use"; Matt was unable to identify the exact reference (personal communication).

13. My reading of the box is altogether different from that offered by Christopher Sharrett in "The Horror Film in Neoconservative Culture," in Barry Keith Grant, ed., *The Dread of Difference: Gender and the Horror Film* (Austin: University of Texas Press, 1996), 253–276. Sharrett sees the box as an updated Pandora's box (p. 262), laying the blame for evil on women; this is an example of how presumptions of standard film theory can lead one to write utter nonsense. Each film has a clear and obvious male villain and an equally clear and obvious female innocent; there are strong, capable female heroes in three of the films (two of them in *Hellraiser II*); and finally, Pinhead, the prime villain and the ongoing basis for the series, is decidedly male. Rather than fobbing evil off on woman, this series individualizes it in ways I have described.

14. Linda Williams, *Hard Core: Power, Pleasure, and the Frenzy of the Visible* (Berkeley and Los Angeles: University of California Press, 1989). Williams refers in turn to Rick Altman, *The American Film Musical* (Bloomington: Indiana University Press, 1987), and Stephen Neale, *Genre* (London: British Film Institute, 1980).

15. Williams, *Hard Core*, 130.

16. Clover, *Men, Women, and Chain Saws*, 132.

17. Ed S. Tan, *Emotion and the Structure of Narrative Film: Film as an Emotion Machine* (Mahwah, N.J.: Lawrence Erlbaum Associates, 1996), 34.

18. This is what Tan, in ibid., would describe as a switch from film emotions to artifact emotions; he proposes to study fans with just such switches and interests in mind (p. 34). But at best, the empirical studies reprinted in Weaver and Tamborini, *Horror Films: Current Research*, link an interest in horror to thrill-seeking activities or to an interest in

other disasters such as the Challenger explosion. See Ron Tamborini, "A Model of Empathy and Emotional Reactions to Horror," 103–123; Glenn G. Sparks, "An Activation-Arousal Analysis of Reactions to Horror," 125–145; Marvin Zuckerman, "Sensation Seeking and the Taste for Vicarious Horror," 147–160; and Patricia A. Lawrence and Philip C. Palmgreen, "A Uses and Gratifications Analysis of Horror Film Preference," 161–178; all in Weaver and Tamborini, *Horror Films: Current Research*. As relevant as all these kinds of things may be, I still maintain that filmgoers have specialized knowledge and interests in types of films they attend. Phenomena like the very witty and self-referential *Scream* and *Scream 2* would seem to bear me out. On the relevance of audience knowledge, see Steven Schneider, "Kevin Williamson and the Rise of the Neo-Stalker," Harvard University, Cambridge, February 1999, and Isabel Cristina Pinedo, *Recreational Terror: Women and the Pleasures of Horror Film Viewing* (Albany: State University of New York Press, 1997).

19. I am grateful to Matt Rexer for making this point about technology—though he did not use the term "geeky"!

20. Strictly speaking, LeMarchand wins at the end by constructing another gigantic puzzle box in space that uses lasers to create a dynamic "Perpetual Light" or the reverse of the Lament Configuration to banish Pinhead back to Hell. I am again grateful to Matt Rexer for the arcane details (but we disagree about whether the movie itself represents this as a permanent defeat of Pinhead).

21. See Weaver and Tamborini, *Horror Films: Current Research*.

22. William Paul, *Laughing Screaming: Modern Hollywood Horror and Comedy* (New York: Columbia University Press, 1994).

23. Friedrich Nietzsche, *The Birth of Tragedy: or, Hellenism and Pessimism*, in *Basic Writings of Nietzsche*, trans. and ed. Walter Kaurmann (New York: Modern Library, 1968), 15–144. See also Nietzsche, *Philosophy in the Tragic Age of the Greeks*, trans. Marianne Cowan (Chicago: Henry Regnery Company, 1962).

24. Nietzsche, *The Birth of Tragedy*, 50.

25. See Williams, *Hard Core*, 131.

fILMOGRAPhY

Chapter 1: Dr. Frankenstein's Progeny

Frankenstein (James Whale, 1931)
Mary Shelley's Frankenstein (Kenneth Branagh, 1994)

Chapter 2: Women and Bugs

Alien (Ridley Scott, 1979)
Aliens (James Cameron, 1986)
Alien³ (David Fincher, 1992)
Alien Resurrection (Jean-Pierre Jenet, 1997)
The Fly (David Cronenberg, 1986)
Mimic (Guillermo del Toro, 1997)
Revenge of the Creature (Jack Arnold, 1955)
Species (Roger Donaldson, 1995)
Species II (Peter Medak, 1998)
Star Trek: First Contact (Jonathan Frakes, 1996)
Starship Troopers (Paul Verhoeven, 1997)
Them! (Gordon Douglas, 1954)

Chapter 3: Monstrous Flesh

The Brood (David Cronenberg, 1979)
Dead Ringers (David Cronenberg, 1988)
The Dead Zone (David Cronenberg, 1983)
The Fly (David Cronenberg, 1986)
Scanners (David Cronenberg, 1980)
Videodrome (David Cronenberg, 1983)

Chapter 4: Seductive Vampires

Bram Stoker's Dracula (Francis Ford Coppola, 1992)
Dracula (Tod Browning, 1931)

Dracula (John Badham, 1979)
The Hunger (Tony Scott, 1983)
Interview with the Vampire (Neil Jordan, 1994)

Chapter 5: The Slasher's Blood Lust

Frenzy (Alfred Hitchcock, 1972)
Henry: Portrait of a Serial Killer (John McNaughton, 1986/1990)
Peeping Tom (Michael Powell, 1960)

Chapter 6: Feminist Slashers?

Repulsion (Roman Polanski, 1965)
The Silence of the Lambs (Jonathan Demme, 1991)

Chapter 7: Uncanny Horror

Eraserhead (David Lynch, 1978)
The Shining (Stanley Kubrick, 1980)

Chapter 8: Graphic Horror

Hellraiser (Clive Barker, 1987)
Hellbound: Hellraiser II (Tony Randel, 1988)
Hellraiser III: Hell on Earth (Anthony Hickox, 1992)
Hellraiser: Bloodline (Alan Smithee/Kevin Yagher, 1996)
The Texas Chainsaw Massacre (Tobe Hooper, 1974)
The Texas Chainsaw Massacre, Part 2 (Tobe Hooper, 1986)

Epilogue: The Appeal of Horror

Nosferatu (F. W. Murnau, 1922)

BIBLIOGRApby

Alford, C. Fred. *What Evil Means to Us.* Ithaca and London: Cornell University Press, 1997.

Allen, Richard, and Murray Smith, eds. *Film Theory and Philosophy.* Oxford: Clarendon Press, 1997.

Anderson, Joseph D. *The Reality of Illusion: An Ecological Approach to Cognitive Film Theory.* Carbondale and Edwardsville: Southern Illinois University Press, 1996.

Arendt, Hannah. *Eichmann in Jerusalem: A Report on the Banality of Evil.* Rev. and enl. ed. New York: Viking Press, 1965.

Auerbach, Nina. *Our Vampires, Ourselves.* Chicago and London: University of Chicago Press, 1995.

Baldick, Chris. *In Frankenstein's Shadow: Myth, Monstrosity, and Nineteenth-Century Writings.* Oxford: Clarendon Press, 1987.

Baudrillard, Jean. "The Masses: The Implosion of the Social in the Media." In Jean Baudrillard, *Selected Writings,* edited by Mark Poster and translated by Jacques Mourrain, 207–219. Stanford: Stanford University Press, 1988.

Baxter, John. *Stanley Kubrick: A Biography.* New York: Carroll and Graf Publishers, 1997.

Berenstein, Rhona J. *Attack of the Leading Ladies: Gender, Sexuality, and Spectatorship.* New York: Columbia University Press, 1996.

_____. "'It Will Thrill You, It May Shock You, It Might Even Horrify You': Gender, Reception, and Classic Horror Cinema." In *The Dread of Difference: Gender and the Horror Film,* edited by Barry Keith Grant, 117–142. Austin: University of Texas Press, 1996.

Bordwell, David, and Noël Carroll, eds. *Post-Theory: Reconstructing Film Studies.* Madison: University of Wisconsin Press, 1996.

Botting, Fred. *Making Monstrous: Frankenstein, Criticism, Theory.* Manchester and New York: Manchester University Press, 1991.

Boyle, Thomas. *Black Swine in the Sewers of Hempstead: Beneath the Surface of Victorian Sensationalism.* New York: Viking Press, 1989.

Bussing, Sabine. *Aliens in the Home: The Child in Horror Fiction.* Westport, Conn., and London: Greenwood Press, 1987.

Carroll, Noël. "Film, Rhetoric, and Ideology." In *Explanation and Value in the Arts,* edited by Salim Kemal and Ivan Gaskell, 215–237. Cambridge: Cambridge University Press, 1993.

_____. "Horror, Helplessness, and Vulnerability: A Reply to Robert Solomon." *Philosophy and Literature* 17 (1993):110–118.

_____. "The Image of Women in Film: A Defense of a Paradigm." *Journal of Aesthetics and Art Criticism* 48:4 (Fall 1990):349–360.

_____. *Mystifying Movies: Fads and Fallacies in Contemporary Film Theory*. New York: Columbia University Press, 1988.

_____. *The Philosophy of Horror, or Paradoxes of the Heart*. New York and London: Routledge, 1990.

_____. *A Philosophy of Mass Art*. Oxford: Clarendon Press, 1998.

Cavell, Stanley. *The World Viewed: Reflections on the Ontology of Film*. Enl. ed. Cambridge and London: Harvard University Press, 1979.

Chion, Michel. *David Lynch*. Translated by Robert Julian. London: British Film Institute Publishing, 1995.

Clarke, James W. *On Being Mad or Merely Angry: John W. Hinckley, Jr., and Other Dangerous People*. Princeton: Princeton University Press, 1990.

Clover, Carol J. *Men, Women, and Chain Saws: Gender in the Modern Horror Film*. Princeton: Princeton University Press, 1992.

Coppola, Francis Ford, and James V. Hart. *Bram Stoker's Dracula: The Film and the Legend*. New York: Newmarket Press, 1992.

Crane, Jonathan Lake. *Terror and Everyday Life: Singular Moments in the History of the Horror Film*. Thousand Oaks, Calif., London, and New Delhi: Sage Publications, 1994.

Creed, Barbara. *The Monstrous Feminine: Film, Feminism, Psychoanalysis*. London and New York: Routledge, 1993.

Cronenberg, David, and Chris Rodley, eds. *Cronenberg on Cronenberg*. London and Boston: Farber and Farber, 1997.

Currie, Gregory. *Image and Mind: Film, Philosophy, and Cognitive Science*. Cambridge: Cambridge University Press, 1995.

Damasio, Antonio. *Descartes' Error: Emotion, Reason, and the Human Brain*. New York: Avon Books, 1994.

de la Motte, Eugenia. *Perils of the Night: A Feminist Study of Nineteenth-Century Gothic*. New York and Oxford: Oxford University Press, 1990.

de Sousa, Ronald. *The Rationality of Emotion*. Cambridge, Mass., and London: MIT Press, 1987.

Dietz, Mary Lou. "Killing Sequentially: Expanding the Parameters of the Conceptualization of Serial and Mass Killers." Paper presented at the First International Conference on "Serial and Mass Murder . . . Theory, Research, and Policy," April 3–5, 1992, University of Windsor, Windsor, Canada.

Dika, Vera. "From Dracula—with Love." In *The Dread of Difference: Gender and the Horror Film*, edited by Barry Keith Grant, 388–400. Austin: University of Texas Press, 1996.

_____. "The Stalker Cycle, 1978–81." In *American Horrors: Essays on the Modern American Horror Film*, edited by Greg Waller, 86–101. Chicago: University of Illinois Press, 1987.

Doherty, Thomas. "Genre, Gender, and the *Aliens* Trilogy." In *The Dread of Difference: Gender and the Horror Film*, edited by Barry Keith Grant, 181–199. Austin: University of Texas Press, 1996.

Dresser, Norine. *American Vampires: Fans, Victims, Practitioners*. New York: Vintage Books, 1989.

Edmunson, Mark. *Nightmare on Main Street: Angels, Sadomasochism, and the Culture of Gothic*. Cambridge, Mass., and London: Harvard University Press, 1997.

Erens, Patricia, ed. *Issues in Feminist Film Criticism*. Indianapolis: Indiana University Press, 1990.

Fisch, Audrey A., Anne K. Mellor, and Esther H. Schor, eds. *The Other Mary Shelley: Beyond Frankenstein*. New York: Oxford University Press, 1993.

Frank, Marcie. "The Camera and the Speculum: David Cronenberg's *Dead Ringers*." *Proceedings of the Modern Language Association of America (PMLA)* 106 (3) (May 1991):459–470.

Freeland, Cynthia A. "Art and Moral Knowledge." *Philosophical Topics* 25 (1) (Spring 1997):11–36.

_____. "Feminist Frameworks for Horror Films." In *Post-Theory: Reconstructing Film Studies*, edited by David Bordwell and Noël Carroll, 195–218. Madison: University of Wisconsin Press, 1996.

_____. "Feminist Philosophy of Film." In *Blackwell's Companion to Feminist Philosophy*, edited by Alison Jaggar and Iris Marion Young, 353–360. London: Basil Blackwell, 1998.

_____. "Plot Imitates Action: Aesthetic Evaluation and Moral Realism in Aristotle's *Poetics*." In *Essays on Aristotle's Poetics*, edited by Amélie Oksenberg Rorty, 111–132. Princeton: Princeton University Press, 1992.

_____. "Realist Horror." In *Philosophy and Film*, edited by Cynthia A. Freeland and Thomas E. Wartenberg, 126–142. New York: Routledge, 1995.

_____. Review of *Men, Women, and Chain Saws*, by Carol Clover. *Afterimage* 20 (8) (March 1993):12–13.

_____. Review of *Visual and Other Pleasures*, by Laura Mulvey. *APA Newsletter on Feminism and Philosophy* 89 (2) (Winter 1990): 52–55.

_____. "The Sublime in Cinema." In *Passionate Views: Film, Cognition, and Emotion*, edited by Carl Plantinga and Greg M. Smith, 65–83. Baltimore: Johns Hopkins University Press, 1999.

Freeland, Cynthia A., and Thomas E. Wartenberg, eds. *Philosophy and Film*. New York: Routledge, 1995.

French, Peter A. *Cowboy Metaphysics: Ethics and Death in Westerns*. London and Boulder: Rowman and Littlefield, 1997.

Freud, Sigmund. "The 'Uncanny.'" In Freud, *On Creativity and the Unconscious: Papers on the Psychology of Art, Literature, Love, Religion*, 122–161. New York: Harper and Row, 1958.

Gane, Mike, ed. *Baudrillard: Critical and Fatal Theory*. London and New York: Routledge, 1991.

_____. *Baudrillard Live: Selected Interviews*. London and New York: Routledge, 1993.

Gelder, Ken. *Reading the Vampire*. London and New York: Routledge, 1994.

Gilbert, Susan, and Susan Gubar. *The Madwoman in the Attic: The Woman Writer and the Nineteenth-Century Literary Imagination*. New Haven: Yale University Press, 1979.

Grant, Barry Keith, ed. *The Dread of Difference: Gender and the Horror Film*. Austin: University of Texas Press, 1996.

Gray, Jeffrey. "Three Fundamental Emotion Systems." In *The Nature of Emotion: Fundamental Questions*, edited by Paul Ekman and Richard J. Davidson, 243–247. New York and Oxford: Oxford University Press, 1994.

Grodal, Torben. *Moving Pictures: A New Theory of Film Genres, Feelings, and Cognition*. Oxford: Clarendon Press, 1997.

Grunenberg, Chris, ed. *Gothic: Transmutations of Horror in Late Twentieth Century Art.* Cambridge, Mass., and London: MIT Press, 1997.

Hammett, Jennifer. "The Ideological Impediment: Epistemology, Feminism, and Film Theory." In *Film Theory and Philosophy*, edited by Richard Allen and Murray Smith, 244–259. Oxford: Clarendon Press, 1997.

Hardcastle, Valerie Gray. "Changing Perspectives of Motherhood: Images from the *Aliens* Trilogy." *Film and Philosophy* 3 (1996):167–175.

Hertz, Neil. *The End of the Line.* New York: Columbia University Press, 1985.

Hoberman, J., and Jonathan Rosenbaum. *Midnight Movies.* New York: Harper and Row, 1983.

Hogan, David J. *Dark Romance: Sexuality in the Horror Film.* Jefferson, N.C., and London: McFarland and Company, 1986.

Hurley, Kelly. *The Gothic Body: Sexuality, Materialism, and Degeneration at the Fin de Siècle.* Cambridge: Cambridge University Press, 1997.

Huss, Roy, and T. J. Huss, eds. *Focus on the Horror Film.* Englewood Cliffs, N.J.: Prentice-Hall, 1972.

Jancovich, Mark. *Rational Fears: American Horror in the 1950s.* Manchester and New York: Manchester University Press, 1996.

Jordanova, Ludmilla. *Sexual Visions: Images of Gender in Science and Medicine Between the Eighteenth and Twentieth Centuries.* Madison: University of Wisconsin Press, 1989.

Kagan, Norman. *The Cinema of Stanley Kubrick.* New York: Continuum, 1995.

Kant, Immanuel. *The Critique of Judgement.* Translated with analytical indexes by James Creed Meredith. Oxford: Clarendon Press, 1957.

Keane, Marian. "A Closer Look at Scopophilia: Mulvey, Hitchcock, and Vertigo." In *The Hitchcock Reader*, edited by Marshall Dentelbaum and Leland Poaque, 231–249. Ames: Iowa State University Press, 1986.

Keeler, Toby. *Pretty as a Picture: The Art of David Lynch.* Calabasas, Calif.: Fine Cuts Video Production, 1997.

Keller, Evelyn Fox. *Reflections on Gender and Science.* New Haven and London: Yale University Press, 1985.

Kellner, Douglas. *Jean Baudrillard: From Marxism to Postmodernism and Beyond.* Stanford: Stanford University Press, 1989.

Korsmeyer, Carolyn. "Gendered Concepts and Hume's Standard of Taste." In *Feminism and Tradition in Aesthetics*, edited by Peggy Zeglin Brand and Carolyn Korsmeyer, 49–65. University Park: Pennsylvania State University Press, 1995.

Krasniewicz, Louise. "Cinematic Gifts: The Moral and Social Exchange of Bodies in Horror Films." In *Tattoo, Torture, Mutilation, and Adornment: The Denaturalization of the Body in Culture and Text*, edited by Frances E. Mascia-Lees and Patricia Sharpe, 30–47. Albany: State University of New York Press, 1992.

Kristeva, Julia. *Powers of Horror: An Essay on Abjection.* Translated by Leon Roudiez. New York: Columbia University Press, 1982.

LeDoux, Joseph. "Cognitive-Emotional Interactions in the Brain." In *The Nature of Emotion: Fundamental Questions*, edited by Paul Ekman and Richard J. Davidson, 216–223. New York and Oxford: Oxford University Press, 1994.

_____. *The Emotional Brain: The Mysterious Underpinnings of Emotional Life.* New York: Simon and Schuster, 1996.

Lo Brutto, Vincent. *Stanley Kubrick: A Biography*. New York: Penguin Books, 1997.

Lucanio, Patrick. *Them or Us: Archetypal Interpretations of Fifties Alien Invasion Films*. Bloomington: Indiana University Press, 1987.

Lynch, David, and Chris Rodley, eds. *Lynch on Lynch*. London and Boston: Faber and Faber, 1997.

Mank, Gregory William. *It's Alive! The Classic Cinema Saga of Frankenstein*. San Diego and New York: A. S. Barnes and Company, 1981.

Maxford, Howard. *The A-Z of Horror Films*. Bloomington and Indianapolis: Indiana University Press, 1997.

McCarty, James. *The Modern Horror Film: Fifty Contemporary Classics from* The Curse of Frankenstein *to* The Lair of the White Worm. New York: Citadel Press, 1990.

_____. *Official Splatter Movie Guide*. New York: St. Martin's Press, 1989.

_____. *Official Splatter Movie Guide*. Vol. 2. New York: St. Martin's Press, 1992.

McLarty, Lianne. "'Beyond the Veil of the Flesh': Cronenberg and the Disembodiment of Horror." In *The Dread of Difference: Gender and the Horror Film*, edited by Barry Keith Grant, 231–252. Austin: University of Texas Press, 1996.

Mellor, Anne K. "*Frankenstein*: A Feminist Critique of Science." In *One Culture: Essays on Literature and Science*, edited by George Levine, 287–312. Madison: University of Wisconsin Press, 1988.

_____. *Mary Shelley: Her Life, Her Fiction, Her Monsters*. New York: Methuen, 1988.

_____. "Possessing Nature: The Female in *Frankenstein*." In *Romanticism and Feminism*, edited by Anne K. Mellor, 220–232. Bloomington: Indiana University Press, 1988.

_____. *Romanticism and Gender*. New York: Routledge, 1993.

Merchant, Carolyn. *The Death of Nature: Women, Ecology, and the Scientific Revolution*. New York: Harper and Row, 1980.

Midgley, Mary. *Wickedness: A Philosophical Essay*. London, Boston, Melbourne, Henley: Routledge and Kegan Paul, 1984.

Miller, Elizabeth. *Reflections on Dracula: Ten Essays*. White Rock, British Columbia: Transylvania Press, 1997.

_____, ed. *Dracula: The Shade and the Shadow, a Critical Anthology*. Westcliff-on-Sea, Essex, U.K.: Desert Island Books, 1998.

Modleski, Tania. "The Terror of Pleasure: The Contemporary Horror Film and Postmodern Theory." In *Studies in Entertainment: Critical Approaches to Mass Culture*, edited by Tania Modleski, 155–166. Bloomington: University of Indiana Press, 1986.

_____. *The Women Who Knew Too Much: Hitchcock and Feminist Theory*. New York and London: Routledge, 1989.

Most, Glenn W. "*Disjecti membra poetae*: The Rhetoric of Dismemberment in Neronian Poetry." In *Innovations of Antiquity*, edited by Ralph Hexter and Daniel Selden, 391–419. New York and London: Routledge, 1992.

Mulvey, Laura. "Afterthoughts on Visual Pleasure and Narrative Cinema Inspired by King Vidor's *Duel in the Sun* (1946)." In Mulvey, *Visual and Other Pleasures*, 29–38. Indianapolis: Indiana University Press, 1990.

_____. "Visual Pleasure and Narrative Cinema." In Mulvey, *Visual and Other Pleasures*, 14–26. Indianapolis: Indiana University Press, 1990.

Nelson, Thomas Allen. *Kubrick: Inside a Film Artist's Maze*. Bloomington: Indiana University Press, 1982.

Nietzsche, Friedrich. *The Birth of Tragedy: or, Hellenism and Pessimism.* In *Basic Writings of Nietzsche,* translated and edited by Walter Kaurmann, 15–144. New York: Modern Library, 1968.

———. *Philosophy in the Tragic Age of the Greeks.* Translated by Marianne Cowan. Chicago: Henry Regnery Company, 1962.

O'Neill, James. *Terror on Tape: A Complete Guide to over 2,000 Horror Movies on Video.* New York: Billboard Books, Watson-Guptill Publications, 1994.

Pappas, Nickolas. "Failure of Marriage in *A Sea of Love*: The Love of Men, the Respect of Women." In *Philosophy and Film,* edited by Cynthia A. Freeland and Thomas E. Wartenberg, 109–125. New York: Routledge, 1995.

Parker, John. *Polanski.* London: Victor Gollancz, 1993.

Paul, William. *Laughing Screaming: Modern Hollywood Horror and Comedy.* New York: Columbia University Press, 1994.

Pinedo, Isabel Cristina. *Recreational Terror: Women and the Pleasures of Horror Film Viewing.* Albany: State University of New York Press, 1997.

Renfroe, Alicia. "Defining Romanticism: The Implications of Nature Personified as Female in Mary Shelley's *Frankenstein* and Charlotte Bronte's *Jane Eyre*." Web site at <http://prometheus.cc.emory.edu/panels/2D/A.Renfroe.html>.

Rice, Anne. "From Anne Rice on the Film, *Interview with the Vampire.*" Web site at <http://www.maths.tcd.ie/pub/vampire/morecomments.html>.

———. *Interview with the Vampire.* New York: Ballantine Books, 1976.

Ross, T. J. "Polanski, *Repulsion,* and the New Mythology." In *Focus on the Horror Film,* edited by Roy Huss and T. J. Ross, 152–161. Englewood Cliffs, N.J.: Prentice-Hall, 1972.

Ryan, Michael, and Douglas Kellner. *Camera Politica: The Politics and Ideology of Contemporary Hollywood Film.* Indianapolis: Indiana University Press, 1988.

Schelde, Per. *Androids, Humanoids, and Other Science Fiction Monsters: Science and Soul in Science Fiction Films.* New York and London: New York University Press, 1993.

Scheman, Naomi. "Missing Mothers/Desiring Daughters: Framing the Sight of Women." *Critical Inquiry* 15 (Autumn 1988):62–89.

Schneider, Steven. "Kevin Williamson and the Rise of the Neo-Stalker." Harvard University, Cambridge, February 1999.

———. "Monsters as (Uncanny) Metaphors: Freud, Lakoff, and the Representation of Monstrosity in Cinematic Horror." *Other Voices* 1 (3) (January 1999). Electronic journal at <http://dept.english.upenn.edu/~ov/1.3>.

———. "Uncanny Realism and the Decline of the Modern Horror Film." *Paradoxa: Studies in World Literary Genres* 3 (3–4) (1997):417–428.

Schuetz, Julie K. "Mary Shelley's *The Last Man*: Monstrous Worlds, Domestic Communities, and Masculine Romantic Ideology." Web site at <http://prometheus.cc.emory.edu/panels/4A/J.Schuetz.html>.

Sharrett, Christopher. "The Horror Film in Neoconservative Culture." In *The Dread of Difference: Gender and the Horror Film,* edited by Barry Keith Grant, 253–276. Austin: University of Texas Press, 1996.

Shaw, Daniel. "*Dead Ringers*: Horror and the Problem of Personal Identity." *Film and Philosophy* 3 (1996):14–23.

Shelley, Mary. *Frankenstein.* New York: Dover Publications, 1994.

Skal, David J. *Hollywood Gothic: The Tangled Web of Dracula from Novel to Stage to Screen.* New York and London: W. W. Norton and Company, 1990.

_____. *The Monster Show: A Cultural History of Horror.* New York and London: W. W. Norton and Company, 1993.

Solomon, Robert C. "Emotion and Choice." In *Explaining Emotions,* edited by Amélie Oksenberg Rorty, 251–281. Berkeley and Los Angeles: University of California Press, 1980.

_____. *The Passions.* Garden City, N.Y.: Anchor Press/Doubleday, 1976.

_____. "Review of *The Philosophy of Horror, or Paradoxes of the Heart,* by Noël Carroll." *Philosophy and Literature* 16 (1992):163–173.

Spark, Muriel. *Mary Shelley: A Biography.* New York: New American Library, 1987.

Spoto, Donald. *The Art of Alfred Hitchcock: Fifty Years of His Motion Pictures.* 2d ed. New York and London: Anchor Doubleday, 1992.

Stoker, Bram. *Dracula.* New York: Bantam Books, 1989.

Stossel, Scott. "The Man Who Counts the Killings." *Atlantic Monthly* 279 (5) (May 1997):86–104.

Tan, Ed S. *Emotion and the Structure of Narrative Film: Film as an Emotion Machine.* Translated by Barbara Fasting. Mahwah, N.J.: Lawrence Erlbaum Associates, 1996.

Testa, Bart. "Technology's Body: Cronenberg, Genre, and the Canadian Ethos." Web site at <http://www.netlink.co.uk/users/zappa/cr_testa.html>.

Thornburg, Mary K. Patterson. *The Monster in the Mirror: Gender and the Sentimental/Gothic Myth in Frankenstein.* Ann Arbor, Mich.: UMI Research Press, 1987.

Timpone, Anthony. *Men, Makeup, and Monsters: Hollywood's Masters of Illusion and FX.* New York: St. Martin's Press, 1996.

Truffaut, Francois. With the Collaboration of Helen Scott. *Hitchcock.* New York and London: Simon and Schuster, 1985.

Tudor, Andrew. *Monsters and Mad Scientists: A Cultural History of the Horror Movie.* London: Basil Blackwell, 1989.

Twitchell, James B. *Dreadful Pleasures: An Anatomy of Modern Horror.* New York and Oxford: Oxford University Press, 1985.

Tyrrell, Kimberly. "Special Effects and Gender in the Films of David Cronenberg." B.A. (honours) thesis in women's studies, Australian National University, August 1995.

Walton, Kendall. *Mimesis as Make-Believe: On the Foundations of the Representational Arts.* Cambridge, Mass., and London: Harvard University Press, 1990.

Weaver, James B., III, and Ron Tamborini, eds. *Horror Films: Current Research on Audience Preferences and Reactions.* Mahwah, N.J.: Lawrence Erlbaum Associates, 1996.

Weiskel, Thomas. *The Romantic Sublime: Studies in the Structure and Psychology of Transcendence.* Baltimore: Johns Hopkins University Press, 1976.

Weiss, Andrea. *Vampires and Violets: Lesbians in Film.* New York: Penguin Books, 1992.

Williams, Linda. "Film Bodies: Gender, Genre, and Excess." *Film Quarterly* 44 (Summer 1991):2–13.

_____. *Hard Core: Power, Pleasure, and the "Frenzy of the Visible."* Berkeley and Los Angeles: University of California Press, 1989.

_____. "When the Woman Looks." In *Re-Vision: Essays in Feminist Film Criticism,* edited by Mary Ann Doane, Patricia Mellencamp, and Linda Williams, 83–99. Los Angeles:

American Film Institute Monograph Series, University Publications of America, Frederick, Md., 1984.

Wood, Robin. "Burying the Undead: The Use and Obsolescence of Count Dracula." In *The Dread of Difference: Gender and the Horror Film*, edited by Barry Keith Grant, 364–378. Austin: University of Texas Press, 1996.

Zimmerman, Bonnie. "Daughters of Darkness: The Lesbian Vampire on Film." In *The Dread of Difference: Gender and the Horror Film*, edited by Barry Keith Grant, 379–387. Austin: University of Texas Press, 1996.

INDEX